DYING

DYING
Facing
the Facts

EDITED BY

HANNELORE WASS
University of Florida, Gainesville

● HEMISPHERE PUBLISHING CORPORATION
Washington   New York   London

McGRAW-HILL BOOK COMPANY
New York   St. Louis   San Francisco   Auckland   Bogotá
Düsseldorf   Johannesburg   London   Madrid   Mexico
Montreal   New Delhi   Panama   Paris   São Paulo
Singapore   Sydney   Tokyo   Toronto

DYING: Facing the Facts

1 2 3 4 5 6 7 8 9 0   L I L I   7 8 3 2 1 0 9

This book was set in Baskerville by Hemisphere Publishing Corporation. The editors were Cindy DeMoss and Christine Flint; the designer was Howard Paine; the production supervisor was Rebekah M. McKinney; and the typesetter was Peggy M. Rote.
LithoCrafters, Inc., was printer and binder.

Library of Congress Cataloging in Publication Data

Main entry under title:

Dying, facing the facts.

Bibliography: p.
Includes indexes.
1. Death—Addresses, essays, lectures. I. Wass, Hannelore.
BD444.D94   128′.5   78-10921
ISBN 0-07-068438-3 (hard cover)
ISBN 0-07-068437-5 (soft cover)

To Harry

Contents

Contributors

Jeanne Quint Benoliel, PhD, Professor of Nursing, Comparative Nursing Care Systems, School of Nursing, University of Washington, Seattle, WA 98195

Barton E. Bernstein, Attorney, Adjunct Assistant Professor, Social Work and Law, University of Texas at Arlington, 700 Southland Center, Dallas, TX 75201

Ronald A. Carson, PhD, Chief, Division of Social Sciences and Humanities, College of Medicine, Assistant Professor, Department of Community Health and Family Medicine and Department of Humanities, University of Florida, Gainesville, FL 32611

Charles A. Corr, PhD, Professor, Philosophical Studies, School of Humanities, Southern Illinois University at Edwardsville, Edwardsville, IL 62026

Glen W. Davidson, PhD, Professor, Chairperson, Department of Medical Humanities, Chief of Thanatology, Professor of Psychiatry, School of Medicine, Southern Illinois University, Springfield, IL 62708

Robert Fulton, PhD, Professor of Sociology, Director, Center for Death Education and Research, University of Minnesota, 1167 Social Sciences Building, Minneapolis, MN 55455

Edgar N. Jackson, PhD, minister, writer, consultant, Washington Road, Corinth, VT 05039

J. Eugene Knott, PhD, Assistant Director, Office of Counseling and Student Development, University of Rhode Island, Kingston, RI 02881

Ralph A. Redding, MD, Department of Family Medicine, School of Medicine, University of Miami, P.O. Box 016700, Miami, FL 33101

Michael A. Simpson, MD, Academic Department of Psychiatry, The Royal Free Hospital School of Medicine, Pond Street, London, N.W. 3 2QG, England

Judith Stillion, PhD, Professor, Chairperson, Department of Psychology, Western Carolina University, Cullowhee, NC 28723

Carol Taylor, Anthropologist-in-residence, School of Nursing, University of Florida, Gainesville, FL 32611

Robert M. Veatch, PhD, Staff Director, Research Group on Death and Dying, Institute of Society, Ethics and The Life Sciences, 360 Broadway, Hastings-on-Hudson, NY 10706

Hannelore Wass, PhD, Professor, Educational Psychology; Associate, Center for Gerontological Studies and Programs, University of Florida, Gainesville, FL 32611

Preface

Why add another book on death and dying to the many volumes that have already been written on the subject? This question must be asked today by anyone who thinks of writing in the field. The primary motivation to proceed with this book was the conviction that there is a need for a volume that focuses on the *basic facts of death* and that presents them comprehensively and in a systematic manner. Much information has emerged over the past few decades from the efforts of researchers, scholars, clinicians, and practitioners in various death-related disciplines and professional fields. This information can be found scattered in various journals and other publications but has not been brought together in one book. Nine chapters, almost two-thirds of this book, are devoted to the discussion of the facts of death.

A second objective was to provide a volume that is structured with *logic and cohesion*, leading from A to B to C. Such a structure is achieved, I believe, by using a simple basic assumption, namely, that we as individuals as well as a society have problems with death and dying, and if our aim is to solve them, we must first clearly identify these problems, then consider all the facts, and use this information in trying to find solutions. Therefore in designing the book, while keeping the discussion of the facts of death as the main focus, I recognized the need to offer a clear statement of the problems we have with respect to dying and death. Moreover, these problems had to be placed within a larger framework, that is, they had to be treated within a broad sociocultural and historical context to provide valid perspective. Thus in Part One the first two chapters introduce and define the problems of death-related attitudes and behaviors in our society and their manifestations and consequences. These chapters probe deeply and do not retreat from presenting complexities and ambivalence. They attempt to capture the problems in the process of change in a changing society. Oversimplification was avoided for the simple reason that it is of little value to those who seriously seek solutions. In Part Three, four chapters dealing with current issues and controversies are included. These chapters give an indication of the efforts by leaders in the field to grapple with contemporary controversies about death and dying. I feel they will stimulate thought as well as inform and thereby help the reader work through the problems and face the facts. In order to further unify the book, I have written a short introduction to each chapter, in which the chapter is discussed in the overall context of the book as a whole.

The contributors have made every effort to write in a straightforward manner, avoiding technical language whenever possible. I hope the reader will recognize that the simplicity of style did not interfere with maintaining high standards of scholarship. Contributors representing the broad spectrum of relevant fields (such as philosophy, psychology, psychiatry, medicine, nursing, sociology, anthropology, law, and education) have drawn upon existing knowledge and in many instances communicated new information and thought they generated in their respective areas.

In designing this volume, I envisioned it to become a comprehensive basic text for the serious student, whether he or she is an undergraduate student, a professional in the field, a parent, or simply an interested person. It should be mentioned that a number of the contributors to this volume have written their own books in the field of death and dying or are in the process of doing so. Their willingness to expend time and energy to write for this book is evidence that such a book is needed. Several contributors have written their chapters while carrying the burdens of personal tragedy, such as a terminally ill child or spouse, the death of a parent, or personal illness. Their dedication and commitment is deeply appreciated.

This book, then, delineates the problems related to dying and death that confront individuals and society as a whole. It presents in systematic fashion the facts of death as we now know them. I hope this book will stimulate the reader's interest and motivation to apply these facts toward achievement of solutions of the problems concerning dying in our society today and that this will be true for the reader who is a student or professional in regular contact with the dying and their families, as well as for the reader who seeks his or her own confrontation with death in an existential way in order to be better able to define life purposes and goals. It should help the reader achieve a clearer sense of self within a larger order. In sum, I hope the reader will find this a compact, comprehensive, and current volume of personal and professional value.

Hannelore Wass

DYING

The Problem:
Denial
and Ambivalence
toward Death

Throughout history human beings have sought to understand the purpose of their existence. Different civilizations and cultures have produced widely varying notions about life's ultimate meaning and so have individuals within these groups. Even though individual perceptions of life and death are strongly influenced by the values and milieu of the culture in which they exist, the realities of personal experience also alter and redefine these perceptions. Thus as individuals we are both dependent on as well as independent of our society's attitudes. We are dependent when we adopt our culture's attitudes and follow its traditions and practices without question. We are independent when we assert the freedom of individual thought and choice. Thus each of us is free to confront (or not to confront) our own finiteness and derive a more realistic perspective, a deeper personal meaning of our existence, more clearly focused personal priorities, and a heightened awareness of the preciousness of life. Similarly, each of us has the capacity, if not the motivation, to examine and critically evaluate collective attitudes and practices, and many individuals through the ages have developed a sense of mission and acted to influence and alter societal trends. Such has been the case in our society in the development, over the past two decades or so, of a *death awareness* movement. This development arose from a critical look at what has been termed society's "denial of death," the tabooing of the subject with all its ramifications and consequences.

Today our society's orientation toward death is in flux; the equilibrium has been disturbed. The conflict between death denial and conscious death awareness is not resolved. Charles Corr, among many others including this editor, feels that negativity still constitutes the dominant posture toward death in our society today. Some death educators view with concern an increasing interest and fascination with death and its superficial treatment in the mass media; they interpret these as symptoms of a passing fad. This phenomenon compounds the problem and adds to the issue.

Part One of this book portrays the problem of death and dying in our society as accurately as possible. It thus lays the foundation of the book and defines its parameters. It is an introduction that offers both definition and overview. The reader is invited to participate throughout the book, from consideration of the problem to the relating of facts to the challenge of seeking solutions.

Part One consists of two chapters that outline death-related attitudes in contemporary society. The fact that attitudes are changing and fluctuating within our changing society with its divergent values contributes a major share to the problematic character of death and dying today. More importantly, societal attitudes manifest themselves and have consequences in behaviors. These consequences, also presented in Part One, comprise the other major factor in making dying and death a societal problem.

Society's death-related attitudes and behaviors pose a complex issue that cannot be evaluated simply and in a global way. Therefore, in Part One the complexities and pluralities of the death and dying problem are separated into what are thought to be its various components. Neither can the issue be examined in isolation, apart from its context. Therefore the death and dying issue is considered in a broad framework, including a historical perspective.

CHAPTER ONE

Reconstructing the Changing Face of Death

CHARLES A. CORR

INTRODUCTION

How Shall We Begin?

Many people believe that talking about death must be unpleasant or bewildering. Some go further and assert that it is impossible to study this subject in any responsible way. There are many reasons offered for such viewpoints. A large number of people are filled with great anxiety or discomfort at the mere mention of the term *death*. As a result, they are reluctant to enter into any discussions that might follow. Others report that they do not know what to think or feel about death, and that this perplexity makes them unsure about

▬▬▬▬▬▬▬

Corr has undertaken the enormous task of broadly surveying the experiences and attitudes about death, in their diversity with all their complexities and ambivalence, that are part of our daily lives. He has at the same time attempted to capture the processes of change that are occurring in both experience and attitudes. He has indicated that a sense of negativity seems to be emerging as the dominant outlook on death in our society. The portrait that results from his survey is an overall picture of the problem we have with dying and death. The author's keen and careful strokes in painting this portrait provide insight into the nature, depth, and breadth of the problem. This chapter makes evident that a search for simple solutions is bound to fail.

taking part in inquiries related to death. Among this group are some whose curiosity overcomes their hesitations, leading them to join timidly in explorations concerned with death. They want to see what can be said about this subject, even though they are unclear about whether there should be such investigations. Still another kind of person can be heard to assert, somewhat flippantly, "I don't know what death is like because I've never been dead." Of course, we study many things that have not been a part of our own direct experience. "Not dead" is a condition that applies to everyone who might take part in our project. As such, it would rule out all inquiries about death before they have even begun. Exceptions to these prohibitions against the study of death are sometimes granted to theologians or philosophers on the ground that their work focuses on the spiritual dimensions of death. But it seems odd that we cannot talk about death as an everyday event until we have cleared up the very difficult questions of its ultimate meaning.

These conflicting points of view have a special importance for those who are about to undertake an examination of death, dying, and bereavement. They remind us of the limitations of our experience and draw attention to the important role our own attitudes and personal concerns play in determining whether and how we will deal with projects concerning death. The conflicting points of view also suggest that a comprehensive treatment of death must provide an appropriate place for religious and philosophical interpretation. But there is a good deal of evidence to indicate that the negative attitudes toward the study of death that we have cited are not warranted. The reason for this is that most of what we have seen thus far depends upon perceiving death in a selective and holistic way.

No one would deny that some aspects of death pose the most baffling questions that human beings are likely to encounter in the course of their lives. These are the questions the French existential thinker Gabriel Marcel (1) calls "mysteries," unfinishable personal inquiries at the very heart of our existence, as distinguished from "problems," which are objective, detached, and always, in principle, resolvable. Many persons may conclude that all questions related to death are too complex for ordinary investigation, too personal for common discussion, and inaccessible apart from a leap of religious faith or a flash of mystical experience. Such a conclusion goes far beyond its premises; it invokes a kind of farsightedness that claims to see things at the greatest distance better than those that are found within our everyday lives. However, those who cannot see the trees for the woods must soon find that their vision of that which is ultimate and difficult is no clearer than their misperception of that which is proximate and accessible. Death is not a single, monolithic

The Problem: Denial and Ambivalence toward Death

entity; it is a complex and many-sided dimension of human experience for which a wide range of affective states can be appropriate. It is important for us to recapture this latter view, not merely for the sake of our appreciation of death, but in order to be able to put life back into proper perspective. This is a far-reaching claim, whose justification may not now be fully apparent. At present, however, my point is only to draw attention to the fact that we are all capable of learning and sharing a great deal about death. To achieve this education I suggest we begin with those aspects that are least mysterious and closest to everyday life.

A Provisional Orientation

Here we can draw a useful lesson from the way that John Keegan treats a parallel problem from the unlikely field of military historiography. In his thoughtful book *The Face of Battle* (2), Keegan asks himself whether a professional historian who is not a member of the military can ever hope to achieve a legitimate understanding of what armed conflict is like, especially in wars that occurred in a previous era and under a different set of circumstances. His answer is that this can be done, but only if we get beyond the study of battle at the level of strategy and grand schemes. The latter is the perspective of battle that is enjoyed by kings and generals and has occupied such a disproportionate share of the work of military historians and of students in their classrooms. Keegan's recommendation is that historians should attempt to reconstruct the much harsher and more immediate experience of the ordinary soldier on foot or in a hole in the ground. In short, Keegan proposes that we have new and possibly more important lessons to learn by studying the proximate face of battle in its concrete historical setting, and he gives three detailed examples of its distinctive visages at Agincourt, Waterloo, and the Somme.

Keegan's method of addressing the study of battle may also be a valuable approach to the study of death. The principal difference is that we shall want to reconstruct not a historical but a contemporary situation. In fact, this seems to be the approach typical of much of the recent interest in questions concerning death, at least insofar as that interest has devoted particular attention to empirical or clinical studies and to concrete autobiographical, biographical, or fictional portraits. This is not the only way to come at the subject of death, but I do propose an adaptation of Keegan's technique as a provisional orientation from which we can begin. Put another way, I think it is helpful to start out, not with large-scale philosophical or religious theories of the ultimate meaning of death, but with a more proximate and prosaic examination of those experiences and attitudes that are related to death and encountered in our daily lives. It is the sum of these experiences and attitudes that constitute the face of death as we know it in our particular temporal and spatial circumstances. To gain an appreciation of the features of this specific image of death, we need only begin by identifying and inspecting as many of its elements as possible.

Death in Our Time

One well-known student of the sociology of death, Robert Fulton (3, p. 85), has said that ours is the first "death-free generation." I think there is an important sense (to be developed below and in the following chapter) in which this observation expresses a keen insight into recent North American contacts with death. But Fulton's point should not be exaggerated. He cannot mean, for example, that we are free of all feelings and attitudes toward death. Even if we have little experience with death and strive to deny its reality, the very idea will generate a variety of emotions. And it is hardly likely that Fulton intended to claim that we have no experience at all of death, for death is present in the cycles of growth and decay that we witness in nature, in the pets and other animals we bury as children, in the cemeteries and funeral homes that we drive past, and in numerous other aspects of our daily experience. What Fulton undoubtedly had in mind is our typical lack of direct contact with natural human death. Here he is correct: people in our society are increasingly likely to be born, grow to maturity, and have children of their own without ever witnessing the natural death of a close relative or friend. This situation is unique in contrast with the experiences of other peoples and of other times in the history of our country.

We often assume that our experiences are universal. But as soon as such an assumption is recognized, it can easily be seen to be false. It is obvious, for example, that the face of battle has changed and continues to change in keeping with time and circumstances. Much the same ought to be expected for the face of death. And that is the first lesson to learn from Fulton's comment: we are a people whose characteristic involvements with death are likely to be different from those of humans who live in a different time or in a different culture. This does not mean that death-related experiences and attitudes are wholly discontinuous from time to time or from place to place. Death is, after all, one of the few common denominators that we all share. But this sharing takes place in different and often distinctive ways from society to society and from individual to individual. That is, death presents us with a variety of interlinked faces evolving in accord with their historical frameworks, differentiated by their cultural settings, specified according to concrete individuals, and united by our common humanity. The plurality of these faces of death is a bit overwhelming at first, but in the long run it serves to increase our access to death and to multiply our opportunities for understanding its meanings. Therefore, in addition to searching out our own experiences and attitudes concerning death, it helps to note contrasting perspectives embodied in data from other times and other cultures. Nevertheless, our primary aim here is not to construct an exhaustive catalogue of historical and cross-cultural materials but to come to know ourselves better from the standpoint of death.

Principal Elements of the Face of Death

One more point to acknowledge explicitly is that the face of death, as we perceive it, is composed both of *cognitive* and *affective* elements. That is, our overall image of death consists of things we claim to know or to have encountered in our experience, together with a variety of feelings or emotions that come along with that knowledge. These two elements are very closely linked. Not only do they originally appear together, they later interact and mutually influence each other. Changes in the ways that we are acquainted with death seem to be associated with changes in our attitudes toward death, just as alterations in our beliefs and feelings about death can be linked with changes in our perceptions of death and with alterations in the historical and social contexts in which death is experienced. The processes by which these changes take place involve a complex flow of mutual interactions, both within the diverse elements of our death-related experiences and between them and a variety of independent forces and values. We do not have a complete description of these processes, much less a causal account of why they occur. We cannot reproduce here their dynamic interplay, but we can point out some of their prominent features.

Our survey begins with a sketch of changing experiences of death and some of the ways in which these experiences appear to be linked with changes in our everyday lives and in our attitudes toward death. In turn, a review of our attitudes about death suggests correlations with shifts in the experiences we permit ourselves to undergo. And a list of some independent factors in the final section will remind us that all these elements in our dealings with death are located within the larger context of the overall events of life. Our immediate aim in the remainder of this chapter is to reconstruct a representative portrait of the face of death as it typically presents itself to people in our society and as we represent it to ourselves. As we go along, the reader can test and amplify much of what we say in the light of personal experiences and attitudes. That will verify or correct the accuracy and adequacy of our portrait—which is necessarily somewhat general in character—and foster the kind of increased self-knowledge that is our ultimate goal.

CONTACTS WITH DEATH

Natural Human Death: Changing Mortality Patterns

Humans strive to influence or control nature and the natural patterns of events around them. One example of this is well known to those who travel in airplanes and have the opportunity to examine the landscape below. The relative order of those portions of the land that are inhabited by humans is a sharp contrast to the spontaneous and somewhat accidental expressions of nature itself. A similar history of increasing influence and control is evident in the vital statistics of birth, life, and death that are the special province of the science of demography. However, one does not need to be a demographer to be aware of the fact that one of the most basic of the vital statistics—average life expectancy—has changed dramatically in recent times. Most of us know that, as a group, females in our society can expect to outlive males and that for the first time in history the average life expectancy for all humans in our society now exceeds 70 years, the well-known Biblical norm of three score and ten.

Calvin Goldscheider is one of those who have been most helpful in explaining the shifting patterns of the human experience of death. In his book *Population, Modernization, and Social Structure* (4), he examines the historical evolution of mortality patterns and begins the task of linking these changes to other long-run social processes. He sees himself as dealing with two major issues in the larger field of sociological demography: "1) the relationship between modernization and mortality, and 2) the consequences of the mortality revolution for the nature of human society" (p. 102). Some have attempted to estimate average life expectancy at various times and places in the ancient and medieval world, suggesting such figures as 20-22 years for ancient Greece and Rome and 33 years for England during the Middle Ages. Although such figures pique our curiosity, they are quite speculative since they do not rest on any systematic body of data of the sort that is available for modern societies. Hence, Goldscheider rejects such specific projections as unscientific and proposes instead a more recent and broader contrast between mortality patterns before and after the Industrial Revolution.

Although Goldscheider's description of mortality experiences in the preindustrial world is not without some historical and demographic basis, in a larger sense his effort is to construct a model of what life and death would have been like in a setting identified as one of "uncontrolled mortality." Such a model is more important for our purposes than an uneven collection of assorted historical data. It reveals three important features of the experience with death in a preindustrial society: "mortality was high, fluctuated over short periods, and varied widely at any point in time between areas and subpopulations" (4, p. 106). That is, not much more than 200 years ago, human beings experienced quite high death rates and correspondingly low average life expectancies. Some individuals did live to a ripe old age—the death of Socrates at the hands of the Athenians occurred in 399 B.C. when he was 70 years old—but most humans died at what now would be regarded as a relatively young age, in fact what we now estimate as the "prime of life." Infants, children, and other vulnerable groups experienced particularly high mortality rates. Further, because mortality rates fluctuated greatly from time to time and from place to place, death was a force shrouded in mystery. Famine, epidemics, and wars sharply increased death rates. Sometimes this took place over wide areas for relatively long periods of time, as in the case of the Black Death that ravaged Europe and Asia in the fourteenth century. Other instances show a much narrower temporal and spatial influence such as the French plague of 1720-1722, which traveled along communication routes, ignoring isolated towns and small villages, to strike hardest in the largest metropolitan concentrations. Because of these high and irregular levels of mortality, and because of the basic impotence of medicine and public health measures at the time, Goldscheider calls these contexts of "uncontrolled mortality." But even in such situations we need not overemphasize the meaning of this phrase, since the availability of warm clothing, shelter, and food did have a favorable influence in warding off death from particular groups and individuals.

If we contrast this model of mortality with that of the "controlled mortality" of the postindustrial world (for which more reliable data are available), the differences are obvious and striking. Goldscheider (4) summarizes a representative set of statistics in a single sentence: "By 1840, the population in the most advanced European countries had a life expectancy of over forty years slowly increasing to forty-five years by 1880, to fifty-one years by the turn of the twentieth century, to over sixty years by 1930, and to over seventy years by the 1950s" (p. 110). This means not only that mortality rates declined in the industrialized world but also that they did so in a steady and continuous way, and that they eventually reached levels that are so low as to have no known precedent in human history. Further, apart from what humans still do to themselves in the form of wars and other sociopolitical disturbances, the great fluctuations that characterized the death experiences of the preindustrial world have virtually been eliminated. Most of this resulted not from dramatic breakthroughs related specifically to death but from overall gains in standards of living: better housing and working conditions, improvements in agriculture, and advances in communications and transportation whereby surplus food could be brought to those who needed it. Somewhat later, public health and sanitation measures became influential, and a growing knowledge of the causes of infant deaths and effective countermeasures compounded this progress by reducing high infant mortality rates. Finally, late in the nineteenth century and especially in the twentieth century, developments in science, technology, and medicine constituted an independent force acting to further reduce the death rate. This first appeared in advanced industrialized countries, but it is even more dramatically evident in many underdeveloped areas of the world. Especially since the 1930s, such countries have experienced sharp alterations in mortality rates that result from applying direct mortality control techniques. A favorite example, chosen because it is such an extreme case, is the island of Sri Lanka (Ceylon) where the introduction of DDT spraying in 1946–1947 virtually wiped out the malarial mosquito and thereby brought about a reduction in the overall death rate from 20 to 14 per 1000 in a single year.

Implications of Contrasting Death Situations

There are two lessons to learn from the contrast between controlled and uncontrolled mortality contexts. The more obvious one is that *quite different death experiences will be found in these two situations*. This is true whether we compare our own current situation in North America with the less favorable experiences of preindustrial Europe, of Latin America before the 1930s, or of many parts of present-day Asia and Africa. Mortality patterns are not the sole factors determining these differences, but they are of great significance. In a context of uncontrolled mortality, annual crude death rates might run around 50 per 1000 members of the population, average life expectancy figures could be in the neighborhood of 30 years of age, and infant mortality rates would be such that on the order of one-quarter to one-third of all infants would die before they completed their first year of life. In such situations, Goldscheider (4) says, death will be ever present, its fluctuations may produce great uncertainties about length of life, it is likely to present a mysterious appearance, and it will particularly affect the very young and other vulnerable segments of the population. In short, uncontrolled mortality is characterized by a set of contacts with death whose quantity and quality would now be regarded as very undesirable.

The second lesson is that *death is not an isolated phenomenon*. As we have already seen, it is linked in many ways to alterations in the overall structure of a society. In turn, we need to realize that a changed context of mortality has implications of its own for the society in which it occurs. The everyday lives of those who find themselves in a context of controlled mortality are quite different from those in a context of uncontrolled mortality. Since the

The Problem: Denial and Ambivalence toward Death

interactions between mortality patterns and society at large are quite complex and interlinked with a variety of other factors, we are not always able to identify direct causal connections between the two. But we can easily compare some typical features of the overall social situation in a context of uncontrolled mortality with those found in a society enjoying controlled mortality. Such a comparison reveals many contrasting and distinctive features. For example, in a context of uncontrolled mortality a society is likely to display qualities of the following sort: an emphasis on kinship groups in view of their relatively long endurance capacities; large family size insofar as high fertility can be seen as a kind of social counterforce to high mortality levels; arranged and relatively early marriages in response to the lack of time for extended bachelorhood or courtship; reduced emotional ties between parents and offspring as a reflection of the inevitable precariousness of the lives of children; the presence in society of a large proportion of orphans and young widows; an emphasis on living in the present; and an orientation toward religious, mythical, or other-worldly explanations of the death that is such a frequent and public feature of daily life. Not all these qualities may appear in every society with uncontrolled mortality, but it seems plausible that the patterns they suggest will characterize such societies and that the appearance of such patterns has a good deal to do with the ways in which the society experiences death.

In societies like ours, however, in which mortality rates are low a quite different lifestyle is usually the norm. People who live until a ripe old age can afford to emphasize individualism and the nuclear family; they can choose to limit family size to one or two children; and they can invest great emotional and financial resources in these children because the children are also expected to have a long life, one that normally exceeds that of their parents. It is possible in these societies to have lengthy courtship practices emphasizing romantic love, marriages at a later age, longer marriages, and serial monogamy—divorces and remarriages; to have more time to devote to formal education and training programs; to have more energy available for research and therapy aimed at curing disease and further extending life; and to foster future-oriented attitudes of planning, saving, and deferred gratification. Finally, a reduction in regular confrontations with death is likely to diminish the felt need for its explanation so as to encourage a more secular or "this-worldly" orientation. Orphans are much more rare (and likely the result of their parents' accidental deaths), death is apt to be thought of largely as the business of the aged, and bereavement is perceived as a condition of elderly women.

In fact, two contrasting images of widowhood typify quite different mortality experiences and social situations: 1) the youngish man of some time ago whose wife died in childbirth and who is now searching for a new mate and mother for his several children, versus 2) the elderly woman of our era whose children are grown and busy raising their own families and who can expect many years of widowhood after the death of her husband, which probably took place shortly before or after his scheduled retirement. The latter is more likely to be a typical feature of the face of death in our time. Furthermore, the very existence of a specific period in life intended for retirement from active work and applicable in principle to the population as a whole is a recent development. Historically, people in the United States had expected to remain "in the saddle" and to die "with their boots on." Only the privileged and the wealthy or the feeble and the sick could have contemplated an extended period after childhood when some form of productive work would not have been the necessary and the normal focus of their lives. However, when life is prolonged and patterns of living are modified, then retirement can be made: a) possible through pension and social security plans, and b) desirable, both as a societal device to create openings for younger workers and as an expression of individual commitment to the goals of leisure enjoyment. We know these and other things to be true of society, but we do not often attend to them explicitly. As a result, we fail to realize that one important factor significant in defining who we are at any given time in history and in any particular social and cultural context is the nature of our experience with death.

Some American Variations

It is important to remember that the foregoing sketches have been painted with a very broad brush. More detailed historical and comparative studies of countries or population groups thus far represented only by the models of controlled and uncontrolled mortality would reveal that each has its own specific set of experiences with death. Three examples from the broad U.S. experience illustrate this point: 1) although U.S. society has benefited from the overall pattern of steady improvement outlined above, the influenza epidemic of 1918, shared with many other countries, caused a sharp interim drop of about 15 years to just below 40 years in life expectancy rates; 2) similarly, the Civil War had a short but dramatic effect upon mortality in the United States during the 1860s; and 3) identifiable subgroups within the population, such as Native Americans, have had and continue to have a significantly different mortality experience at any given time in contrast with the society as a whole. This last point is developed by Goldscheider along with many others who have studied the relationships between socioeconomic status and mortality experiences within U.S. society. These relationships generally manifest an inverse ratio between social class indicators (however defined) and mortality. No matter how much their absolute situation is improved, poverty populations are always relatively less well off than upper-class groups in such matters as average life expectancy and neonatal, infant, and maternal mortality rates. The obvious reason is that the lives of those who live in poverty are poorer in quality in such key matters as food, housing, education, and access either to public health facilities or personal health care within the private medical system.

Two other facts also seem noteworthy in comparing recent mortality patterns in advanced societies. First, about 30 years ago in the United States as well as in many other industrialized areas of the world the rate of increase in average life expectancy began to decline, and it seems to have continued to taper off since that time. We might well ask if this means that life expectancy in these countries has reached or is approaching an upper limit or an extended plateau somewhere beyond 70 years for men and a bit higher than that for women? Second, several other countries (notably Australia, New Zealand, and the Scandinavian countries) have discernibly higher average life expectancies than those of the United States, which is not at all the leader in the valued statistic of infant mortality rates. It seems likely that a large, heterogeneous country such as the United States cannot expect to match the statistics of smaller, homogeneous societies, but we ought not to concede that without a critical examination of the major contemporary determinants of mortality. There is every reason to believe that at least some of those determinants are influenced by decisions we have made about the nature of our society, decisions that we might alter if their consequences seem sufficiently important to motivate us to do so.

Causes and Locations of Death Today

Some of the topics in the previous section are addressed in a seminal article by Monroe Lerner entitled "When, Why, and Where People Die" (5). But it is even more interesting to note what Lerner has to say about changes in the causes of death and in the places where death occurs. His review of causes of death in the United States during the twentieth century shows a notable shift in relative importance from the major *communicable* diseases (e.g., influenza and pneumonia, tuberculosis, and the "gastritis grouping") to what he calls the chronic *degenerative* diseases (those occurring mainly in later life and generally thought to be somehow associated with aging, such as diseases of the heart and malignant neoplasms or cancer). As Lerner (5) says: "Whereas formerly people died on the average much earlier in life, victims primarily of the communicable diseases, they survive today to a much later age, only to succumb in due time to the degenerative conditions" (p. 16). Lerner's comment helps us to understand why so much contemporary attention is given to what are commonly called heart attacks and cancer, even though influenza and pneumonia still cause the deaths of many individuals and remain with us both as a special threat to certain groups and as a widespread menace to the general population from time to time. Our present sense of the awesome power of the degenerative diseases is, at least in part, a function of the reduced influence of the communicable diseases. This is not to diminish the significance of the degenerative diseases, but only to place them in the context of our society's overall experience with death.

A similar lesson is evident in the statistics concerning deaths that result from accidents. This category advanced from seventh to fourth rank among the leading causes of death during the period from 1900 to 1966. But accidents are not like the flu virus migrating from the east or a swarm of killer bees invading our country from the south; fatal accidents are not propagated like a contagious germ, although panic in large crowds may result in a succession of deaths from trampling or suffocation. Nor are accidents the result of a kind of inner degeneration within our bodies, although a decrease in mental or physical alertness, strength, and coordination may make us more prone to accidents. Instead, accidents have become more apparent as a lethal force in our society because other categories have declined in efficacy, because we now live over 50 percent longer than we did in 1900, and because the affection of most Americans for their automobiles and for other forms of risk-taking has led to a more high-speed and dangerous style of living. These same reasons (less competition from other factors, longer life, and a more tension-filled mode of living) also play a large part in the increased incidence of murder and suicide as contemporary causes of death.

Another prominent change in our mortality patterns has to do with the location or place of death. Many can remember a time when most of the deaths in our society routinely occurred in the home. But Lerner cites data to show that by 1949 approximately 50 percent of the deaths in the United States took place *in an institution.* Furthermore, additional data show that by 1958 the percentage of institutionalized deaths had risen to just over 60 percent. Some of this reflects the growth of nursing homes and homes for the aged, but the largest number involves a shift in the location of death from the home or some public place to a general hospital. The trend is continuing and knowledgeable observers estimate that 70–80 percent of the deaths in our society now occur in an institutional setting. This is an unusually high proportion, especially when we consider that many deaths (for example, a large share of those resulting from heart attacks, cerebral hemorrhages, accidents, suicide, and homicide) take place rapidly and often effectively resist institutionalization.

More importantly, locating death in institutions is a major social change from those times when death ordinarily occurred at home. Above all else, it means that *death is removed* in one more way from the midst of our lives. This comes about because the institution, by imposing limited visiting hours and prohibitions against certain kinds or numbers of visitors, tends to segregate death from the rest of society. As a result, individuals in our society are now much more likely to die alone, in unfamiliar surroundings, or among strangers than they are to die at home in the company of those they love. This has important and often negative implications for the way dying will be experienced, for survivors, and for the institutions into which death is increasingly thrust, especially if many of those institutions view themselves (as they increasingly do) as "health centers." In such institutions dying is very likely to be regarded as an unhealthy or undesirable thing to do.

What all this teaches us is that people in our society live different lives, in part because their experience of death is not the same as that encountered by human beings who lived at other times or who are alive today in a different mortality situation. Whereas death has become for us less erratic and mysterious, more predictable and understandable at the objective level, it is also increasingly an experience that has grown apart from the mainstream of everyday life. Death has become less natural and familiar to us and thus increasingly appears to be *less appropriate* as a part of a person's lot in this life. Here we find the real import of what it is to be a "death-free generation." Direct contact with natural human death is a more and more unusual event in our experience, and we seem to have arranged our lives—intentionally or unintentionally—in ways that tend to decrease further the opportunities for us to confront the realities of death.

Fantasized Death

A remarkable characteristic of our times is that whereas the natural death of human beings has become a less familiar part of our lives, death has achieved a startling return to prominence as an insubstantial fantasy in the mass media and popular culture. Throughout human history death has been a frequent subject of legends, poetry, drama, and literature. This reflects the basic realities of life and accords with the momentous part that death plays in human existence. But now we find death appearing in a quite different form, as the staple fare of popular entertainment fantasies. This sort of death is a pervasive feature of the cowboy, police, medical and other adventure stories (war being temporarily out of fashion) depicted on television and in the movies. It is said, for example, that before the age of 20, children in our society witness some 20,000 deaths of various sorts on television. However, this kind of death has very special qualities. It is usually incidental to the plot or is the fate of lesser characters who do not merit our full attention or concern; rarely does it apply to the central figures of the story who need to remain alive simply in order to be able to return for next week's episode and who are subtly portrayed as too important to die.

This kind of fantasy death often occurs either in such casual ways as to be indistinguishable from other events in the action or in such exaggerated forms that it bears little connection with real life. As a result, the fantasized apparition of death may excite and thrill audiences, but it does not represent the actual facts of life and death. Perhaps the most insistent of these fantasized versions of death appear in cartoons for children. In this setting, death displays very few of its natural qualities. It occurs with great frequency, happens only to deserving villains, is over in a flash, and is hardly ever mourned. The villains regularly fall victim to their own traps or to accidental retributions of an extreme nature, but they do not die, they just keep getting killed. In these animated allegories of the conflict between good and evil, death is portrayed, perceived, and understood in a very special and artificial way.

It would be wrong to conclude from this that all romanticism is undesirable. Fantasy compensates for the tedium in our daily routines and offers temporary release from the tensions of living and thus is quite healthy. It becomes unhealthy and deserving of critical scrutiny only when it is excessive and when it supplants a balanced appreciation of life. This is what seems to be happening with the contemporary experience of death: fantasized surrogates are replacing natural reality. We are bombarded with images of death that are apart from and inconsistent with the realities of life. As a result, we find more and more that the sum total of our experiences with death includes divergent and sharply conflicting elements. The danger is that our representations of death will thereby become increasingly distorted.

Another sort of media representation of death can be found in news reports, especially those appearing on television. Here reality *is* being represented, though in a highly selective way. For many reasons, it is the extraordinary event—a death chosen from a very limited variety of types—that commands attention, not the prosaic happenings of ordinary life. But violent deaths caused by suicide, homicide, and armed conflict are foreign to most peaceful neighborhoods, just as the death of a prominent person is remote from the life of the average citizen. Both are perceptions at a distance. I call these fantasized deaths because of their *selectivity* and *remoteness*, and I draw attention to them because their sheer volume gives them a certain prominence in the context of a relative absence of natural death experiences. Once in a while, our individual lives are touched intimately by the death of a special person (e.g., John or Robert Kennedy, Martin Luther King, Jr., Elvis Presley) or a particularly striking event (e.g., the brutal death of a child, the havoc left by a terrorist attack, or the carnage following a commercial airline crash). But more often fantasized deaths remain outside the world that we inhabit. Simple repetition makes them appear monotonous and in-substantial. For example, television news reports have made us all aware of the slaughter that takes place every day on our highways. We can even predict with a high degree of accuracy the automobile death toll on a long holiday weekend. But we hardly pay attention to this prominent contemporary form of death in our society unless it somehow forcibly breaks into our personal lives.

Unnatural Forms of Death

Automobile mayhem brings us directly to the topic of unnatural forms of death, that is, violent deaths human beings bring upon themselves. We have already mentioned several cases in which one human being more or less deliberately commits suicide or kills someone else, but most of our examples, such as suicide and murder, have involved a single death or a small number of deaths. Now we need to consider unnatural death as it has occurred in our time on a much larger scale, usually in connection with war or some sort of civil disturbance. In an eerie volume, *The Twentieth Century Book of the Dead* (6), Gil Elliot has estimated that there have already been 110 million unnatural deaths in this century. The sheer size of this figure (to the extent that we can comprehend it) is staggering. Even though humans have always been involved in the grisly business of killing one another, the volume of these deaths hardly suits our self-image of growing humaneness and concern for others. It does not take much study of these statistics to learn that the largest number of the unnatural deaths in our time have occurred in quite undramatic ways. More humans have recently killed each other through various privation techniques (ghettos, prisoner-of-war and labor camps, sieges, dislocations, etc.) than through the direct use of bombs, guns, and other weapons. But Elliot argues that our century is distinguished, not only by the fact that more people have died at the hands of others, but also by the altera-tion in the quality of many of these deaths. We will use two exam-ples taken from World War II, Auschwitz and Hiroshima, to illus-trate these quantitative and qualitative aspects. In his own unique language, Elliot (6) comments on these two examples in the following way:

> There are two kinds of total-death machine. One is the system of the atom and hydrogen bombs. What makes that a total-death machine is the hardware of the system—the exploding bomb itself. The other kind of total-death machine is the system which crushed the Jews of Europe. The "hardware" of that system is, as we all know, gas-chambers and guns. But that system is not primarily dependent upon its hardware. What makes it a total-death machine is the *organization* of the system, or, in our modern language, the software technology. This is the important difference between the two kinds of total-death machine. (pp. 64–75)

Auschwitz

There is a form of unnatural death, symbolized by hand-to-hand combat and the stylized encounters of medieval knights, that displays important personal qualities and occasionally even the opportunity for heroism. Some elements of this form of conflict can undoubtedly be found in all wars, but they are idealized types and not at all typical of unnatural deaths in this century. The reason for this is that past assaults of one side on another were usually not conducted so as to obliterate all traces of human community. Even in the grueling trench warfare of 1914–1918, both professional and citizen soldiers could admire the heroism of an opposing individual or group, treat a captured or wounded enemy with decency and respect, and arrange temporary truces for the purpose of removing the maimed and dead from a battlefield. And elsewhere, as war increasingly spilled over or deliberately came to include civilians, it did so simply by treating them as contributors to the enemy combat effort.

But at Auschwitz and the other extermination camps it became the official and systematic policy of a government to direct a new kind of macroviolence at a noncombatant population on ideological and racist grounds (7). The phrase, "the Jewish question," implies that the very existence or the right to exist of the Jewish people (and of some other groups) had been redefined as questionable. Only in this context can we make any sense at all of a "final solution" that depends upon a total alienation between the aggressor and a victim identified as subhuman (8). Technology plays an important part in this process for, when shooting and burial proved to be unwieldy methods of dispatching large numbers of people, it was the intervention of the more "advanced" techniques of the gas chamber and the crematory that "solved" the problem. This is how the move was made from random brutality, to execution squads, to ghettos and concentration camps, and finally to extermination camps, of which Auschwitz was simply the largest and the most notorious. But the more important influence of that technology depends upon the way in which some of the attitudes that accompanied it reinforced the impersonal objectification and ideological estrangement at the core of the war against the Jews.

Some (e.g., 9, pp. vi and x) have raised the difficult and agonizing question of whether contexts like Auschwitz produced, not only an *inter*personal alienation *between* the SS guards and the civilian victims, but also an *intra*personal alienation *within* the victims themselves. If so, this might be seen especially in those who survived for a brief period in the work details, upon which the gassing, the salvaging of economically valuable materials, and the cremations depended. Passive acquiescence or even active cooperation among the various death-bound populations (Jews, Slavs, Gypsies) might be interpreted as implying that some suffered the death of their humanity prior to their loss of biological existence, which then helped to bring about the deaths of themselves and of their comrades as well. It is undoubtedly easier to raise this question from the comfortable perspective of history than it must have been to live through the unprecedented horror of the actual events. I mention this point here not to add to the burden of those who were forced to live in such terrifying circumstances, but to suggest the unparalleled potential for interaction between quantitative and qualitative aspects of unnatural forms of death in the twentieth century. Many people aptly employ the term *holocaust* to convey our sense of awe at the scale of this assault, the completeness of the resulting fiery devastation, and the dreadfulness of the personal and social alienation it embodied.

Hiroshima

The other great signpost of the changes in unnatural forms of death during the twentieth century is represented by the explosion of the atomic bomb over Hiroshima on August 6, 1945. At Hiroshima, and 3 days later at Nagasaki, a quantum leap of technology unleashed a power new to the world. That power not only annihilated vast numbers instantaneously, it also established what Robert Jay Lifton (10) has termed a new experience of "death in life," the sudden, unexpected, and overwhelming immersion of a people in death. With no apparent enemy in sight, it is estimated that at least 100,000 persons died instantly at Hiroshima, 50,000 more at Nagasaki, and a like number were injured or impregnated with invisible radiation. In both Japanese cities, the horror of survival and its attendant experiences of psychic numbing or closing-off, guilt, and contamination may even have been worse than the flash of vaporized extinction that left behind rubble, some shadows etched on roads and walls, and a ghastly silence. As before in Europe, the alienation between aggressor and victim was complete, and again the target was essentially civilian, chosen mainly for strategic and psychological reasons. But at Hiroshima there was also the element of a new *alienation from nature*. Days after the blast, as humans died from the residual effects of the bomb and its radioactivity, nature burst into a frenzy of bloom and growth! And all of this preceded much more enduring personal and intergenerational consequences such as the stimulation of cancers and the transmission of genetic defects.

Lifton has argued that the experience of the atomic bomb constitutes a fundamental threat to, if not an irreparable shattering of, the very fabric of meaning in our lives as previously established by a continuity between life and death. His argument is framed in terms of the psychological mechanisms he believes we employ to anchor our sense of meaningfulness in the face of inevitable biological death. According to Lifton there are four such "modes of symbolic immortality": 1) the biological or biosocial, whereby we expect to live on through the biological chain of our descendants and family or social continuity; 2) the theological, in which one looks forward to survival or release into a higher form of existence through a God or divine force; 3) the artistic or creative, whereby one's work or influence is viewed as the enduring legacy of one's life; and 4) the natural, in which we anticipate that we shall persist not as individuals but as a part of nature itself. The nuclear era appears to weaken if not actually sever these symbolic bridges to immortality: it threatens to destroy our biological and creative posterity, undermines the security of our belief in a good God, and even seems to devour or deform life and nature. Thus "nuclear weapons confront us with a kind of death that can have no meaning" (11, p. 209). If this is true, how can words convey our current enlarged ability to destroy humanity, life, and nature in a still more cataclysmic doomsday?

If the quantitative and qualitative aspects of unnatural forms of death in the twentieth century have been altered in ways whose potential exceeds our human ability to imagine or to comprehend in rational terms, then death seems to have escaped our grasp once more. Recognizing this, writers such as John Hersey (12, 13) and Arnost Lustig (14) have sought to capture what is communicable in experiences like Auschwitz and Hiroshima through the concrete images of fiction and documentary reporting. However, the real validity of Lifton's contention that "nuclearism" is a failure of the imagination that still afflicts us may be better tested in the recent discussion of plans to develop a neutron bomb. Advocates of this weapon argued that it would have its main effect upon humans. Some opponents argued against all such devices. Others called for a bomb that would destroy buildings and weapons but leave people untouched. A third group suggested a bomb that would destroy only clothing, leaving people intact but naked! The aim is to jolt us into some realization of the bizarre quality of what passes for conventional and rational discussion. Until we find some way to gain control over these new forms of unnatural death, we must continue to exist under the shadow of total nuclear destruction checked only by the unstable threat of mutual terror. In the meantime, the excess of violence caused by humans constitutes a most important and terrifying element in the contemporary face of death. Such an element is sufficient in itself to require us to ask how death has come to be this way and what responsible people can do about it.

Nonhuman Forms of Death

Our effort to flesh out the contemporary face of death has taken us from historical remarks on its changing human patterns to reflection on some of its current inhuman manifestations. Anything following an account of unnatural death must suffer by comparison, but it is still worthwhile to consider nonhuman forms of death. This is not merely an idle play on words or a pedantic insistence on the minutiae of morbidity. Instead it is an acknowledgment that death presents itself to us in various forms, including those found in animals, plants, and other vital things. Some of these experiences are significant in the contributions that they make to our overall portrait and in what they teach us about death. Children in our urban society, for example, often meet real death for the first time in a chance encounter with the cold and rigid body of a small wild animal or in the death of a domestic pet. These are important and potentially valuable educational experiences, especially since natural human death has become less evident and less accessible. In our society the death of a household pet is a much more frequent and personally disturbing event for most than the demise of an unfamiliar relative living hundreds of miles away. Somewhat less vivid but still instructive experiences of death can also be found in the withering and decay of flowers and household plants, in the stark images of bare trees and bushes during winter, and in the crumbling decomposition of a rotting log or stump. Those who live in rural areas witness all this through the magnifying prism of farm animals, crops, and their closeness to the regular cycles of nature. But everyone shares in such observations to some degree and we will not appreciate all that we know about death if we discount such experiences. They signal our involvement in a community of living things, each of which is mortal and destined to die. Our special advantage rests in the ability to survey this community, to realize the qualities its members share, and to reflect on their meaning before we are called to confront our own death.

Analogues to Death

Beyond this, other events in our experience serve as partial analogues contributing to our understanding of death. These are the experiences of cessation, loss, and deprivation found throughout our lives. They include extended illnesses, the loss of a limb, retirement from an active career, extended separation from close friends, the end of a love affair, sunset on a pleasant day, grief over some misfortune, and suffering of various kinds. Some find going to sleep or being anesthetized prior to surgery to be like dying, and it is thought that insomnia is centrally related to a fear of death. Being caught in a stalled elevator and other claustrophobic experiences can suggest the confinement of death, and near-death experiences in accidents have brought many "to death's door." The ability of such episodes in life to serve as precedents for, or preliminary representations of, death depends on the degree of continuity that they, as interim events, exhibit with the final event in our lives. That such continuity does exist is evident in the way death is naturally received into a life that has witnessed a good deal of hardship and distress. Death is a familiar partner to those whose journey through life is filled with poverty, pain, and suffering. Such people do not need to reach out to history, other cultures, media fantasies, formal education, or animals and plants in order to know firsthand what death is like. Similarly, those who wonder how they will deal with death when it comes are often advised to consider how they are now coping with the lesser traumas that appear throughout life. This is sound counsel, for death is not merely a single bold period at the end of life; it is also a series of lesser terminations during life. The passage of time in an existence marked by temporality and transience is a reminder of the inevitable passing of life. To follow these leads from whatever "is no more" in our experience is to discover the continuity between many common occurrences within life and what Elisabeth Kübler-Ross (15) has called "the final stage of growth."

Difficult Cases

Especially in the United States, though not exclusively so, problems related to death have manifested themselves in the last few years in a series of difficult cases. For many people these cases constitute very unsettling kinds of experiences that need to be included in our review of the changing face of death. The cases in question mainly originate in a medical context or at the juncture of medicine and law, religion, morality, or social custom. It would be impossible to list all such cases, but we can at least indicate their variety in a series of examples: a) the transplantation of a nontwinned organ such as the

The Problem: Denial and Ambivalence toward Death

heart, which had historically been viewed as fundamental to the individual's humanity, seems to put into question some aspects of the enduring life of a recipient who is using someone else's vital organ; b) transplantation from a cadaver donor has also brought new attention to the timing of a declaration of death; c) the ability to sustain the appearance of life without much, if any, of its substance also prompts questions about the definition of death; and d) instances of defective newborns or terminally ill patients who can achieve only a very limited quality of life with no prospects for recovery or normalcy have led to debate over prolonging or terminating life. All of these have been widely reported in the news media: the rash of heart recipients in the late 1960s; the growing need for kidney donors in the 1970s; proposals for definition of death legislation; cases of irreversible coma (Karen Ann Quinlan); hydrocephalic, spina bifida, and other severely deformed newborns; living wills, the "right to die"; and euthanasia. A few people have seen their way to a reasoned moral, social, or legal position on some or all of these cases, but for the general public the new situations have had the effect of increasing the mysteries of life and the perplexities of death. For example, in 1976 in St. Louis a young woman was involved in a severe automobile accident, following which she displayed no measurable brain activity and no spontaneous respiration or circulation of blood. Because of disagreements within her family and a cloudy legal situation, ventilation and circulation were artificially maintained for 23 days, until her body deteriorated so far as to render even this impossible. Kidney specialists in the area claim that the publicity accompanying this case was an important factor in a major drop in the number of people willing to sign uniform anatomical gift cards or to agree to body donations from newly dead next-of-kin. Yet after an autopsy the county medical examiner found sufficient evidence to backdate the time of this woman's death to the day after her accident. In retrospect there is little question about the accuracy of this declaration of death, though the prospective situation was much less clear, and the ramifications, such as the willingness of third-party insurors to pay for "treatment" imposed on a corpse, are complex.

These examples are cited to show the problematic character that some aspects of death have assumed for many people, largely as a result of advances in the art and science of medicine. While this progress has generally been of great benefit, some of its consequences have been far less desirable in themselves and in our ability to cope with them. It is not easy to reconcile such cases with existing patterns of knowledge, feeling, and behavior. Nor does it help to say that these examples are relatively rare and that some have been exaggerated in the media. Both assertions are true, but the data remain a

part of our experiential panorama. Since they will not disappear or supply their own solutions, they provide an impetus for the development of a comprehensive philosophy or *unified outlook on death* within which they can be understood and interpreted. We need more than a jumble of ad hoc postures and prejudices. Our reconstruction of the changing face of death is intended to contribute to such a philosophy, in the hope that it might eventually help to guide both what we think and how we feel about death.

Dying

One final matter that deserves attention in this survey of our experiences with death is the distinction between death and dying. Very often when we use the term *death* what we really have in mind is *dying*. Thus "the death of Socrates" really refers to those dramatic moments before he drank the poisonous hemlock and his life ended, the time during which he was facing death. Similarly, when we compare the deaths of two individuals we are most often drawing attention to the ways in which they died. When precision is demanded, it is not difficult to acknowledge that *death* properly refers to the state or condition of being dead (that is, of having died and no longer being alive), while *dying* applies to someone who is about to die, who is at the point of death, or who is engaged in the process of ceasing to live. Obviously the two are closely related, and that explains our tendency to slip from one to the other. But there are a number of circumstances in which it is useful or necessary to keep in mind their difference. Probably the most pressing instance in our society is the need to distinguish dying persons from those who are already dead. One might think that would be self-evident, but when we look more closely at our treatment of the dying or at examples of useless therapy imposed on a corpse we find that sometimes we have made a subconscious elision between *dying, all-but-dead, as-good-as-dead*, and *dead*. To prevent this, we need not alter the ways in which we speak about death and dying, but we must realize that they rest upon a very important underlying conceptual difference. It is a distinction that has some relevance for the ways in which we describe our changing experiences of death, and one that will grow in prominence as we turn to an analysis of attitudes and feelings in the following section.

ATTITUDES CONCERNING DEATH

The Place of Feelings

In addition to cognitive dimensions, the changing face of death is also composed of a set of *feelings or affective components*. In the

The Problem: Denial and Ambivalence toward Death

previous section we sought to confine our discussion to various sorts of contacts with death and to what we know or believe we know about death. However, even there it was not possible to exclude all reference to what we *feel* about death. In this section we want to look more directly at the many ways in which death touches, excites, and affects our emotions. Some claim that these affective components ought to be understood as a response to the stimulus of experience, whereas others contend that experience is itself, from the very outset, shot through with both cognitive and affective elements. However, for our purposes here it is only necessary to concede that tonal dimensions are an essential part of our overall perception of death. That lesson can be taught by very simple experiments such as word association tests or free pictorial depictions of death.

If we accept that humans are not impartial and objective observers when it comes to confrontations with death, then it follows that an important ingredient of subjectivity is involved in our experience of death. Different individuals, groups, and societies may have different perceptions of death, and the same individual, group, or society may have different feelings about different kinds of death. Moreover, because death rouses and sways us profoundly, many deep-seated emotions may not be immediately apparent to us. This is one reason why a course on death and dying can be an exercise in self-discovery. In the present investigation we cannot examine every possible attitude toward death, any more than we could list every individual encounter with death in the preceding section. Instead we will undertake to scan some of the most prominent social and personal feelings found in our contemporary representation of death. As always, natural human death is the paradigm case. It sets the standard for other experiences of death because of the importance of human forms of life and because the workings of nature are the foundation upon which fantasy and the effects of human action are superimposed. We shall begin then with the shifting attitudes that have evolved in a kind of rough tandem with the changing patterns of our contacts with natural human death.

Tamed Death: Familiarity and Resignation

A thoughtful guide in this part of our investigation is the French social historian Philippe Ariès (16). Ariès describes four prominent attitudes toward death that he has found in the history of the West and that we can confirm in individual examples. The first and oldest of these is what Ariès calls "tamed death." Such a title fits an era when death was a common and ordinary fact of life. In those circumstances, life and death were close companions, and their association led to what Ariès calls "the old attitude in which death was both familiar and near, evoking no great fear or awe" (16, p. 13). Perceived as a customary fact of human destiny, death aroused little play of sustained emotion beyond a kind of grudging acquiescence and general resignation. It was as if humans said, "we shall all die, and we all know it." Anything familiar may generate attitudes of this sort, and death is no exception. In the time under discussion, death had many recognizable aspects and often gave advance warning. That is, death was often not instantaneous, but it was also not protracted as it can easily be today. Medical skills and familiarity with the signs of death's approach might not have been sufficient to restore health or to prevent the inevitable outcome, but they enabled many to foresee its arrival. Death in this era was often sad and painful, but it did not appear to threaten the regular order of life's events as death often does at present.

One's Own Death: Acceptance

Ariès observes that during the twelfth through the fifteenth centuries, the period of the late Middle Ages, "death became the occasion when man was most able to reach an awareness of himself" (16, p. 46). The "decent interval" of dying gave the individual an opportunity to assemble his or her family, set important affairs in order, dispose of property, and "prepare to meet my Maker." An encompassing religious framework emphasized the divine judgment that would follow shortly after death. The dying person and those in attendance sought to do whatever they could to get ready for the momentous event. And the cult of the *ars moriendi*, the "art of dying," encouraged calmness, solemnity, and a sense of awe. Such a death could be the high point of an individual's life. It was consistent with the relative shortness of the lifespan and the perceived fragility of living things. Repeated encounters with suffering and hardship throughout life might have prepared the way for death, and there was little opportunity to suspect that death might have been prevented if only a particular medical regimen or other sort of external intervention had been undertaken. In short, the general attitude was: This is my own death, and I am ready to meet it with a relatively high degree of acceptance. It is a culmination in which I am a full and often dominant participant, and it results in a loss that is not without its consolations for my survivors.

Death of the Other: Fascination and Fright

By the time of the eighteenth century Ariès (16) observes an important shift in Western attitudes concerning death: Death was seen as a rupture or break with life, something frightening and yet obsessive.

The Problem: Denial and Ambivalence toward Death

What had previously been perceived as an ordinary and even banal event turned into an object of morbid attention. From a drama revolving about the self, the emphasis shifted to a fascination with the death of the other. Ariès finds indicators of this sort of outlook in the reincorporation of cemeteries into urban areas, in the tendency of mourning to become hysterical, and in the growing practice of erecting monuments and memorials to the dead. Many of the same feelings are illustrated in the bygone spectacle of the public execution. This kind of death was once viewed as a popular social event for people of all ages and a form of moral and social education. Now it would be thought ghoulish and macabre. In many Western countries, capital punishment is currently out of favor and prohibited. But even where the principle is legalized and supported by the populace, the practice is likely to be attended only by a very few observers, most of whom are compelled to be present by virtue of position or official function.

Forbidden Death

The final set of attitudes that Ariès discusses revolves around the concept of *forbidden death*. Developing in the midnineteenth and twentieth centuries, this involved a growing feeling of distaste concerning death, a sense of death as shameful and prohibited. Ariès (16) exemplifies the shift to this way of looking at death by considering motivations behind lying about the true state of the dying person's condition.

> The first motivation for the lie was the desire to spare the sick person, to assume the burden of his ordeal. . . . [But later,] one must avoid—no longer for the sake of the dying person, but for society's sake, for the sake of those close to the dying person—the disturbance and the overly strong and unbearable emotion caused by the ugliness of dying and by the very presence of death in the midst of a happy life. (pp. 86–87)

This tension between the professed interests of the dying person and the presumed needs or desires of family, friends, staff, and society continues as a source of difficulty today. It is a witch's brew of evil consequences compounded from a pair of misconceived ingredients. On the one hand, there is the assumption that others have the right to lie to an individual about the imminence of his or her death in a way that will prevent that person from anticipating the moment and living through it in his or her own way. On the other hand, the wrong is compounded by exercising that "right" on behalf of someone other than the dying person. Death can impose heavy burdens on all the living, but frequently the principal stress results from our unwillingness to perceive it as anything other than unpleasant and discomforting. However, when death is near, it is questionable whether the feelings of others can fairly be taken to outweigh the interests of the dying person. And it is always dangerous to assume that deliberate deceit is a good basis for dealing with, much less assisting, another individual. The notable fact about these practices, however, is their dependence upon an increasingly negative attitude toward death and its implications.

Death as Inappropriate and Distant

Once again we find the emergence of a dominant pattern: as natural human death becomes less and less a part of our common experience, it is perceived as less and less appropriate to our lives. To some extent, this is true whether or not we have had several individual encounters with this form of death as personal or particular experiences. What is important is the image of death we have constructed, an image that the rude fact seems to violate. Of course, we know in an abstract, intellectual way that death is a general fact of life, but the specific event becomes so unusual that it is subconsciously eased out of our lived experience and regarded as not quite real. Tolstoy (17) makes this point well in *The Death of Ivan Ilych* when Ivan realizes that "the syllogism he had learnt from Kiezewetter's Logic: 'Caius is a man, men are mortal, therefore Caius is mortal,' had always seemed to him correct as applied to Caius, but certainly not as applied to himself" (pp. 131-132). This syllogistic inference may provide a kind of retrospective "explanation" of the death of a figure from the past. It also concedes something about the human race in general or man in the abstract. And it can even go so far as to anticipate that we (always the vague plural, never the definite singular) will all eventually die. But this does not yet come home to the concrete self in the present tense. It is little more than a loose eventuality in some remote future. What a shock, as Tolstoy's Ivan discovered, when these airy reveries are punctured by the sharp truth of reality!

A curious kind of widespread, but rarely acknowledged, socialization process mirrors these attitudes. It began with natural human death becoming less and less frequent a part of our lives. We were comforted by that fading presence and we encouraged the process whenever we could. Partly because we wanted to, we began to believe that death was not really a legitimate part of life and somehow should not break in on us. Death came to be regarded as unfortunate, undesirable, and even improper. When it had to be recognized, we treated it as something that ought to apply only to the elderly, a group to which none of us happened to belong. By such methods, we proceeded not only to reduce the frequency of death, but also—since it would continue to insist on striking some of those among us—to put it out of our sight wherever possible. In other words, we have coupled increasing distance with decreasing frequency. This is undoubtedly reflected in social practices that deal with death through *specialization* and *functionalization.* For example, in the recent past we have transferred a very large portion of the responsibility of caring for the elderly, the dying, and the dead to a select set of institutions and professional functionaries. Of course, specificity and division of function are characteristic of many complex societies and are associated, in the case of dying persons, with the factors that favor institutionalizing most treatment of serious illnesses. But it cannot be denied that, as death and dying have become increasingly distasteful to our society, we have acted to segregate from our daily lives the elderly, those who manifest a high risk of mortality, those who are actually dying, and the bodies of the dead. Making a place in the household for elderly grandparents, tending to or at least keeping company with the sick and the dying, and washing and dressing the corpse of a dead relative have traditionally been the right, the responsibility, and the privilege of family and close friends. For some individuals and groups these traditions and practices continue in force today, but our society as a whole typically employs custodial institutions, general hospitals, nurses, and funeral directors to perform most of these tasks for us.

Children and Death

A good example of the outcome of this growing negativity is presented in the way we deal with children and death. In general, we try to separate the two because we believe that the idea—much less the experience—of death is necessarily bad and harmful, and that children are too pure and fragile to be able to deal with such traumatic matters. Confusing ignorance with innocence, we have made great efforts to shield children from any contact with death. Our conviction seems to be that lack of communication, evasion, sanitized explanations, or outright lies are preferable to the contamination of truth and reality. At other times, when death was a prominent and recognized feature of human life, things were quite different.

> Men of that period were profoundly and rapidly socialized. The family did not intervene to delay the socialization of the child. Moreover, socialization did not separate man from nature, with which he could not interfere short of a miracle. (16, p. 28)

But now we can and do interfere with the order of nature, sometimes with favorable results. In the case of death, however, the attitudes we have formed lead us to try to "protect" children and adolescents from some of the basic lessons of life. Many adults appear determined not to introduce children to death, despite its omni-presence in nature. In the long run, this is impossible, though we may succeed in leaving children unprepared to deal with death. Children raised in artificial greenhouses are bound for difficulty when, as we all must sooner or later, they are required by circum-stances to cope with actual reality.

The Pornography of Death

Ariès' account of forbidden death is parallel to, and partially depen-dent upon, the work of Geoffrey Gorer, a British anthropologist. Gorer captured the core of this cluster of contemporary attitudes toward death in his celebrated little essay entitled "The Pornography of Death." Writing in 1955, Gorer (18) argued as follows:

> Traditionally, and in the lexicographic meaning of the term, por-nography has been concerned with sexuality. For the greater part of of the last two hundred years copulation and (at least in the mid-Victorian decades) birth were the "unmentionables" of the triad of basic human experiences ... During most of this period death was no mystery, except in the sense that death is always a mystery. . . .
> In the 20th century, however, there seems to have been an unre-marked shift in prudery; whereas copulation has become more and more "mentionable," particularly in the Anglo-Saxon societies, death has become more and more "unmentionable" *as a natural process.* (p. 195)

Gorer's analysis of death as pornographic rests on his conviction that we have come to view it as a subject inherently abhorrent, one which can never be mentioned openly or discussed directly. Like all disgust-ing subjects, death can only be introduced into polite conversation obliquely or euphemistically. As Gorer (18) says:

> Our great-grandparents were told that babies were found under gooseberry bushes or cabbages; our children are likely to be told that those who have passed on (fie! on the gross Anglo-Saxon mono-syllable) are changed into flowers, or lie at rest in lovely gardens. (p. 196)

It is typical of this view of death as pornographic that the attitude should be projected into the event itself. There are many things that we dislike but do not regard as intrinsically repellant; Gorer wants us to realize that we have come to attribute our negative feelings to the event of death itself. This is a good example of the interplay between contacts and attitudes. It shows once more that attitudes are not simply passive products but active participants in a changing set of experiences.

Institutionalization and Death

By looking once more at the institutionalization of death, we will be able to see how changing experiences and attitudes intertwine to produce a *synergistic effect*, one which is more powerful than either of its elements alone. As death occurs more and more in institutions, both the ways in which it is encountered and the attitudes associated with it are altered. From the very beginning, the institution will act to fit death into its own structures and routines. Its intention will be to serve its own best interests and the interests of its overall client population. But it may not achieve this goal and larger concerns may be ignored. As Ariès (16) says:

> Death in the hospital is no longer the occasion of a ritual ceremony, over which the dying person presides amidst his assembled relatives and friends. Death is a technical phenomenon obtained by a cessation of care, a cessation determined in a more or less avowed way by a decision of the doctor and the hospital team. Indeed, in the majority of cases the dying person has already lost consciousness. (p. 88)

Barney Glaser and Anselm Strauss (19) have shown how the simple act of entering a hospital transfers a high and usually unexpected degree of responsibility to the institution. Admission is only the first step in transforming a previously autonomous individual into something now called a "patient." This label is revealing, for it does not only mean one who waits calmly. Etymologically, it derives from a Latin root that suggests bearing or enduring pain, undergoing care or receiving treatment from another. Indeed all institutionalization involves some degree of submission, particularly when the person involved is dying and when the institution is a hospital established for the very purpose of mobilizing a wide range of equipment, technical skills, and other resources to combat illness and death.

In such an environment one finds many signs of efforts to hide death and to pretend that it is nonexistent. For example, some institutions try to remove from their premises the person who is about to die, so that the actual event will occur elsewhere. This can be particularly cruel and thoughtless in a nursing home or other long-term care facility, where the staff and other residents may be the dying person's only remaining friends. Removal denies the opportunity for human fellowship at the moment of death and for healthy grieving immediately thereafter. Another practice of some hospitals is to transfer a dying person to a single room, ostensibly because this provides privacy for the person and for his or her close relatives at this great moment. But it is worth noticing that this apparent act of altruism also has the effect of separating the distasteful fact of death from other patients, staff, and visitors. Even more obvious are institutional regulations that require the closing of hall doors and the isolation of elevators for the removal of a corpse, as if such behavior did not itself indicate what is taking place. This sort of misguided cleverness is now aided by improved equipment—wheeled carts that appear to be empty but actually conceal the dead body on a hidden lower level. All these practices suggest an emphasis on one particular aspect of the changing face of death.

> The accent has been placed on "acceptable." . . . [that is, a death] which can be accepted or tolerated by the survivors. It has its antithesis: "the embarrassingly graceless dying," which embarrasses the survivors because it causes too strong an emotion to burst forth; and emotions must be avoided both in the hospital and everywhere in society. One does not have the right to become emotional other than in private, that is to say, secretly. (16, p. 89)

We see here how a narrow range of attitudes has become increasingly prescriptive of how individuals ought to feel, how they should behave, and what society will tolerate. In other words, the changing patterns of our attitudes toward death have stimulated an internal dynamism that reinforces the negative ways in which we have come to view the face of death and that encourages the further restructuring of our experiences of death.

Unexpected Death

Another example of the interaction of knowledge and attitudes can be found in deaths that are unexpected, either because of their swiftness or because they strike those whom we regard as tender and unlikely victims. Today, the sharpest of these cases may well be that of *Sudden Infant Death Syndrome* (SIDS), often referred to as "crib death." This sort of death has become the leading cause of mortality in the United States among children from 1 to 12 months of age, taking some 7,500–10,000 lives annually in this country alone (20). SIDS is particularly troublesome to us because its victims are helpless infants, because we have no real understanding of its causes, and because it strikes swiftly and without advance warning. SIDS is especially paradoxical because improvements in pediatric medicine have eliminated or sharply reduced other formerly lethal ailments, and because we are increasingly able to identify this syndrome retrospectively through postmortem examinations. Parents who have to deal with the aftermath of SIDS often believe that something could or should have been done to prevent the death. The problem is to know what that might have been. Medicine, science, and life, which formerly seemed to offer so much, now appear to have betrayed us. Lack of understanding among relatives, neighbors, and those whose work involves them with such deaths often adds to the trauma in various ways. For example, callousness and charges of child abuse can result from ignorance and insensitivity. The stricken parents usually find themselves unable to remedy this unfortunate situation or even to strike back at its causes effectively. Hence, their impotence often turns to frustration, which can add to the problem and which seems to be an important factor in the high divorce rate among parents following an experience of SIDS. SIDS evokes a special range and depth of emotional reaction that can instruct us about all our attitudes toward death. Unlike other sorts of natural human death (even those involving children) that can be foreseen and perhaps mitigated by anticipatory grieving, the experience of SIDS is concentrated in the repercussions of a single sharp and final blow. And unlike some other quick-acting deaths, such as those resulting from an automobile accident or a heart attack, the experience of SIDS is aggravated by feelings of betrayal, guilt, and accusation.

Even though we cannot explain the causes of SIDS, researchers and counselors try to recreate some measure of intelligibility by identifying it as a *syndrome* or grouping of concurrent and characteristic symptoms. The point is to show that it is more than a series of unrelated and wholly capricious deaths. Counselors also try to explain to family and friends the common patterns of grieving and related difficulties following an SIDS experience. Self-help groups composed of individuals who have themselves had an earlier encounter with SIDS attempt to reassure the parents that they were not at fault. In short, there is an effort to create some degree of normality in an otherwise abnormal and still fundamentally inexplicable event.

The Unreality of Death

Many who are forced to confront a death—especially a disturbing one like SIDS—find themselves thrust into a state of disbelief. In part, this is a normal way of creating a pause or temporary buffer against traumatic shock, but it often goes further in a time when many forms of natural human death have assumed a quality of unreality. Confronting death violates our implicit sense that we shall simply go on and on, living as we are at present. This conviction is largely unspoken, perhaps because of our subliminal awareness that it cannot be sustained under the scrutiny that would follow explicit articulation. Nevertheless, Freud (21, pp. 304–305) thought that this attitude is quite fundamental in humans and that it results from the inability of our unconscious to believe in our own death. Regardless of whether Freud's explanation is correct, surely many are troubled by thoughts of death that convey intimations of our own mortality. Death touches us all because its finality and absoluteness escape our power either to change the fact or to do anything more for the person who has died. The problem of helplessness was not so significant in an era when people did not expect to influence or control the events of life very much. It is far more challenging in our present condition. Yet the inability to continue or to remedy past failures in our relationships with a dead person has always been with us. It has inspired various efforts to reestablish contact with the dead, and it creates a universal possibility for guilt, since we are all open to the charge that we might have done more to better the lives of our fellow human beings before their deaths. That holds reality to an ideal standard, which is hardly a fair measure, but it is a frequent dimension of our affective response to death. In short, there are many understandable reasons why we are likely to become angry, confused, disoriented, or discomforted when death and its consequences are thrust into our lives.

Some of these qualities of our perceptions of death are reinforced by the ways death is represented in the mass media and in its current unnatural forms. As shown earlier, these fantasies rarely confront death as an authentic part of human existence. Instead, they exploit it indiscriminately for other purposes and misrepresent its actuality through mindless repetition and outright distortion. Life and any realistic sense of death pale before the caricatures of James Bond or the wanton slaughter of "bad guys" in early John Wayne movies. In her thoughtful study of children and television, Marie Winn (22) takes this point a step further by emphasizing the *fact* of watching rather then the *content* of what is watched.

> To a certain extent the child's early television experiences will serve to dehumanize, to mechanize, to make less *real* the realities he encounters in life. . . . once television fantasy becomes incorporated into the viewer's reality, the real world takes on a tinge of fantasy— or dullness because it fails to confirm the expectations created by televised "life." The separation between the real and the unreal becomes blurred; all of life becomes more dreamlike as the boundaries between the real and the unreal merge. . . . A disturbing possibility exists that the television experience has not merely blurred the distinctions between the real and the unreal for steady viewers, but that by doing so it has dulled their sensitivities to real events. For when the reality of a situation is diminished, people are able to react to it less emotionally, more as spectators. (pp. 10 and 70-71)

If one has a reliable framework of understanding and appreciation for death as it really is, then these extravagances may provide a harmless escape from drudgery and a therapeutic release of tension. But in an era when we rarely encounter or come to terms with natural human death, these fantasies may serve to diminish the meaningfulness of human life. Thus, they also have the effect of denigrating the importance of death and flattening out or evacuating our affective responses to its occurrence.

This is excessively evident in the changing face of violence and unnatural forms of death in the twentieth century. In these forms of death, above all, we find our own behavior to have exceeded our comprehension of its nature and consequences. A kind of spiritual myopia makes us indifferent to the premature deaths inflicted by some humans on others, as long as they do not impinge on our own personal happiness and well-being. Like the survivors at Hiroshima, we experience a kind of psychic numbing, preferring to avert our eyes or depend on appeals to abstract principle rather than to confront real tragedy in flesh and blood. Both the microviolence of rape, robbery, and assault in the ghetto and the macroviolence of nuclear destruction display a peculiar mindlessness that is essential to what is going on. There is, in other words, a kind of alienation of understanding from knowledge and of feelings from experience. In terms of our topics, this can be looked at in two complementary ways. On the one hand, death will be thought to be unimportant wherever we lack the imagination or the sensitivity to see and to feel the importance of life. And on the other hand, by distancing ourselves from death and losing respect for its significance, we also find ourselves drawing away from a sense of the value of life. This is why the *fantastic* qualities of natural and unnatural human death are matters of such urgent concern, why we need to reconstitute them once more as *real* components of our vision of the changing face of death.

INDEPENDENT FACTORS

Our thesis throughout this chapter has been that the face of death is a shifting image of many hues, a portrait combining both cognitive and affective elements. In the introduction we argued for the need to reconstruct a contemporary representation of death and suggested that the way to do so was to identify and explore some of its principal elements. This led to a survey of changing contacts with death, and then we undertook an examination of evolving attitudes toward death. For the sake of discussion, we have attempted to deal with each of these components of our death-related experiences separately, but we have also tried to show that there is an ongoing internal dialogue between them that influences everything else that is taking place. Now we want to look at some examples of external factors and values that are not in themselves concerned with death but have an important impact on the ways we experience death. Several of these have already been touched on briefly in the course of our previous discussions. We need not repeat them all here; it will be enough to cite those forces that appear to be most influential in shaping our perceptions of the changing face of death.

One very obvious factor is that ours is a youth-oriented society. Youth, health, vigor, and vitality are all highly prized by most Americans. Thus our discomfort with the mentally ill and the handicapped often adds a social problem to the original mental or physical disability that they live with. Some Americans even seem to view illness and death as a kind of moral fault of the dying person. The seriously ill are sometimes made to feel that they have done wrong in getting sick or that the sickness is a punishment that they somehow deserved. In our society it is the death of an infant or a young person that appears as most painful and unfair. Conversely, we see evidence of the uncritical feeling that death is all right for the elderly. This is quite different from the viewpoint of a society that values wisdom, learning, and experience, or one that regards its oldest members as living links to the history of the group and to those who are now dead. In our society, one can even come across a kind of prejudicial "age-ism" that pits young against old with little recognition that both are living human beings. But why should we concede that the elderly should politely give up their claim to life? Who has the right to say that such individuals have lived their lives and that anything left is no longer important? And what is the basis for the belief that anyone who dies at a young age has somehow been cheated out of an entitlement to a long life? By emphasizing youth and health as we do, we structure a certain perception of death and a view of life that concentrates on quantity almost to the exclusion of quality.

A second important factor is our emphasis on individual freedom. Like youth and health, there is much that is inherently desirable in individualism and in freedom. They become unsatisfactory when they are made to bear more weight than they can and when their use is not tempered by a consideration for other important values. In our society, for example, the interpretation of individual freedom as a kind of social liberty sometimes leads to what has been called the "oppressive toleration" that we practice toward the behavior of others. This is a viewpoint that argues that as long as the actions of another person do not directly and adversely affect my own interests, I should tolerate (or even be indifferent to) his or her behavior. The danger of this viewpoint can be seen, for example, when it is applied to cases of suicide. Many people who threaten to commit suicide are really crying out for help. In response, we often ignore their real needs and sometimes we actually encourage their self-destructive tendencies. That is, we sometimes employ our freedom to convey to suicidal persons our agreement that their lives *are* without worth, when what is really called for is an effort to aid them to identify and to promote the values inherent in their lives. This is not the only instance in which freedom can have a bearing upon death, but it may help us to see how one dimension of life can have an important impact upon another.

Happiness is another central value in our society, closely related to freedom, that can have a significant influence upon our perception of death. Listen to Ariès (16) and Gorer (18), respectively: "It is henceforth given that life is always happy or should always seem to be so" (p. 87); "The right to the pursuit of happiness has been turned into an obligation" (p. x). Since death intrudes on our happiness and abrogates this right, it is an unwelcome visitor that must be fended off. While dying of leukemia, Lauren Trombley (23) came to realize that,

> . . . some of the people with whom I have had fairly close contact in the past found it almost impossible to deal with me and my illness because of their own fears and fantasies concerning death. One almost amusing idea came to light through one of my supervisors, namely, that some of my colleagues might very well be wishing that I would drop dead and get it over with rather than continue to torment them as I was. (p. 29)

Trombley's amusement must be ironic, but the discomfort felt by some of his colleagues that his dying should be tormenting them is surely real. It provides a good illustration of how powerfully our own egocentric needs can enter into our dealings with the death of another. One wonders whether happiness is or should be the ultimate value in our lives. If so, then we should surely abandon love, since intimate involvement with other human beings inevitably brings pain as well as happiness. Those who care for dying persons cannot avoid being hurt; they will not always be happy, but they can find a great deal of satisfaction in what they are doing.

Freedom, the pursuit of happiness, and a more affluent lifestyle have stimulated the creation of a mobile society built around individuals and nuclear families. Mobility, and the associated tendency to relocate for a better job, fragments extended families who live hundreds of miles apart. It forces each member of the society to turn inward to his or her own resources, rather than outward to larger and more stable groups. This tends to weaken the strength and extent of communal and social bonds. As a result, we simply have less opportunity for, and less understanding of, familial and other forms of informal emotional sustenance in times of stress. Self-help groups are coming into being in response to the felt need to build new systems of support in a changed environment. A closely related development is the deritualization of many practices that used to mark the occurrence of a death. This seems to depend upon our feeling that we no longer need long wakes, formal visitations, and prescribed mourning periods. But custom and ritual are not necessarily confining; they can free us from distractions and channel our energies so as to accomplish the work that really needs to get done.

Our discomfort with sadness and unhappiness is also fostered by a kind of overarching intellectualism, in which all strong feelings are suspect and the emotional needs of humans are deemphasized or suppressed. During the funeral ceremonies for President Kennedy, for example, his wife Jacqueline was widely praised for her stalwart and controlled behavior. But is such stoicism a wise model for everybody? Should it not be acceptable to scream and cry out when a terrible and shattering event has taken place? Did we really admire Mrs. Kennedy because she eased the demands made *on us* at a difficult time and because she conformed to our ideal of superhuman behavior? My point is not to censure Mrs. Kennedy for her behavior. I only want to suggest that quite different patterns of bereavement may be appropriate for others. More importantly, I want to draw attention to a widespread inclination to subject personal and emotional needs to certain intellectual and conceptual models that represent a one-sided interpretation of humanity. Better than any others, the experiences of mourning and bereavement bring home the lesson that human beings are more than disembodied intellects.

Another factor that contributes to making death a more difficult experience is the dominant scientism and agnosticism of our times. We live in a society that increasingly finds itself without a creedal or mythic framework in which to understand life and interpret death. As a result, that final event in our lives becomes, as Herman Feifel (24, p. 4) has said, less and less an opening to the future and more and more a wall into which we collide. And yet, the lesson that Gil Elliot (6) draws from his long review of the statistics of unnatural forms of death in the twentieth century is that our needs go exactly in the opposite direction: "Fact, is not superior to myth. Technology is not more efficient than religion. However much factual and technical knowledge we acquire, we shall always have to live with the unpredictable" (p. 203). It is our failure to realize this demand of life and to accommodate it in any other effective framework of interpretation that leads us to see death as a thief who cheats or an enemy who defeats. These are metaphors of interpretation, but they are not adequate to our needs. We have overestimated our claim to the future and our power to control it. Consequently, we feel betrayed by death and subjected in some nameless fashion. It is not enough to throw over the philosophies and religions of the past and to become a secular society, without creating new systems of meaning or adapting traditional ones to the new situation. Humans cannot function effectively without some framework in which to make sense of the events of life and the power of death.

One myth system that served its adherents for a long time was the Protestant ethic of faith and hard work. Like similar systems, it constituted a set of values that provided security and direction in the midst of the problems of life. It seems now, however, to have become debased into a crude bartering for success, where success is not thought to be compatible with death except on some vague and unspecified terms. This is why the intrusion of death into a life of faithfulness and diligent striving often causes people to accuse God of not fulfilling His assigned role. Such people, like many of their humanistic and nontheistic cousins, have somehow come to feel that human beings have a right to their expectations of a pleasant future in this life. It is thought unjust that such expectations should not always be satisfied. This is a very basic misunderstanding of the character of human life and of its transciency and limitations. It is also rather bad theology. Those who persist in being frustrated and defeated by death, in decrying its injustice and lack of equity, are really struggling with their own conceptions of life and death. As the great signpost of human finitude, death can be the master teacher that sets these misconceptions aright, but only if we apply ourselves to the lessons it has to teach.

This brings us to our well-known impatience with issues that are complex and difficult. Most of us prefer, and are accustomed to dealing with, problems that are manageable and easy to solve. We become discouraged and angry when we cannot gratify this desire. Our tendency is to assume that there are relatively simple, accessible, and universal answers to all questions. When our own efforts to find such answers are not successful, we assume there must be some authoritative source that knows the answers and can supply them to us without much difficulty. If that does not prove to be the case, we suspect that there is something wrong or unfair about the initial problem. Death puts all these assumptions to the test. Despite our best efforts, it will not go away. Nor does it admit easy solutions, although there are many competing "authorities" who claim to have resolved its difficulties. Even if we find one or more of their lessons to be plausible, we soon discover the age-old lesson that any answer that is to have enduring value for an individual must ultimately be appropriated, interpreted, and made into one's own achievement. Otherwise it is merely a shaky prop borrowed from its rightful owner. The moral is that maturity is not a gift, it is a continuing task, an undertaking in which one learns to live with a certain amount of ambiguity and incompleteness. This is how death drives away shallow perceptions of life and leads us to look more deeply into the true character of our humanity. And the first step in that process, insofar as death is concerned, is to try to discover the various elements that make up the changing face of death in our own lives. It may even be that death presents more than one integrated pattern or face to each of us.

In these last two sections we have traced a substantial shift in attitudes toward death, reinforced by a variety of independent values, all of which move us sharply in the direction of a less accepting and more hostile outlook on death. As a result, many insist that we have come to be a pure example of a death-denying society. Others (and I include myself among this latter group) believe that this is too simple and unequivocal a diagnosis, despite its obvious basis for justification. But all can agree on two evident conclusions. First, there is quite a high proportion of discomfort and denial in our attitudes and in those aspects of our behavior that are concerned with death. And, second, the results of this increased negativity constitute a new and distinctive posture towards death as the dominant perspective of our society. That is not the whole story of our contemporary dealings with death, but it must be the primary affective theme in any reconstruction of the changing face of death in our time. To complete our portrait, we need to go on to Chapter Two where we can examine in greater detail what it is like to live with this new and evermore spectral visage of death.

REFERENCES

1. Marcel, G. On the ontological mystery. In *The philosophy of existentialism* (2nd ed.), trans. Manya Harari. New York: Citadel, 1962.
2. Keegan, J. *The face of battle.* New York: Viking, 1976.
3. Fulton, R. *Death and identity* (Rev. ed.), in collaboration with Robert Bendiksen. Bowie, MD: Charles Press, 1976.
4. Goldscheider, C. *Population, modernization, and social structure.* Boston: Little, Brown, 1971.
5. Lerner, M. When, why, and where people die. In O. Brim, H. Freeman, S. Levine, & N. Scotch (Eds.), *The dying patient.* New York: Russell Sage Foundation, 1970.
6. Elliot, G. *The twentieth century book of the dead.* New York: Random House, 1972.
7. Dawidowicz, L. *The war against the Jews 1933-1945.* New York: Bantam, 1976.
8. Reitlinger, G. *The final solution: The attempt to exterminate the Jews of Europe 1939-1945* (2nd rev. and augmented ed.). London: Vallentine, Mitchell, 1968.
9. Bettelheim, B. Foreword to M. Nyiszli, *Auschwitz: A doctor's eyewitness account.* (Trans. Tibere Kremer and Richard Seaver). Greenwich, CN: Fawcett, 1960.
10. Lifton, R. J. *Death in life: Survivors of Hiroshima.* New York: Random House, 1967.
11. Lifton, R. J. On death and death symbolism: The Hiroshima disaster. *Psychiatry*, 1964, 27, 191-210.
12. Hersey, J. *The wall.* New York: Bantam, 1967.
13. Hersey, J. *Hiroshima.* New York: Bantam, 1948.
14. Lustig, A. *Darkness casts no shadow.* New York: Inscape, 1977.

15. Kübler-Ross, E. *Death: The final stage of growth.* Englewood Cliffs, NJ: Prentice-Hall, 1975.
16. Ariès, P. *Western attitudes toward death: From the Middle Ages to the present.* (Trans. P. Ranum.) Baltimore: Johns Hopkins University Press, 1974.
17. Tolstoy, L. *The death of Ivan Ilych and other stories.* New York: New American Library, 1960.
18. Gorer, G. The pornography of death. In *Death, grief and mourning.* Garden City, NY: Doubleday, 1967.
19. Glaser, B., & Strauss, A. *Time for dying.* Chicago: Aldine, 1968.
20. Bergman, A., Melton, J., Baker, R., and others. *Sudden unexpected death in infants.* New York: MSS Information Corp., 1974.
21. Freud, S. Thoughts for the times on war and death. In E. Jones (Ed.), *Collected papers* (Vol. IV). New York: Basic Books, 1959.
22. Winn, M. *The plug-in drug.* New York: Viking, 1977.
23. Trombley, L. A psychiatrist's response to a life-threatening illness. *Life-Threatening Behavior,* 1972, 2, 26–34.
24. Feifel, H. (Ed.) *New meanings of death.* New York: McGraw-Hill, 1977.

CHAPTER TWO

Living with the Changing Face of Death

CHARLES A. CORR

DEATH SYSTEMS AND THE CHANGING FACE OF DEATH: MANIFESTATIONS AND CONSEQUENCES

One of the most knowledgeable writers in the field of death and dying, Robert Kastenbaum, coauthor of *The Psychology of Death* (1), has developed in a recent book, *Death, Society, and Human Experience* (2), the notion of a "death system," which he first proposed several years earlier. By *death system* Kastenbaum means a

---

While the first chapter is concerned with the dynamics of negative and ambivalent views and attitudes toward death, we now see how these attitudes manifest themselves in many types of negative behaviors. We see that negative behaviors have a number of consequences that are detrimental to the well-being of individuals and to society as a whole.

However, even though attitudes toward death are by and large negative, there are coexisting positive views with resulting positive consequences. Ambivalence itself can have a positive component in that one sometimes feels positively about death and at other times feels negatively depending upon circumstance. These factors are noted to avoid oversimplification. The author does not shy away from the question of value judgments and personal meanings involved in deciding what is negative, positive, or ambivalent in the first place.

The Problem: Denial and Ambivalence toward Death

"socio-physical network by which the relationship to mortality is mediated and expressed." Nothing sinister or extraordinary is contemplated; Kastenbaum's focus is on the patterning or orderliness of our everyday relations with death. Thus a death system is the total complex of people, places, times, objects, and symbols that any given group of humans employs to organize its dealings with death. There can be many death systems, each suited to a particular population and set of circumstances. All such systems serve a number of functions: warning and prediction, prevention, care of the dying, and even, in various ways, killing. According to Kastenbaum, the existence of a death system does not challenge the uniqueness of individual responses to life and death. But he does contend that individual encounters with and feelings about death will not be properly understood unless they are also seen as occurring within broader patterns of time, place, and culture. To that extent, death systems are more comprehensive and more specific versions of Goldscheider's models of uncontrolled and controlled mortality, which we saw in the previous chapter. And our own metaphor of "the changing face of death" is another way of suggesting that death has numerous features that present themselves in a variety of ways in different circumstances. All these models and metaphors are intended to draw attention to the complexity and the pervasiveness of our relations with death. Death and its implications permeate our lives. Sometimes its presence is obvious and accessible; often it is disguised or hidden from immediate view. Its aspects can be commonplace or unusual, but it is never wholly absent from human experience.

In Chapter One we reconstructed large-scale patterns in the changing face of death. Now we need to develop the portrait in more detail, acknowledge diverse elements, and give more particulars about our modes of *living with* the changing face of death. To use Kastenbaum's language, in this chapter we will be primarily interested in those manifestations and consequences of the changing face of death that define the dominant, contemporary North American death system. First we will consider a series of negative manifestations in attitude and behavior. We cannot mention all such cases, but we can cite representative examples in each of the three primary areas: death, dying, and bereavement. Each reveals the high degree of discomfort and avoidance that is typical of this society. Note that such manifestations are initially termed *negative* because of the orientation of rejection or denial that they display toward death. This does not mean that they are inherently bad or dysfunctional. Negativity in this sense might be an appropriate way of dealing with death for a particular society, individual, or set of circumstances. However, in our society there is so much facing away from death, and its consequences are often so counterproductive, that the term *negative* usually takes on a second sense of *undesirable*. In this chapter we will also look at more positive examples of acknowledgement or acceptance of death. These aspects of the ways we have come to live with death correct the too-simple stereotype that we live in a society that is exclusively death-denying (3). These aspects also suggest that both positive and negative elements can coexist in a single death system and that this ambivalence can exist within individuals as well. Finally, we will consider some of the consequences that follow from our accommodations with death. Here the argument is twofold: 1) that these are natural consequences of the strategies we have adopted for dealing with death; and 2) that, in large part, they are symptoms of an undesirable death system. If that is correct, then we must either accept such consequences as an unavoidable price for the accommodations we require, or we must alter our modes of coping with death in the hope of achieving a more desirable set of consequences. The chapter concludes with a suggestion for a point of view that might help us move in the latter direction as we study the remainder of this book.

NEGATIVE MANIFESTATIONS

Avoidance

As noted in the previous chapter, Gorer (4) and Ariès (5) have argued that our society views death as pornographic and forbidden. If they are correct, then our death system can be expected to manifest a heavy reliance on various techniques of avoidance. Surely it would be natural to turn away from, or to try to arrange our lives so as not to come into contact with, anything regarded as unpleasant or distasteful. So far as we can, most of us try to avoid having anything to do with death, whether before or after the fact. Our efforts are not always successful—we cannot always hermetically seal death out of our lives—but it is the attempt that reveals the motive. In the following parts of this section, we will give evidence of avoidance attempts in our dealings with death, in matters related to dying or other events preceding death, and in postdeath activities concerning funeral practices and bereavement.

Talking about Death

One of the significant things about human beings seems to be the ability to create and use language systems. Consequently, *language patterns* are often important indicators of underlying attitudes. For example, many feel that death is not a pleasant subject for conversation, but they admit that it is a fact of life that must be faced. They

The Problem: Denial and Ambivalence toward Death

are likely to talk about death in an honest, though somewhat reluctant, manner. Their outlook might be epitomized in the trite remark that in this life we can only be sure of two things, death and taxes. When we examine this comment, it appears that the real purpose may be to express a muted complaint about taxes, but it does also have something to say about death. One senses elements of resignation, self-deprecation, and even a small bit of intended humor. The language of death is often used in these ways to add drama or emphasis to ordinary speech. "She worries me to death," a mother will say about her obstreperous child. Or someone will exclaim, "I was so embarrassed, I wished I was dead." An obnoxious person who accosts us at a party will be told to "drop dead." Orville Kelly (6), a courageous man with a life-threatening illness, was once told by a friend over the telephone, "I'm just dying to see you again!" (p. 186). And there are dead batteries; things that are deader than a doornail; alcoholics who are dead drunk; people who are scared to death, dead on their feet, or dead right; marksmen with a dead eye; nighttime hours that are dead quiet; and dart throwers who hit the target dead center. A particularly curious phrase speaks of "killing time," as if we had nothing better to do with it and should want it to be dead and past. These patterns of speech testify to the marvelous adaptability of language. Usually harmless, they may signal the user's inability or unwillingness to find other ways to achieve linguistic emphasis. But they also show that, when all is said and done, we see death as absolute or final and we often associate with death a sense of undesirability.

A quite different vocabulary is brought into play when we have to speak of death itself. This vocabulary is characterized by *euphemisms*, which employ indirection and camouflage to soften direct references to death. Thus people rarely "die"; they "pass away," "expire," "kick the bucket," "pass on," "go to meet their Maker," or "go to receive their reward." Familiar metaphors of "laying someone to rest" or "sleeping in heaven" invoke soporific concepts that children often use for death. This makes one wonder whether adults have taught these "softer" concepts to children or if we are more comfortable borrowing their childlike terms? All these expressions provide a relatively good or auspicious way of referring to that which is perceived as distasteful or offensive. Many euphemisms were once vigorous and graphic, now they are typically trite and conventional. Sometimes they are appropriate to a particular context, or matters of style and individual choice. But they can also be misleading and unfortunate. Hospital staff members who tell their replacements on the next shift that they "lost" Mr. Smith last night might prompt a literal-minded observer to wish that they would hurry out and try to find him again. A youngster who inquires about a sick pet is likely to learn that it has been "put to sleep" by the veterinarian—whereupon the child may well be told to stop asking annoying questions and to go take a nap! Evelyn Waugh so deftly exploited a once-popular phrase used in the title of his satirical novella *The Loved One* (7), that it is now heard much less frequently. But a dead body will still be referred to as a "person," instead of as a corpse. In the funeral home, the corpse is placed in the "slumber room," and the change in terminology from *undertaker* (quite a graphic and literal title) to *mortician, funeral director*, and *grief therapist* is more than just a substitution of equivalencies or a reflection of changing duties.

When presented with a situation involving death, many protest, "I don't know what to say." This may reflect disorientation in an unfamiliar or uncomfortable situation for which little social guidance has been provided. Or it may go further to indicate a desire for a cookbook theory of human interaction in which specific formulas and recipes would be provided for every imaginable context. For many, this desire is satisfied by clichés, familiar phrases that offer conventional responses to a wide variety of events. However, clichés achieve their versatility through overuse and an impoverishment of meaning. They are hackneyed substitutes for thought, reflecting lack of commitment instead of sincere concern. That is why it does not seem very satisfying to announce to a dying person that "we all have to go sometime." Even though true, the remark is unhelpful because it is distant and empty of feeling. Likewise, the stereotyped greeting, "How are you?" is often accompanied by a moment of embarrassment and a desire to recall the words when it is inadvertently put to a seriously ill person. In our society, "How are you?" is akin to "Hello," a conventional greeting rather than a serious request for information about one's state of health. Clichés provide something to say in a passing moment, but while they may fill an uncomfortable silence, they do not stand up to a serious or sustained interchange. That is why those who come to depend upon clichés experience a sense of increased inadequacy when these resources fail to serve their needs. Clichés buffer us from death and other events, but they do so by fostering inattention and insensitivity to the realities of life.

Death and Morbidity

When death is mentioned directly, some people in our society will exclaim, "I just don't want to talk about that." If pressed, they may tell us that it is morbid to talk about death. This seems to mean that there is something inherently disagreeable or repulsive about death, a viewpoint that associates two related misapprehensions. First, death is a natural and, from a biological standpoint, an essential part of life. Thus the complaint can be sustained only by showing that life itself is repellant, and if we look closely at the character of our existence we will discover that the possibilities for meaningfulness in being human are closely related to the fact that life is essentially transient and temporal. It is not a life of continuous and unending bliss such as might be typical for an angel or some sort of deity. We are death-bound from the moment of our birth. Our lives, as shown in the previous chapter, are thoroughly permeated with death and death-related experiences. One can complain about this situation, but it is not realistic or consistent to accept life without also accepting the necessity of death that comes along with it.

Secondly, the term *morbid* properly denotes an unhealthy concentration on death, a kind of death fixation. But paying attention to death need not be harmful to our well-being. It is the balance of qualitative and quantitative factors that determine whether the involvement is or is not healthy. There are examples, as in cases of necrophilia, when death is given too much attention or the wrong sort of attention. But there are also cases in which it is our aversion, our thanatophobia, that is unhealthy. The prohibition against morbidity cannot be allowed to rule out all investigation or discussion of death. As a practical matter, that could hardly be achieved, since death is a fundamental part of our lives. But what we want to foster is a constructive look at death. We study death not so much for its own sake, but as an inescapable fact of our existence and as an important perspective from which life can be understood, assessed, and valued. The seventeenth century French moralist La Rochefoucauld said, in an oft-quoted statement, "one can no more look steadily at death than at the sun" (8). That is undoubtedly true, but it does not mean that we can find no way at all to look either at death or at the sun. We obviously do look at the sun in many ways, often obliquely or through filters, and we live our lives in its necessary warmth and light. There is no a priori reason why we cannot do the same with death. We need to confront death openly from time to time, and then to face away in order to live our lives with full awareness of the lessons of that confrontation.

Callousness and Defiance

In situations in which one cannot successfully avoid death, negative attitudes are often expressed through forms of callousness. These are devices that employ indifference or hardness as a way of protecting ourselves from the impact of death. For instance, soldiers in battle often employ language that erases or reduces the humanity of their opponents. And medical students confronting their first cadaver in a gross anatomy class—possibly the first time that they have ever seen a dead body—frequently resort to a crude gallows humor (9). Both are ways of protecting us from empathizing with the cadaver and the enemy; these behavior patterns free us from responding to such deaths as human events. Another approach involves defiance or direct confrontation with death. This involves risk taking for its own sake, not the braving of hazards in the interest of advancing knowledge or improving our lives. For a previous generation that had just discovered the thrill of powerful automobiles, this appeared in games of "chicken," in which opposing vehicles were driven toward each other at high speed to see which would give way first. Similarly, one still hears of occasional cases of Russian roulette, in which a person loads a revolver with a single bullet, spins the cylinder so that the position of the bullet is unknown, puts the barrel to the head, and pulls the trigger. A prominent contemporary example is Evel Knievel, the daredevil motorcycle rider. What motivates his attempts to ride a motorcycle over canyons and artificial obstacles? And what motivates those who pay to watch him put his life in jeopardy? In these cases, death is seen as a malignant and hostile force, essentially apart from and opposed to life. This vision of death apparently compels some to try to master or to vanquish it like a dragon of old. Even otherwise sophisticated medical circles have absorbed some of this ethos, as can be seen in their refusal ever to "give up" treatment and their sense of "failure" when death arrives. The phrasings are significant: one "surrenders" or "fails" in a contest against an alien force.

Death: The Ultimate Evil?

The question posed by all this avoidance, callousness, and defiance is whether or not death is the ultimate evil. Is this sort of estrangement from death necessary or appropriate? Or is it misconstrued and sometimes even pathological? Could there ever be, under any circumstances, another value (fidelity, altruism, integrity, humanity, patriotism, or whatever) that I would choose at the cost of death? Throughout history, many have in fact made such choices. One case involves those who have been martyred for refusing to recant religious or other beliefs, preferring allegiance to a "higher" cause over the price to be paid for remaining alive. Another example is that of soldiers who have thrown their bodies over a hand grenade to muffle its explosion, thereby saving the lives of their comrades. Ours is a cynical era that tends to devalue such instances because we emphasize short-term, personal success over long-range altruism. Even when we do favor deferred gratification, it is usually egocentric and this-worldly rather than other-directed and abstract. But we need to find some way of putting to ourselves the hard question: Is our over-riding aim the mere extension of life at all costs?

Gillian Martin offers us a penetrating example of choosing be-tween competing values. In *The Goat, the Wolf and the Crab* (10), Martin describes a middle-aged Englishwoman who is informed that she has cancer. The alternatives are surgery, which offers a very high expectation of success, as against the option of doing nothing and dying in about 2 more years. The "obvious" choice is surgery, but the protagonist decides to take her 2 years. Her explanation is that she is choosing, not death, but one free deci-sion of her own after a lifetime of conformity to the conduct that others expected of her. We need not agree with this interpretation, but then we must be prepared to say just what we would have done and exactly why we would have behaved in a different way.

Others have imagined an endless life extending on and on while generation after generation of family, friends, and acquaintances are born, experience life, and die. Would such a life be desirable, or would it be boring, meaningless, and absurd? If we say that interminable existence is good, how does that reflect on our own limited life? If we reject a life of endless endurance, what is the element that turns it sour? We should not think that this is too fanciful an example, for it has a partial analogue in the *cryonics movement* (11). First advocated by Robert Ettinger (12), this program seeks to place newly dead bodies in a state of suspended animation at supercool temperatures. By replacing blood with a glycerol solution, placing the body in a capsule, and reducing temperatures to those of liquid nitrogen, the Cryonics Society proposes that cadavers can be sustained indefinitely without fur-ther decay. Obviously, such a frozen cadaver is neither lively nor lifelike, but suspension is not viewed as an end in itself. The aim is to make possible the rejuvenation of the frozen bodies at some unspecified future date when medical and scientific advances might have corrected the causes of their deaths. One implication is that death occurs only as a result of some specific cause, that it is not an essential part of life. Apart from high costs and other practi-cal problems, which appear to be forcing the cryonics movement into virtual nonexistence (13), some critics have raised ethical questions about the propriety of bequeathing a heritage of defec-tive corpses to future generations. But our concern is only to in-quire whether the zeal to extend life in this way is commendable or overwrought. Shall we join with the motto of the group, "Never Say Die"? Or shall we try to determine the conditions under which death can be regarded as legitimate and appropriate in a human life?

Religion and Death

Some regard religion as a kind of omnibus attempt to deny the reality of death. Thus John Fowles (14) argues that religion is but one more attempt to *domesticate* death. This is achieved, he thinks, by making death subservient to a doctrine of afterlife, immortality, resurrection, or reincarnation. Fowles sees this as setting a promise of some future life against our present form of existence. Instead, he contends that we should reject all hope of anything beyond this life and commit ourselves solely to the values to be found within our present state of existence. Otherwise, he believes, value and meaning will be siphoned away from this life through the hope of the future. This seems to conform, for example, to popular accounts of Christian Scientists who are said to deny the reality of death and of Hindus or Buddhists who believe in reincarnation. But we might ask whether the former denial goes so far as to claim that the lives of a married couple are completely unchanged after one of them stops all breathing for an extended period of time? And doesn't *re*incarnation involve the cessation of one life, the inauguration of another, and the lack of remembered continuity between them? More importantly, the well-known Jesuit theologian Karl Rahner (15) insists that a Christian theology of death depends upon an acknowledgment of the definiteness and finality of death as a natural and personal conclusion to this life. For Rahner, death is the universal and necessary end to the human state of pilgrimage. My point in raising these diverse and apparently conflicting positions is to suggest that much that is said concerning religious interpretations of death, both pro and con, is uninformed and superficial. We need to look much more closely at the meanings of particular religious doctrines that have to do with death. That is the only way to learn what those doctrines have to teach us about death and is the indispensable condition for making our own test of their soundness in each case.

Dying

Another set of manifestations of avoidance and negativity has to do with dying. More than one study (16, 17) has shown that physical ailments may not be the most stressful aspects of dying for many people in our society. Good medical and nursing care must address themselves to the alleviation of discomforting symptoms, such as nausea and diarrhea, and to the control of physical pain. But pain, especially in its chronic forms, is a complex phenomenon not limited merely to bodily aspects. Total pain includes other important factors (18). A dying patient is not just an individual who happens to contain a heart or other organ that is losing its ability to perform properly; he or she is also a total person who has psychological, social, and spiritual, as well as physical needs. The dying person is, until death has actually occurred, also a living human being. The fact that the person is dying may confer a distinctive character upon the life that he or she is living while dying, but we should not permit this special time or condition in an individual's life to divert attention from the continuing needs of the total person.

And yet that is often exactly what we do allow to happen. For the special poignancy of dying, as so many have found it in our society, rests in separation, loneliness, and loss of sustaining human contact. It has been said that our death is something that each of us can only experience alone. Whether or not that is true, dying is something we can share in many ways. And the sharing of that experience is often a process of great significance, both for the dying person and for the others who are privileged to participate. That is the great lesson Elisabeth Kübler-Ross and the members of her seminar on death and dying have put before us (19). Though hardly a new lesson, it seems to be one that especially needs to be reaffirmed for our generation. For we have consigned the dying to institutions in unprecedented numbers; we have reduced and sometimes eliminated both the number and the length of our visits to them; and we have fostered or permitted the imposition of restrictions that tend to keep children and grandchildren from enjoying the mutual comfort of being together with their parents and grandparents in the precious time right before death.

Professionalism and Other Barriers

Those who cannot detour around dying individuals sometimes construct barriers of one sort or another to limit such interactions or to control their consequences. Orville Kelly tells of a particularly obvious example from his own experience (20). Some time after the diagnosis of his cancer, Kelly went to a party with his wife where he found enjoyment overcoming his depression for the first time in several months. "Then I noticed that everyone else in the room had his drink in a glass. Mine was in a paper cup (p. 26)." Here the problem clearly is not with Kelly but with his hosts. What could they have been thinking, and what in fact did they do to him? What fears prompt some to treat dying as if it were a contagious disease? With professional care givers, barriers are likely to be more subtle or even unconscious. For example, Lawrence LeShan (21, pp. 6–7) conducted a comparative study that showed it took some hospital personnel much longer to respond to call button signals from those who were near death than to signals from other patients.

The individuals involved were startled when LeShan gave them his report on their own behavior. *Professionalism* has aspects that can be turned into barriers. Thus physicians have been known to say, "There is nothing more that we can do." This is particularly significant since it demonstrates a double failure. Professionally, there is always something more that good medicine and nursing have to offer to a sick person, even if no cure is to be had and the resources of a narrow specialization are no longer applicable. And as humans, there is never a time we cannot lend our concerned presence to a fellow comrade on the road of life.

Other sorts of barriers surrounding many dying persons result from varying attitudes toward truth-telling. In this situation, similar results can follow from contrasting attitudes of noncommunication, candor, and lying. Some choose to deal with dying persons by reducing or eliminating direct communication. Whether that applies to communications about the person's state of health or to more general forms of interaction, it has much the same effect. One or more of the principal realities in the individual's life is put off limits for discussion. Relationships are constricted, and the individual is at least partially isolated. Others respond to the dying person's need for truth with a kind of brutal candor. The brutality need not be intentional, but where truth is delivered in ways that are hurtful the wound becomes a barrier to further intimacy. Another possibility relating to truth-telling involves the distortion or actual misrepresentation of the truth. This can be carried to the point of outright lies, spoken, it is usually said, so as not to take away the person's hope. All these tactics involve a corrosive mixture of three elements: 1) an insistence on perceiving death as irredeemably evil, so that news of its impending arrival must be either suppressed or hastily transferred to someone else; 2) lack of creativity to develop alternative forms of communication that might better fit the situation of the dying person; and 3) an undue focus on the personal needs of the second party who must communicate with the dying individual and who, as a result, is also coping with a difficult (though somewhat different) problem. The presence of each of these elements is understandable but does not excuse their intrusion into a setting that may already be difficult enough. If we are to deal effectively with dying persons, we need to look more closely at our own perceptions of death and how we permit our attitudes and limitations to aggravate the problems of dying. Furthermore, many of these difficulties might be eased if we realized that the demands of truth and hope need not force us into sharp either/or dichotomies.

Oversimplification: Truth and Hope

The difficulties outlined in the previous two paragraphs misrepresent the realities of dying because they depend upon undifferentiated and quite simplistic notions of truth and hope. We flounder in imparting truth because we proceed from the belief that all the relevant knowledge is possessed by only one of the members participating in the dialogue. One can only ask, "Should I tell the truth to this patient?" when it is assumed that I alone know what the situation is and the patient does not. That is rarely the case. It may well be, for example, that a professional person in such a dialogue does have a significant kind of intellectual and technical understanding of the presence or absence of a certain disease process. But there is also an important sense in which most of us have some sort of awareness that something is or is not going wrong within our own minds and bodies. Avery Weisman (22) has termed this latter condition a state of "middle knowledge." Drawing on self-awareness, it may extend anywhere from a nagging suspicion to explicit consciousness. The point is that in the model physician-patient relationship, as in most other forms of significant dialogue, the two human beings ought to be partners in sharing. They ought to be able to guide each other in a process of mutual information. Further, when the dialogue concerns death, the dying have an important existential stake in having their inner suspicions instructed by the categories and interpretations of the best available medical knowledge and judgment. After all, it is their life and health that are under discussion. And many have testified that reliable knowledge of their impending death is far preferable to the loose ends of ignorance and the anxieties of an unbridled imagination. The real question, as many astute physicians, counselors, and friends have learned through precious experience, is not *whether* to tell a person the truth, but *when* and *how* to convey what must be communicated (23, 24). Here the dying person may be the best leader. Truth-telling is not a matter of simplistic absolutes but a process serving the ends of our shared humanity by respecting the needs and capacities of the parties involved.

Similarly, *hope* is a supple and highly individual thing. It ought not be confused with mere wishing or with a desire for miracles. Hope is an orientation or state of being that can be directed to a variety of ends. For a dying person, that might encompass long life, relatively good health, a minimum of pain and other forms of discomfort, some new form of therapy or treatment, some significant accomplishment, and the love and companionship of relatives and friends. Ultimately, we can always hope that our lives will be valuable and meaningful for having been lived as well as they could be. None of these hopes are unrealistic. Indeed, this sense of hope is fully compatible with truth, as well as with impending death. Thus, if properly understood and respected, hope can and should always be preserved. It will be sustained—not subverted—by the truth, when that truth is conveyed with intelligence, imagination, and sincere concern. Thoughtlessness, brutality, and deceit unnecessarily betray both truth and hope, in the last analysis because they repudiate our shared humanity.

Communication, Presence, and Caring

Our tendency for avoidance in the face of death frequently leads us to encourage false hopes or to lapse into an uncomfortable and unaccustomed silence. That need not be the only mode of interaction with dying persons, as Barney Glaser and Anselm Strauss (25) have shown in their analysis of "open," "closed," and "mixed" ("suspicion") *awareness contexts.* But no tragedy is greater than that which comes about when a lifetime of love and honest sharing between husband and wife, parents and children, relatives and friends ends in a final period of deception and inability to communicate. That is the great game of mutual pretense so familiar in our society. Such a ritual drama can serve positive values in certain circumstances. For example, it can provide time to mobilize one's psychic resources, or it can supply temporary relief from the task of facing overwhelming difficulties. However, it is more often employed as a counterfunctional prohibition against beneficial human intercourse. The desire to avoid honest confrontation with death is so strong and pervasive in our society that some dying people have internalized it and made it into the basis for their own conduct. But many more testify to their loneliness and frustration at being unable to speak frankly about the implications of the process that is most important in their lives. They tell of the need for a sympathetic comrade with whom to share their thoughts and feelings as death approaches. Others praise those who do provide them with an opportunity to speak what is on their mind or to vent pent-up emotions. Not everybody will want or need exactly the same forms of assistance. But what is striking in our society is the degree to which we have withdrawn from the venerable traditions of making ourselves available to the sick and keeping company with the dying.

Sometimes well-meaning people protest that they are uncomfortable during visits with the elderly, the sick, the dying, and the bereaved. They complain that they just don't know what to say. A young college student once told me how she had handled a similar situation. Her father was dying, and while she was with him words

The Problem: Denial and Ambivalence toward Death

seemed to fail her. Instead, she held his hand and they cried together. It was what some theologians might call a *witness of presence*, an unmistakable profession of concern and open sharing of emotions. Much the same kind of communication is dramatized in the powerful film *Peege*. In this story a married couple and their three sons of college age or slightly younger visit the boys' elderly grandmother in her nursing home for perhaps the last time. The viewer observes the cheery phoniness of the staff nurse and a forced and artificial relating of news and conventional trivialities on the part of the family. But at the end, after everyone else has left, there are a few moments during which the oldest son puts his arm around Peege and reminds her of warm memories of their shared adventures from his childhood. Though Peege appears to be blind and nearly senile, the smile on her face as the young man leaves is an unforgettable testimony to what can be achieved if our concern is genuine and if we are willing to risk the hurt that is a part of caring. No one can replace loving family and friends, but if we rightly understood the needs of dying persons—especially those in institutions—volunteers could offer an important supplement to professional care givers. Because of their freedom from other duties, empathetic volunteers could be available as active listeners at a time when such fellowship is greatly needed and appreciated.

It may seem odd that the praiseworthy desire to *avoid* pain and suffering should become a *source* of just those qualities in our society. But the explanation is not far off: avoidance of discomfort on the part of well persons and society in general is increasing the difficulties experienced by dying persons. Throughout human history, pain and suffering have been familiar parts of life. As such, they have been appreciated both as natural phenomena and in the context of an overall interpretation of human existence. Pain served as a signal that something was wrong or as a sign that some curative process was working its proper course. Suffering was a part of being born, experiencing life, and facing death. Now it appears that our antipathies toward death are paralleled by a phobia of pain. We seem to prefer an antiseptic existence to one that includes any kind of hurt. It may be possible to prevent the pain of saying "goodbye" by never saying "hello." But the price is high. Not caring, not getting involved may preserve us from one sort of hurt, but it effectively isolates us from loving and being loved and from the riches of life. The harm that results is much deeper and longer lasting.

After Death: Funeral Practices

Earlier we illustrated a process of placing death at a distance by the growing institutionalization of dying and of other events that occur before the fact of death. Now it may be helpful to look at the parallel instance of institutionalization after death, in the form of American funeral practices. As Vanderlyn Pine (26), himself a fifth-generation funeral director and a trained sociologist, has said: "For present-day Americans, one of the common features of death is the employment of a funeral director" (p. 21). In the language of the title of Pine's book, the American funeral director has become the *Caretaker of the Dead.* But why is this so? Throughout history there have been individuals who helped, for one reason or another, with washing and preparing the corpse, with mourning, and with the disposition of the body. Still, the emergence of a semiprofessional, secular class of individuals combining service and business interests is a recent and in many ways distinctively North American phenomenon. How did it come about? Pine's (26) answer is quite simple and direct: "American undertaking evolved by gradually adding to itself specific tasks previously carried out largely by other occupational groups or by the family" (p. 16). Despite much public confusion and some vehement criticism, it seems that we have created the system that now serves us.

In general only a very small range of the activities of the care-taker of the dead are mandated by law. Most depend upon custom (defined by a not very clear or lengthy historical perspective) and subtle psychosocial pressures. In the main, the corpse is no longer "laid out" in the home; embalming takes place, restorative cosmetology is practiced, and "viewing" or "visitation" occurs in a funeral home; caskets have replaced coffins; cemeteries have become independent operations; mausoleums have been built; and costs have risen because we have sought or permitted these practices and because we have hired others to carry them out on our behalf. Where we have chosen to withdraw even further, viewing hours have been reduced and processions of automobiles to a cemetery have been shortened. Memorial societies came into being to help reduce costs or to eliminate certain expenses by encouraging prompt burial or cremation without embalming or viewing (27). Their program usually recommends a subsequent memorial service in the absence of a corpse or casket. But some criticize this approach also, especially for being overly intellectual and insufficiently responsive to the needs of individuals and of a society that has survived a death (28). Similarly, some view cremation as a way of eradicating even the burial plot to which we might otherwise feel obliged to return periodically (29). Perhaps the only safe thing to say here is that our values in this area are neither fully clear nor wholly stable.

This can be illustrated by looking a bit more closely at selected "postdeath activities" in North America with the realization that they would be regarded as quite unusual in many other parts of the

The Problem: Denial and Ambivalence toward Death

world. As Geoffrey Gorer (4) says, "the most striking contrast between the British and the American handling of death lies in the treatment of the body between death and disposal, and in the expense involved in the funeral or cremation" (p. x). High costs are typical of many aspects of American life, but in this case they seem to have a great deal to do with what we purchase and how we obtain the services we desire. It has been argued that while funeral costs usually represent the third largest monetary decision most of us make in our lives, we normally come to such decisions in periods of great emotional stress, without time or much inclination for reflection or comparative pricing. And it is contended that we are served by an excessive number of funeral homes, whose individual overhead costs and business practices tend to drive prices upward (30, 31). There are some obvious remedies for these conditions, but the central issue seems to be our uncritical acquiescence in such practices as embalming, the facial restoration of the corpse, and open coffin viewing.

It is true that the Egyptians, who are often mentioned in these discussions, practiced embalming. But they did so in a specific religious or philosophical (and climatic!) context that we do not share. Their aim seems to have been long-term or indefinite preservation of the body (32). That goal is sometimes suggested as a justification for present-day embalming practices, but most of us know that embalming only delays or inhibits biological decomposition; it cannot prevent this natural process forever. Another rationale has to do with considerations of public health and social welfare, but immediate burial, or prompt cremation would largely serve the same ends more cheaply. Apart from their utility in these cases or when the corpse is to be shipped by a common carrier, airtight caskets present a mixed value, since while effectively preserving the corpse from external contamination, they subject it to the confinement of internal organic agents. Perhaps the real reason for embalming in our society is that it is the indispensable condition for the kind of restorative cosmetology and open coffin viewing practices that seem so typical (33, 34). One could choose prompt burial without viewing as do many orthodox Jews, visitation of the body with a closed casket as sometimes occurs in cases of severe mutilation, temporary preservation by refrigeration, or viewing of an unrestored corpse. Some of these suggestions may seem shocking, but they are not necessarily impractical. Funeral directors often argue that open coffin viewing has a salutary psychotherapeutic effect in confirming the reality of death. Also, it is contended that a "beautiful memory picture" is desirable and valuable for the survivors. And extended viewing periods are said to be mandatory in a society in which relatives and friends must come from great distances. Thus the popular claim is that funeral practices in our society are primarily intended for the living.

There is much heat in disputes over these practices, but very little light or hard evidence (35). One wonders, for instance, how well the reality of death is conveyed by a body that gives no visible evidence of death or of the wasting illness that turned it into a corpse? Is it desirable for adults to fashion a representation of death that employs a resting or sleeping posture? Alternatively, is it good to avoid contact with the dead body at all costs or to refuse to join in the community that assembles for the funeral service? Perhaps no single set of rules would be adequate for every individual and group. My purpose is certainly not to insist on any specific set of practices. Nor do I necessarily mean to condemn the practices chosen for discussion here. But I do want to observe that the practices that seem to typify our society are not observed by all its members, and they certainly are not universal to the human species. Our funerary practices are the products of a complex scheme of attitudes and motivations that deserve careful attention and that are open to critical reassessment. Whether or not they constitute the optimum form of post-death activities, as they appear to for Howard Raether and Robert Slater (36), is perhaps a matter that is not yet and may never be fully settled.

After Death: Bereavement

The other primary activity after death in which evidences of discomfort and avoidance are unmistakable is bereavement. Gorer (4) summarized the findings of his study in England in ways that are likely to be even more true of North America over 20 years later.

> I think my material illustrates the hypothesis that this lack of accepted ritual and guidance [for dealing with grief and bereavement] is accompanied by a very considerable amount of maladaptive behaviour, from the triviality of meaningless "busy-ness" through the private rituals of what I have called mummification to the apathy of despair. (p. 127)

Bereavement is not just a phenomenon of the period to which we give nearly exclusive attention, the time between death and the burial or cremation; careful study has shown that it continues for some time thereafter and may even be more intense months later (37). "Grief work" can take on different forms in different circumstances, and it can have damaging consequences if it is prevented from following a natural course of catharsis, reconstruction, and reintegration. A society that is uncomfortable with death and its consequences will give little comfort to those who are grieving, and may even deny their mourning needed outlets and assistance. Certainly we are all too ready to tranquilize the grieving person in order to silence unwelcome outcries and anesthetize undesirable feelings. Colin Murray Parkes (38) has addressed this problem by showing that, in addition to loss and deprivation, bereavement usually calls forth an experience of social stigma. But to whom are bereavement and its manifestations so unwelcome and undesirable? And what are the consequences of such suppression of feeling and modification of behavior? The results are all too evident for those who wish to see them. And the notable fact is that in this area, as in so many others, the conduct of our society is unusual, not normal. That is the most important lesson that Gorer, the anthropologist, has to teach us. Can we be comfortable with ourselves as individuals and as a society when we have so far submerged the natural human sympathy for those suffering from grief? Why do we now find ourselves in the curious position of having to struggle to understand such basic facts as what it is to be bereaved and how we can be helpful to those in mourning?

POSITIVE MANIFESTATIONS

Reality and Complexity

Although our characteristic attitudes and behaviors have strongly shifted toward a negative relationship with death, it would be incorrect to believe that our contemporary experience holds no positive aspects. In fact, there are manifestations of recognition and acceptance existing side by side with the more obvious and quite different elements that we have already outlined. These positive manifestations seem to be a result of two important converging factors in the human situation. The first is that death occurs and is inevitable. That is, the facts of life, among which death is one of the most basic, exert a coercive influence upon us. We may be able to distance ourselves from some aspects of death and to deny other facets either partially or completely, but we cannot hope to shut death totally out of our lives. It pursues us relentlessly and rises up at unexpected moments or in unanticipated situations. The second key point is that individual human beings and the societies they create are much too complex to be captured in a single posture or attitude. As we have already shown, death and dying are intricate and many-sided phenomena with wide-ranging implications. Consequently, there is every reason to expect that our encounters with them and our related attitudes and behaviors will be every bit as complex. It would be quite startling if all our relationships with death could be reduced to a single form. There may well be motifs that dominate our outlook and actions, but that does not imply that manifestations of other sorts cannot also be identified.

Body Disposal and Social Consolidation

For example, because death will always be found wherever there is life, every society has to develop some way of responding to the event of death and of dealing with its consequences. Ordinary biological decay in a dead organism usually requires some form of disposal of the corpse; we are typically obliged to make some arrangements for separating the living from the dead. Frequently, this need is joined to the desire to record or mark the fact of passing from life to death. For instance, even when the corpse is abandoned to the elements and scavengers, one cannot conclude that the motivation necessarily involves disinterest or antipathy to the meaning of a human death. Closer inspection may show that this is part of a larger creed and cult that sees life as involved in a natural cycle in which the dead are to be solemnly returned to nature. In our society, death is marked by the legal devices of the death certificate and burial permit, by the social custom of newspaper obituary columns, and by religious practices of prayer and ceremony. As long as a society or an individual makes some provision for sacred or profane logistics and rites of passage, they cannot be said to deny wholly the reality of death.

Further, we have already seen various ways in which particular aspects of death and dying have been separated and apportioned among specialized institutions and functionaries. That is, a good deal of dying is given over to the care of hospitals, nursing homes, and their staffs, while much of the care of the body after death is assigned to morgue attendants, funeral directors, and cemetery operators. This brings about a transfer of responsibility from the individual and his or her family and friends to the new agents. As a result, a certain distancing develops that may reflect or bring about denial concerning these aspects of death. But at the same time, relief for the individual is not necessarily relief for the society. To the extent that the society as a whole continues to deal with these implications of death, it is evident that they are not wholly ignored. After all, the existence of these functional subgroups within the society manifests *some* recognition of the demands of death. Undoubtedly, this brings about a more impersonal approach to death, but it also entails a degree of candid recognition of death that ought not be overlooked.

Lately our society has given signs of a more positive reawakening of interest in matters of death and dying. One can now find books, films, and television dramatizations, whether biographical or fictional, that present more honest and realistic portrayals of death. This may be a reaction to excessive emphasis on sex and violence and a simultaneous realization that dying and death need not always be portrayed in shocking or offensive ways. Death, which has long been a familiar part of folklore and fairy tales, is beginning to reappear in more authentic ways in literature for children (39, 40). The short history of teaching and research on death shows a burgeoning growth that threatens to sweep us away in its dynamism (41, 42). Once at the top of the list of taboo topics (43), death and dying are now popular subjects for courses, workshops, discussion groups, and public talks. Lael Wertenbaker (44) and C. S. Lewis (45) provide examples of the many thoughtful individuals who have permitted us to share their struggles with a terminal illness or with grief. For some, the act of sharing has been therapeutic, and for the rest of us it has improved our understanding of death and dying. As a result we may learn a heightened appreciation of the needs of others, and we might hope for a renewed grasp on our own humanity.

Some have gone further to act on these realizations. One example involves the founding of *self-help groups* to provide a machinery for making available lay help to those who need it. The implicit premise of such groups is that self-help may be all that is required in many cases and that it can complement rather than compete with professional assistance. Orville Kelly founded Make Today Count for individuals with life-threatening illnesses; Phyllis Silverman (46) encouraged widow-to-widow groups; and Simon Stephens (47) established the Society of Compassionate Friends to aid bereaved parents. These are only three of the many similar organizations that have recently sprung up in our society. Their rapid spread is clear evidence that they are responding to some felt need. At least they provide a constructive alternative for those under stress and an opportunity for ordinary people to show that they care in an increasingly cold and aloof society. Another recent example is a program of home care for the dying child in Minnesota (48). Already there is growing evidence that this project has made easier a very difficult situation and its consequences. But it is significant that this sort of program is unusual in our society, and that it was necessary to argue for the home as an "alternative health care center." One notable outcome is that children dying at home seem to prefer to do so in the *living* room in the midst of familiar activity, not alone in an upstairs bedroom. What does this tell us about the recommended place of death in life?

The past 10 years have also witnessed the development of a new mode of attention to dying in the form of the hospice movement. Hospices are places of rest and succor for those in the last stages of the journey through life. Originating in England, they are best known in the example of St. Christopher's Hospice, London, and in the person of its medical director, Dr. Cicely Saunders (49, 50). Hospices view dying as more than a physical process. In addition to expertise in symptom control and the treatment of chronic pain, hospices also seek to respond to psychological, social, and spiritual needs. They attempt to engage family and friends in caring for the person who is dying, and they usually operate an outpatient or home care program. Bereavement follow-up, staff support, and education are other important hospice goals. They insist that they are not merely a place to go to die, but a resource that helps improve the quality of the life that remains. Hospice principles are now being imported to North America where they seem more likely to be found operating within existing structures rather than as free-standing or separate institutions (51, 52). Hospices are not without problems: a) they require fairly high staffing levels and rather special personnel even though they put aside certain forms of expensive therapy, b) they take on some services that may be new to hospital-based units, c) in this country they are confined by prohibitions against the use of heroin and restrictions on other medications, and d) here (versus England or Canada) they have the special problem of justifying their charges to third-party sources of payment. But in the main, hospice principles foster a return to a praiseworthy wholeness in our integration of dying and death with life.

Most of these recent positive developments seem to be largely a reaction to what has gone before. They appear to represent a growing awareness that we have drawn so far away from contact with and understanding of death that we are unprepared to deal with it effectively. My own feeling is that there are undesirable elements and superficial emphases in some of the ways that death has lately been rediscovered, but that the basic concern is authentic.

SOME CONSEQUENCES

Systemic Dysfunction

The previous two sections have shown that our society has chosen to live with death in a way that is dominated by attitudes of denial and negativity, although leavened by elements of resignation and acceptance. In other words, we find ourselves living in the face of death with a good deal of tension expressed mainly in terms of denial, ambivalence, and discomfort. What we want to do in this section is look at some of the consequences of this contemporary and distinctive mode of dealing with death. There are many such consequences and they are of various kinds, but a single central theme runs through all of them. In my experience, no professional thanatologist or scholar of death has captured this theme more precisely than an Englishwoman who lived through the dying and the death of her 33-year-old husband. In a single sentence Jocelyn Evans (53) has cut to the very quick of our death-related attitudes and behavior: "We have created systems which protect us in the aggregate from facing up to the very things that as individuals we most need to know" (p. 83). In the previous chapter we noted Philippe Ariès' contention (5) that the principal changes in recent Western experiences with death were of two sorts: 1) a shift away from a concern over the death of one's self and toward an interest in the death of the other, and 2) a shift away from attending to the appropriateness of death from the standpoint of the dying person and toward an emphasis on the acceptability of that death to the survivors and the surrounding society. Now we can see the full import of those shifts in the light of Evans' comment and of what we have learned in the meantime about *systemic dysfunction.*

At bottom, what every one of us needs to know is that *we shall all die sooner or later.* This insight must permeate and illuminate our lives. Though certainly not all that we need to know, it is a realization that every human being ought to achieve. Many of us are disturbed by this fact of life, and we appear to have chosen to deal with our discomfort by easing its implications as far out of our lives as possible. Thus as individuals we create for ourselves the presumption that we have a right to expect to live to or beyond the point of average life expectancy. As a society we have erected social barriers that prohibit, reduce, or render into an impersonal and unobtrusive form our contacts with death. What we are really witnessing here is the largely unspoken development of a certain perception of what is tolerable in death. But this perception incorporates more or less subtle prohibitions, whose effect is largely to suppress recognition of death as an essential and central element in life. We need to look to the consequences of this death system if we are to evaluate fairly its desirability.

Loss of a Sense of Community

The most evident result of the ways we have chosen to live with death can be seen in a loss of a sense of community. This occurs in three ways, the first of which has to do with the *relationships between people*. If death is regarded as odious and distasteful, it imposes a kind of stigma upon those with whom it comes to be associated. Dying human beings, for example, are so much identified by the process of coming-to-be-dead that they are often physically and mentally set apart from the living. Such treatment ignores both the truism that one must be living as long as one is dying, and the realization that there is a sense in which we are all moving inexorably toward death. In a similar way, those who are bereaved may find themselves isolated, though they will commonly come under pressure to rejoin the living by casting aside external evidences of association with death. An aura of social disapproval may also hover around certain occupations that particularly deal with death, such as morgue attendants and funeral directors. The same unfavorable attitude does not seem to apply to nurses who wash the body or to ministers who conduct the graveside services, probably because this portion of their work is overbalanced by a larger and more acceptable field of activity. Burial locations are set apart from the spaces of the living, and efforts are made to keep children at a distance from the facts and the realities of death. There are many other examples, some of which have been mentioned above, but all share in some degree the tendency to fragment our interpersonal community.

A second and quite similar consequence concerns the sense of *wholeness within a person*. Loss of this sense comes about when we are obliged to restrain our natural feelings for other persons and adapt our behavior toward them in terms of certain conceptions of professionalism, specialization, or maturity. For example, Tolstoy's (54) protagonist Ivan Ilych trained himself "to exclude everything fresh and vital, which always disturbs the regular course of official business, and to admit only official relations with people, and then only on official grounds . . . something that could be expressed on officially stamped paper" (p. 117). Such a viewpoint not only directly affects interpersonal attitudes but also results in divisions within the person who adopts such a mode of behavior. That is, our lives become compartmentalized and we fail to appreciate the natural affinities between the different aspects and phases of our existence. In order to satisfy a particular model of conduct, we restrain our natural sensitivity and imagination, sometimes to the point of permitting a certain atrophy of our personhood. Like adolescents, we focus on the immediate present together with what we assume to be the assured future, neglecting all thought both of an unromanticized past and of where that future will eventually lead. But the past could reveal that parts of our lives have already ended, that our existence is shot through with events that are over and with times that will be "nevermore." And even a short

The Problem: Denial and Ambivalence toward Death

moment in the present, as biologists tell us, is sufficient for the death and birth of countless cells within the organic community that is our body. Reawakening ourselves to these elements of transience and temporality is a first step toward the recovery of wholeness within ourselves.

A third kind of consequence occurs in the *relations between persons and nature*. This was suggested by the reference to human cell destruction and generation. In this regard it is noteworthy that when Earl Grollman compiled his anthology *Explaining Death to Children*, he invited a zoologist, Claiborne S. Jones, to contribute a chapter. Jones (55) offers two related observations. The first is that partial death is necessary for normal human development. This repeats the point made above about the interior or microcosmic senses of death within an individual. The second is that there can be no life without death. It enlarges our scope to the macrocosm. It instructs us that our lives must be seen in the broader context of life itself. There are many distinctive aspects to the human mode of existence, but there is also a good deal that we share with other forms of life. Nature is a community of which we are a part and from which we can learn, as long as we are open to its instruction. Our problem is the tendency to withdraw from nature and construct an artificial living space populated by plastic flowers, glass figurines, and pet rocks—none of which will ever die.

These three kinds of loss of felt community—alienation from other people, from self, and from nature—add up to a *diminution of our humanity*. Our attitudes and our behaviors do not manifest the full potentiality of our humanness because we are less in touch with ourselves as creatures in nature, as complete and total individuals, and as members of a societal fellowship. By holding death at a distance and not permitting it into our lives, we have failed to realize the guidance it could provide as a steering force in helping to determine the ways we might live. Death need not be the only, or perhaps even the primary, principle of instruction in life. Nor should it be allowed to overwhelm and paralyze the remainder of our existence. But death is, as Kastenbaum (56) has so aptly put it, "not just our destination; it is a part of our 'getting there' as well" (p. 43). Whether it is a biological imperative, a result of the sin of Adam and Eve, or a necessary implication of the wheel of eternal recurrence, death is a part of our lives. We may choose to ignore that fact, but by doing so we pay a heavy price of distorting our humanity.

Physicians: The New Priestly Class

Death, dying, and bereavement are not primarily medical problems. They are much broader in their import and much more fundamental in their origin. But in a society that values professionalism and functionalism, one that tends to define its difficulties in terms of existing institutions, it is not unusual that many of the issues we have considered in these two chapters should have assumed a medical connection in the popular mind. Nor is that wholly improper. However, it has important consequences that can be illustrated in two closely related topics, the status of physicians in our country and the development of a document called the "living will." Western physicians proudly trace their heritage back to Hippocrates (460?–377? B.C.), the so-called Father of Medicine, and to other ancient healers. This is a rich tradition in which knowledge, skills, and prudence are brought to the aid of mankind. But historically it was tempered by other sources of insight and wisdom, such as religion, philosophy, and literature. For many today this is no longer true. We live in a society that has abandoned many of its former religious values and most of its patience with the search for wisdom, in favor of more manageable technical procedures and quicker answers. Physicians are the professionals who deal with us most intimately and significantly. Well rewarded financially, they have come to be a premier professional class. Because of their special authority over matters of life and death, they have in many ways become our new priestly class.

It is to physicians that we turn for treatment and advice when life is threatened or seems to hang in the balance. Only after they can do no more, do we and they (with or without much real conviction) turn to the clergy or other sources of assistance. In this way, we oversell the abilities of medicine and elevate physicians to an undeserved and undesirable status. We need some sort of authority to rely on when life becomes threatening, and physicians have earned our gratitude in many ways. But the overestimation of physicians is more a reflection of our own ignorance, our desires, and the lack of viable competition. Thoughtful physicians recognize their own fallibility in these matters and the many limitations in the science and the art of medicine. For various reasons, however, not enough has been done to convey these limitations to the general public. Some physicians have even internalized this inflated image by making the title *Doctor* (whose root meaning is *teacher*) into an essential part of their name and identity. A realistic sense of proportion is lost. The degree to which things are out of balance is evident in our sense of betrayal when medical skill can no longer ward off death. It seems unfair that "success" should elude our grasp in an atmosphere of high expectation. Tomorrow's cure has come so often that we are prone to rebel when it develops that we shall not live that one more day until it arrives.

That is true for physicians as well, at least some of whom may have entered medicine partly because of above-average fears of death and their desire to do something about it (57). We have all subtly come to view death itself as a disease to be cured. This misapprehension of the nature of death is one central element in our faulty estimation of the capacities of physicians and the role of medicine.

The Living Will

A living will is an attempt to express one's desires about the kinds of treatment one would want or not want if one were dying and could not, for any reason, take part in the process of making those important decisions. Living wills usually ask that dying not be unduly prolonged and that medication be given to reduce pain, even at the risk of shortening life. They frequently assert that death is less to be feared than useless pain, suffering, or expense. Sometimes they disavow the direct taking of life.

For our purposes what is most significant about living wills is their very existence as a symptom of social concern. Living wills result from the convergence of two factors. The first is that dying is now perceived as likely to be painful, arduous, and lengthy. Many wish to get through it quickly, even if death is the outcome. This is quite different from the view that dying is a precious time for getting ready and saying goodbye. Second, there is a popular image of a time in our country when the family doctor was a personal friend who knew us as individuals and was trusted as a reliable personal advisor. Whether or not this nostalgic portrait is accurate, many now believe they face a much different system of medical treatment. It is simultaneously exalted, depersonalized, and mistrusted. Further, the news media have publicized cases in which it appears to the lay public that the person was unable to make decisions about desired treatment or to get them communicated effectively. Some are even afraid that their individual desires will be overruled by an arbitrary medical authority. It is as if we have promoted physicians to such heights that we are no longer confident they, like the Wizard of Oz, will hear or respect our wishes about the ways we want to be treated. In short, many people are apprehensive about the experience of dying and the system which provides them with terminal care. They are wary of finding themselves in circumstances in which they might have to struggle on their own to regain control over death and dying, either without the assistance of others or even against their earnest efforts.

The living will is a device to stimulate prior discussion about death and dying. Executing such a document is a way of articulating one's preferences about treatment and an effort to get them respected. Even when it has no legal force, the living will attempts to exert a kind of suasive force and to share the moral responsibility of those who are called upon to honor it. But living wills are not simple or unproblematic documents. Nor is it easy to fix their principles in legislation, as is evident from the debates that preceded and continue after the enactment of the precedent-setting Natural Death Act in California. Some of the difficulties have concerned who is entitled to execute a living will, when and under what circumstances that can be done, how far rights to refuse treatment can be extended, and what the implications of such rights are for family, care givers, and insurors. One might have thought that after careful deliberation any competent adult could legally refuse even life-preserving therapy. But that is evidently often not so in practice, whether or not it is true in theory. We must note how difficult these aspects of death have become in our time and how this partly reflects larger problems in our dealings with death. It is said that elephants instinctively go off alone to a private graveyard when they sense the approach of death. Human anticipations of death are not always so clear. More importantly, they are often complicated by a variety of acquired perceptions and attitudes that frequently lack harmony. As we have seen, there are many potential sources of disharmony and they can only be brought into tune by a careful examination of the ways we are living with the changing face of death.

A CONCLUDING REMARK

In these first two chapters we have undertaken an introduction to the changing face of death. Its main features will be examined in greater detail in succeeding chapters by other contributors. I have also sought to identify certain difficulties within our death system and to suggest some general directions for its improvement. But whatever is to be done will ultimately depend upon the efforts of concrete individuals and their realization that death is a constitutive part of human life. Death is the ultimate limit in our lives, the point at which we have no further control. But we often fail to realize how much freedom and control we have before we come to that point. Although we shall inevitably die, awareness significantly redeems the fact and permits it to impart value and preciousness to our lives. In this way, death can offer us occasions for far-reaching instruction about the meaning of our own life and about the humanity that we share with others.

The Problem: Denial and Ambivalence toward Death

REFERENCES

1. Kastenbaum, R., & Aisenberg, R. *The psychology of death.* New York: Springer, 1972.
2. Kastenbaum, R. *Death, society, and human experience.* St. Louis: Mosby, 1977.
3. Dumont, R., & Foss, D. *The American view of death: Acceptance or denial?* Cambridge, MA: Schenkman, 1972.
4. Gorer, G. *Death, grief and mourning.* Garden City, NY: Doubleday, 1967.
5. Ariès, P. *Western attitudes toward death: From the Middle Ages to the present.* (Trans. P. Ranum.) Baltimore: Johns Hopkins University Press, 1974.
6. Kelly, O. Make today count. In H. Feifel (Ed.), *New meanings of death.* New York: McGraw-Hill, 1977.
7. Waugh, E. *The loved one.* New York: Dell, 1948.
8. La Rochefoucauld, Réflexions ou sentences et maximes morales, #26. In his *Oeuvres,* ed. D. Gilbert & J. Gourdault. (3 vols.) Paris: Hachette, 1868–1881; I, 41.
9. Langone, J. *Vital signs: The way we die in America.* Boston: Little, Brown, 1974.
10. Martin, G. *The goat, the wolf and the crab.* New York: Scribner's, 1977.
11. Bryant, C., & Snizek, W. The iceman cometh: The cryonics movement and frozen immortality. *Society,* 1973, *11,* 56–61.
12. Ettinger, R. *The prospect of immortality.* New York: Doubleday, 1964.
13. Berman, S. Frozen immortality: An idea whose time has gone. *Science Digest,* 1976, *80,* 72–77.
14. Fowles, J. *The Aristos.* Boston: Little, Brown, 1964.
15. Rahner, K. *On the theology of death.* New York: Seabury Press, 1973.
16. Feder, S. Attitudes of patients with advanced malignancy. In *Death and dying: Attitudes of patient and doctor.* New York: Group for the Advancement of Psychiatry, 1965, pp. 614–622.
17. Cartwright, A., Hockey, L., & Anderson, J. *Life before death.* London: Routledge & Kegan Paul, 1973.
18. Melzack, R. *The puzzle of pain.* Harmondsworth, England: Penguin, 1973.
19. Kübler-Ross, E. *On death and dying.* New York: Macmillan, 1969.
20. Kelly, O. *Make today count.* New York: Delacorte, 1975.
21. Bowers, M., Jackson, E., Knight, J., & LeShan, L. *Counseling the dying.* New York: Thomas Nelson, 1964.
22. Weisman, A. *On dying and denying: A psychiatric study of terminality.* New York: Behavioral Publications, 1972.
23. Hinton, J. *Dying.* Harmondsworth, England: Penguin, 1967.
24. White, L. Death and the physician: Mortuis vivos docent. In H. Feifel (Ed.), *New meanings of death.* New York: McGraw-Hill, 1977.
25. Glaser, B., & Strauss, A. *Awareness of dying.* Chicago: Aldine, 1965.
26. Pine, V. *Caretaker of the dead: The American funeral director.* New York: Irvington, 1975.
27. Morgan, E. *A manual of simple burial.* Burnsville, NC: Celo Press, 1971.
28. Jackson, E. *For the living.* Des Moines, IA: Meredith, 1963.
29. Irion, P. *Cremation.* Philadelphia: Fortress Press, 1968.
30. Mitford, J. *The American way of death.* Greenwich, CN: Fawcett, 1973.
31. Harmer, R. *The high cost of dying.* New York: Crowell-Collier, 1963.
32. Habenstein, R., & Lamers, W. *Funeral customs the world over* (2nd rev. ed.), Milwaukee: Bulfin, 1974.

33. Habenstein, R., & Lamers, W. *The history of American funeral directing* (Rev. ed.). Milwaukee: Bulfin, 1962.
34. Irion, P. *The funeral: Vestige or value?* Nashville: Abingdon, 1966.
35. Leviton, D. The scope of death education. *Death Education*, 1977, *1*, 41–56.
36. Raether, H., & Slater, R. Immediate postdeath activities in the United States. In H. Feifel (Ed.), *New meanings of death*. New York: McGraw-Hill, 1977.
37. Parkes, C. *Bereavement: Studies of grief in adult life*. New York: International Universities Press, 1973.
38. Glick, I., Weiss, R., & Parkes, C. *The first year of bereavement*. New York: Wiley, 1974.
39. Marshall, J. & W. The treatment of death in children's books. *Omega*, 1971, *2*, 36–45.
40. Bertman, S. Death education in the face of a taboo. In E. Grollman (Ed.), *Concerning death: A practical guide for the living*. Boston: Beacon, 1974.
41. Pine, V. A socio-historical portrait of death education. *Death Education*, 1977, *1*, 57–84.
42. Leviton, D. Death education. In H. Feifel (Ed.), *New meanings of death*. New York: McGraw-Hill, 1977.
43. Feifel, H. Death. In N. Farberow (Ed.), *Taboo topics*. New York: Atherton, 1963.
44. Wertenbaker, L. *Death of a man*. Boston: Beacon, 1974.
45. Lewis, C. S. *A grief observed*. New York: Bantam, 1976.
46. Silverman, P. et al. *Helping each other in widowhood*. New York: Health Science Publishing Corp., 1975.
47. Stephens, S. *Death comes home*. New York: Morehouse-Barlow, 1973.
48. Martinson, I. *Home care for the dying child: Professional and family perspectives*. New York: Appleton-Century-Crofts, 1976.
49. Saunders, C. *Care of the dying*. London: Macmillan, 1959.
50. Saunders, C. Dying they live: St. Christopher's Hospice. In H. Feifel (Ed.), *New meanings of death*. New York: McGraw-Hill, 1977.
51. Rossman, P. *Hospice: Creating new models of care for the terminally ill*. New York: Association Press, 1977.
52. Stoddard, S. *The hospice movement: A better way of caring for the dying*. New York: Stein and Day, 1978.
53. Evans, J. *Living with a man who is dying*. New York: Taplinger, 1971.
54. Tolstoy, L. *The death of Ivan Ilych and other stories*. New York: New American Library, 1960.
55. Jones, C. "...In the midst of life ..." (Reflections on some biological aspects of death). In E. Grollman (Ed.), *Explaining death to children*. Boston: Beacon, 1969.
56. Kastenbaum, R. Death and development through the lifespan. In H. Feifel (Ed.), *New meanings of death*. New York: McGraw-Hill, 1977.
57. Feifel, H. The function of attitudes toward death. In *Death and dying: Attitudes of patient and doctor* (Vol. 5, Symposium No. 11). New York: Group for the Advancement of Psychiatry, 1965.

The Data:
The Facts
of Death

Death, or more accurately its prevention, has long been a primary concern of the medical profession. Death has also been central in every religious belief system. But the scientific exploration of dying and death is a twentieth-century phenomenon. Seeking knowledge about all unexplained events, phenomena, and processes is characteristic of our era, and death and dying are not exempt. Nevertheless, no matter how keen and curious scientists have become, the experience of the transition from dying to being dead has not been recorded. There is no scientific evidence of human beings having returned after death to report what it is like to die and become dead and what happens afterward. The closest we have come are the accounts of persons near death who have been resuscitated and lived to tell of their extraordinary experiences. However, even here no controlled systematic study has been undertaken; indeed what little evidence there is suggests that only a portion of persons in life-threatening situations have fantastic experiences as reported by Moody and Kübler-Ross. Where science stops, belief takes over.

This book is titled *Dying: Facing the Facts,* and Part Two is called "The Data: The Facts of Death"; however, it is necessary to alert the reader to important distinctions. The factual content presented in the nine chapters that follow varies not only in substance but also in the degree of validity. The degree of validity ranges from material that is absolutely certain to material that is tentative. For example, in Chapter Eleven ("Death and the Law") the laws discussed are definitive and there can be no speculation about them. It is a definitive fact, for instance, that in the United States upon death a human body becomes the property of the next of kin. In "Physiology of Dying" (Chapter Three) much of the material is based on systematic medical research involving large numbers of subjects. This kind of material has high validity although it may be somewhat less definitive than legal statutes. However, when we consider the psychological and social aspects of dying, the information is less definitive. This is so for several reasons. First, the sciences concerned with human individual and group behavior are relatively new (less than 100 years old) and incompletely developed. Second, study in these fields deals with complex systems making the isolation of variables difficult. Third, studies in psychology and sociology often preclude direct systematic observation and are plagued by other methodological problems, such as the achievement of representative sample groups, avoidance of attrition, and the development of valid and reliable measures for the variables under study. Finally, ethical considerations dictate limitations in the nature of experimental treatments. However, in every instance the authors of the relevant chapters have sought out and presented the best information available to date.

CHAPTER THREE

Physiology of Dying

RALPH A. REDDING

INTRODUCTION

Living in health is a most wondrous and precious state. As younger persons filled with our own immortality, we often laugh at such trite phrases. But as we age, and especially when a few infirmities ensue, the collection of phrases similar to the above assume a more profound meaning that eventually stirs us all to sit and think for a

━━━━━━━━━━━

This is, to our knowledge, the first chapter ever written by a physician about the physiology of dying that centers around the person *rather than* the disease process *and that is written for readers that do not have medical training. Redding is to be congratulated for this achievement. Stressed is the close interaction between mind and body in the causation and timing of illness and death. The chapter is unique in other respects as well. Redding not only discusses the common mechanisms of dying but also the processes of decay and decomposition of the body. Where else can the nonmedical reader find such information? The facts of bodily decay may not be pleasant to ponder, but they are made available. The discussion of body preservation or the inhibition of decay is also enlightening because the data provided have implications for the common practice of embalming the corpse and for the advertisement claims made by many casket manufacturers.*

The Data: The Facts of Death

moment, pondering our own destiny. Why begin a discussion about the physiology of dying with a philosophical statement about health or living? Some consider living and dying or life and death as being poles apart, while another hypothesis suggests they are but two sides of the same coin. But which is the correct simile? Homo sapiens, above all animals, have delighted in their ability to reflect, ponder, and essentially manipulate ideas into an integrated and well-organized pattern that may provide them with the meaning of their very being. So when a title comes along like "Physiology of Dying," which implies a study of the mechanisms or processes by which dying occurs, I think it is very right and proper first to understand the semantics of the words we will be using.

Like other English words (*drowning* and *drowned*, *hanging* and *hanged*), *dying* and *dead* have been used as if they were a process leading to a final event. Here I will contend that the term *dead* (or *death*) falls closely into what A. N. Whitehead (1) called the "fallacy of misplaced concreteness." In essence, he suggested that because of the unique sort of minds that humans possess, we prefer to define and relate all kinds of miscellaneous data into concepts, rather than leave them disorganized, in order to bring us into a state of better understanding. We often forget that this process of understanding is really our effort to simplify that which is initially unfathomable. Our mind artificially separates or classifies most processes in order to provide meaning. Robert Morrison (2) defined living as that which "we observe (as) some unusual set of objects, separated from the rest of the world by peculiar properties such as reproduction, growth, and special ways of handling energy . . . we elect to call living things."

It is but a short step from this kind of concept to invent an entity we call "life" as distinguishable from "nonliving" things. This additional step may erroneously add a new dimension to living things, implying that life must be more definable since it is indeed more substantial for the mind to assimilate. And as we come to think of life as having a dimension of its own, so too can we think of death as a thing unto itself, moving around and extracting or taking away life, and we begin to adjust our thinking upon hearing ominous terms such as "death came for my father and took him away." In our particular civilization, only old soldiers seem to just fade away.

The point here is to suggest that people have personified or reified the words *life* and *death* as if they were actual things with certain qualities that are absolute and definable. While poetry, art, and music all provide special meaning by symbolizing these nouns in a number of ways, it is very difficult in fact to define or qualify the continuing process of conception through putrifaction of organic matter. Such comic expressions as "from sperm to the worm" or "from womb to the tomb" try to define limits when in fact there may well be none.

Some people would profoundly state that the process of dying begins with birth, so must this dissertation start at that point? That would certainly lengthen the chapter. Even the definition of death has undergone turbulent debate in the past decade, a debate perhaps largely stimulated by recent technological advances of medicine and other concepts. The trajectory of dying to death for all of us is really an interrelated compendium of psychological, sociological, and physiological variables, gradually but sometimes abruptly provoking our awareness. Sometime, somewhere, the process will simply demand our attention.

The process is so complex that each individual probably has a unique style or developmental pattern of thought about dying. In our society, however, fewer and fewer people are able while dying to maintain quality of living at home in their own beds, within their own surroundings, amidst their own loved ones. More and more people are labeled *patients* and subjected to all kinds of medical intervention that interrupt, delay, but seldom reverse the process of dying, while merely existing in an unfamiliar, sterile hospital or nursing home bed isolated from his or her kin folk. This latter phenomenon of our times will be examined elsewhere in this book.

What I have chosen to do is to begin our study of dying physiology at or about the time that the person becomes *aware* of the process. This specifically ignores the question of definition but does suggest that, in its fullest meaning, awareness of our finiteness often comes as an emotional explosion associated with, or accompanied by, a medically defined disease process that is the triggering mechanism. At this point there is indeed the onset of dis-ease or extreme discomfort of mind and body. It is interesting to note, as this point, that a medical dictionary has borrowed the term *disease* and modified its meaning in order to depersonalize or reify this word as well. Disease is defined by Dorland (3) as "a definite morbid process having a characteristic train of symptoms; it may affect the whole body or any parts, and its etiology, pathology, and prognosis may be known or unknown" (p. 428). This semantic slip of the medical tongue has forgotten completely about the person who experiences the dis-ease associated with the "definite morbid process." Probably this lessens the dis-ease in the medical reader who has to study the myriad of morbid processes.

Health and *disease* also have both become labels that are as personified as any others mentioned above. *Health* has been variously defined: negatively as the absence of disease (to be lost when disease is encountered) or in a more positive vein, by the World Health Organization, as a state of emotional and physical well-being. The problem now exists that we tend to view these terms as polar opposites, with disease being in direct violation or confrontation with health. I would like to propose that, as a natural resource, disease will be a likely phenomenon in all our lives at some point, and we do not necessarily lose our health because of it. Rather it provides us with a unique opportunity (and often the responsibility) to reconsider our life values in order to learn and grow.

HISTORICAL BACKGROUND

Physicians have been very interested in death and dying since time immemorial, in spite of pronouncements to the contrary by some experts in this field. Physicians have dealt with their discomfort about death in less than overt ways, but they have nevertheless dealt with it. One writer, Erwin Ackerknecht (4), after exploring medical writings extensively, suggested that medicine has rarely discussed the essence of death. From his viewpoint, physicians have treated death or dying in an artisan-like rather than a philosophical manner. Medical interest in death and dying, according to Ackerknecht, has progressed in three main arenas: 1) *The assignment or pronouncement of death so that grief processes can begin.* This particular interest is of historical value in that obtaining absolute proof that death had occurred provided practical prevention against burying or even brutally treating (as corpses frequently were in the thirteenth through fifteenth centuries) people who were still alive. In ancient times people were so afraid that loved ones might be buried alive that they initiated the historical practice of placing a long rope from within the casket underground to a bell above the ground. 2) *The fixing of the time of death.* This question has been of particular interest to anthropologists and to those interested in legal medicine. With regard to the latter, the linking of the exact time of death of a homicide victim with his murderer's visit has obvious practical legal implications. More recently, death definitions have taken on other important considerations, such as in transplantation surgery or the allocation of scarce medical resources. 3) *Prognosis, or predicting when death might occur.* (Please note that portion of Dorland's definition of *disease* dealing with prognosis.) Among doctors' textbooks, no description of a disease process seems complete without a prognosis being given. It has always been fascinating to me to hear medical colleagues ask immediately upon being told of an incurable process in a patient "how long has he got?" In contrast, patients or family seldom pose such questions immediately. Many doctors seem to feel more secure about a disease process if they have some feeling for the time period their patient will have to endure the disease.

If one considers only a strict interpretation of discussion about death and dying, Ackerknecht may be correct. But I believe that, with ever-accelerating anxiety, physicians have pursued death and dying with great vigor and attention. Every day, the number of medical textbooks being written and published increases. While most do not deal with death directly, they do after all discuss the problems associated with the morbid process and sometimes discuss opportunities for the physician to intervene with some helpfulness. For the physician the body has been constantly divided into ever smaller parts (organ systems, cells within organs, subcellular organelles, and biochemical and enzyme kinetics) in order to search for the causation and process that might lead to dying or death. The unwritten statement of intent has always been to contravene the process through finding the cure. Death has always been the physician's enemy. For most of us in the medical profession, the fact that death inevitably comes seems to suggest that we have been unsuccessful and therefore are failures, which only compounds our anxiety.

PRESENT MODEL OF DISEASE

Our current biomedical model assumes that a *disease process* is a deviation from health fully accounted for by abnormal biochemical or neurophysiological aberrations (5). Hopefully, by diligent study of these chemical and physiological phenomena, reversible processes will soon be discovered leading to new methods of successfully treating illness. Perhaps the present medical model of investigating disease processes has been overly restrictive in that it has not paid more attention to processes other than chemicals, enzyme systems, organs, or body function in the dynamic process of living. Within the framework of the biochemical model there is very little emphasis presently placed on the social, psychological, or behavioral dimensions affecting an illness, although there is general agreement that these factors play minor supplementary roles. But according to the hypothetical model mentioned above, these latter entities play no part in causation and certainly make no major contribution to the pathogenesis of disease.

One way of examining our emotional appreciation of disease that conceivably could lead to death is to divide it up into categories that assign responsibility or blame to someone (6). The first category of medical diseases includes those for which we can assign blame directly to the individual. In this situation the behavior of the deceased caused his or her own demise. One example is a heart attack, which is largely believed to be caused by poor attention to diet (overeating), poor exercise habits, smoking, and other

The Data: The Facts of Death

controllable behavioral patterns. Other examples include alcohol abuse, dangerous maneuvers with a motorcycle, or neglecting to wear seat belts and the increase in mortality associated with automobile accidents. The most common cause of cancer in men, bronchogenic carcinoma of the lung, would be almost totally preventable if cigarette smoking were to cease immediately.

A second causal group of diseases is the result of abnormal heredity traits, and thus clearly the blame can be assigned genetically to our parents. Excellent examples of this include such diseases as juvenile-onset diabetes mellitus, epilepsy, sickle cell anemia, and Tay-Sachs' disease.

The third and last category of diseases includes those accidents or processes for which no one is apparently responsible or to blame. Examples are fires, earthquakes, floods, and hurricanes, all of which fall into the category of "acts of God" that randomly pluck certain members of our society out for an early grave. Unfortunately, in Judeo-Christian tradition, some undercurrent of blame has still been placed upon the individual himself. The accident was his punishment for bad behavior or not leading a moral life. Nevertheless, these causes of death are generally conceived of as accidental and completely out of the hands of the individual.

Aging

The current medical biological model of disease includes the premise that a "medical disease" overtakes the individual and either threatens or takes his life. However, this premise may be only partially true because, coexisting with the disease process, is a second process of human *aging* continuously progressing in each of us. There is little disagreement among experts in the field that individual members of our society, after reaching sexual maturity, begin to accumulate physiological decrements in the functional capacity of all organ systems, leading to an increased risk of dying. After age 30 there is about a 0.8 or 0.9 percent loss in functional capacity, which occurs in a linear fashion (with much individual variation) each year.

There is also a common impression that medicine has provided outstanding contributions leading to a lengthening of our human life span, but this supposition is not presently supported by either vital statistics or biological evidence. What has happened is that improved medical treatment of illness in the early years of our life has prevented early deaths and thus allowed most people to reach what appears to be an immutable upper limit. Thus while life expectancy has increased, the traditional three score and ten years of life span has not changed during recorded history. As deaths in earlier years become less frequent, graphs of life tables simply become more rectangular in shape (see Figure 1). The graph shows a comparison of the number of survivors by age from a variety of countries including the United States at different time periods. Note that as of 1941 New Zealand had the largest number of people surviving to old age. Since 1900 the United States has improved its vital statistics such that in the white population in 1941 its survivor curve closely approximated that of New Zealand. In many privileged countries such as ours, most people can reasonably expect to grow old before they die.

Let us fantasize for a moment that, through remarkable medical achievements, all disease states could be cured or eliminated. Our life span would then be increased to about 100 years (see "ultimate curve" in Figure 1). If the two leading causes of death (heart disease and stroke) were eliminated, we could expect about 18 years of life in addition to our present 70. With the elimination of cancer only 2 more added years would result. If we look historically at the above theory, we can see on the graph that the net gain in our life expectancy at age 65 and 75 since the year 1900, respectively, was only 2.9 and 2.2 years. Thus we are not gaining life span but simply living until we are old.

Presently the large majority of our research monies are directed toward the cause and treatment of disease states. The above concepts would suggest that although this kind of orientation may slightly increase our life expectancy, it will never change our life span. The data suggest that the fundamental causes of death (especially beyond age 70) may be as much the decremental loss of functional capacity as the three main causes usually listed (heart disease, stroke, and cancer). Biological evidence about aging cells comes from a number of interesting studies; the reader who wishes to pursue this further is directed to the writings of Hayflick, Comfort, and others (7, 8).

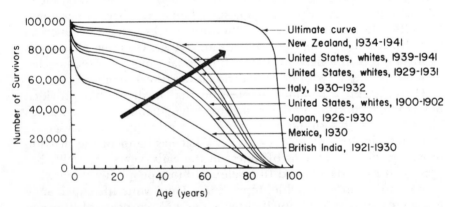

FIGURE 1   *Number of survivors by age in various countries at different time periods. Reprinted by permission from* The New England Journal of Medicine, *295:1302, 1976.*

The Data: The Facts of Death

Homeostasis

Having pursued the relationship between medical disease and biological aging, let us move first to general then more specific physiological concepts about the whole body. Through functional integration of its component organ systems, the body tries to maintain a constant internal environment, sometimes termed the *milieu interne*. The process of maintaining this stability has been called *homeostasis*. While each organ system contributes its share to maintain a harmonious balance, there is also available a reserve capacity in case of extra needs. Even though humans are separated and protected from the environment by our skin, there are many invasions from the environment (for example viruses and bacteria), upsetting this delicate balance of integrative processes. The functional reserve capacity of the body's component parts reacts in such a way as to counter the disruption, returning the body to a normal state through the process of homeostasis.

Host and Invader: The Eternal Conflict

Let us assume that a particularly virulent strain of virus particles suspended in droplets of moisture are inhaled while we normally breathe. Impaction and deposition of these virus particles occur largely in the nose and the posterior aspects of the throat, called the *nasopharynx*. Whether or not the virus is successful in invading the mucous lining of the nasopharynx depends, not just on the numbers or invasiveness (virulence) of the virus, but also on the quality of a variety of defense mechanisms of the host. Examples of defense mechanisms in the nose include a sneeze (which would expel the virus particles) and the mucociliary blanket of the nasopharynx, which acts as a physical barrier and, through its ciliary action, moves material into the back of the throat where it can be swallowed. An intact mucosa cell layer with a barrier of mucopolysaccharide secretions, adequate numbers of surface antibodies that kill bacteria, and surface cells that can engulf and kill the virus particles can together marshall a successful defense. Resolution of the problem may occur when the invasion of virus particles has been successfully stonewalled by the aggregate cooperation of these defense mechanisms. If, however, the mucosa has been damaged and inflamed by irritant gases or smoke (as from cigarettes) or the other defenses are diminished, the penetration of viruses may proceed. Once the invading virus gains access across the mucosa barrier, another series of integrated events from the body's lymphatic system produces a local inflammatory reaction resulting usually in containment of the infection; this reaction of the body is well known as the common cold.

However, the possibility also exists that a superimposed bacterial infection can utilize the foothold gained by the virus infection in breaking down defense barriers. The net balance of forces between the presence, numbers, and virulence of the invading bacteria and the quality of the above-mentioned host defense mechanisms determines what the outcome will be. Once again let us suppose that the balance favors the bacteria proliferating and spreading to invade the lungs. An acute inflammatory reaction (called *pneumonia*) takes place in the lungs and impairs the reserve capacity of the lungs themselves. If the lungs had already been damaged by previous insults (for example tuberculosis, pneumonia, or smoking effects-emphysema), less reserve functional capacity would be available to transfer oxygen through the bloodstream to the other important body organ systems. This in turn might impair other organ systems' contribution to fight the infection. In an integrated system such as ours, each system has reserve capacity to help should another system begin to fail. In the example stated above, although the bloodstream may have to carry less oxygen per unit volume, increased heart action may increase the transit time or blood volume per unit time and make up for the oxygen deficiency. Moreover, preferential distribution of blood to important organs in the body considered vitally necessary for survival also occurs. By rallying several more vital organ systems, survival of the host may be achieved.

The above explanation was not meant to be exhaustive in defining all the defense processes, but hopefully was illustrative in suggesting that disturbances in our homeostasis and our subsequent ability to cope with these disturbances is possible because of a complex interplay between host body systems and the invader. There are various lines of defense the body can marshal against the invader. And indeed, although one line of defense may be overcome by the invader, the result may simply allow the host to provide a wider spectrum of defense mechanisms, enabling the host ultimately to overcome the invader. It is perhaps a happy fact that throughout our life span the body's defense mechanisms ultimately win their multiple encounters with the environment every time but one.

The defense of the body cannot be explained just by biochemical, cellular, or neurological events. Since smoking, alcohol, and drug abuse all impair the defense of the lung against infection, the overall personality of the individual determines to some extent his or her ability to handle the environmental insult.

Body System Relationships

The body can be divided into a number of systems that operate in an integrated and cooperative way to maintain our health and

TABLE 1   Body Systems and Their Functions

Physiological Function	System
Thought, movement, and coordination	Central nervous system
Circulation	Cardiovascular system
Gas exchange	Pulmonary system
Oxygen delivery	Hemopoietic system, red blood cells
Excretory system	Kidneys
Digestion	Gastrointestinal system
Hormonal changes	Endocrine system
Locomotion	Musculo-skeletal system
Reproduction	Genital system

vigor (see Table 1). With the exception of the first three systems in Table 1, the body can tolerate considerable disruption or destruction of the other systems without death. The disruption of any system can cause considerable trouble (we call this *morbidity*), perhaps even reducing the person's quality of life. However, if substantial damage to any of the first three organ systems occurs, it is extremely unlikely that meaningful life can be maintained.

Oxygen, the Vital Ingredient

There are approximately only 4 minutes of reserve oxygen storage capacity in all of us (largely carried on the hemoglobin molecule within red blood cells). Oxygen as a molecule can only be transferred by passive diffusion across cell membranes utilizing the physical laws of diffusion (partial pressure gradients). At sea level our atmosphere contains a partial pressure for oxygen of 150 mm of mercury that, through diffusion gradients, is gradually reduced to about 2 mm of mercury at the level of most cells of the body. As room air is ventilated in and out of the lungs, the partial pressure for oxygen in our alveolar air sacs is about 100 mm of mercury. By the time it is transferred across the alveoli into the hemoglobin molecule within red cells leaving the pulmonary capillary it is 90 mm of mercury. If circulation of blood is adequate because of normal cardiac output and peripheral vessel (vascular) tone, the systemic tissue capillary oxygen partial pressure for oxygen is about 40 mm of mercury. From the capillaries, oxygen diffuses a distance of 1 to 2 mm into the tissues to reach cells furthest from the capillaries. At this point it may reach a partial pressure of only 2 mm Hg.

We can see from the brief explanation above that oxygen deprivation to all tissues (*hypoxia*) might occur in a number of conditions, which can be logically sequenced. These conditions include a) low oxygen pressure in the ambient atmosphere (above 10,000 feet altitude), b) lung dysfunction such that partial oxygen pressures from ventilated fresh air are not distributed evenly to an adequate blood stream flow passing in juxtaposition to the air sacs, and c) disorders of circulation that either fail to distribute blood evenly to ventilated lung for oxygenation or to systemic capillaries within vital tissue.

MECHANISMS OF DYING

The above discussion leads us into the concept of mechanisms of dying. In medico-legal terms, the *mechanism* of dying is quite different from the *cause* of death. The cause of death is that process responsible for initiating the series of events that leads to death (for example, myocardial infarction or a gunshot wound). The series of events culminating in death are called *mechanisms.* That is, if the heartbeat became irregular and the outflow of blood became ineffective, we would say that two mechanisms leading to death were ventricular fibrillation and shock (or low blood pressure). A less common term, the *manner* of death suggests whether the cause was natural or unnatural (or violent). If unnatural, the manner of death may have been suicidal, homicidal, accidental, or even undetermined.

Although there are many causes of death, only three major mechanisms of disturbed function can be identified as immediately life threatening. These revolve about the brain, the cardiovascular system, and the pulmonary system. These three organ systems are intricately entwined in providing and distributing oxygen to the various parts of the body in such a way that best serves the total system.

Let us deal in some detail with the three main mechanisms of dying, that is, failure of the brain, heart, or lungs. Simply stated, the series of events leading to death are: a) the brain ceases to supply information vital for controlling ventilation, heart action, or muscular tone of arteries; b) the lungs are unable to supply adequate fresh air for gas exchange with the blood stream; c) the heart or blood vessels are unable to maintain adequate circulation of blood to vital tissues.

Before modern technological achievements, the heart, lungs, or brain failed rapidly in concert with each other, no matter which was first seriously affected. More and more often in modern times, however, technology can support the vital function of any of these organs, disconnecting or overriding their time failure relationship. The intent has always been to support these systems until the primary initiating disease can be allowed to resolve.

Central Nervous System

Within the brain are centers primarily concerned with promoting the rhythmicity and adequacy of breathing air in and out, with maintaining vascular tone of blood vessels so that the capacity of the container (the circulatory system) is never larger than its content (the blood volume within it), and with stimulating a regular effective heartbeat to pump blood. Since the brain and spinal cord are encased in rigid bony structures (skull and vertebrae), with essentially no expansibility, it is obvious that any swelling or space occupation within the central nervous system (CNS) would seriously affect function. Increased cerebrospinal fluid pressure is usually a manifestation of brain or spinal cord swelling. Causes of alteration in CNS function include the following: a) Infection of the brain or brain lining (*meninges*), usually caused by bacterial, viral, fungal, or other invading organisms, seriously disrupts normal brain synchronization of electrical circuitry by inflammatory swelling. Terms such as *encephalitis*, *meningitis*, or *brain abscess* are used to describe this subgroup. b) Blood vessel disruption: In this instance, blood flow continuity to portions of the brain is interrupted by traveling clots of blood or tumor to the head (thrombi or tumor emboli), by intravascular clotting of blood in vessels whose walls are damaged, by congenitally aberrant vascular malformations that burst, or, lastly, by blunt trauma to the skull itself. In the latter case, bleeding beneath the cranium, by space occupation, may seriously damage or impede brain function. Cerebrovascular episodes (CVE's), or *strokes* as they are also called, are included as one of three main causes of death and rank second only to heart attacks. Only when major vessels within the brain are occluded is the vascular supply to the brain sufficiently impaired to cause death. Thus, in reality, the first stroke very rarely kills; more often a series of ministrokes lead to a person's final demise. It is noteworthy that high blood pressure is frequently a precipitating factor in the evolution of this process. c) Malignant tumors: Within the brain most tumors, whether slow or fast growing, are very dangerous both because of their direct interference with brain function and their occupation of space. Whereas many cancers (from lung, colon, breast, etc.) can spread to the brain (called a *metastasis*), primary brain tumors seldom spread outside the skull. d) Metabolic disruption: There are many metabolic causes that can seriously interfere with normal integrative function of the brain. They first alter general body function or metabolism which eventually affects the brain's vital centers as well. Disorders of acid-base balance such as kidney failure (uremia), liver failure (hepatic encephalopathy), or pancreatic failure (diabetic ketoacidosis) drastically alter brain function. Inadequate hormone secretion by thyroid, adrenal, or pituitary seriously affects brain function. An overdose of barbiturates, tranquilizers, or other sedatives markedly depresses cerebral function leading to neurological decompensation.

These four mechanisms all initiate progressive decompensation, which contributes to the disruption of vital functions and the delicate interrelationship of brain, heart, and lungs. Classic signs of neurological decompensation indicating progressive alteration of the state of consciousness include *confusion*, or inability to orient as to where you are, who you are, who your familiar loved ones are, or about the time of day, month, season, or year. More serious decompensation includes *lethargy*, a state of apathy with reduced ability to perform simple cognitive functions such as simple arithmetic. When *obtunded*, attention can be stimulated or gained only by tactile, auditory, or visual stimuli; otherwise a state of sleep prevails. In *stupor* there can be withdrawal, defensive maneuvers, or purposeless movement in response to the above mentioned stimuli, but no arousal or wakefulness occurs. In *semicoma*, movement can be elicited only in response to deep pain, while with *coma*, the last stage of consciousness, no communication is possible at all.

Postural effects can be observed that correlate well with the level of consciousness. In *decorticate* posturing, stimulation of the person will cause lower extremity extension with toe pointing while upper extremities reflex onto the chest. This kind of posture is often observed in the lethargic or stuporous stages. Thereafter, with deeper states of unconsciousness, a *decerebrate* posture ensues with both legs and arms extended. In this situation the palms are turned out from the body in an extended position and the back may even be arched (called *opisthotonos*). Philosophically perhaps, the posture connotates the body's resignation to its loss. In the early stages of CNS decompensation, the pupils, which normally briskly constrict upon exposure to light, become sluggish. When one side of the brain is compressed more than the other side, the corresponding pupillary light reaction may antidate the fellow pupil, but eventually both pupils lose their reactivity to light and dilate into a fixed position. Opiates, like morphine or heroin, can produce pinpoint pupillary constriction. If severe brain depression occurs, barbiturate overdose tends to produce fixation of the pupils at about midpoint (that is, halfway between maximal constriction and dilation). As brain hypoxia becomes worse, dilated, fixed (that is, unresponsive to light) pupils are observed. At this point the pulse rate gradually climbs while the blood pressure gradually falls.

Pulmonary Failure

Simply stated, pulmonary failure is the inability of the pulmonary system to adequately supply oxygen and remove carbon dioxide from the bloodstream. In mild pulmonary failure, inadequate oxygen supply is observed first. Only much later does excretion of carbon dioxide become a problem, so that it accumulates in the blood in the advanced stages of conditions that result in pulmonary failure. Interestingly, the early symptoms and signs of inadequate oxygenation of the brain (*hypoxia*) or decreased carbon dioxide removal (*hypercarbia*) are rather similar. They include confusion, hyperexcitability, irritability, a sense of fear ranging from mild anxiety all the way to a feeling of impending doom. At first, shortness of breath occurs with heavy exertion as an increased breathing rate and depth. As the disease process continues, shortness of breath occurs with diminished degrees of exercise until finally it may occur at rest. Interestingly enough, when smoking is the cause, morning cough and sputum production may be the first symptoms observed in the individual, heralding but for a few years the onset of a more serious process to come, that of emphysema. Examples of the causes of pulmonary failure would include four major abnormalities: interruption of pulmonary vascular supply (pulmonary thromboembolism), emphysema, alteration of the chest wall, and CNS alterations. The lung acts as a remarkably good filter, preventing all particles traveling in the bloodstream larger than red and white blood cells from reaching the systemic circulation. This sieve-like function is very useful for straining out abnormal intravascular material. In some situations, however, large blood clots from venous thrombosis in the legs or thighs is a serious source of mortality. Commonly called *pulmonary thrombo-embolism*, this disease process ranks behind heart attacks and strokes as the third commonest mechanism of death. Fortunately, the disease process is serious enough to kill only 10 to 30 percent of the time, depending upon accurate diagnosis and specific treatment with anticoagulants such as heparin. Pulmonary thrombo-emboli are known to occur more commonly in individuals who have congestive heart failure, emphysema, or have recently undergone surgery.

In emphysema large numbers of alveolar air sacs are destroyed so that the net surface area for air-blood exchange of gases is gradually but progressively reduced. As cigarette smoking is by far the commonest cause of emphysema, this preventable disease has become a major sociological problem of our time. Smoking is largely irrational, therefore its prevalence must be related to behavior patterns or the affective side of each of us. Other examples that cause impaired gas exchange include pneumonias. These are caused by virus, bacterial, or fungal agents, all of which have in common a significant inflammatory cellular replacement of alveolar sacs impeding oxygen transfer.

The chest wall, or diaphragm, can be altered effectively to disturb its bellows action of moving air in and out of the lungs. Examples of this kind of problem include fluid or air accumulation within the pleural space, which by simple space competition prevents the lung from expanding properly. Fluid accumulation within the pleural space can occur from congestive heart failure, infection, or cancer metastasis. Another cause of mechanical alteration in the chest wall are those situations where deformity of the ribs or spine occurs (severe *kyphoscoliosis*) or, alternatively, muscle weakness such as might occur either in poliomyelitis or multiple sclerosis.

CNS alterations, previously mentioned, can impede rhythmical breathing patterns. In essence, depression of the respiratory centers in the lower medullary portion of the brain can lead to all the characteristics of pulmonary failure and ultimately to death.

Inadequate Circulation of the Blood

Circulation and distribution of blood to all body tissues is the responsibility of the cardiovascular system with its unique connections with the brain and lungs. The blood volume (about 80 ml per kg body weight) is always less than the capacity of the circulatory system to hold it. In order for the vascular system to maintain a pressure gradient for blood flow to occur, tissue arteries and capillaries are selectively constricted in order to reduce tissue blood supply until special circumstances prevail. A good example might be the decreased blood supply to the gastrointestinaly tract until a meal is eaten. At selected times, improved blood supply would aid digestion and assimilation of food. Nevertheless, such vital organs as the lungs, heart, brain, and kidneys always have priority for ample blood flow, which is maintained by both the pumping action of the heart and the compliant (elastic) great vessels such as the aorta, femoral, and iliac branches. The walls of these large vessels are very elastic and are able to maintain a pressure gradient insuring continual blood flow downstream to all tissues. The failure either of heart action or the vascular tree to maintain pressure results in decreased blood supply to any or all vital tissues. In response to hemorrhage or altered heart action, our homeostatic mechanisms enable us first to selectively vasoconstrict or reduce blood supply to nonessential organs such as the skin, gastrointestinal tract, muscle, or fat. Finally, vital tissue blood supply may be altered when nothing else can be done. Alterations leading to failure of the cardiovascular system include either abnormalities of the heart itself or the great blood vessels supplying the vital tissues:

Disturbed heart action or rhythm
The heart itself has precious conduits for its blood supply (commonly called the *coronary arteries*) that insure an adequate supply of oxygen and nutrients to the myocardial muscles. Should athero-

sclerosis narrow the lumen of one of the main branches of the coronary arteries, there will be loss of functional reserve of the myocardium to contract when extra demands are required. Moreover, acute occlusion or spasm narrowing one of the coronary vessels may abruptly interrupt blood supply and cause irregular heart rhythm, necrosis (death) of part of the heart muscle, or both, leading to acute pump failure. This we commonly know as *coronary occlusion* or *myocardial infarction*; when muscle mass is destroyed as a result of acute loss of oxygenated blood supply. A "coronary" or heart attack ranks as the number one killer of our population. It is a most dreaded event, since the first attack may kill nearly 25 percent of those afflicted.

Alterations of vascular supply

Within this category are included a variety of events that lead to loss of adequate blood supply to vital tissues. Loss of blood volume through hemorrhage would be paramount among examples of this situation. Blood vessels bleed because of injury, inflammation, infection, or from chronic erosion or disruption of their walls from cancer invasion or atherosclerosis. Occasionally, general impairment of vasoconstriction homeostasis can accompany generalized or localized infection, because of release of toxic substances into the bloodstream. The resultant problem is termed *shock*, a condition in which, for any of the reasons mentioned above, there becomes a progressive disparity between the circulating blood volume and the ability of the vascular tree to maintain an adequate pressure for adequate oxygenation through blood perfusion to vital structures. If the process is not relieved early enough, irreversible shock leads to death.

SUDDEN AND UNEXPECTED DEATH

In most United States' communities where sound governing laws prevail, about 25 percent of all deaths are investigated by the coroner's office. These are almost uniformly sudden or unexpected (or both) deaths, that is, rapid trajectory dying under unexpected or unexplained circumstances. More than two-thirds of these deaths are natural and will be dealt with shortly. The remaining third are violent deaths (see Table 2), that is, deaths that occur from unnatural and accidental circumstances, the major locale being attributed to the motor vehicle (9). Less than 0.5 percent of violent deaths remain unexplained.

Although no age group is exempt, sudden and unexpected deaths from all causes are relatively uncommon between ages one and thirty and after age seventy. The causes of death for the latter group

TABLE 2 Causes of Death by Percent of All Deaths Investigated by Cleveland, Ohio Coroner's Office, 1943–1969 (9)

Type of death	Percent
Industrial accidents	1.5
Home accidents	7.4
Vehicular accidents	6.5
"Other" accidents	5.8
Suicides	5.6
Homicides	3.8
Unexplained	.5
Total (Violent deaths)	31.1
Total (Natural deaths)	68.9

are most commonly degenerative diseases, which are infrequent in early life. Conversely, the older age group has usually provided overt indications of the disease that will prove fatal; thus the death is not unexpected. Men outnumber women by far as victims of sudden death, and the economically depressed are more likely to succumb than the affluent.

Of the natural sudden or unexpected deaths, the cardiovascular system is by far the most common site; the most vulnerable structure is an artery. Thrombosis, occlusion, spasm or narrowing of a coronary artery, embolic occlusion of a major pulmonary artery, or rupture of an artery within the skull are the most common causal factors in the adult sudden death syndrome. One study (10) suggested that of approximately 500 white males who died within an hour of the onset of their terminal trajectory, 90 percent succumbed to narrowing or occlusion of their coronary arteries due to a degenerative disease known as atherosclerosis. Other diseases in which large or small arteries are involved include a sudden tear or rent in the major artery leading from the heart (aorta) and vascular malformations of the intracranial arteries known as berry aneurysms (saccular ballooning of these vessels). The latter may account for about 3 or 4 percent of all rapid and unexpected deaths. It is most unusual for bleeding from vessels located in the lungs, gastrointestinal tract, or other organs to cause sudden unexplained death since the vessels bleeding tend to be smaller, allowing a longer time interval for observation. Moreover signs are readily apparent, such as massive coughing up of blood (as has occurred in advanced tuberculosis), vomiting of blood (from peptic ulcer disease), or bloody bowel movements (from a variety of inflammatory or infectious diseases of the colon).

Among the rarer causes of sudden death, brief mention should be made of a few that occur in the younger age group. Epilepsy, as one example, can occasionally lead to death either because of prolonged seizure activity preventing adequate ventilation and gas exchange, or to aspirating vomitus obstructing the airways. Both situations of course lead to asphyxia (suffocation). Acute pneumonia from any infectious agent (viral, bacterium, etc.) or the accidental inhalation of noxious gases or fumes (phosgene, kerosene, muriatic acid, or hydrochloric acid) may be so overwhelming as to produce asphyxia or multiorgan disturbance (heart, brain, kidneys) leading to death. The recent outbreak in Philadelphia currently known as Legionnaires' disease was one such example of a hitherto-unknown infectious bacterium (11). Another example is carbon monoxide poisoning. Although carbon monoxide enters the body through the lungs, its lethality is related to displacement of vital oxygen from hemoglobin within the red cells, which in turn leads to hypoxic death to all tissues. Another unusual and unfortunate cause of sudden death occurs in young people who have asthma. They may, in unusual circumstances, develop such severe spasm of their central tracheobronchial tree as to produce asphyxia before help can be obtained.

Brief mention of an extremely rare circumstance, called "instantaneous physiological death," should be included because of its bizarre, yet interesting nature. These deaths, involving all age groups but predominately the young, are a rapid process of but a few minutes leading to death initiated by relatively minor trauma or peripheral stimulation of a relatively simple and ordinarily innocuous nature. Culminating evidence of circulatory failure, possibly explained by reflex slowing or stoppage of the heart, reflex dilation of all blood vessels with profound fall in blood pressure, or both, is all that is found at autopsy. A typical story might read as follows: "An 8-year-old boy collapsed and died in a public playground immediately after having been struck on the front of his chest by a ball, batted by a playmate. The incident, observed by the playground supervisor and other spectators, was felt to be of the most innocuous trauma. No abnormalities save circulatory failure were observed at post-mortem examination." Other examples initiating this syndrome have included a blow to the larynx, pressure on carotid sinus (in the neck), shower massage to the neck, a kick in the scrotum, or canalization of the cervix.

Psychological Aspects of Premature Death

Simply to lay out a groundwork of somatic pathology such as the above as a description of dying, belies the obvious union of mind and body in all of us. What part does the emotional or affective side of our everyday living play in precipitating sudden, unexpected and presumably premature death? The answer probably is that "our emotions play a bigger part than at first glance," and some supportive evidence is available. G. L. Engel (12) collected 275 cases of sudden death and performed a psychological autopsy, that is, investigated the affective side of their dying. There was a total of 186 males and 89 females in the study. Among 135 individuals there had been recent loss of an intimate loved one by death or divorce. Engel sustained an acute myocardial infarction and survived on the eleventh-month anniversary of the death of his brother, also a heart attack victim. In another 21 individuals, there had been losses of great emotional impact (such as loss of a valued position or possession) or particular events that symbolized defeat, failure, or disappointment.

In another 103 cases, a recent episode of extreme danger involving attack or struggle had occurred. One example of this kind of emotional impact involved a lady who, while waiting for a bus, was attacked and her purse taken. After the episode she slumped over dead while sitting in a car explaining the event to a policeman. Lastly, happy reunions or public recognition were encountered in the purview of 16 additional people who encountered sudden death.

That deeply felt emotions may be an important ingredient in many sudden deaths is illustrated by the death of Lyndon Johnson. It is known that his last days in office were filled with bitter disappointment and frustration, largely unexpressed. Deprived of his accustomed power and influence, the retired president was harshly criticized for his Vietnam policy, even by former close associates and admirers. In discussing the Nixon administration effort to substantially cut funds for his domestic policies, Johnson compared his Great Society to a starving woman. "And when she dies," said Johnson, who had served the presidency in remarkable health despite a coronary in 1955, "I too will die." Nixon was inaugurated for his second term of office on January 20, 1973, and the next day his administration announced plans for a complete dismantling of the Great Society. The following morning, January 22, 1973, Lyndon Johnson died of a myocardial infarction. Or was it a broken heart?

Other studies have raised our consciousness level about the interplay between behavior and medical textbook diseases. Caroline Thomas (13) performed a prospective study of medical students from Johns Hopkins University graduating between 1948 and 1964, following some of the graduates for nearly 30 years. During their medical school years the students were given questionnaires that coded the number of habits of nervous tension (excessive fatigue, tension, insomnia, nausea, shakiness, etc.), attitudes about closeness to parents, the common Rorschach Test, and a human figure drawing test. Results of these questionnaires were evaluated in 109 male individuals who later were affected by 5 disorders: suicide, cancer, hypertension, myocardial infarction, and mental illness (defined as a psychological disorder involving some period of hospitalization). As a control group, 123 individuals were matched by age, sex, class, and race. In medical school, the total disorder group had more insomnia, smoked more cigarettes, and drank alcohol and coffee more frequently than did the control group. The suicide and mental illness group showed the most nervous tension, depression, and anger under stress and the malignant group the least. Suicide, mental illness, and malignant tumor groups had lower mean scores for closeness to parents, while the hypertension and myocardial infarction group means were higher than the control group. One could conclude from this brief synopsis of Thomas's study that psychological differences measured even in youth have group (but not necessarily individual) predictive potential in regard to premature disease and death.

Additional information has become available about cancer from another study by S. Greer and T. Morris (14). They interviewed 160 consecutive women arriving at the hospital who had a breast lump and were preparing for a biopsy. Neither patient nor interviewer therefore knew what the eventual diagnosis might be. Among the 69 patients subsequently found to have breast cancer there was a significant association with a past behavior pattern, persisting through adult life, of abnormal release of emotions. Compared to the 91 found to have benign breast disease, the cancer patients demonstrated predominantly an extreme suppression of anger and other feelings. Much less commonly, an overreactive expression of feelings was observed.

Schmale et al. (15) found similar kinds of results in a group of women about to have a biopsy to determine whether or not they had cancer of the cervix. From the interview results of a cohort of 51 patients, he was able to conclude that the 18 women found to have cervical cancer had a lifetime behavior pattern of "feeling cornered" during episodes of stress and tending to give up rather than fight. There were indications of increased tendency toward depression in the group of women found to have cervical cancer.

Thus we can see that already within the literature are glimmerings of an association between mind and body when encountering disease states. It is conjectural as to what comes first, the mind or the body, in the causation of disease, and probably not relevant. But one conclusion that immediately comes to mind is that by altering one's behavior characteristics, a richer and fuller life can be achieved.

Voodoo Death

There has been described among primitive peoples, especially those aboriginal tribes who are isolated, uneducated, and filled with superstitions in a land of hostility among tribes, an unusual kind of premature death, variously named as *voodoo death*, *self-willed death*, or *bone pointing* (16). Although descriptions are largely anecdotal from a variety of regions such as South America, South Africa, Australia, New Zealand, Micronesia, and other islands of the Pacific, the phenomenon is so incredible and foreign to most civilized peoples that it deserves some attention.

The testimony usually revolves around a person who, when subjected to particular spells, sorcery, or the use of "black magic," rapidly dies within days without evidence of organic disease. The possibility of poisons often is raised by critical observers, but this cause has often been ruled out (16). One account cited by W. B. Cannon is of an aborigine Maori woman, who, having eaten some fruit, was told by a medicine man that it had been taken from a tabooed place; she exclaimed that the sanctity of her chief had been profaned and his spirit would kill her. The incident occurred in the afternoon and within 24 hours she was dead. No cause was found at autopsy. Another account cited (16) was of a native of North Queensland, Australia who came to a physician, saying he would be dead in a few days because a spell had been put upon him and nothing could be done about it. The doctor had known the man for some time. A thorough physical examination, including tests of the blood and stool, revealed no abnormality. Puzzled, the western doctor called in a foreman of the tribe to give the man reassurance, but the tribal relative leaned over the victim for a brief moment and merely confirmed the poor man's self-willed prophecy. The next morning the man was dead. A post-mortem examination revealed nothing that could account for the fatal outcome.

Another anecdote from a mission in North Queensland, described a reversal in the trajectory. A young male convert was found in great distress, wailing and excited, and told the missionary physician that a famous local witch doctor had pointed the bone at him and he would die for his conversion. Although the young man had no fever, pains, or other symptoms of disease, he looked seriously ill and extremely weak. The witch doctor was immediately called and threatened that his food would be cut off and his people driven away from the mission. At once the witch doctor agreed to remove the spell and went to see the young man. The relief, the mission doctor testified, was almost instantaneous; that evening the young man was back at work, quite happy again, and in full possession of his physical strength.

To be sure, such citations are very difficult to document as proof that a psychological self-willed and socially-in·luced death is possible, and a conservative viewpoint should be maintained. T. X. Barber has written a critical note of evaluation of these phenomena (17).

The Data: The Facts of Death

Nevertheless, reports from all over the world have been compared and found to be fairly similar.

A person as a social and gregarious animal thrives upon interpersonal relationships, likes to be sought after, nurtured, and esteemed by colleagues. Three major events occur in the process of voodoo deaths. The first of these is the immediate establishment of a new social contract, in unconscious accord with the medicine man, whereby the community withdraws its social support from the victim. This becomes a very effective action. If no one returns a knowing glance, answers a spoken word, pays attention to what the victim does; if every person he meets "cuts him dead," then no alternative but death might seem plausible to the victim. The second event is the victim's unconscious acceptance of the medicine man's wishes reinforced by total societal deprivation. In the illness that ensues, the highly suggestible victim makes no effort to live or stay within the group, but also may, through the multiple negative suggestions of his kinship, cooperate by withdrawing from them. He assists in committing a primitive form of suicide, by becoming what the attitudes of the fellow tribesmen will him to be—dead.

Before death takes place, however, the community returns to the victim with a new form of attention that marks the third and last noteworthy event in the process. This attention is in the form of rituals and ceremony that help the community to debond itself from the victim through mourning and anticipatory grief. The process also reinforces the victim's trajectory by cutting him off from the ordinary world and placing him in his rightful and proper position in the sacred world of the dead. By his death, the victim ultimately acknowledges and reciprocates this feeling.

Analogous situations in our western society may lead to premature death through the use of many highly emotional and stigmatized labels such as "cancer," "dying," or "terminal," through "barriers of silence" initiated by the family upon being told of an individual's cancer, dying, or terminality, and by premature debonding and anticipatory grief processes. G. W. Milton (18) talks about the comparison in discussing individuals who come to his melanoma clinic. At one end of the spectrum, some individuals, upon being told of their malignancy, change their whole personality, becoming physically and mentally transformed. They turn their face to the wall, lie inert in bed, often covering their face with a bed sheet (paralleling a shroud). They do not appear terrified but are instead vague, evasive, and show blanket indifference. They may eat or drink a little to please their spouses, but they derive no pleasure from it. Such individuals do not lament their fate nor look abjectly miserable, rather they remain indifferent to all attempts at communication or social connection. Within a month of the onset of this syndrome the person is usually dead, and although the autopsy may show widespread malignancy, there will often appear to be no adequate explanation for the cause of death. Such a trajectory can be enhanced if there are relatively few or extremely poor quality social contacts with other people (whether relatives or hospital personnel).

At the other end of the spectrum are individuals who enter a hospital with an attitude within themselves and their relatives of total despair and all the above features of self-willed death. As soon as the patient feels that something can be done for him, even it all that can be achieved is a revitalized interest in himself and relief of such agonizing symptoms as pain, his mental attitude changes. By reinforcing more family visits and honest sharing of feelings among all family members, a remarkable improvement in the patient can frequently be observed. Short-term remissions such as the above, through psychological and social support of the individual and his family, can sometimes be misinterpreted by the medical staff as occurring as a result of chemotherapy or other somatic treatments.

MORBIDITY AND MORTALITY AMONG THE BEREAVED

In considering the above heading, a poignant story comes to mind about a man who abruptly gave up his avid lifetime avocation of goose hunting and sold all his shotguns. In the story the man and a few friends, huddled in a blind early one beautiful New England fall morning, were finally gratified to see a flock of Canada geese flying in to alight upon a nearby salt-marsh. Just as they were coming in, he and his friends opened fire, but in spite of many shots only one goose fell from the sky. All but one of the other geese immediately veered off to escape the hunters' fire. As you may know, Canada geese mate for life, and that one goose slowly circled downward, placing itself in jeopardy by following its wounded mate's trajectory into the water. Additional fire from the hunters eventually succeeded in killing the second goose, but the man was so touched by this one wild bird's act of utter concern and devotion for its mate, even though increasing the risk for itself, that he never hunted again.

The death of a spouse usually represents the loss of a person's most meaningful source of interaction and support. The ensuing process of grief, which may last an indefinite time period, can be an unhealthy state that involves untold suffering and impairment characterized by loneliness, despair, role confusion, relative poverty, sexual frustration, and societal alienation. It would not be illogical therefore to expect that individuals are placed in morbid and mortal jeopardy during this bereavement period. P. J. Clayton (19) reviewed

The Data: The Facts of Death

much of the data presently available concerning increased morbidity of individuals entering the bereavement period. There is evidence that these individuals seek more medical attention both for non-psychiatric and psychiatric symptoms. The symptoms include depression and its component parts, insomnia, anxiety, headaches, restlessness, and inability to function well at work. There is usually an escalation in prescriptions given for drugs, both sedatives and tranquilizers, to both widows and widowers. Increased alcohol intake also has been recorded.

D. N. McNeill (20) studied a cohort of 9000 widows and widowers whose spouses died in 1965 in the state of Connecticut to see if there was an increased risk of dying in the bereavement period. He did indeed find that the risk increased beyond statistically expected death rates; 3.7 times expected in the widowers and usually during the first 6 months, and 2.0 times expected in the widows, usually during the second and third 6-month periods. Even though the risk of conjugal bereavement rose exponentially between ages twenty and seventy, there was an inverse relationship in the spouse also dying within 18 months of the loss. Among those aged 20 to 29 years, the spouse died 7 times more frequently than the expected rate, while in those aged 60 to 69 years, the risk factor was only 0.9. Among widowers, deaths due to suicide were 12 times expected, while atherosclerotic heart disease and stroke were each greater than 4 times expected. Among widows the increased risks of dying in the second and third 6-month periods were from liver cirrhosis and alcoholism (6.5 times expected), atherosclerotic heart disease (2.3 times expected), and cancer (2.0 times expected). The collective data seemed to indicate that the suddenness of a spouse's death may modify the mortality risk for the surviving spouse. A prolonged terminal illness in the spouse may permit the survivor to prepare for the loss through anticipatory griefwork, thus ameliorating his increased risk of dying.

The mechanisms whereby the survivors of a spouse loss are placed in morbid and mortal jeopardy are unknown, but several possibilities can be entertained. These include physiological changes that may increase vulnerability to disease, psychological changes (such as depression) that may lead to suicide, failure to detect or seek help for cancer early (personal neglect), decreased attention to or management of such chronic diseases as diabetes or hypertension, or other changes such as increased alcohol consumption. Nevertheless, awareness of the data should direct the medical field and indeed alert societal concern to provide better support facilities for the unfortunate individuals who gradually or suddenly are faced with "going it alone;" there is a need for personal revitalization and growth during the bereavement period.

DEATH PROCESSES

We have purposely avoided writing about the usual fanfare surrounding the definition of death because it is the philosophical contention of this author that the label *death* is an arbitrary line during a continuum of events in process. As stated earlier, it is essentially the progressive decompensation of the brain, lungs, and heart that leads us toward death and the next series of events that deserve description.

During ultimate failure of the above-mentioned organ systems a number of processes begin (21). One such process is *rigor mortis*, in which the muscles of the body gradually become hardened due to accumulation of lactic acid and other products of anaerobic metabolism within muscle fibrils. The process begins within 2 to 4 hours of death but may be hastened by high fever, convulsions, or extreme muscle activity in the pre-mortem period. In contrast, the onset of rigidity may be delayed for hours by rapid cooling in a chilly environment or by refrigeration. Rigor mortis sometimes is absent or much attenuated in the very old or young or in those severely debilitated with paucity of muscle tissue. Because shorter muscle fibers develop rigidity sooner than longer extremity muscle fibers, it is commonly stated that rigor mortis starts in the face and neck before spreading over the body. The persistence of rigidity is also directly influenced by body temperature, which in turn may be a function of surrounding temperature. Rigor mortis may disappear within 9 to 12 hours if the body is in an extremely hot environment and if decomposition begins early (e.g., following generalized bacterial infection or septicemia).

There are several superstitions regarding body or eyelid movement in the process of death that should be dispelled. People frequently die with their eyelids in a semiclosed position and, if the eyelids are artificially closed, they will usually remain so during the process of rigor mortis. Rigidity occurs from hardening of the muscles and not from muscle contraction. Thus eyelids do not open if they have been closed. Also, stories about bodies sitting up in coffins or moving limbs simply are not true. In some situations, the legs or arms may fall to a resting position from being fully flexed as rigor mortis dissipates, but this occurs as a result of gravity.

A color change often occurs in dependent positions of the body that has been termed *livor mortis*. This purplish discoloration of the skin is caused by gravitational settling of blood cell hemoglobin into dilated capillaries. Though it depends upon gravity, livor mortis is usually absent where skin has borne the body's weight, a factor that prevents the surface capillaries from accepting the deoxygenated hemoglobin. A halo of livor mortis can often be seen around these pressure points, revealing the exact body position during the death process. In carbon monoxide poisoning, hemoglobin retains a cherry red coloring lending that hue to dependent skin parts. Of course, in severe hemorrhage or anemia, livor mortis may be so pale as to be inapparent. Formation of livor mortis begins from the moment blood circulation stops, is perceptible usually within 2 hours, and reaches a maximum between 8 and 12 hours after death.

Body cooling in the early hours following death may give some useful information approximating the time of death. Based on an initial rectal or liver temperature of 98.6° Fahrenheit, the temperature falls about 1.5 degrees per hour in most bodies exposed to moderate ambient temperature. The rate of fall of course depends not only on ambient temperatures, but on wind chill, relative humidity, and the insulating ability of clothing. Sometimes during poisoning or heat stroke the initial body temperature may be 5 to 10 degrees warmer than normal, making calculations much less reliable.

The process of decomposition leading to putrefaction (decay and bacterial decomposition) of the body, like other parameters mentioned above, is subject to enormous time variation depending upon circumstances of the death, ambient temperature, and preexisting condition of the corpse. *Autolysis* refers to the action of digestive enzymes in the body, breaking down complex proteins, carbohydrates, and fats into simpler molecules. Most noteworthy are the gastrointestinal tract enzymes, which may cause such autolysis as to result in post-mortem rupture of stomach or bowel wall. The large bowel is normally colonized with quantities of bacteria that, following death, also aid in digestion of abdominal contents, reducing the tissues to a fluid consistency and producing large amounts of foul-smelling (putrid) gas. Sometimes discharge of fluid and gas occurs through orifices (anus, vagina, mouth) previously continent by virtue of sustained sphincter hardening during the period of rigor mortis. Movement of the body after death often initiates this odorous event.

As bacteria spread throughout the body's blood vessels and gas is released within the tissues, the body becomes distended, skin color changes from green to purple and black, and the eyes and tongue may protrude. Gradually the skin softens and slips, revealing underlying structures. Skin slippage may be so complete that the entire skin of a hand or foot may be detached in glovelike fashion.

Although obese bodies tend to decompose more rapidly, warm ambient temperature is the single most important factor in determining the putrefactive process. It is not uncommon to see advanced decomposition within 12 to 18 hours. The body has become generally discolored and swollen to two or three times normal size, with loss of facial contour, displacement of scalp hair, and loss of integument (skin). Death from poisoning, particularly within the abdomen or bloodstream, accelerates the process. During putrefaction and the liquifaction processes, the body loses water content at a rate that again depends upon the relative humidity and temperature of the ambient air. As dehydration proceeds, the tips of the fingers and toes, and facial skin retract, with apparent production of more nail or hair. This has given rise to the erroneous lay belief that the hair and nails grow after death. Body decomposition need not occur so rapidly. We have all heard or read about prehistoric animals found perfectly preserved for hundreds of thousands of years by rapid freezing during the glacial ice ages.

Adipocere: Inhibition of Decay

One variant of the putrefaction process that deserves consideration is a process called *adipocere.* This change, though observed historically, has not received much attention until recent times; the word *adipocere* was introduced in 1786 (22). The term applies to spontaneous preservation of corpses through unusual alterations in their fatty tissue. The body of St. Cuthbert, who died in A.D. 687, was recorded as being relatively well preserved for over 850 years. Presumably his remains were preserved because of this process.

In cool moist soil or in cool water, the fatty soft tissues of the body decay much more slowly and are instead converted into a peculiar grayish-white cheesy material, consisting principally of hydrolyzed fats, which resists decay for much longer periods. The material is firm or hard when cold, and softer and greasy at room temperature. On warming, the greater part of the substance melts, to set again on cooling. Fatty tissue normally contains neutral fats such as triglycerides or cholesterol. After death, the fatty acids from these fats are liberated by enzymes, and their fatty acids (mostly palmitic, stearic, and oleic acid) are hydrolyzed under anaerobic conditions with some soap formation. There is an offensive and powerful smell associated with this decomposition, probably related principally to ammonia production. The water required for fatty hydrolysis comes mainly from body tissues, which consequently become more and more dehydrated. Conditions favoring the slower decay of fatty tissue into hydrolyzed fatty acids include adiposity (occurs in women more than men), moisture, still air or water, inadequate oxygen supply, and cessation of bacterial growth. The process begins within a few weeks after death but is not fully developed before 6 months have elapsed. The distribution of fat within the human body is nearly universal, although to some extent excessive appetite may increase its distribution percentage. When adipocere is widespread, other soft tissues of the body become remarkably dry, decreasing their weight considerably. The intestines and lungs are commonly parchmentlike in consistency and thinness, and hearts are reduced to 40 grams or less (normally about 350 grams). The most prominent abdominal organ is usually the liver whose weight is perhaps halved though retaining its shape.

On the limbs and back, a line of demarcation between sub-cutaneous adipocere and muscle is usually impossible to ascertain, but deeper parts of bulkier muscles may retain a beefy pink to red color. The color is due mostly to myohemoglobin and is relatively stable once exposed to air.

Historical Preservation of the Body

There is ample evidence that ancient man was very aware of body decay after death; he likely became very interested in reproducing some of the natural processes as well as supplementing them in order to prevent or retard putrefaction (22). One of these processes, *mummification*, was slowly developed into a specialty in ancient Egyptian times. It began with the observation of corpses interred in hot, dry sand. They observed the bodies drying very quickly and converting into dry leathery parchmentlike masses of skin, tendons, and bones.

The development of artificial mummification progressed from this simple environmental exposure to more elaborate methods that included separate processing of internal organs. Doubtless, observations of putrefaction led to the discovery that destructive processes commenced with widespread bacterial dissemination from the large bowel. In order to retard this process, the body was disemboweled as soon as possible after death, although heart and kidneys were often left intact. Then a highly stylized ritual was developed for the socially elite of the times. The body was first washed in water from the Nile (for this river was the source of life to the Egyptians). Then the remains were immersed in dehydrating saline solutions or natron (an alkaline mixture of sodium salts) for 2 to 6 weeks before exposure to the drying sun and sand for an equal length of time. Body organs were also preserved separately in this manner, then treated and wrapped either for eventual return to the thoraco-abdominal cavity or for storage in special urns or jars. Following dehydration, different kinds of resins or hot bitumen (pitch) were used along with elegant oils and ointments, with inter-mittent wrappings of linen cloth. Hot resin or bitumen applications sealed the surface of the body but damaged outer tissues. However, the application of these substances was used to improve skin color and preservation and to obscure putrefactive odors.

Numerous exhumations of Egyptian mummies clearly reveal that the ancient practices, although elegant, elaborate, and prolonged, did not achieve a very high standard of preservation. Although facial configuration was usually apparent, skin, bone, and muscles were usually so dry and brittle that even minor disturbance to the corpse caused the remains to collapse within its wrappings. In other mummies, however, an outer shell of hardened and matted tissue remained that could be occasionally cut off in blocks, but usually cracked, flaked, or broke apart.

Another more striking account of ancient funeral practice comes from the examination of a remarkably preserved Chinese woman disinterred in 1974 from a tomb over 2100 years old. Her yellowish-brown skin was still moist and much of the soft tissues retained some elasticity. Post-mortem findings revealed that the abdominal contents and organs, although shrunken, were still intact. In all organs however, cellular definition was largely lost. The breakdown of tissue had proceeded remarkably slowly over the 2000 years! How was such preservation accomplished? The remains had been wrapped in 20 layers of silk cloth and was half immersed in a reddish preserving fluid, containing salt buffers, several organic acids, and a mercury compound. Slightly antiseptic and disinfecting, the liquid had helped to prevent decay. However, the fundamental reason for body preservation was that it was contained within the innermost of four sealed containers, buried under 5 tons of charcoal and sealed within a 4-foot layer of clay. The oxygen within the innermost chamber was quickly used up by aerobic bacteria decomposing meat that had also been placed within the tomb, rapidly creating an oxygen-poor environment. The tomb was about 50 feet underground, providing excellent conditions for the hermetic seal.

In modern times, preservation of bodies for medical, scientific, or funereal practice has proceeded along the lines mentioned above. In medical schools the body is usually rapidly cooled after death to inhibit digestive enzyme release and bacterial growth and dissemination from the large bowel. As soon as convenient, the circulatory system of the body is used to infuse and distribute preservative embalming fluids. These fluids generally contain aldehydes, such as formaldehyde or glutaldehyde, along with buffer salts to maintain body pH. One of the major arteries is cannulated and the embalming fluid distributed to all body parts under a gravity-dependent pressure gradient system. The embalming fluids operate as a disinfectant, killing bacteria as well as denaturing protein as they diffuse out of the circulatory system into tissues of all parts of the body. In medical school a carbolic acid immersion vat is also used to improve preservation. Once fixation of tissues is accomplished and the bodies stored in a constant, cool, and dry place, long periods (years) of preservation can follow. One funeral director's school recorded a 10 percent weight loss after 11 years of observation. The loss of weight was from water loss (dehydration) in the stable laboratory environment.

Funeral homes also use major arteries for their embalming procedures as described above. The corpse is usually placed in a casket of variable quality insofar as its seal from air and general construction is concerned. Thereafter, the casket and its contents are burned (cremation), placed in an above ground mausoleum, or buried in the ground. Depending on which of the latter two procedures is used, the corpses deteriorate at a variable rate in spite of embalming procedures. The rate of decay is of course, delayed beyond the natural process, but is highly dependent beyond the natural process, but is highly dependent upon preservation techniques and prevailing weather conditions, i.e., variations in temperature, humidity, and wind.

SUMMARY

Considerable effort has been made in this chapter to avoid the usual process of overly defining, categorizing, and otherwise demarcating the continuum of living while dying. In spite of this effort, the reader will recognize a large number of terms that label events. Many processes have received a rather cursory evaluation, but, alternatively, an attempt was made to broaden perspective by including the mind and body as a unit in their continual interaction with nature.

Aspirations to immortality have long intrigued homo sapiens. Adam may have created the precedent for his ephemeral descendents when, despite considerable difficulties in his early marriage and trouble between his two sons, he managed to live to the scriptural age of 930 years. After much arduous research, Ko Hung, an alchemist who lived in the fourth century A.D., proclaimed that a mixture of liquid gold and pure cinnabar, nine times transmuted, produced the one true elixir of life. He further recorded his regret that he personally was too poor to afford the necessary expensive ingredients to extend his time. Other life-lengthening potions prescribed over the years have included royal jelly from bees, gland grafts, bizarre injections, yogurt consumption, and other dietary eccentricities. Most modern attempts may perhaps include the unabashed medical and political community's war against cancer, heart disease, stroke, or whatever disease you would care to name.

Seeds of doubt about the virtue of immortality were fortunately sown by Jonathan Swift in *Gulliver's Travels,* when his leading man encountered the Struldbrugs, a remarkable race of peculiar people who never died. Though invested with immortality, the Struldbrugs were not protected from growing old. And so they lived on and on, losing hair, teeth, strength, taste, or memory, multiplying their senescent infirmities as inexorably as the passage of time. It has been said of our own race that "millions have longed for immortality who do not know what to do with themselves on a rainy Sunday afternoon." In *Catch 22* Dunbar sought to extend his years by cultivating boredom. Once, when lying motionless in bed and staring at the ceiling, he worked so hard at increasing his life span that suddenly he actually thought he was dead.

Maurice Chevalier was once asked about his personal reaction to his advancing years. His reply I think deserves some consideration. "I really prefer old age to the alternative!" However, would it not be wiser, and less vulnerable to disappointment for all of us, if we were to adopt the humble and simple reality principle of someone who said "I intend to live well into my years, or die in the attempt."

REFERENCES

1. Whitehead, A. N. *Science and the modern world.* New York: Macmillan, 1967.
2. Morrison, R. Death: Process or event? *Science,* 1971, *173,* 694-698.
3. Dorland, W. A. *American illustrated medical dictionary* (22nd ed.). Philadelphia: Saunders, 1965.
4. Ackerknecht, E. H. Death in the history of medicine. *Bulletin of History of Medicine,* 1968, *42,* 19-23.
5. Engel, G. The need for a new medical model: A challenge for biomedicine. *Science,* 1977, *196,* 129-136.
6. Veatch, R. M. *Death, dying, and the biological revolution.* Cambridge, MA: Schenkman, 1976.
7. Hayflick, L. The cell biology of human aging, *New England Journal of Medicine,* 1976, *195,* 1302-1308.
8. Comfort, A. *Aging: The biology of senescence.* New York: Holt, Rinehart and Winston, 1964.
9. Adelson, L., & Hirsh, C. S. Sudden and unexpected death from natural causes in adults. In W. U. Spitz & R. S. Fisher (Eds.), *Medicolegal investigation of death.* Springfield, IL: Thomas, 1973.
10. Spain, D. M., Bradess, V. A. & Mohr, C. Coronary atherosclerosis as a cause of unexpected and unexplained death. *Journal of the American Medical Association,* 1961, *176,* 129.
11. McDade, J. E., Shepard, C. C. et al. Legionnaires' disease: Isolation of a bacterium. *New England Journal of Medicine,* 1977, *297,* 1197-1203.
12. Engel, G. L. Sudden and rapid death during psychological stress. *Annals of Internal Medicine,* 1971, *74,* 771-781.
13. Thomas, C. B. Precursors of premature disease and death. *Annals of Internal Medicine,* 1971, *85,* 653-658.
14. Greer, S. & Morris, T. Psychological attributes of women who develop breast cancer: A controlled study. *Journal of Psychosomatic Research,* 1975, *19,* 147-153.
15. Schmale, A. et al. Hopelessness as a predictor of cervical cancer. *Annals N.Y. Acad. Science,* 1966, *125,* 807-811.

16. Cannon, W. B. Voodoo death. *American Anthropologist*, 1942, *44*, 169-182.
17. Barber, T. X. Death by suggestion: A critical note. *Psychosomatic Medicine*, 1961, *23*, 153-155.
18. Milton, G. W. Self-willed death or the bone-pointing syndrome. *Lancet*, 1973, *1*, 1435-1436.
19. Clayton, P. J. The clinical morbidity of the first year of bereavement: A review. *Comprehensive Psychiatry*, 1973, *14*, 151-157.
20. McNeill, D. N. *Mortality among the bereaved.* Abstract presented at the 105th Annual Meeting of the American Public Health Association, November, 1977.
21. Fisher, R. S. Time of death and changes after death. In W. U. Spitz & R. S. Fisher (Eds.), *Medicolegal investigation of death.* Springfield, IL: Thomas, 1973.
22. Evans, W. E. D. *The chemistry of death.* Springfield, IL: Thomas, 1963.

CHAPTER FOUR

Social and Psychological Aspects of Dying

MICHAEL A. SIMPSON

THE CONTEXT OF DEATH

The social and psychological context of death has changed in many ways in recent years. A century ago, the experience and expectation of death was commonplace in each family, while sex was socially unmentionable. During the unprecedented carnage of the first decades of the twentieth century, Western men and women overturned the taboo of sex and discovered that almost everybody

---

This chapter provides a comprehensive and careful review and analysis of a complex subject about which a great deal has been written in various publications. Simpson's extensive knowledge of the fields of sociology and the psychology of death and their interaction, combined with his scholarly rigor and incisiveness have made this a unique contribution that presents facts and issues with a clarity and straightforwardness seldom found anywhere.

A physician himself, the author gives special emphasis to the issue of lying or telling a patient of his or her impending death. Most physicians use a variety of evasive responses to the patient's question. Simpson's own clinical experience as well as his analysis of the available research lead him to believe that honest discussion with the dying is not only needed but is also possible though it may differ qualitatively from other forms of interpersonal communications.

The Data: The Facts of Death

does it and worries about it, that it is a valid subject of study, and that much can be done to alleviate the worry and suffering associated with its related problems. Much later in the century, amid increasingly unbridled exploration and expression of sex, we have begun to make a similar rediscovery of death.

Death is a very badly kept secret. I have over 700 books about death on my shelves and thousands of articles on file, mostly announcing that ours is a death-denying society, and congratulating themselves on breaching that denial. The growth of the death literature during the 1960s and 1970s has been a remarkable cultural phenomenon. Until then, the subject's absence from the literature was very striking; now so much is being published that no one person can keep fully aware of it all. Exploitation of the theme in books, audiotapes, and cinema—often in very shoddy products—has become frequent. Two recent primary guides to the literature have become essential for any attempt to cope with this mass of material, organizing the published articles (1) and books and other media (2).

A new breed of researchers, clinicians, philosophers, and educators has developed. Death has become an area of exciting and creative interdisciplinary exploration. There are societal trends suggesting that like blacks, women, homosexuals, the insane, and the old, the dying have come out of the closet in turn. The death taboo has been lifted. But what occurs may not be the brave existential confrontation of life and its inevitable end that we fondly imagine, for this new zealous interest may be merely another variety of denial.

There are interesting parallels with an earlier historical period of comparable social preoccupation with death and dying centuries ago. Then—following the plague of the Black Death and prolonged warfare, during the breakdown of feudalism, and amid the turmoil of the early Renaissance—there was a similar concern with the problem of how to die properly. A similar genre of books emerged, dealing with the art and craft of dying, the *ars moriendi*. Now we have handed the care of the dying and the dead to professionals, having lost the simple folk arts and basic domestic skills of doing it for ourselves. We have largely lost our traditional spiritual and psychological moorings of shared beliefs and rituals, and we drift through marked social disorganization.

Our grandparents had a larger, functioning, extended family, embedded in the nexus of an active and communicating community of kinfolk, which could provide mutual support in the event of the loss of any one member. The high infant mortality rate and the frequent loss of young adults from infectious diseases meant that they could become practiced and adept at coping with loss and grief. In our time we have more often shrunk to the nuclear family (husband, wife, and children) and even to the postnuclear family (one-parent families, one-child or no-child families, and single people). Each death can diminish us more profoundly. "No man is an island" is no longer strictly true. In the age of alienation, many men are islands, and we each belong to a smaller archipelago.

THE SOCIOLOGY OF DEATH

Social Determinants of Mode of Death

When and how you die will depend in part on your social class and position in society. The classic illustration is the sinking of the Titanic in 1912. The official casualty lists showed a clear social-class selectivity in the death of the women on board. Only 4 of 143 first-class female passengers were lost (and 3 of these had insisted on staying on board); 15 of 93 women in second class drowned; and 51 of the 179 women in third class died. The mortality varied from under 3 to some 30 percent, depending on the class of passage (3).

The social inequality of death has been well reviewed by Goldscheider (4). The poor show higher infant, child, and young adult death rates and more deaths from severe childhood infections. The rates of infant death among the lowest social classes lag some 30 years behind the infant mortality rates of the higher classes (5). In mid- and later life the white-collar middle-class worker shows higher death rates from heart disease, cancer, and stroke; the diseases of affluence. Hunt and Huyck (6) showed a higher infant and maternal mortality rate in areas with low income and high incidence of social problems and in areas of low quality housing as compared with areas of good housing. Another study (7) showed higher mortality rates over the age of 25 among groups with less schooling and among those with low family incomes.

Other studies, by Sudnow (8) and Simpson (9), have shown the influence of other social factors. Should you collapse, suddenly and critically ill, there are broadly two ways you might be treated. Those who find you may regard you as a cardiac arrest or similar emergency case and begin the attempt to resuscitate you. You would then be rushed to a hospital, where energetic resuscitation would be continued. Or you may be assumed to be dead already, taken to a hospital in a more leisurely fashion, and declared Dead on Arrival or "BID" (Brought in Dead). The most crucial decisions about you will not have been made by a doctor, and there may be little major difference in the clinical condition of people treated in either fashion—but other distinctions may be clear. The older the patient the more likely it is that tentative death will be accepted without resuscitation (and the less likely it will be that resuscitation, if begun, will be prolonged). Social class and perceived moral character also influence such life-or-death decisions. The moribund patient who appears to be of low social class, is shabbily dressed, unwashed, or smells of alcohol, seems to be less likely to receive vigorous attempts at resuscitation, as will the patient with perceived social deviancy—the addict, the suicide, and the vagrant. On the other hand, the great and powerful—like Generalissimo Franco—may be denied the possibility of an unharassed death and may receive bizarrely prolonged and desperate resuscitation attempts.

The Sociological Study of Death

One might have expected death to be a major topic of study of modern sociology as it developed, but the discipline has never attempted or produced a systematic exploration of problems relating to death. Durkheim's *Suicide* (10) was an early classic but not followed by further organized studies for many years. Only very occasional sociologists attended to the issues, for example, Eliot (11) in the 1930s. In 1953 Faunce and Fulton (12) identified death as a "neglected area of research" and cogently argued the need for further work but to little avail. Anthropologists, by contrast, have retained an interest in death and its attendant rituals, as evidenced by such works as Tylor (13), Evans-Pritchard (14, 15), Malinowski (16), Radcliffe-Brown (17), van Gennep (18), Hertz (19), Gluckman (20, 21), Bendmann (22), Frazer (23), and more recent writers such as Goody (24).

Only in the 1960s were detailed and competent sociological studies of the phenomena of death first published. Most notable was the work of Barney Glaser and Anselm Strauss (25, 26), and their methods of study (27) have been influential. Another brilliant and perceptive study was that of David Sudnow (8).

Using a flexible participant observation technique, Glaser and Strauss, in their first study, *Awareness of Dying* (25), focused on the systems of communication surrounding the dying person and the *awareness context*, which they defined as "what *each* interacting person knows of the patient's defined status, along with his recognition of the others' awareness of his own definition." They delineated four typical awareness contexts: closed, suspected, mutual pretense, and open.

In *closed awareness* the patient does not know he is going to die. The staff does know but tries to maintain the patient's unsuspecting ignorance by a complex variety of ploys including misdirection and avoidance, evasion and lying, and inventing a fictional future for the patient. In the situation of *suspected awareness* the patient is between full ignorance and full awareness, as in Weisman's state of "middle knowledge" (28), suspecting but not knowing for sure. The patient has to engage in a sort of tug-of-war for information, seeking confirmation of suspicions from direct and indirect cues that everyone tries to avoid providing. He must try to catch people off-guard, to overhear, to snatch at inadvertent clues. If the patient tries direct questions, direct avoidance is the result. The staff will tell the patient in various ways, directly and indirectly, that he is behaving unacceptably and going too far. This is a very unstable state, insecure and with uncomfortably oscillating hopes.

Then there is the state Glaser and Strauss called the ritual drama of *mutual pretense.* Here the patient and the staff both know that the patient is dying, yet both in some way tacitly agree to act as if this is not so. The details of this highly intricate game are not always fully visible even to the players, for one of its rules is to pretend that we are not pretending. All participants are extraordinarily careful not to embarrass the others and may only talk about risky subjects so long as there is no risk of breaking through the pretense. Conversation may concentrate on safe topics—food, sleep, minor symptoms and their management. The pretense may offer some privacy and protection for individuals' feelings, while limiting the possibility of genuine intimacy. Richard Kalish (29) has emphasized how impossible it is to have a warm personal relationship with a dying person if one is unable to relate to that person in terms of their dying as well as their living. He has described the "horse on the dining-room-table" syndrome. At a pleasant dinner party, a horse is sitting in the middle of the table. The guests talk as if it were not there, for to mention it might embarrass the host; and the host doesn't mention it lest it embarrass the guests. Though it is studiously ignored in everyone's conversation, the horse still sits there and is in the center of everyone's thoughts all night.

When the mutual pretense breaks down, as is likely eventually, there may be no other means of support available for patient, family, or staff to help them cope with the loss of pretense.

The context of *open awareness* exists when patient and staff both know and acknowledge that the patient is dying. There may still be different mutual expectations, but they may be openly revealed and discussed.

In their subsequent study, *Time for Dying,* Glaser and Strauss (26) introduced the concept of the *dying trajectory*—the length, course, and shape of the dying patient's last phase of life (lingering or quick, certain or uncertain)—and the differing perceptions of the trajectory that patient and staff may hold. They suggest four major types of trajectory.

1. *Certain death at a known time,* with minimum uncertainty and often a rapid course, as in some acute leukemias or following severe trauma.

2. *Certain death but at an unknown time*, which is the typical course of a more chronic fatal illness, with the problem of maintaining authentic living in a time scale that is uncertain and ambiguous.
3. *Uncertain death, but resolved at a known time*, as in major surgery or after a cardiac infarct, where following a period of acute crisis and risk, the outcome will become clear, and one will have died or survived.
4. *Uncertain death and at an unknown time of resolution*, which is the position most of us are in, though it will be more uneasy in the presence of illnesses of fluctuating menace, such as multiple sclerosis.

Sudnow's ethnographic study (8) of the social organization of dying, the techniques of breaking "bad news," the handling and processing of dead bodies, and the behavior of doctors, nurses, technicians, and other personnel involved, is uniquely detailed and vivid; while Ann Cartwright and her colleagues (30) have made the most thorough survey of the terminal phase of life, the patterns of problems and care, and they demonstrate the high proportion of unrelieved symptoms and the inadequacy of quantity, quality, and coordination of community services and resources.

Dying and Lying: On Telling and Knowing

Dying, like VD, is a social disease; it is impolite to talk about it. The evidence shows that most people want to know about their illness and its seriousness, and yet most doctors prefer not to tell them. When asked, some 80 percent of people state that they would want to be told if they had a mortal illness (numerous studies have shown this, including [31]); some 80 to 90 percent of doctors say that they rarely, if ever, tell patients (several studies, including [32], show this). The desire to know the gravity of one's illness is not limited to people asking in a secure state of health. In a survey reported by Hinton (33) of over 500 patients at a tumor clinic who were asked if they wished to know of a potentially fatal diagnosis, 80 percent said they wanted to know, 12 percent did not; and 8 percent were unsure. Aitken-Swan and Easson (34) found a similarly high proportion of patients being treated for cancer were glad that they had been told, only 7 percent disapproving. Other studies have reported similar findings (35, 36).

Only one study, by McIntosh (37), has argued that patients generally know all they want to know and do not need to be told about their illness. But this research study has such major methodological and conceptual flaws as to require that its findings be disregarded. Much of the data cited in the book contradict the conclusions its author bases thereon. The typical doctor's approach (and naive sociology as exemplified in this study) is littered with serious misconceptions and oversimplifications. It is assumed that the patient's attitudes and wishes are likely to be congruent with those of the doctor, though this is demonstrably untrue. It is assumed that patients who are not "told" will not "know"—whereas even where no formal attempt is made to tell the patient, a high proportion of patients know (30, 31). It is assumed that patients who are told will know—whereas it is clear that people often fail to hear or remember what they do not want to know. In one series (34), 19 percent of a group of patients denied having been told, despite having been carefully informed. Studies of doctor-patient communication (well reviewed by Ley [38]) demonstrate the complexity of the situation.

Doctors often justify their refusal to tell patients on the basis of clinical experience that patients lose all hope, and go to pieces or break down when told explicitly of their terminal status. Yet close examination usually reveals that they are not referring to genuine experience, grounded in reality, but a species of personal mythology related at most to one or two bad experiences and usually based only on incidents about which colleagues have talked. The ill-effects they expect are in fact extremely rare in practice.

Doctors often explain that though they may not routinely tell patients, they do make exceptions according to the individual circumstances of each patient and judge each case on its own merits. Yet observational studies have shown a completely stereotyped response (such as, "Well, it's a little growth and we've decided to remove it in case it becomes troublesome") to every patient (37).

Doctors tend to maintain double standards. While 80 percent may decline to tell their patients, generally 80 percent or more indicate that they themselves would want to be told if they were gravely ill. Similarly, if one observes the characteristics of the patients who are the exceptions, who do get told what they ask, they are usually mature people, of relatively high social class, well educated, wealthy, and with considerable business and other financial affairs to settle, and they may show other striking similarities to the doctor, who can readily identify with them.

It is also commonly assumed that not telling or not knowing is an option; that the choice is between crudely forcing awful and unexpected news upon a patient or keeping her in happy ignorance of the disease and its likely outcome. In practice, total nondisclosure is simply not possible. It is like attempting not to let a pregnant woman know she is pregnant. Your choice is less whether she will find out than how she will find out.

The author's studies (39) have shown that patients discover the nature of their terminal status in many ways. If the patient is patently ill, feels awful, has many investigations, and is given no convincing explanation, the silence can be deafening—if the doctor says nothing, that says a lot.

Patients become very sensitive to the significance of indirect communication. They notice their failure to respond to treatment, or that they are moved into high-dependency beds close to the nursing station. They know or learn the meaning of terms such as *radiotherapy* and *oncology* used by professionals. They look up their specialists' qualifications in directories or investigate the uses of the drugs they receive; they read medical textbooks in public libraries or bookstores. They read their own charts or medical records. They notice the almost palpable decrease in the interest of the staff once they have been diagnosed as "terminal." (As one patient remarked to the author, "I feel like a railway station that's been closed—the Ward Round doesn't stop here any more.") They notice that other patients with the same condition weaken and disappear. They know the significance of red-eyed, stuffy-nosed visitors making hearty and evasive conversation.

When patients do raise the question of their dying, they meet determined evasion on the part of those around them. Doctors often seem to operate a variant of Catch-22, believing that the patient who does not ask for the truth does not want to know, and that the patient who does ask does not want to know either, but is seeking reassurance to the contrary. Doctors and nurses use varieties of evasive response. Kastenbaum (40) asked 200 attendants and nurses at a geriatric hospital to describe their usual reactions to patients' explicit comments on the imminence or desirability of their death. There were five general types of response:

Reassurance: "Don't think like that—you're doing very well"; "You'll soon be your old self again—you'll not feel that way when you're feeling better." Reassurance is almost always more comforting for the reassurer than for the reassured.

Denial: "You don't mean that!" "Oh no!—you're going to live to be a hundred! You won't die!"

Changing the Subject: "Let's talk about something more cheerful"; "Isn't your daughter visiting this week?"

Fatalism: "Well, we'll all die some day"; "God will take you when he wants to"; "Yes—I may fall under a bus on my way home."

Discussion: "Why do you feel that way today?" "Has someone upset you?" Discussion is often the rarest type of response.

Honest and genuine discussion with the dying is possible, though it may differ qualitatively from other types of interpersonal communication (39, 41). Knowing, realizing, and acknowledging that you know are epistemologically complex phenomena, not readily or usefully amenable to the crude oversimplifications used in so many studies of these events. *Realization* has two very apt meanings. It can mean noticing and perceiving something that is already extant; and it can mean the process of making something real, of converting it from potential to actual existence. Some people use these meanings strategically and interchangeably, as if by not realizing (in the sense of recognizing that something is there) we can avoid making it real; as if what we do not acknowledge will not exist; as if external reality (whatever that may be) can be managed by controlling our own cognition, our internal reality. In a sense, that is true.

Death and the Health Professional

It appears that health professionals may have particular difficulty in dealing with death. While the position has improved somewhat, it has been the common experience of those who pioneered clinical, research, and educational work in this area in the 1960s, that colleagues regarded our interest in the subject as deviant and threatening, frequently refused to cooperate with studies, and even actively sought to oppose and prevent such work.

From his studies, Feifel (42, 43) suggested that their own above-average fears about death might be one of the main reasons why some physicians enter the medical profession. Kastenbaum (44) has suggested that the unspoken sentiment might be: "I am protecting others from death, therefore, I myself must be invulnerable." In an empirical study based on depth interviews of physicians, medical students, terminally ill patients, and apparently healthy "normal" individuals, Feifel and his colleagues found that death was an especially salient personal problem for the doctors and medical students. While others tended to describe themselves as "feeling bad" or "sorry" when learning of the death of another person, the physicians were more inclined to "reflect on my own mortality." They showed more negative death imagery and blocked more frequently on death questions compared to other subjects. Though they stated that they now feared death less than they had in the past, they were still more disturbed by it than other people, and their fears appeared to have begun at a younger age. They showed a significantly less religious orientation regarding the idea of life after death and a more vigorous response against the idea of a personal death than even the terminal patients. Feifel (42) commented on the physicians' continuing vulnerability to death fears and how this might alter their behavior toward patients: "In those instances where the physician's professional narcissism comes under attack—particularly in encounters with the fatally ill—his reawakened anxieties about death may lead him to unwittingly disinherit his patient psychologically at the very time he enhances attention to his physiological needs" (pp. 201-202).

There are many reasons why this may be so. The physician's professional role is, stereotypically, as a healer. Throughout the professional socialization that occurs before, during, and after medical school, this role is reinforced and forms an important component of his or her self-esteem. It is success as a healer that the individual comes to expect will form the basis of his or her reputation among patients, public, and colleagues. In medical school the collective myth of teachers and students suggests that mastery of the subject is achievable, expected, and probably being achieved by fellow students (45). In actual practice, of course, the range and extent of material basic to medicine is far beyond the capacity of any individual to master, and the practice of medicine is replete with object lessons in fallibility. Students learn to simulate more knowledge than they possess and greater mastery of the situation than they could actually achieve. This century has seen the rise of the scientistic ideology in medicine and medical education, which sees medicine as an applied science and places preeminent value on "scientific objectivity" (which is usually neither scientific nor objective). This further encourages an attitude of counterphobic bravado. Yet there is an inherent contradiction, as Kasper (46) points out: "There are some very useful similarities between science and medicine, but whereas a scientist is interested in death, a doctor is against it."

The author's studies of medical students in several countries have emphasized the importance students place on dealing with the sequence of challenges to their ability to cope with pain, suffering, death, and disfigurement. Many students state how important it is to deal with these things in a cool, matter-of-fact manner. Students encounter dissection of the cadaver in anatomy class and often cope with it better than they expected by reifying the body, making it an interesting object of study. This is made easier by its state of preservation, which makes it look, smell, and feel very unlike a human being. Still, some parts of the body remain stubbornly "person" rather than "thing"—hands (especially with nail polish or a ring), faces, eyes, genitalia—and may be more difficult (for some students, impossible) to deal with and dissect. Counterphobic joking and conspicuous nonchalance may be displayed, representing not callousness but attempts to avoid an excess of feeling. Later, there are the encounters with the autopsy (particularly the autopsy of a patient previously known to the student) and with the dying patient.

Medical textbooks and teaching emphasize the necessity to explain and understand the cause and natural history of disease rather than to understand the people inhabited by disease. Cure, actually a comparatively rare event in medical practice, is seen as the major therapeutic aim, rather than management of the attendant problems of the illness and care for the individual. Doctors come to feel a frustrated and impotent failure when facing patients they cannot cure. "There is nothing more we can do" is a common comment at times when there is still a great deal to be done for the patient but when cure has been recognized as no longer likely to be achieved. The modern physician is having to relearn the art of medical care.

Getting Rid of the Body

A final illustration of the social problem of death is seen when death occurs in a public institution such as a hospital. The body is an embarrassment and a threat to hospital and medical staff, and it must be disposed of in a seemly fashion. While the official explanation for the elaborate subterfuge generally used is to avoid upsetting the other patients, it is clear that the patients are often disturbed by the deception, which is mainly for the benefit of hospital staff.

On a typical occasion (47), a death will occur in a single room or at least behind screens, for the sake of the patient's privacy. After due preparation and wrapping of the body, the ward will be prepared and wrapped too. The curtains may be pulled around the other beds and the doors to other rooms closed. As this usually happens on no other occasion, patients familiar with the ward culture know just what it means. Patients are asked to stay at their beds, and a nurse checks the bathrooms and lounge, so that no one should walk in at the wrong time. The staff of neighboring wards may be warned and close their doors to avoid inopportune intrusions. Finally, two porters will arrive with the mortuary trolley. Older models may have a hooped metal and canvas top to hide its occupant (the "covered wagon"), and in some pediatric departments a child's body may be removed in a laundry cart. Often, the more recent concealment trolley is used. It resembles an ordinary hospital trolley, except that the superstructure swivels over to reveal a narrow stretcher between the wheels where the body can be hidden. The apparently empty trolley leaves, and the ward returns to its usual activity—with an empty bed.

Most patients realize that a death has occurred, but it has also been made clear that nothing has happened. The implication is that death is too horrible to be seen or talked about. Death has been made socially invisible and psychologically obscene.

Symbolic Death and Immortality

In addition to the biological definitions of death discussed elsewhere, one may also recognize varieties of symbolic death, such

The Data: The Facts of Death

as what Kalish (48) has called *psychological death*: the point at which the individual defines himself as dead or "as good as dead," giving up all hope and regressing into himself. Goffman (49) has described *civil death*, the point at which the individual loses most or all of the normal civil rights, temporarily or permanently (such as the losses incurred when one is committed to prison or to a mental hospital). Several authors also describe *social death*, when a person is treated for social purposes "as if" dead. This may occur when someone is comatose or senile and demented (they may live as if dead, in institutions, for years); or even during the course of a terminal illness, while the person is still sentient. The family may begin to settle the socially "dead" person's business affairs, and to dispose of her belongings; they may talk about her as if she were already dead, while no longer visiting her. If the anticipated biological death does not follow soon, the family may find it difficult to deal with their impatience.

When Kalish (48) asked a group of psychology students when a person was "dead" for them, only 55 chose "when the heart stops beating," while substantial numbers chose such alternatives as: "when a person loses self-awareness," "when a person wishes to die," "on entering a hospital knowing he will not leave alive," or "on entering a nursing home."

Similarly, there can be belief in symbolic immortality, which allows us possibilities of personal continuance. The incidence of such beliefs varies widely and is not very closely or predictably tied to traditional systems of religious belief. Indeed, some people who claim to adhere to no recognized religious faith still express or demonstrate a belief in an afterlife. There are few satisfactory or pertinent research studies in this area. An early British public opinion survey (50) found that 49 percent of a general population sample claimed to believe in life after death, 33 percent denied such a belief, and 18 percent were unsure or expressed no opinion. Of a group of students who said they did not believe in an afterlife, 45 percent expressed a wish that they could have such a belief (50). Nelson (51) in a more recent study of Appalachian Presbyterians found that 82.7 percent claimed a definite belief in life after death, 15.9 percent indicated uncertain belief that there is probably life after death, and only 1.4 percent considered that there is probably no such thing. The belief was more common in those from rural and open country than in those from urban areas.

Other research, including his own, reviewed by Vernon (52), suggests that belief in an afterlife is commonest among spiritualists, Mormons, Catholics, Baptists, and Lutherans, and that such beliefs are less common among people of higher occupational status. A 1961 American Institute of Public Opinion poll (53) suggested national differences in belief in an afterlife, ranging from the United

States, where 74 percent of the population sampled indicated such a belief (14 percent disbelieving), and Canada (68 percent believing and 19 percent disbelieving), to West Germany (38 percent believing and 29 percent disbelieving).

Robert Lifton (54, 55) has elegantly outlined the varieties of symbolic immortality that may be recognized. There is *biological* or *biosocial immortality*, when you live on through your children and their children. Extending this, one may draw comfort from the continuation of one's tribe, people, nation, or even species. *Creative immortality* occurs when one lives through one's works and cultural traces—creating objects (by art or craft), building, repairing, teaching, writing, discovering, or healing. *Theological* or *religious immortality* has been offered by many churches and beliefs throughout history. *Natural immortality* is available through your sense of continuity with nature, "dust to dust," recycling your ingredients by rejoining the elements from which you ultimately came. Finally, Lifton describes *experiential transcendence*, a psychological state of attainment of rapture and trance providing a sense of psychological unity with th world, attainable through contemplation and meditation, music, battle, dance, art, and creation.

Each variety of immortality has been altered since we entered the Nuclear Age, as Lifton has emphasized. After the Bomb, you might have no descendants (or they might be so mutated as to be not representative of you). Your works would be destroyed, and none would remember you, for we could kill history. Rejoining the natural cycle seems even less appealing if you are to become merely another slowly decaying isotope, swapping a life for a nuclear half-life.

Experiential transcendence, demanded urgently in the here and now, has become more popular and more urgently sought after at these times; and its techniques have included experimental toying with the risk of death, even more obviously and elaborately than previously.

One must also recognize the political functions of immortality. It is obviously easier to maintain a social and political system that tolerates injustice and inequity and provides poverty and promises, when there is a shared public belief in an afterlife of infinite opportunities for rewarding the faithful folk who humbly accept their lot in life. Such beliefs are useful to oppressors, keeping the workers cowed in anticipation of the big bonus scheme in the sky. The fear of death has the biologically useful function of persuading people to invest in their present existence, however wretched. Belief in a paradise is a useful supplement to natural aggression in encouraging the soldier too.

Religion and Death

The literature on the relationship between religion and attitudes toward and the experience of death is conflicting. Some studies (12, 56, 57) have reported a negative influence of religion, others (58-61) report a positive influence; while further studies (62-65) have found no religious differences in attitudes and behavior. Comprehensive reviews of the subject (66, 67) have concluded that religion as such is not a critical factor in determining attitudes or responses to dying and death. Hinton (68) looked at the relationship between the degree of religious faith and anxiety during the terminal illness. Of those with firm religious faith, attending their church weekly or frequently, only a fifth showed substantial apprehension. Those who frankly had little or no faith were almost as calm, only a quarter showing anxiety. He found significantly greater anxiety, though, among those of tepid faith, who professed to belong to a religious group and yet showed few observances of the faith. They were twice as commonly apprehensive as regular church-goers or nonbelievers. While faith may be beneficial, the brand or denomination does not seem so important. Someone who has a personally worked out and relatively coherent philosophy of life (whether they be a devout Christian or Jew, or a devout atheist or Socialist) seems to find it easier to incorporate and make sense of their own death.

Similar personality factors may influence the responses to religion and to death. Religion may be used constructively or destructively, in death as in life. If it has previously given rise to anxiety and guilt, it will do so in dying; if it has been a consistent comfort, it will probably remain one. Major philosophical and theological debates are less prominent among the dying than might be expected (69); they may be more the prerogative of the healthy.

THE PSYCHOLOGY OF DEATH

Except for occasional speculative comments by psychologists, usually on matters relating to immortality, it was only in the late 1950s that death began to be more generally accepted as a relevant matter for psychological study. Major pioneers in the area include Feifel (70, 71), Kalish, Kastenbaum, Fulton, and, in the area of suicide, Farberow and Shneidman. More recently, the standard text reviewing and integrating the research on the subject has been produced by Kastenbaum and Aisenberg (44); the field has achieved its first critical survey in the Annual Review of Psychology (72); and, apart from some evanescent publications with uncertain and uncritical editorial standards, an authoritative journal *Omega* (73) has reached its ninth year of publication and has been joined by *Essence* (74) and *Death Education* (75).

THE EXPERIENCE OF DEATH

We have begun to learn something about what the experience of death may be like from the accounts of people who have approached it and returned, such as the survivors of cardiac and respiratory arrest. Similar experiences are at times recalled by those who have undergone anesthesia, which may mean that it is not a specifically terminal experience. There are, though, sufficient similarities between the reported experiences of large numbers of patients for us to seriously consider the existence of a *Lazarus syndrome.*

Reports range from single case studies such as Hunter's (76), to series such as those described by Heim in 1892, Pfister in 1930 (77), Kalish (78), Moody (79), Canning (80), and Osis (81). Among the experiences commonly reported during near-death episodes are: out-of-the-body experience, a sense of displacement of the conscious self from the physical body, possibly watching the resuscitation attempts; a sense of rapid travel through space, a tunnel, a passage; awareness of a comforting presence, being, or light; a feeling of peace, calm, and acceptance, perhaps with sympathy for others; a sense of rapid review of scenes from one's life; awareness of approaching but not crossing some sort of barrier or frontier; and perhaps some mild reluctance to return. Osis (81) collected deathbed observations from 640 physicians and nurses and concluded that terminally ill patients not uncommonly hallucinate the presence of dead persons known to them, who may "claim to aid the patient's transition into post-mortem existence." In most cases he felt able to exclude disturbance of the patient's mentality by medication, high body temperature, or other potentially hallucinogenic states.

Kalish (78) assembled 323 reports and concluded, "It strikes us as less remarkable that 23 percent of the sample were fearful or in a state of panic than that 77 percent did not mention fear." About half of those describing reactions of panic were drowning, and others were trapped, healthy, in other helpless and perilous situations. Some 12 percent of his respondents reported the classic flashback, life review experience.

Of the various explanations that have been proposed for the recurrent phenomena, purely physical causes are not very convincing. All the circumstances under which such experiences occurred would, however, be likely to enhance the tendency for brain and mind to perceive images and emotions determined by psychological mechanisms, including well-recognized defense mechanisms, screen memories, and wish fulfillment. There is a need for better studies with more careful and unbiased collection and interpretation of the data, with precautions to avoid interviewers suggesting the nature of the responses they expect; and cross-cultural comparisons would be valuable. In recent years, some collections of unscientifically assembled anecdotes have been widely read, grossly overpraised, and misrepresented in publicity as "evidence of the survival of the human spirit beyond death." There is certainly not any scientific proof of life after death, though interesting features of life before death. Death is beyond the point from which any normal subject can return and tell us anything.

THE EXPERIENCE OF DYING

Hinton (82) has described some of the stresses experienced by patients with cancer, including pain, disfigurement, concern over the future, loss of work role, dependency and the fear of being a burden on others, and a sense of alienation, feeling that many people no longer cared about them as individuals, while others wanted nothing more to do with them. Achté and Vauhkonen (83) studied the psychological problems of cancer patients, describing among the overlapping symptoms—tenseness in 65 percent of the group, fear of death in 58 percent, depression in 58 percent, aggressiveness in 39 percent, labile affect in 30 percent, paranoid trends in 25 percent, reduced interest in life in 15 percent, and hypomania in 12 percent.

The Stages of Dying

The most widely known and influential account of the psychological needs of the terminally ill has been that of Kübler-Ross (84). She described a sequence of five "stages of dying" through which patients approached their fate. The initial response to awareness of terminal illness was *denial* ("No, not me!"). It could be replaced by *anger* ("Why me?"); which can be hard for doctors, nurses, and family to handle. There can be great bitterness and a projection of resentment onto people and conditions surrounding the patient. The patient may then enter the subsequent stage of *bargaining* ("Yes, me—but . . ."). This may be seen as a strong desire to live long enough to achieve a particular ambition or to complete some specific unfinished business, or as a hope that one might avoid one's fate if one is a good husband/wife/Christian/patient. It is a phase of negotiation with reality, seeking to improve the terms and conditions of the contract with the inevitable. This would be followed, in the Kübler-Ross model, by a stage of *depression*, which is normal and appropriate; and finally by a relatively emotion-free stage of *acceptance*.

While this model describes five common components of the total emotional response to death, it is too narrow and overgeneralized a theory to encompass the very complex patterns of states of knowing and avoiding and their attendant emotional responses; and its use has far too often led to uncritical, simplistic, and overliteral applications. While it has been invaluable in generating widespread interest in and concern for the dying patient, the five stages model is only belatedly receiving appropriately critical attention. Though arising from the extensive practical experience of a warm and humane clinician, the stages are relatively poorly defined and lack any data base to indicate their derivation, frequency, and relations. There are too frequent shifts, in many people's use of such models, from the descriptive to the prescriptive—from an account of what many people happen to do to an account of what they should do. Such models do not adequately take account of the patient's previous personality, ethnic and cultural context, earlier life experiences, the nature of the particular disease and treatment, nor the interrelationships with significant others in the family and the caring team.

Denial

Denial is a clinically ubiquitous and multifaceted phenomenon that we are only just beginning to understand, aided by such classic studies as Avery Weisman's *On Dying and Denying* (28). Denial may be a temporary and fluctuating defense or may become a complex system for consistent evasion of reality; it is frequently revisited during an illness, when one faces new aspects of loss and needs a rest from remorseless reality. Denial is not all-or-nothing. You may deny that there is anything wrong at all. You may accept that you are ill, but deny that it is serious. You may accept that it is a serious illness but deny the actual diagnosis, or accept that but deny that it could be fatal. Even if one accepts the prospect of mortality, one may deny that this bothers one at all or ignore its implications and consequences.

Denial is an interpersonal as well as an intrapersonal act and may lie in the eye of the beholder; it may be found because the observer needs it and wants to find it. It is too often assumed that denial is bad and that we must do something about it. In fact denial is an essential defense and enables the patient to leave aside the gloomier aspects of life and attend to more constructive aspects of living. It may enhance the patient's enjoyment of life and should not be interfered with by amateur meddling (not even by professionals!). Only when denial is so exaggerated as to isolate the patient from family and friends or to endanger the patient's treatment and best interests may it need to be modified.

The Data: The Facts of Death

Hope

Hope is a valued and much misunderstood commodity. It is enormously therapeutic but more hardy and flexible than is generally assumed. Those who ignore the patient's desire for information usually insist that once the patient knows about the illness, he or she will lose hope and succumb, as if to a hemorrhage. Yet hope may remain active to the moment of death, though its point of focus may alter. It may become smaller and more specific, but still sturdy. One may no longer hope for eternity or for 20 years but hope for tomorrow, for a pleasant meal, for peace. It is not a matter of rational predictions and projections. Hope is a way of being.

Simplistic Classifications

There is a great deal of seriously simplistic abuse of such terms as *denial* and *knowledge* throughout the sociological and psychological literature on death. The human mind is capable of so many levels of knowing, acknowledging, and ignoring, not only in rapid succession but even simultaneously, as to completely elude the naive classifications that are usually applied. In the hands of some writers on the subject, anything short of persistent direct statements of unequivocal certainty of one's imminent death is regarded as clearcut denial. Failure to continually contemplate mortality must not be regarded as denial or as pathological, too many of the models implied by studies and commentaries in this area reflect their authors' own fears and needs to a greater extent than the patients'. Remember that however mortally ill one is, dying is not all one is doing, and failure to pay due attention to many other aspects of living would be truly inappropriate and would certainly represent denial of reality. Terminally ill patients have a lot of waiting about to do and must be allowed to occupy their time with more than anxiety. Dying is like war—98 percent pointless waiting about and 1 or 2 percent fear.

PSYCHOSOCIAL CAUSES OF DEATH?

Obviously all deaths, like all lives, result from an interaction between physical, biological, social, and psychological processes, but some deaths occur when psychosocial factors are notable and physical causes obscure. The first serious scientific study perhaps was Cannon's (85) survey of examples of "voodoo deaths" from many countries; of the sort later discussed by Barber (86). Such deaths occur within a specific cultural belief system shared by the victim and the person or persons originating the bewitchment or "bone-pointing." Similar instances are described in the absence of such structured belief systems. In concentration and prisoner-of-war camps, hospitals, and similar institutions, it is recognized that some people "turn their face to the wall," lose the will to live, and die (87). Seligman's work (88) on the *learned helplessness syndrome* is clearly relevant to understanding these occurrences and is also germane to studies of psychosomatic aspects of cancer (89, 90), stressing the effects of separation and loss, leading to the person giving up and running out of psychological resources to cope (91). In one experiment Schmale (92) interviewed women having a biopsy for possible gynecological cancer. Whenever he found evidence of both recent loss and feelings of helplessness or hopelessness, he predicted that the woman would prove to have cancer; and in 71 percent of the cases his prediction was correct. The effects of the stress of bereavement on health have been summarized by Parkes (93).

Statistical studies of large populations have shown declines in the death rate just before holidays, birthdays, and other days of special significance, with a "catching up" to normal rates after the special day has passed (94–96). There is now also a good deal of research showing the increased mortality seen in old people after being relocated in a new environment (97–98).

DEATH ATTITUDES

We think of death quite frequently. One early study (100) found that most Americans think of death somewhere between "once a month" and "daily" and suggested that the only time they never think about death is "during, before, or after sexual intercourse."

We can regard an attitude as a relatively long-lasting system of organization of what we believe about the world, what we value in the world, and what we expect from the world, with regard to a particular situation or phenomenon; and tending to influence the way that we behave and respond to the world. Let us consider some of our present understanding of death attitudes.

The primary emotional response to death that has been studied is "fear of death" or "death anxiety." Ordinarily, we would perhaps use the term *fear* with a specific referent (one fears an attacker, an earthquake, a lion) and *anxiety* for a less concrete threat. More recently we have tended to subsume both terms under *anxiety* but to recognize both specific and free-floating anxiety. Death is a sufficiently specific menace to give rise to fear or specific anxiety and vague enough for free-floating anxiety, and the terms seem to be used synonymously in most work. The distinction can be worth making, however. Some psychological research fails to clarify whether it is talking about attitudes toward death as a very broad and general concept or toward one of its more specific components.

Among the fears of death are:

Fear of dying: including fear of the associated biological and social processes of pain; loneliness; shame; dependency; impairment and loss of functions, roles, objects, and people; loss of control and of consciousness; fear of deformity; and altered body-image.

Fear of death: including fear of being dead, fear of nonbeing, of loss of self, of loss of identity; like Leveton's (101) existential ego-chill, "a shudder which comes from the sudden awareness that our non-existence is entirely possible".

Fear of the results or consequences of death: including fear of what will happen to those one leaves behind, to one's property, plans and projects, fear of the unknown, and fear of what might happen to one in an afterlife, of judgment and punishment, of Hell or Hades.

Fear of the death or dying of others: including fear of separation from and loss of loved ones and fear of repetition of an unpleasantly experienced dying of another.

Fulton (102), for example, found that fear of dying was greater than fear of death. Some of the apparent differences may be due to the greater social acceptability and apparent reasonableness of claiming fears of dying rather than fear of death. Combinations of all these fears are usually present, in personally varying proportions, and each may generalize to the others. A group of college students (103) rated their fear of snakes and of cancer higher than their fear of death, though it would seem likely that the former fears arise at least in part from a fear of death.

It has become a commonplace to insist that the fear of death is essentially universal (or so prevalent as to be effectively universal). Such diverse luminaries as Seneca, Tillich, Choron, Malinowski, and Klein seem to agree on this. Though this supposition has not yet been empirically or experimentally established, it is widely relied upon to the extent that absence of manifest fear or anxiety seems to be assumed to be synonymous with defensive denial. Zilboorg has described death anxiety as "present in our mental functioning at all times"; Klein saw it as the basis of all human anxiety; Stekel saw every fear as a disguised fear of death; and Becker claimed it as the source of all creativity.

What explanations are offered for the fear of death? A very wide range of causes have been suggested, including infantile separation anxiety, fear of aggression by others, most of the component fears of death already mentioned, guilt about the aggressive deaths one has wished upon others, fear of suffocation stemming from breathing difficulties in earliest infancy, learning from the fears and superstitions of others, sibling rivalry, the castration complex, and even masturbation guilt (104), and fear of the dark!

These explanations are nebulous and circular in so far as many of the "causes" are also described as "effects." As Dumont and Foss (105) ask, for example, "does one fear death as a consequence of a prior fear of the dark, or does the fear of the dark develop in response to the death fear?" It appears that significant factors in the maintenance of fears of death probably do include fear of the unknown, of permanently losing consciousness and self-mastery, of losing the chance to achieve goals (those who have already attained most of their aims in life seem to fear death less [106]), and the expectation of separation from all we value in this life, especially our attachment to individuals.

We may speculate as to the cultural effects of a lack of fear of death. Marcuse (107) considered that "it would lead either to mass suicide (since for a great part of mankind life is such a burden that the terror of death is probably an important factor in keeping it going) or to the dissolution of all law and order. . . . "No domination is complete without the threat of death and the recognized right to dispense death—death by legal verdict, in war, by starvation" (p. 70). Without fear, the threat would be empty.

Fear is not the only approach to death. There may be a death wish (distinguishable from a wish for suicide). Death has been seen as excellent and beautiful or as an adventure. Freud postulated a death instinct, *thanatos*, balancing the desire for life, *eros*; but this was a concept he developed imperfectly and it has never been widely accepted. Yet he was not very far wrong. Surveys such as that by Bromberg and Schilder (100) have shown that most people have consciously wanted to die at some point in their lives, usually in response to frustration.

It has been suggested that women show a more positive view of death, being more likely to look forward to it "with a sense of excitement" and being both frightened and thrilled by the prospect. It may have sexual connotations for women and may be viewed as a "lusty, but evil, seducer of women" (108). The "gay seducer" is one of the personifications of death most chosen by college women, according to one survey (109); like most other major personifications of death (butcher, doctor, grim reaper, etc.), it is male.

Changes in Death Anxiety

Murray (110) has made a pioneering attempt to measure changes in death anxiety levels produced by death education. He found no significant decrease in death anxiety during a 6-week course that used a wide variety of educational experiences, from lectures to sensitivity groups. Yet a significant decrease in death anxiety was reported during the 4 weeks after the course ended. Considering the recognized complexity of the processes of attitude change (111), this should not surprise us. It is also important to consider when evaluation of the effects of such educational programs would be most appropriate. Attitudinal changes are unlikely to be complete or consolidated (if achieved at all) immediately after the cessation of the teaching; and it is presumably lasting rather than evanescent change we wish to produce.

Zuehlke and Watkins (112) have attempted to study the effects of psychotherapy with dying patients—a very important and much needed endeavor. They provided six sessions of Frankl's logotherapy over 2 weeks to six terminally ill patients. There were significant increases in both Purpose in Life Test and Death Anxiety Scale mean scores, while a control group showed no significant change. This is an intriguing finding, suggesting that while life came to be seen as more meaningful, admission of fear of death also increased (not necessarily a direct therapeutic aim).

Further research is needed to explore the interrelations of such relevant measures as death anxieties, modes of denial, purpose in life (112), and locus of control (113). Goldstein (114), for instance, has described some promising studies of denial and locus of control in serious chronic medical illness. (People with an extreme external locus of control see their own actions as having no effect on what happens to them, the environment acting on them randomly or maliciously; while those with a high internal locus of control see whatever happens to them as the result of their own actions.) Goldstein found a significant relationship between denial (measured by the R-scale of the Minnesota Multiphasic Personality Inventory) and external locus of control for ill, long-term hemodialysis patients but not among controls. While both denial and external locus of control may be seen as adaptive mechanisms and defenses, they may be counterproductive or even dangerous in serious illnesses in which the patient is expected to play a role in his own treatment process or where compliance with the therapeutic regime is mandatory.

Many studies seem to have assumed that their small group of subjects, often people attending a "Death and Dying" elective course, will be typical of the population at large and that their results will be readily generalizable. This underlying hypothesis is rarely if ever tested. Summarizing studies thus far in other areas of behavioral research, Rosenthal and Rosnow (115) have shown substantial differences between volunteers and nonvolunteers.

Generally, volunteers tend to have higher educational and occupational status, higher intelligence, a greater need for social approval, and a lower degree of authoritarianism than nonvolunteers. Mahoney and Kyle (116) have looked at volunteers for thanatological research (172 out of 237 college students opting to complete a Do-It-Yourself Death Certificate) and found the student volunteers to be a reasonably representative cross-section of the student group as a whole. Further studies of this sort are obviously needed.

Death: Adolescence and Adulthood

There has been a widespread assumption that an "adult" point of view is reached some time during adolescence and persists without much modification through the rest of life. There have been few attempts (117) to understand later cognitive and attitudinal development. A prominent concern among studies in young adulthood is the relationship between death anxiety and futurity and time perspective (118-120). Studies (121-124) have shown that a significant proportion of adolescents and young adults expect to die within a few years, often by violence, and the *subjective life expectancy*, the proportion of life the person sees as remaining to them, may be a relevant variable. This is implied also by Tillich (125) who suggests that perception of time depends on recognition of our mortal end: "Time runs from the beginning to the end, but our awareness of time goes in the opposite direction. It starts with anxious anticipation of the end. In the light of the future we see the past and present." Similarly, Rheingold (126) held that "attitudes are affected by the time the person conceives to exist between the present moment and the moment of death."

Simpson (123) has shown how some young people, on contemplating their own death and completing their own death certificate, seem to minimize its threat by either declaring that death has already occurred or by postponing it to very advanced age; and they have very unrealistic perceptions of the likely cause, even when in possession of the relevant facts and statistics. They omit "dying" by predicting instantaneous death by accident, violence, or by cardiac arrest. This is in agreement with earlier findings by Feifel (127) and Vernon (128) that Americans would prefer to die quickly, with no suffering, in bed, at night, at home, while sleeping; and Feifel and Jones (129) report a frequent preference for a quick and painless heart attack.

There is a great paucity of research on death attitudes in adults, with few exceptions (128) that indicate that the attitudes are complex and operate at different levels, influenced by varying situations in each individual. Studies (130) in relation to the proposal that in midlife one moves from visualizing one's age in terms of distance from birth to seeing it in terms of distance from death are interesting; as well as attempts to incorporate the disengagement theory of aging (131).

While we are still far from a comprehensive understanding of the sociology and psychology of death, we understand more clearly what it is that we do not understand. We can reach no final conclusions about The End, but we have made a substantial beginning.

REFERENCES

1. Fulton, R. (Compiler) *Death, grief and bereavement: A bibliography, 1845–1975.* New York: Arno Press, 1977.
2. Simpson, M. A. *The critical, annotated bibliography on death, dying and bereavement.* New York: Plenum Press, 1978.
3. Antonovsky, A. Social class, life expectancy and overall mortality. *Milbank Memorial Fund Quarterly*, 1967, *45*, (Pt. 1, p. 31).
4. Goldscheider, C. *Population, modernization, and social structure.* Boston: Little, Brown, 1971.
5. Stockwell, E. G. Infant mortality and socio-economic status: A changing relationship. *Milbank Memorial Fund Quarterly*, 1962, *40*, 102–103.
6. Hunt, E., & Huyck, E. Mortality of white and non-white infants in major U.S. cities. *Health, Education & Welfare Indicators*, January 1966, 1–18.
7. Kitagawa, E., & Hauser, P. Education differentials in mortality by cause of death, United States 1960. *Demography*, 1968, *5*, 1, 318–353.
8. Sudnow, D. *Passing on. The social organization of dying.* Englewood Cliffs, NJ: Prentice-Hall, 1967, pp. 95–107.
9. Simpson, M. A. Brought in dead. *Omega*, 1976, *7*, 3, 243–248.
10. Durkheim, E. *Suicide.* Glencoe, IL: Free Press, 1951.
11. Eliot, T. D. The adjustment behavior of bereaved families: A new field for research. *Social Forces*, 1930, *8*, 543–549.
12. Faunce, W. A., & Fulton, R. L. The sociology of death: A neglected area of research. *Social Forces*, 1958, *36*, 205–209.
13. Tylor, E. B. *Primitive culture.* (Vol. 1) London: J. Murray, 1913.
14. Evans-Pritchard, E. E. *Theories of primitive religion.* Oxford: Clarendon Press, 1965.
15. Evans-Pritchard, E. E. *Witchcraft, oracles and magic among the Azande.* New York: Oxford University Press, 1965.
16. Malinowski, B. Death and the integration of the group. In *Magic, science and religion and other essays.* New York: Doubleday, 1954.
17. Radcliffe-Brown, A. R. *"Taboo" in structure and function in primitive society.* London: Cohen & West, 1952.
18. van Gennep, A. *The rites of passage.* Chicago: University of Chicago Press, 1961.
19. Hertz, R. (Trans. R. & C. Needham) *Death and the right hand.* Glencoe, IL: Free Press, 1960.
20. Gluckman, M. Mortuary customs and the belief in survival after death among the South-Eastern Bantu. *Bantu Studies*, 1937, *11*, 117–136.
21. Gluckman, M. (Ed.) *Essays on the ritual of social relations.* New York: Humanities Press, 1962.

22. Bendmann, E. *Death customs.* New York: Knopf, 1930.
23. Frazer, J. G. *The fear of the dead in primitive religions.* London: Macmillan, 1933.
24. Goody, J. *Death, property and the ancestors.* Stanford: Stanford University Press, 1962.
25. Glaser, B. G., & Strauss, A. L. *Awareness of dying.* Chicago: Aldine, 1965.
26. Glaser, B. G., & Strauss, A. L. *Time for dying.* Chicago: Aldine, 1968.
27. Glaser, B. G., & Strauss, A. L. *The discovery of grounded theory.* Chicago: Aldine, 1967.
28. Weisman, A. D. *On dying and denying.* New York: Behavioral Publications, 1972.
29. Kalish, R. A. Dying and preparing for death. In H. Feifel (Ed.), *New Meanings of Death.* New York: McGraw-Hill, 1977.
30. Cartwright, A., Hockey, L., & Anderson, J. L. *Life before death.* London: Routledge & Kegan Paul, 1973.
31. Gilbertsen, V. A., & Wangensteen, O. H. Should the doctor tell the patient that the disease is cancer? *Cancer,* 1962, *12*, 80–85.
32. Oken, D. What to tell cancer patients. *Journal of the American Medical Association,* April 1961, *175*, 1120–1128.
33. Hinton, J. Facing death. *Journal of Psychosomatic Research,* 1966, *10*, 22.
34. Aitken-Swan, J., & Easson, E. C. Reactions of cancer patients on being told their diagnosis. *British Medical Journal,* 1959, *1*, 779–783.
35. Kelly, W. H., & Friesen, S. R. Do cancer patients want to be told? *Surgery,* 1950, *27*, 822–826.
36. Kline, N. S., & Sobin, J. The psychological management of cancer cases. *Journal of the American Medical Association,* 1951, *46*, 1547–1551.
37. McIntosh, J. *Communication and awareness in a cancer ward.* London: Croom Helm, 1977.
38. Ley, P. Psychological studies of doctor-patient communication. In S. Rachman (Ed.), *Contributions to medical psychology* (Vol. 1). Oxford: Pergamon Press, 1977.
39. Simpson, M. A. *The facts of death.* Englewood Cliffs, NJ: Prentice-Hall, 1979.
40. Kastenbaum, R. Multiple perspectives on a geriatric "Death Valley." *Community Mental Health Journal,* 1967, *3*, 21–29.
41. Shneidman, E. S. (Ed.) *Death: Current perspectives.* Palo Alto: Mayfield, 1976, pp. 277–279.
42. Feifel, H., Hanson, S., Jones, R., & Edwards, L. Physicians consider death. *Proceedings of the 75th Annual Convention of the American Psychological Association,* 1967, 201–202.
43. Feifel, H. The functions of attitudes toward death. In *Death and dying: Attitudes of patient and doctor.* New York: Group for the Advancement of Psychiatry, 1965, pp. 632–641.
44. Kastenbaum, R., & Aisenberg, R. *The psychology of death* (Concise edition). New York: Springer, 1975, p. 172.
45. Simpson, M. A. *Medical education: A critical approach.* London & New York: Butterworths, 1972.
46. Kasper, A. M. The doctor and death. In H. Feifel (Ed.), *The meaning of death.* New York: McGraw-Hill, 1959.
47. Simpson, M. A. The lady vanishes, or, Getting rid of the body. *World Medicine,* October 6, 1976, *12*, 1, 93–95.
48. Kalish, R. A. A continuum of subjectively perceived death. *The Gerontologist,* 1966, *6*, 73–76.

49. Goffman, E. *Asylums*. Garden City, NY: Doubleday, 1961.
50. British Institute of Public Opinion, December 1947. Cited in M. E. Mitchell, *The child's attitude to death*. New York: Schocken Books, 1967, pp. 88–89.
51. Nelson, H. M. The Appalachian Presbyterian: Some rural-urban differences. *Research Bulletin No. 5*, Western Kentucky University, College of Commerce, Office of Research and Services, Bowling Green, February 1968.
52. Vernon, G. M. *Sociology of death*. New York: Ronald Press, 1970.
53. American Institute of Public Opinion. Cited in G. M. Vernon, *Sociology of death*. New York: Ronald Press, 1970, p. 76.
54. Lifton, R. J. The sense of immortality: On death and the continuity of life. *American Journal of Psychoanalysis*, 1973, *33*, 3–15.
55. Lifton, R. J., & Olson, E. *Living and dying*. New York: Bantam, 1975.
56. Alexander, I. E., & Adlerstein, A. M. Studies in the psychology of death. In H. P. David & J. C. Brengleman (Eds.), *Perspectives in Personality Research*. New York: Springer, 1960.
57. Feifel, H. Religious conviction and fear of death among the healthy and the terminally ill. *Journal for the Scientific Study of Religion*, 1973, *13*, 353–360.
58. Jeffers, F. C., Nichols, C. R., & Eisdorfer, C. Attitudes of older persons toward death: A preliminary study. *Journal of Gerontology*, 1961, *16*, 53–56.
59. Martin, D., & Wrightsman, L. Religion and fears about death: A critical review of research. *Religious Education*, 1964, *59*, 174–176.
60. Martin, D., & Wrightsman, L. The relationship between religious behaviour and concern about death. *Journal of Social Psychology*, 1965, *65*, 317–323.
61. Swenson, W. M. Attitudes toward death in an aged population. *Journal of Gerontology*, 1961, *16*, 49–52.
62. Kalish, R. A. Some variables in death attitudes. *Journal of Social Psychology*, 1963, *59*, 137–145.
63. Lester, D. Religious behaviour and fear of death. *Omega*, 1970, *2*, 181–188.
64. Templer, D. I. Death anxiety in religiously very involved persons. *Psychological Reports*, 1972, *31*, 361–362.
65. Templer, D. I., & Dotson, E. Religious correlates of death anxiety. *Psychological Reports*, 1970, *76*, 895–897.
66. Lester, D. Religious behaviours and attitudes toward death. In A. Godin (Ed.), *Death and presence*. Brussels: Lumen Vitae, 1972.
67. Spilka, B., Pelligrini, R. J., & Daily, K. Religion: American views and death perspective. *Sociological Symposium*, 1968, *1*, 57–66.
68. Hinton, J. M. The physical and mental distress of the dying. *Quarterly Journal of Medicine*, January 1963, *5*, 1–21.
69. Berman, A. L. Belief in afterlife, religion, religiosity and life-threatening experience. *Omega*, 1974, *5*, 127–135.
70. Feifel, H. (Ed.) *The meaning of death*. New York: McGraw-Hill, 1959.
71. Feifel, H. (Ed.) *New meanings of death*. New York: McGraw-Hill, 1977.
72. Kastenbaum, R. & Costa, P. T. Psychological perspectives on death. *Annual Review of Psychology*, 1977, *28*, 225–249.
73. *Omega: Journal of death and dying*. R. Kastenbaum (Ed.). Farmingdale, NY: Baywood Publishing.
74. *Essence: Issues in the study of ageing, dying and death*. S. Fleming & R. Lonetto (Eds.). Toronto: Atkinson College Press.

75. *Death Education: Pedagogy, counseling, care. An international quarterly.* H. Wass (Ed.). Washington, D.C.: Hemisphere Publishing.
76. Hunter, R. C. A. On the experience of nearly dying. *American Journal of Psychiatry*, 1967, *124*, 122-126.
77. Pfister, O. Schockdenken und schockphantasien bei hochster todesgefahr. *Zeitschrift fur Psychoanalytische Pädogogik*, 1930, *16*, 430-455.
78. Kalish, R. A. Experiences of persons reprieved from death. In A. H. Kutscher (Ed.), *Death and bereavement.* Springfield, IL: Charles C Thomas.
79. Moody, R. A. *Life after life.* Atlanta: Mockingbird Books, 1975.
80. Canning, R. R. Mormon return-from-the-dead stories, fact or folklore. *Utah Academy Proceedings*, 1965, XLII, 29-37.
81. Osis, K. *Deathbed observations by physicians and nurses.* New York: Parapsychology Foundation, 1961.
82. Hinton, J. Bearing cancer. *British Journal of Medical Psychology*, 1973, *46*, 105-113.
83. Achté, K., & Vauhkonen, M. Cancer and psyche. *Monographs from the Psychiatric Clinic of the Helsinki University Central Hospital*, No. 1, 1970, pp. 3-44.
84. Kübler-Ross, E. *On death and dying.* New York: Macmillan, 1969.
85. Cannon, W. B. "Voodoo" death. *American Anthropology*, 1942, *44*, 169-181.
86. Barber, T. X. Death by suggestion. *Psychosomatic Medicine*, 1961, *23*, 153-155.
87. Engel, G. L., & Schmale, A. H. Psychoanalytic theory of somatic disorders. *Journal of the American Psychoanalytic Association*, 1967, *15*, 344-365.
88. Seligman, M. *Helplessness.* San Francisco: Freeman, 1975.
89. Greene, W. A. The psychosocial setting of the development of leukemia and lymphoma. *Annals of the N.Y. Academy of Sciences*, 1966, *125*, 794-801.
90. Schmale, A. H., & Iker, H. P. The psychological setting of uterine cervical cancer. *Annals of the N.Y. Academy of Sciences*, 1966, *125*, 807-813.
91. Schmale, A. H. Relationship of separation and depression to disease. *Psychosomatic Medicine*, 1958, *20*, 259-277.
92. Schmale, A. H., & Iker, H. P. The affect of hopelessness and the development of cancer. 1. Identification of uterine cervical cancer in women with atypical cytology. *Psychosomatic Medicine*, 1966, *28*, 714.
93. Parkes, C. M. *Bereavement.* New York: International Universities Press, 1973.
94. Fischer, H. K., & Dlin, B. M. Psychogenetic determination of time of illness or death by anniversary reactions and emotional deadlines. *Psychosomatics*, 1972, *13*, 170-173.
95. Marriot, C., & Harshbarger, D. The hollow holiday: Christmas, a time of death in Appalachia. *Omega*, 1973, *4*, 259-266.
96. Phillips, D. P., & Feldman, K. A. A dip in deaths before ceremonial occasions: Some new relationships between social integration and mortality. *American Sociological Review*, December, *38*, 678-696.
97. Aldrich, C., & Mendkoff, E. Relocation of the aged and disabled: A mortality study. *Journal of the American Geriatric Society*, 1963, *11*, 185-194.
98. Lieberman, M. A. Relationship of mortality rates to entrance to a home for the aged. *Geriatrics*, 1961, *16*, 515-519.
99. Novick, L. J. Easing the stress of moving day. *Hospitals*, 1967, *41*, 64-74.

100. Bromberg, W., & Schilder, P. Death and dying. *Psychoanalytic Review*, 1933, *20*, 154–155.
101. Leveton, A. Time, death, and the ego-chill. *Journal of Existentialism*, 1965, *6*, 69–80.
102. Fulton, R. L. *The sacred and the secular: Attitudes of the American public toward death.* Milwaukee: Bulfin, 1963.
103. Means, M. H. Fears of one thousand college women. *Journal of Abnormal and Social Psychology*, 1936, *31*, 291–311.
104. Alexander, I. E., & Adlerstein, A. M. Affective responses to the concept of death in a population of children and early adolescents. *Journal of Genetic Psychology*, 1958, *93*, 167–177.
105. Dumont, R. G., & Foss, D. C. *The American view of death: Acceptance or denial?* Cambridge, Mass.: Schenkman, 1972.
106. Diggory, J. C., & Rothman, D. Z. Values destroyed by death. *Journal of Abnormal and Social Psychology*, 1961, *63*, 205–210.
107. Marcuse, H. The ideology of death. In H. Feifel (Ed.), *The meaning of death*. New York: McGraw-Hill, 1959.
108. McClelland, D. C. The harlequin complex. In R. White (Ed.), *The study of lives*. New York: Atherton Press, 1963.
109. Greenberger, E. S. Fantasies of women confronting death: A study of critically ill patients. Unpublished doctoral dissertation, Radcliffe College, 1961. Summarized in R. White (Ed.), *The study of lives*. New York: Atherton Press, 1963, pp. 107–113.
110. Murray, P. Death education and its effect on the death anxiety level of nurses. *Psychological Reports*, 1974, *35*, 1250.
111. Triandis, H. C. *Attitude and attitude change.* New York: Wiley, 1971.
112. Zuehlke, T. E., & Watkins, J. T. The study of psychotherapy with dying patients: An exploratory study. *Journal of Clinical Psychology*, 1975, *31*, 729–732.
113. Rotter, J. B. Generalized expectancies for internal versus external control of reinforcement. *Psychological Monographs*, 1966, *80* (1, Whole No. 609).
114. Goldstein, A. M. Denial and external locus of control as mechanisms of adjustment in chronic medical illness. *Essence*, 1976, *1*, 1, 5–22.
115. Rosenthal, R., & Rosnow, R. L. The volunteer subject. In R. Rosenthal & R. L. Rosnow (Eds.) *Artefact in behavioral research*. New York: Academic Press, 1969.
116. Mahoney, J., & Kyle, D. Personality characteristics of volunteers for thanatological research. *Omega*, 1976, *7*, 1, 51–57.
117. Riegel, K. Dialectic operations: The final period of cognitive development. *Human Development*, 1973, *16*, 346–370.
118. Dickstein, L. S., & Blatt, S. Death concern, futurity and anticipation. *Journal of Consulting Psychology*, 1966, *30*, 11–17.
119. Hooper, T., & Spilka, B. Some meanings and correlates of future, time, and death among college students, *Omega*, 1970, *1*, 49–56.
120. Kastenbaum, R. Time and death in adolescence. In H. Feifel (Ed.), *The meaning of death*. New York: McGraw-Hill, 1959.
121. Handal, P. T., & Rychlak, J. F. Curvilinearity between dream content and death anxiety. *Journal of Abnormal Psychology*, 1971, *77*, 11–16.
122. Sabatini, P., & Kastenbaum, R. The do-it-yourself death certificate as a research technique. *Life-Threatening Behavior*, 1973, *3*, 20–32.
123. Simpson, M. A. The do-it-yourself death certificate in evoking and estimating student attitudes toward death. *Journal of Medical Education*, May 1975, *50*, 5, 475–477.

124. Teahan, J., & Kastenbaum, R. Subjective life expectancy and future time perspective as predictors of job success in the "Hard Core Unemployed." *Omega*, 1970, *1*, 189-200.
125. Tillich, P. The eternal now. In H. Feifel (Ed.), *The meaning of death*. New York: McGraw-Hill, 1959.
126. Rheingold, J. C. *The mother, anxiety and death*. Boston: Little, Brown, 1967.
127. Feifel, H. Death. In A. Deutsch (Ed.), *The encyclopedia of mental health* (Vol. 2). New York: Franklin-Watts, 1963.
128. Vernon, G. M. A study of attitudes toward death. Unpublished but cited at length in G. M. Vernon, *Sociology of death*. New York: Ronald Press, 1970.
129. Feifel, H., & Jones, R. B. Perception of death as related to nearness to death. *Proceedings of the 76th Annual Convention of the American Psychological Association*, 1968, 545-546.
130. Feifel, H., & Branscomb, A. B. Who's afraid of death? *Journal of Abnormal Psychology*, 1973, *81*, 282-288.
131. Lieberman, M. A., & Caplan, A. S. Distance from death as a variable in the study of aging. *Developmental Psychology*, 1970, *2*, 71-84.

Editor's note: This chapter originally included material on the psychology of death in relation to childhood and old age. Because these subjects are covered in depth in Chapters Seven and Eight, the discussion of them was omitted here. Simpson's critique of research strategies in this field will be included in a future issue of the journal *Death Education*.

CHAPTER FIVE

Dying in an Institution

JEANNE QUINT BENOLIEL

INTRODUCTION

Death and dying are experiences known in all human societies. How people manage these important social transitions is determined by a composite of the society's values and beliefs, the technology at its disposal, and the types of death most commonly encountered.

━━━━━━━━━━

While the last chapter focused mainly on the dying person and significant others interacting with him or her, the present chapter zeroes in on the larger environment—the institutions—particularly the hospital, where most people in the United States die today.

In Western societies the hospital originated in the fourth century on religious order as a place for the needy traveler, the infirm, the poor, or the elderly. Benoliel traces its development to the present time. The widely known expert tersely raises the question: How effective are today's hospitals in providing care for the dying? In analyzing institutional structure and organization she finds that dying in a hospital or nursing home is a major social problem. Her indictment is blunt and unencumbered by emotional outpour: The institution dehumanizes the dying process. It does so by the very factors that maximize its structural and organizational efficiency. Hospitals function on an ethic of saving lives so committedly that the care-oriented services are neglected.

Sudden death has undoubtedly always been a part of the human condition. Prolonged dying by large numbers of people is a phenomenon of the twentieth century closely related to the emergence of urban industrial systems and prolonged life expectancy.

In any society, cultural belief systems determine the procedures and rituals established for handling the transition of dying, the settings in which it takes place, and the persons likely to be present during its passage. These institutionalized practices are also reflections of the complexity of lifestyle required of a people, as well as the meaning of death in everyday experience.

In the hunting and gathering societies of earlier times, human beings moved about in small bands exploiting the surroundings for food and sustenance. Their relatively simple technology was used primarily for survival, and their social structures and social relationships were organized around the achievement of that goal. Life expectancy was short, and death was a commonplace event in the daily lives of the people. Not uncommonly people in such societies surrounded the dead with an aura of terror, buried them quickly, and utilized procedures that erased their names quickly from the memories of survivors (1).

Cross-cultural studies of societal practices for coping with death reveal several commonly observed customs, including the use of ritual specialists such as priests or special functionaries at the funeral ceremonies, isolation or separation of the bereaved from other members of society, and final ceremonies that bring the mourning period to a close after a culturally prescribed period of weeks, months, or sometimes years (2). These common customs, as well as others more unique in character, provide social mechanisms for dealing with emotional reactions to death and dying, for breaking relational ties with the departed or departing, and for bringing closure to the bereavement process. Yet despite the observed commonality of many customs, the actual behaviors of people in response to death, dying, and bereavement have been noted to vary a good deal reflecting in each case the values of a particular cultural configuration. The Pueblos of New Mexico, for instance, practiced moderation in the expression of strong emotions and used detailed technical rituals for assisting survivors to maintain self-control and restraint throughout the mourning process; sharply in contrast, many tribes among the Plains Indians engaged in open and uninhibited expressions of grief and anguish as the preferred mode of coping with loss through death (3).

Cultural configurations also determine the customs to be used for the care of the sick, including the places set aside for ill persons. Separate institutions for this purpose probably did not appear until agriculture replaced hunting and gathering as the major style of

The Data: The Facts of Death

human living, thereby setting the stage for the emergence of civilization, complex social and hierarchial structures, and specialized occupations of many kinds. Expansion of population to meet the social demands of civilization created the need for these special places. The evidence available suggests that the earliest hospitals—whether in ancient Egypt, Buddhist India, or Judaic Palestine—were associated with temples or other institutions concerned with religious beliefs and practices. Military operations also fostered the appearance of hospitals, as is shown in historical documents describing the Roman Empire (4).

INSTITUTIONS FOR DYING:
A PRODUCT OF CIVILIZATION

In Western society both religious and social considerations contributed to the growth of care-providing facilities. Following the fall of Rome, Christianity became increasingly influential through the activities of Paul and other teachers of the new religion. By the fourth century the Christian values of faith, hope, and charity were translated into religious obligations such that care for the sick became not only a Christian duty but beneficial for the salvation of the soul. On order of religious authority, hospitals were constructed in every cathedral city, and services were provided to a range of those in need—travelers, the infirm, the elderly, and the indigent. As time went by, support for these institutions came from many benefactors including kings, lords, merchants, and guilds, yet the hospitals continued to be managed and run by members of religious communities. Closely tied to the development of Christian monasticism, the hospital in medieval times existed not as a place solely devoted to the care of sick people but rather as a Center committed to medical care, philanthropy, and spirituality (4).

The Impact of Industrialization

With the development of specialized crafts, mercantilism, and trade came the appearance of a middle class. Industries began to appear, and small villages were replaced by towns and cities to house the workers in these new systems of work. As agricultural lands were taken for industrial and other uses, the conditions of the poor worsened. Increased numbers of sick and poor people placed a heavy strain on charity-providing institutions since the society at the time had no mechanisms for helping those in need to better their condition.

The Catholic church was pressured to change, and by the late Middle Ages differences in religious interpretations precipitated the Reformation and the movement toward secularization of society. Powers once held by church authorities were taken over by secular leaders, and in time the state replaced the church as the primary controlling influence over peoples' lives. Responsibilities once assumed to be religious became the province of the community; and under the guidance of a new set of values, public assistance and welfare emerged as societal approaches for responding to the needs of the sick and the poor.

The changing times impinged on established care-giving institutions and created the need for new kinds of services. The old philanthropic institution sponsored by the church gave way to hospitals and institutions designed for special purposes—venereal disease, smallpox, mental illness, and many others. Physicians began to be associated with hospitals on a regular basis, and public institutions were created for care of the sick and the poor. From the seventeenth century on, hospitals came more and more to be seen as places specifically for the treatment of disease. It also should be noted that the death-preventing capabilities of medical treatments were negligible, and mortality rates in hospitals were high rather than low, with infection and cross-contamination contributing heavily to these outcomes (5). Regardless of the development of hospitals, the majority of deaths occurred outside of these establishments for many centuries—taking place in private homes and on the streets, close to the daily lives of the people.

Influence of Science on Medical Care

The ties between physicians and hospitals were strengthened by the emergence of science and the application of the scientific method to the study of the human body and its ills. As knowledge relevant to medicine accumulated, hospitals came to be places for the study and teaching of medicine as well as for the treatment of the sick. The decline of religious involvement in the running of hospitals affected the availability of manpower to provide direct care to an expanding population of people in need, and the use of hospitals was increasingly limited to sick patients with treatable diseases. Persons with chronic, incurable, and terminal diseases were relegated to almshouses, poorhouses, and other forms of public institutions; and these settings came to be known as undesirable places set aside for the dying of those with limited means.

Separation of Dying from Daily Existence

As the culture of Western society changed from a religious orientation toward life and death to a perspective dominated by the values of science, trade, and business, the act of dying underwent changes such that control over its management shifted progressively from the dying person to the family and eventually to the physician and the hospital team (6). The rise of science was accompanied by a progressive spread of religious disbelief, and over time fear of death emerged as *the* pervasive attitude (7). Direct experience with death and dying disappeared for many members of society as new occupations appeared to take care of the many death-related tasks associated with an expanding population. Management of dying as a social process shifted from the family to the larger society, and the necessary services associated with death became bureaucratized as was also true for many other activities essential to the ongoing flow of human social affairs.

Under the influence of science, death changed from being defined as a supernatural phenomenon to a natural one—an event capable of being conquered by human ingenuity and the application of societal resources for all classes of society (8). With this shift in values ordinary people were increasingly removed from direct experience with death and dying as human transitions and therefore had little opportunity to learn how to handle themselves in these situations. The pattern of "protecting" the dying person by not talking about the fatal disease replaced the traditional religious obligation of informing the dying person so that preparation for death could be completed. Eventually, changes in attitudes and practices led to patterns of withholding information about diagnosis and prognosis of disease from the individual with the terminal illness.

THE NEW CULTURE
OF THE TWENTIETH CENTURY

The influence of science and technology on Western societal attitudes and practices increased progressively between 1700 and 1900, paving the way for a takeover of applied technology in the twentieth century. By the turn of the century human existence had already been altered by secularization, urbanization, and industrialization as these affected work, family, and life-style possibilities; but the changes were minor compared to what the next 70 years would bring. The creation of mass transportation brought a shift to a mobile society. The development of mass communication radically changed the flow of information and knowledge, facilitating thereby a movement toward industrialization of the world.

Contributing to these changes in the United States was the creation of the assembly-line model of work production, which operationalized the historical values of hard work, pragmatism, control over nature, and active doing and eventually made the products of technology readily accessible to ordinary members of society. On the other side of the coin, however, the assembly-line model encouraged a depersonalization of work through fragmentation of the tasks to be done, leading thereby to monotony of daily effort for many people. In time the model came to be applied to service agencies as well as to factories, and the one-to-one provider–client relationship gave way to the emergence of social, educational, and health care services provided by multiple workers.

Population Pressures and Social Control

The advent of science and technology also contributed to growth of the population through a progressive increase in the general standard of living and the application of public health measures to problems of food, water, and waste disposal. Population expansion would be exacerbated tremendously in the new century—not just in terms of people in general but more particularly in terms of groups with special needs—and the society would respond with institutions to regulate and control the social problems created by these groups. Thus the growth in numbers of young people and the need to educate them for work in an industrial society led to the phenomenon of mass education and the public school. Increases in the populations of persons breaking the laws of society expanded the need for prisons and similar institutions to isolate such lawbreakers from regular contact with society. New institutions had to be created to meet the needs of new populations, for example, the mentally retarded and the growing body of elderly persons unable to provide care for themselves.

Population increases also brought increased numbers of people with various illnesses, but the character of hospitals in the twentieth century was as much influenced by changes affecting the practice of medicine as by the needs of sick patients. By 1900 science and technology had already altered the practice of medicine as a result of such discoveries as bacteriology, anesthesia, and prevention of disease through public health measures (9). At the same time the life-saving capabilities of physicians was relatively limited, and the primary killers of people continued to be the infectious diseases. The next 50 years brought major changes in the ailments contributing to morbidity figures and mortality statistics, as the chronic and long-term diseases took primacy over communicable disease. This period also saw the increasing application of science and technology to the diagnosis and treatment of disease, the rapid development of scientific medicine, and the institutionalization of the life-saving ethic in hospital practices (10). More and more, hospitals came to be places designed and organized for the purpose of controlling death.

Dominance of Science over Medical Practice

The influence of science on medicine came in two ways. Scientific discoveries, such as the discovery of X-ray and radiation, led to the direct application of technology to methods of diagnosis and treatment. The creation of a scientific model (known as the *biomedical model* of disease) for applying the reductionist principles of the physical sciences to the study of disease led to the objectification of the doctor–patient relationship and a disregard for social and behavioral factors affecting illness. Expansion of knowledge led to expansion of specialized fields of medical practice; for the patients this change would lead to services offered by many doctors instead of one. The movement of medical schools into universities brought increased control over medical education by the scientific community, and the hospital became as much a medical laboratory for the study of disease as a setting for patient care.

By 1945 the biomedical model of disease had become the dominant influence in the practice of medicine and the education of new practitioners. This model defines disease in terms of physical and biochemical deviations from established norms and treats disease as a breakdown in machinery subject to recovery through replacement or repair of body parts. Since 1945 there is much to suggest that this belief system has become a cultural imperative, that is, that all members of society are influenced to a greater or lesser extent by these beliefs (11). Within such a framework the expansion of the life-saving ethic and the deployment of resources into life-prolonging activities can be understood as socially adaptive devices to resolve the uncertainties surrounding disease and to control death, now defined as an enemy.

The industrialization of disease management and death control moved rapidly after the end of World War II, and the hospital became in short order a technical life-saving establishment. In the United States this change was facilitated by the government's active movement into financial support for medical research and social legislation expanding the availability of health care services to certain high-need members of society. Out of medical research came a variety of life-sustaining and supporting procedures and machines, and new paramedical occupations were developed to implement the new and specialized functions created by the new technology. Responding to the pressures imposed by the discovery of kidney dialysis machines, respirators, transplant surgeries, and other life-prolonging techniques, hospitals reorganized use of staff and space to accommodate these changes (5). Between 1960 and 1970 there appeared a number of kinds of critical care settings all emphasizing medical control over death (12). Training programs evolved to prepare nurses and other workers for coping with the demands of this highly technical work, and nurses in hospitals increasingly found their daily activities dominated by the pressures and stresses of recovery-oriented medical procedures (13). Over a very short span of years dying in the hospital became a technologized, often dehumanizing, experience.

New Patterns of Dying

For much of the history of humankind the deaths of children have been commonplace events. At the beginning of the twentieth century the loss of one or more children in a family was not unusual, and generally speaking these deaths occurred at home. Progressive control over the communicable diseases resulted in a sharp decline in childhood deaths such that by 1960 or thereabouts the death of a child, especially from infectious disease, was a rare occurrence carrying a special kind of poignancy. Although children do die today of cancer, poisons, and accidental injuries, their numbers are small compared to adult deaths, and peoples' reactions are disproportionately intense.

Over the same span of years, increased life expectancy in the adult population created a new social phenomenon—that of large numbers of people living to be 70 years of age and older. This rise in numbers of elderly persons changed the model character of dying by making chronic illness and the deteriorations of aging the primary causes of death in Western society. As a result of this change, associated with a major population shift, the relatively short time periods formerly taken for dying from acute infectious processes were replaced by a new norm—that of prolonged dying over a period of weeks and months, sometimes even years.

In the 1970s a social problem of serious dimensions emerged when it became clear that the numbers of elderly over the age of 80 years were rising faster than those over 65 in general. This old-old group contains proportionately large numbers of "frail elderly" with limited capacities to take care of themselves, and society faces a growing need for caregiving services for these and other partially or completely socially disabled human beings. Improvements in the life-saving capabilities of modern medicine meant that for many older people dying rather than living was the stage being prolonged. Thus the technical advances capable of postponing death brought negative as well as positive consequences to the quality of living for many people—perhaps especially the elderly. Indeed, with the advent of antibiotics and other chemotherapeutic agents, pneumonia, once known as the old man's friend, could no longer function easily as the "friend" of those who were ready to die (14).

The new life-saving techniques and procedures also kept alive other people who in years gone by would have died at an early age, and new populations in need of special services appeared. For instance, children with Down's syndrome (mongolism), long known to have a high susceptibility to respiratory infection, have shown an increase in life expectancy greater than that of the general population, in great measure due to the application of medical technology to the physical defects formerly leading to death in the first year of life. For the first time in history Western society must plan for the special needs of a population of elderly mongoloid people, a situation unheard of prior to 1950. In a more general sense the prevalence rate of severely retarded people is growing rapidly, bringing with it a demand for special institutions capable of providing services to those with limited capabilities to care for themselves (14).

In a similar way the products of medical technology were found capable of keeping alive many newborn infants with severe congenital deformities or other physical problems as well as premature infants whose vulnerability to early death has always been high. Special settings designed for the intensive treatment of these and other high-risk infants and children began to appear in many medical center hospitals, and nursing staffs found themselves faced with the tensions and strains of work in constant contact with dying babies as well as living ones.

Medical technology also made possible the prolongation of life with chronic diseases that in days gone by would have led to early death. The discovery of insulin by Banting and Best in 1922, for example, meant that children with juvenile-onset diabetes mellitus no longer were subject to childhood dying due to ketoacidosis and an inability to control the metabolism of carbohydrates and fats but instead could live to die from the vascular complications of diabetes prone to occur in the middle and later years (14). People with chronic kidney failure were able to have their lives extended by spending part of their time attached to kidney dialysis machines, but their living styles were radically altered by the requirements of this time-consuming medical regimen. Thus, although advances in medical technology made it possible for many people with these and other forms of chronic disease to live longer, they often spent part of that time in the hospital because of complications and acute exacerbations of illness (15). In many cases prolongation of life with chronic disease brought periods of near-death and institutional dying, not just an extension of time. Hospitals and other institutions, defined by society as places for sustaining life, also became settings in which a good deal of dying took place.

INSTITUTIONAL DYING TAKES
SEVERAL FORMS

It is clear that many people who are dying in institutions are not defined as dying by the personnel providing care. It is also clear that institutional dying takes many different forms with particular patterns of dying associated with particular types of settings. Each pattern of dying is determined by an interplay among several interacting factors: the physical state of the person who is dying, the social and spatial arrangements of the setting, the patterns of social interaction around and with the dying person, the patient's defined state, the methods of treatment and care giving provided, the availability of advocates or allies for the dying person, and the number and types of caregiving personnel involved.

Dying in a Nursing Home: The Forgotten Ones

The nursing home industry expanded rapidly after World War II to meet a growing demand for institutional services for the incapacitated elderly. These and other custodial institutions became places for the prolonged dying of individuals with low social value, and they effectively served to remove these "reminders of death" from open visibility by other members of society. In the United States this segregation of the elderly can be viewed as a direct reflection of the youth-oriented, death-denying values of the society at large. The allocation of resources to these institutions appears to coincide with the low social value accorded its occupants. Often the people hired for positions of direct patient care are both poorly trained for the work and poorly paid. In some instances the situation is one that encourages practices of patient abuse, sometimes contributing to a patient's death (16).

Although the majority of people sent to nursing homes are undergoing the process of prolonged dying, observations of the staff in interaction with their elderly clients shows very little open discussion about the reality of death (17). Where the institution must provide services for large numbers of senile and physically disabled elderly patients, the work of keeping them bathed and fed and mobile is organized in regimented ways, removing many of the personal touches enjoyed by elderly people. The organization of work and the typical patterns of communication in many nursing homes create nonstimulating and depersonalized living environments in which elderly persons unable to negotiate other living arrangements for themselves undergo a prolonged process of impersonal dying. Assuming that institutional dying is a social process defined and influenced by the perceptions of those involved—the recipients of services, their families, the providers of care, and those who allocate resources—people who die in nursing homes might be viewed as socially dead long before they reach the point of biological death.

Even in its organization the nursing home tends to be a model of the larger society. The sick elderly are segregated from those who are physically well. Often patients who become critically ill are sent to the hospital for active treatment. For others the final period of dying means placement in a room alone so that the event of death will not be disturbing to other patients, and the staff keeps quiet watch hoping to prevent the end from taking place without another human presence. Although dying is an ever-present phenomenon in the nursing home, its existence is seldom acknowledged openly, and activities around the elderly dying patient are managed by the staff to keep the possibility of emotional disruption under control.

Complex Patterns of Dying
in Urban Medical Centers

Whereas in previous centuries the treatments available to patients in hospitals were the symptomatic and comfort activities commonly classed as nursing care, in the twentieth century highly specialized and technical medical procedures have become the dominant form of therapy and hospital services were altered to accommodate to this change. During the 25 years immediately following the end of World War II, urban hospitals not only increased in size but also became intricate multipurpose social structures to accommodate to the pressures of three interrelated goals: research, instruction, and patient services (5). The work was accomplished by a new division of labor made necessary by the demands of specialization in medicine, and the hospital came more and more to resemble an assembly-line model of services to patients (10).

Dominated by the continually growing power of the biomedical model of disease, the practice of medicine came to be structured and organized around the primacy of the cure ethic. Life-saving procedures and machines became increasingly important in the daily activities of physicians, and the solo practice of general practitioners rapidly gave way to group practice provided by specialists. Heavily influenced by these changes in the practice of medicine, the work in hospitals came to be organized around the diagnosis and treatment of disease, and the focus of nursing work was altered by the pressures of medical technology and the demands for attention to activities for maintaining control over death. As the day-to-day activities of physicians, nurses, and other hospital workers came to center on the primacy of life-saving tasks, services to meet the human needs of patients and families came to be tangential and secondary processes. These changes appeared not because the various professional groups lacked concern but rather because the work to be done was organized for the purpose of saving lives, and the dying patient represented failure.

The primacy of the *cure goal* over the *goal of care* institutionalized the secular value of control over death and facilitated the objectification of practitioner–patient relationships (11). Despite the emergence of mental health concepts and knowledge about the psychological needs of patients and families, the education of new practitioners in nursing was strongly influenced by the power of death control and was relatively ineffective in preparing them for the psychosocial aspects of implementing care (18). Yet the work in hospitals brought them face-to-face with the dilemmas of care and cure, and sometimes they found themselves faced with choices involving conflicts between personal and professional values. The technologizing of death in the hospital increased dehumanizing outcomes for dying patients, but it also added greatly to the stresses and strains of hospital work. The stresses and strains associated with death and dying are not the same in all parts of the hospital, however, for specialization has led to different forms of death-related work.

A major outcome of specialization in medicine has been the emergence of special purpose hospital wards. The "death work" observed in different settings becomes regularized around several interrelated elements: the types of dying most characteristically found there, the types of death-related tasks expected of the workers, the primary emphasis attached to the work to be done, the frequency of death, and the staffs' preparation for the tasks they must perform. Investigators of dying in various institutions have noted some common problems in social relationships and personal experiences regardless of differences in ward characteristics. These common problems include a tendency for the staff to avoid open conversations with dying patients about their dying, communication difficulties among the staff associated with differences in expectations and failures in the flow of information, and strong emotional reactions to difficult choices and decisions (23). Depending on how the work of death is organized, these problems may or may not lead to explicit role conflicts and interpersonal difficulties involving patients, families, and members of the staff. The more that death work is routinized and regularized, the more can the disruptive effects of death be minimized and controlled (19).

DIFFERENT TYPES OF HOSPITAL DYING

The concept of the *dying trajectory* has been coined to refer to dying as a social process perceived and modified by the social interactions and decisions of the various people involved (20). According to this definition, dying is a process that takes time—sometimes only a matter of minutes but more often measured in days and weeks. Dying can also be described by its shape—a graphic pattern of the events that serve as markers of the dying patient's movement away from or toward the final event. These events function as indicators of the certainty (or uncertainty) that death is forthcoming at a predictable (or nonpredictable) time.

In its simplest form the dying trajectory is one in which all persons involved have the same perceptions about the speed and certainty of death's arrival and share a common perspective of the proper activities to perform during the final period of life. In reality, however, the process of dying is often much more complicated because the people involved have different expectations about whether or not the patient is actually dying. Many communication difficulties related to dying are directly tied to these different perceptions of what is taking place.

Among the common types of dying trajectory found in hospitals are three: the lingering pattern of dying, the quick trajectory leading to expected death, and the sudden trajectory leading to unexpected death. These different types are characteristically associated with particular types of hospital units, and they typically produce different patterns of staff activity. The actual process of dying in any one situation, however, reflects the influence of societal values and individual choices as well as organizational structure and medical treatment goals.

Hooked to Machines: Dying in Intensive Care

Critical care settings are typically organized to prevent the occurrence of death in patients whose physical conditions can suddenly worsen thereby moving them rapidly onto the trajectory toward sudden death. Some of these settings deal only with special problems such as cardiac surgery or extensive burns. Others provide services for a range of medical and surgical conditions, and the patients can be children as well as adults. Some settings offer care for only a few patients; others are available to large numbers of critical patients.

Regardless of size and established purpose, critical care settings are structurally and spatially organized to maximize the application of life-sustaining medical technology. Nurses who work in such settings tend to be highly committed to life-saving goals, and their activities are organized around the primacy of preventing death. Often their work involves tending the machines that monitor the patients' conditions or assist them in maintaining their vital functions. Nurses in these settings must maintain constant vigilance to pick up early cues that something might be wrong, and they must be ever ready to move into rapid action when an emergency occurs. Their situation has been compared to that of soldiers serving in an elite combat team for they are never able to remove themselves from the stresses of battle (21).

Because these wards are organized to prevent death, they are spatially arranged so that the doctors and nurses can easily maintain observation of all the patients assigned to the setting. To accomplish this goal, privacy for the patients gives way to the need for constant vigilance, and contacts with patients are done mainly for the implementation of technical tasks and the performance of medical procedures. Relationships between patients and providers are centered around the life-saving activities of the ward, and contacts are frequently short because the staff carry responsibility for many patients. The ward regulations are commonly designed to minimize disruption of staff activities by controlling the family's presence at the bedside, and disclosure of information to the family by members of the staff is more likely than not to be minimal and controlled.

These structural and organizational conditions create a depersonalizing situation for many patients. Those who recover from their critical states ordinarily remain in intensive care for only short periods, but others who remain in serious condition may be kept there for prolonged periods. Those who die there generally end their lives hooked up to all manner of life-prolonging apparatus, and often death occurs following intensive heroic activity by the staff. Dying in intensive care is one of the new rituals of transition in a technologically sophisticated society, and it treats the central participant as something of an object.

Although outsiders tend to view the doctors and nurses in intensive care as detached and unfeeling people, the reality is that work in these settings results in many situational and psychological stresses. The staff is faced with frequent exposure to death and dying, daily contact with unsightly patients, heavy work loads, intricate machinery, and many communication problems involving physicians, nurses, patients, and families (13). The work is easiest when patients are comatose. It increases in complexity when patients are alert and young, have likeable personalities, or stay long enough for the staff to become involved with them. Among the coping mechanisms used by doctors and nurses for adapting to the pressures

The Data: The Facts of Death

of work in settings devoted to critical care are detachment, increased activity, and humor (22). Yet even these adaptive methods cannot protect them completely from feelings of sadness and anger and frustration as they confront the daily uncertainties of their work, nor can they eliminate feelings of negligence associated with errors in judgment or lack of needed supplies at a time of emergency.

The context of critical care is one of recurring crises involving patients, families, and members of the hospital staff in complicated and tension-producing interactions and decisions. Often mechanisms evolve for attempting to maintain a sentimental order of composure and restraint in the face of these difficulties, but the people involved cannot help but be affected by the stresses of the situation and the impossible task of maintaining composure in the face of conflicting pulls and pressures (23).

In and Out: The Prolonged Dying of Cancer

Although patients with cancer occasionally end their days by means of an expected quick trajectory on an intensive care ward, they are much more likely to die on a general medical–surgical ward or one designed specifically for the care of cancer patients. Typically, patients dying of cancer have been undergoing treatment for some time, and many have been in and out of the hospital several times before arriving for the final stay. This history of several hospitalizations means that dying cancer patients and hospital staff have already established a pattern of involvement such that efforts at detachment are difficult to maintain.

Sometimes the end of a lingering trajectory lasts only 1 or 2 days. The patient is brought to the hospital to die usually because the family is unable to manage the situation at home. Sometimes the dying cancer patient is sent from a nursing home unable to provide for the final period of care. In either case the patient is clearly known to be dying, and usually the treatment consists of comfort measures and symptomatic support. The situation for the staff is often one of watchful waiting and is easiest to perform when the patient is comatose and not a social being. Far more difficult for all concerned is the situation of the fully alert dying cancer patient who is capable of initiating conversation that may be awkward or unsettling. Equally upsetting is the family that has not come to terms with the forthcoming death and insists on active life-saving treatment even though its use is clearly to no avail.

Very difficult for the patient and staff alike is the prolonged hospital dying of a person with far advanced cancer, particularly when the patient is not to know the diagnosis and prognosis (23). When either the physician or the family makes this kind of judgment, the nurses feel trapped by an unrealistic situation that they frequently handle by minimizing their contacts with the dying patient. The problem for the patient is social isolation, often brought into being by well-intentioned relatives who believe they are offering "protection" through preventing the dissemination of bad news about forthcoming death. The consequence, of course, is that the person facing death is effectively barred from bringing closure to life by communicating openly with those who are near and dear and by participating in decisions about the context of his or her dying.

Cancer is notably a tension-producing disease, and many of the difficulties encountered in the hospital are directly tied to problems in communication associated with progression of disease. Patients with advanced cancer have high levels of anxiety associated with fears of painful dying and abandonment by other people, and they often reach out for opportunities to express these fears and concerns. The problem is that other people experience difficulty in listening to these expressions of concern, for the situation of the cancer patient triggers a variety of strong and difficult feelings including helplessness, anger, guilt, sadness, and depression. Family members and staff alike protect themselves by using many behaviors designed to maintain control over strong emotional reactions (23).

These problems of communication can be compounded by the physical changes associated with advancing cancer and the difficulties encountered in helping the patient achieve a comfortable death. One of the most tension-producing problems encountered on a cancer ward is the patient whose pain is not amenable to control, and situations of this nature exacerbate tensions among the staff, often leading to interpersonal conflicts. Feelings of helplessness are intense when nothing can be done to help the patient, and the tensions produced by such a situation permeate the atmosphere of the ward.

The problem for the staff working on cancer wards is that they are functioning in a setting in which dying is an ever-present process, even though not explicitly acknowledged. Cancer wards typically have patients at different stages of living with cancer and undergoing difficult kinds of oncologic treatments, and the doctors and nurses must constantly interact with patients and families at different points on the living–dying timetable. It is a context in which uncertainty about the future and tension about the present are constant themes affecting patient and staff alike and molding their interactions so as to control the underlying stresses. It is a difficult context for both living and dying.

The Patient Whose Family Cannot Let Go

One of the most tension-producing problems encountered by nurses in the hospital is the situation of the patient whose family insists on active life saving when the patient is clearly on the way toward death. This situation happens most commonly when the movement toward death has been precipitated suddenly—as with an accident or heart attack—and the members of the family are not prepared for the shocking possibility of death. Often the physicians and nurses may be aware of the seriousness of the person's condition soon after his arrival at the hospital, but the actual decision to discontinue active treatment generally is delayed until the family has had time to agree with the medical recommendation.

Much of the time the period of dying in situations such as these is 1 or 2 days at the most. The process of dying can be extended, however, if the patient is attached to life-support machines that keep the vital physiological systems functioning, and the family and staff are faced with the interpersonal complexities of maintaining composure and control in a context of uncertainty and tension. When this form of dying extends for a long time, the nursing staff carries the burden of care—a task that can be additionally burdensome if members of the family withdraw from contact with the patient.

There are also occasions when a member of the family (most commonly a spouse) cannot face up to the possibility of death during a process of prolonged dying and insists on the patient's being given active medical treatments even to and including intensive care. If the patient is young, the staff are often in sympathy with the fight for life; and active participation in treatment provides a mechanism for counteracting prevailing feelings of helplessness. If the patient is elderly, the nurses are likely to view the action as somewhat inappropriate and particularly if the patient has indicated on previous occasions a personal wish not to have his or her life prolonged.

The undercurrent of unspoken and unresolved feelings and tensions associated with this type of dying trajectory makes it one of the most problematic in nursing work. Yet it also speaks of the lack in many hospitals of effective services for helping families cope with the complex personal and social problems that the process of dying brings into being.

The Special Poignancy of Dying Children

In some hospitals the dying of a child is a rare occurrence, and the staff are unprepared for the stresses and strong feelings that this difficult problem provokes. In other hospitals the dying of children is fairly commonplace, and the staff must cope with these same stresses and feelings on a regular basis. In the first instance the staff often react in a manner very similar to people in general, and they frequently cope by recounting the history of the events of dying over and over again. In the second case the staff are likely to have developed a number of routines for distancing themselves from the stresses.

As is also true when adults are dying, nurses and doctors are better able to keep themselves detached from involvement when the child is in a coma. When the child is alert and capable of social interaction, contacts include conversation as well as treatment, and withdrawal from involvement is difficult to achieve. The care of dying children is always complicated by the reactions and behaviors of parents, and many of the difficulties described by hospital staff are associated with the problematic nature of relating with parents living under constant stress.

Hospital wards providing services for multiple numbers of dying or potentially dying children carry their own special poignancy for on wards such as these, children cannot help but be aware of the deaths of other children. They may or may not talk openly about their concerns about death. Some kinds of dying are distressing to be around because of their effects on the body as in the case of massive burns (24). Others are distressing because they drag on and on or serve as reminders of certain tragic aspects of the human condition. Providing care for dying children is a difficult task for probably the majority of nurses, for it triggers a sense of professional failure along with strong personal reactions associated with the loss of a child (25).

INSTITUTIONAL DYING:
A MAJOR SOCIAL PROBLEM

Just as styles of living have been diversified in the twentieth century, so too have styles of dying. For the most part, dying has been removed from public visibility into the private realm of institutions. At the same time its characteristics as a personal and interpersonal process have become more variable, as medical technology and social values have interacted with new causes of dying to create new rituals of transition. Under the influence of industrialization, dying has moved from being a tribal or familial ritual to becoming an organizational procedure governed by bureaucratic rules and dominated by impersonal strangers. The change is quite understandable when viewed as simply another reflection of the secularization and technologization of Western society. Yet it has introduced

The Data: The Facts of Death

a range of complex problems including the allocation of scarce resources to the living and the dying and the dehumanizing effects of applied technology on the experiences of people whose lives are ending (26).

Values in Conflict

Despite the reality that dying has become a phenomenon organized and controlled primarily by institutional goals, it also continues to be a singular experience in the personal and interpersonal lives of those for whom a forthcoming death carries significant meaning. The problematic nature of the various types of institutional dying can be explained, at least in part, as a collision between two systems of values.

From the institution's perspective, services for dying people comprise a portion of the work to be done, that is, the tasks to be accomplished. The tasks associated with dying need to be regularized and routinized to maximize efficiency and to assist the staff in the maintenance of self-control (19). The problem, of course, is that dying is also a human transition with significant meanings in the cultural, social, and personal sense. The tasks associated with this definition of dying have much more to do with bringing closure to life in an acceptable way and completing unfinished business with persons who are important. The values at issue here are particularistic, having much to do with the relationships of the dying person to nature, to other people, and to the community of which he or she is a part.

The institutions for patient care in Western society have clearly been organized around the primacy of the life-saving ethic, and the value accorded to control over death has impeded the development of care-oriented services (10). Specialization of tasks has created establishments with complex social structures in which channels of information among such concerned groups as patients, families, and providers are often inadequate or missing. The health care system has evolved as an extension of the biomedical model of disease, and there is much to suggest that the impact of medical technology on patients' experiences will expand rather than lessen in the years ahead (27).

A Counterculture for Care

Despite the tremendous power of medical technology and the life-saving ethic, recent years have seen the emergence of a counterculture clearly at odds with the death-avoiding practices of the twentieth century. This counterculture has been manifest by a proliferation of publications—both professional and lay—dealing with many of the complex problems and issues relating to death and dying in this century.

Public interest in finding alternatives to hospitalization has been demonstrated in the creation of *hospices* for terminal care, demands for new legislation permitting consumer participation in decisions about the use of life-prolonging methods, and a plethora of voluntary groups devoted to helping people with various life-threatening disorders and situations. Professional interest in creating alternative forms of care for those who are dying has commonly taken the form of federally funded demonstration projects such as the Minnesota home care program for children with leukemia (28).

Others have taken the tack of attempting to bring about changes in the institutions themselves, and among the groups working in this direction have been a number of nurses. One way the nursing profession has tried to counteract the depersonalizing influences of institutional routines is to introduce well-prepared nurses to assist patients and families with the situationally derived stresses and strains that institutionalization brings. These nurses are known by a variety of different names (such as *clinical specialist* or *nurse practitioner*) but their achievements have been variable depending on whether their activities were perceived as nonthreatening or threatening by physicians, other nurses, and other members of the institutional staff (29). Although in some settings the introduction of clinical nurse specialists has led to discord between the medical and nursing staffs, in other settings it has paved the way for the creation of new and important services—for example, a program out of which evolved a protocol and procedures for providing regular support to the grieving spouses of patients hospitalized in a coronary care unit (30).

These efforts to change societal policies and organizations appear to reflect a growing concern with basic human values. Yet the power of scientific medicine and the life-saving ethic permeate the society in ways that make the introduction of change very difficult. People still look to physicians for miraculous ways of curing them from their ills, and, despite the numbers of books published on the subject, people still continue to be uncomfortable around dying patients. What the future will bring in the balance between technology and humanism remains to be seen, but whatever the outcome it will show in the services available to those who are dying.

REFERENCES

1. Downs, J. F. *Cultures in crisis.* Beverly Hills: Glencoe Press, 1971.
2. Rosenblatt, P. D., Walsh, R. P., & Jackson, D. A. *Grief and mourning in cross-cultural perspective.* Minneapolis: HRAF Press, 1976.

3. Benedict, R. *Patterns of culture.* New York: Houghton Mifflin, 1934.
4. Rosen, G. The hospital: Historical sociology of a community institution. In E. Freidson (Ed.), *The hospital in modern society.* New York: Free Press, 1963.
5. Knowles, J. H. The hospital. In *Life and death and medicine.* San Francisco: W. H. Freeman, 1973.
6. Ariès, P. *Western attitudes toward death.* Baltimore: Johns Hopkins University Press, 1974.
7. Toynbee, A. *Man's concern with death.* London: Hodder and Stoughton, 1968.
8. Illich, I. *Medical nemesis.* New York: Random House, 1976.
9. Wilcocks, C. *Medical advance, public health and social evolution.* New York: Pergamon Press, 1965.
10. Benoliel, J. Q. The changing social context for life and death decisions. *Essence,* 1978, *2*(2), 5-14.
11. Engel, G. L. The need for a new medical model: A challenge for biomedicine. *Science,* 1977, *196,* 129-136.
12. Hilberman, M. The evolution of intensive care units. *Critical Care Medicine,* 1975, *3,* 159-165.
13. Benoliel, J. Q. The realities of work. In J. Howard & A. L. Strauss (Eds.), *Humanizing health care.* New York: Wiley, 1975.
14. Gruenberg, E. M. The failures of success. *The Milbank Memorial Fund Quarterly,* 1977, *55*(1), 3-24.
15. Strauss, A. L. *Chronic illness and the quality of life.* St. Louis: Mosby, 1975.
16. Stannard, C. I. Old folks and dirty work: The social conditions for patient abuse in a nursing home. *Social Problems,* 1973, *20*(3), 329-342.
17. McGinity, P. J., & Stotsky, B. A. The patient in the nursing home. *Nursing Forum,* 1967, *6*(3), 238-261.
18. Quint, J. C. *The nurse and the dying patient.* New York: Macmillan, 1967.
19. Sudnow, D. *Passing on: The social organization of dying.* Englewood Cliffs, NJ: Prentice-Hall, 1967.
20. Glaser, B. G., & Strauss, A. L. *Time for dying.* Chicago: Aldine, 1968.
21. Hay, D., & Oken, D. The psychological stresses of intensive care nursing. *Psychosomatic Medicine,* 1972, *34,* 109.
22. Swanson, T. R., & Swanson, M. J. Acute uncertainty: The intensive care unit. In E. Mansell Pattison (Ed.), *The experience of dying.* Englewood Cliffs, NJ: Prentice-Hall, 1977.
23. Glaser, B. G., & Strauss, A. L. *Awareness of dying.* Chicago: Aldine, 1965.
24. Seligman, R. The burned child. In E. Mansell Pattison (Ed.), *The experience of dying.* Englewood Cliffs, NJ: Prentice-Hall, 1977.
25. Suarez, M. M., & Benoliel, J. Q. Coping with failure: The case of death in childhood. *Issues in Comprehensive Pediatric Nursing.* New York: McGraw-Hill, 1976.
26. Brim, O. G., Freeman, H. E., Levine, S., & Scotch, N. A. (Eds.), *The dying patient.* New York: Russell Sage Foundation, 1970.
27. Benoliel, J. Q. A comparison of technological influences on dying characteristics in one hospital during 1966 and 1971. *Communicating Nursing Research,* Vol. 10. Boulder: Western Interstate Commission for Higher Education, 1977.
28. Martinson, I. M. Why don't we let them die at home? *RN,* 1976, *6,* 58-65.
29. Benoliel, J. Q. Nurses and the human experience of dying. In H. Feifel (Ed.), *New meanings of death.* New York: McGraw-Hill, 1977.
30. Dracup, K. A., & Breu, C. S. Strengthening practice through research utilization. *Communicating Nursing Research,* Vol. 10. Boulder: Western Interstate Commission for Higher Education, 1977.

CHAPTER SIX

Hospice Care for the Dying

GLEN W. DAVIDSON

What is hospice care? *Hospice* is a medieval term that refers to the wayside inns for pilgrims and other travelers, particularly at those places of greatest vulnerability and hardship. The *hospice movement* represents the development of a variety of programs designed to better assist terminally ill patients for whom aggressive medical treatment is no longer deemed appropriate in travel through life.

Care of the dying is not new. Concern about what constitutes

The hope for alternatives Benoliel expressed in Chapter Five in what she terms the emerging "counterculture for care" is the subject of this chapter. The hospice is one of the most rapidly developing movements in the human services fields. The movement has been inspired mainly by Cicely Saunders' work at St. Christopher's Hospice in London. Its objective is simple: to provide compassionate care for the dying.

Davidson very ably discusses the philosophy of the hospice and describes four models of hospice care that he has observed crystallizing and that are now operating. He pinpoints the advantages and disadvantages of each model. Common to all, Davidson concludes, is the aim to affirm the autonomy and dignity of dying persons and their families.

appropriate care is found in mythic and symbolic dimensions of language and tradition. Whether it is the ritualistic storytelling of Navajo tribal identity in North America or the 3000-year-old Vedic texts of ancient India, humankind has been concerned about dying for as long as we can remember. Care for the terminally ill is one of life's major responsibilities.

Like other aspects of living in mass society, patterns of health care, even while offering better and more widespread services, have so disrupted traditional rituals of care known by our grandparents that this generation has had to radically reexamine how best to preserve human dignity in the closing moments of life. Advocates of the hospice movement argue that we not only have the opportunity to bring to the terminally ill new medications, new skills, and new understandings but also the obligation to restore a unified and humane approach to terminal care.

Much of the inspiration for the hospice movement in North America comes from Dr. Cicely Saunders who founded St. Christopher's Hospice in London. Dr. Saunders is an exceptionally trained person. She earned an Oxford degree in philosophy, politics, and economics, and holds diplomas or degrees in the fields of nursing, social work, and medicine. While she was a Fellow in the Department of Pharmacology at St. Mary's Medical School, she carried out research on analgesics and other drugs that could be more effective in controlling intractable pain of patients with terminal illness.

St. Christopher's Hospice was developed outside of the National Health System through the philanthropic generosity of a large number of people. The specialized facility was built at Sydenham, London, in 1967. Today there are more than 30 hospices throughout Great Britain (some are referred to as Marie Curie Homes).

While some of the hospices offer unique services and are organized differently, they have in common a philosophy of compassion in terminal care. As institutions, the hospices attempt to raise the nursing process to its greatest height. They dispense a knowledge of pharmacological control of pain and organize a team that involves the patient and the entire family.

Contrary to many visitors' expectations, St. Christopher's Hospice does not convey an environment of a "death house" where patients are bedridden, narcotized, depressed, or obtunded. One hears the sound of laughter, sees a variety of creative activity including that of the children of staff and patients, and perceives a homelike environment. Each patient brings some personal belongings and is encouraged to maintain as much self-care as possible.

St. Christopher's dedication to "total care of the dying patient" refers not only to the medical–symptomatic management, but also, as importantly, to the concept that anything that produces distress or pain for the patient or the family is a concern for the hospice staff. The total psychosocial impact on the dying patient and the family is addressed, including the grief reaction of the family subsequent to the patient's death.

One way of describing the hospice philosophy of patient care is that should the patient need care in the hospice rather than at home, the space he occupies is his so long as needed. Even after death the space is not filled for 24 hours in order to permit other patients and the staff to mourn the unique place the deceased patient had in their lives.

Dr. Saunders' philosophy is not restricted by the principles of quality nursing, home care, and medicine. She frequently refers to the "spiritual dimension" of care. Her increasingly sophisticated way of articulating what that means is symbolized by the one architectural change made to St. Christopher's Hospice since its opening. It has been necessary to expand the chapel, which is centrally located in the facility.

We can find the antecedents for the hospice movement as early as the time of Emperor Asoka in India (d. 238 B.C.). Cultural exchange across the trading routes of Asia Minor suggest Asokan influence on the earliest health care facilities in the Mediterranean areas. A good example is the early Christian Monastic Hospice in Turmanin (A.D. 475) located in what today is Syria.

Turmanin architecture suggests a facility used as an inn for pilgrims as well as wards for the sick and dying. Such inns were founded upon the biblical mandate: "For when I was hungry, you gave me food; when thirsty you gave me drink; when I was a stranger you took me into your home; when naked you clothed me; when I was ill you came to my help; when in prison you visited me" (Matt. 25:35-36, *The New English Bible*). To these injunctions a seventh work of mercy was identified—burying the dead (see Tobit, 1:16-17). The earliest hospitals did not specialize; specialization is a modern characteristic. As Thompson and Goldin (1) explain: "Since in the guiding text all categories of social assistance were jumbled together, Christian charitable foundations might cater to one, some, or all of the victims of wretchedness: aged, infirm, dying, diseased, wounded, blind, crippled, idiot, insane; orphans, paupers, wanderers, pilgrims" (p. 6). At Turmanin, travelers would receive the monks' hospitality overnight or for as long as they required. Almost by definition a traveler was a pilgrim who would be more or less sick, having undertaken the journey as a form of penance. The metaphor of the pilgrim or wanderer is used extensively in modern hospice literature. Unlike the ancient hospices, however, no modern facility provides space for graves.

From the monastic model in the Mediterranean we can trace both the architectural and organizational influence to North America where the first institutions for the sick were also concerned for both the traveler and the settler. Some of the first monasteries established in sixteenth-century New Spain and seventeenth-century New France and New England had "hospitals" that provided multiple services, but all had in common care for the dying. In the nineteenth and twentieth centuries, various religious communities in both Canada and the United States have long maintained palliative care facilities, of which the most famous still in existence is probably Calvary Hospital in the Bronx, New York.

HOSPICE CARE IN NORTH AMERICA

While prototypes for North American health care institutions can be found throughout a long and honorable history, the unique needs and values of people on this continent have reshaped, reorganized, and reapplied European institutions. A reshaping of Dr. Saunders' vision has been inevitable. With rare exceptions the people trying to organize hospices in North America are inspired by but not trying to duplicate St. Christopher's Hospice in London.

Until the 1950s, most needs of the sick and dying in North America were taken care of in the home. Rituals of care among the general population must be seen in that context. However, by the 1950s a majority of acute diseases were cared for in hospitals. Care of chronically ill patients and convalescent care began to be provided in what has evolved as nursing homes. By 1970, over 70 percent of Canadians and Americans dying would do so in one of the two types of institutions. When one confines those generalized statistics to a given state like California, more than 80 percent die in hospitals or nursing homes. And in specific metropolitan cities in both countries, as many as 90 percent of the people who die spend their last days in hospitals or nursing homes.

While earliest hospitals and nursing homes in North America provided a variety of services, since the implementation of national health care in Canada and Medicare funding for health services in the United States, utilization of hospitals has become more and more confined to the curing of acute diseases and nursing homes have been restricted to care for the chronically ill or those needing rehabilitation. This is not to ignore the fact that as many as 30 percent of all nursing home patients die in a year. Rather it is to make the point that the objectives for the institutions and the protocols of care are organized for cure or rehabilitation, not for terminal care.

The Dying Role: A Sociological Perspective

Where people die and how well they are cared for may be explained in part by the way the dying role is understood by the patients, their families, and the staff who serve them. Talcott Parsons first described the sick role from a sociological perspective (2). Like other roles in society the ill person has both rights and obligations. Those who are ill are excused from their usual responsibilities and obligations, but only for a limited time. They take on the obligation to will themselves back to health.

The ill person also has the right to be cared for, with primary obligation falling to next of kin. But the patient is obligated in turn to seek competent medical help in an effort to regain health and to demonstrate good intentions. A further right of the patient is to avoid conditions that might aggravate being ill. In turn, the patient is obligated to cooperate with treatment modalities prescribed by health care authorities, even if that means being subservient and dependent on care givers.

What Parsons described, without being explicit, is the sick role for the acutely ill. Acute illness strikes quickly and, it is popularly assumed, occurs through no fault of the patient. Such notions are the products of the impact made on human memory by the great epidemics when fear of infectious diseases symbolized *illness*.

The primary institution for caring for the acutely ill is the hospital, particularly as accrediting boards and statutory bodies define institutional authority by narrower expectations. Since the adoption of Medicare in the United States and the national health scheme in Canada, hospitals by definition are acute-care facilities. Consequently, the authority, responsibilities, and roles of competence that health care staff working in hospitals perceive themselves having, exclude the needs of patients who do not fit the roles of the acutely ill.

The chronically ill, by contrast, have received primary attention only in recent times. Preventive and rehabilitative medicine are still looked upon in most schools of medicine as luxuries and are suspect as appropriate within the science of medicine. Confusion abounds over whether to treat cancer patients as having acute or chronic pathologies.

Chronic illnesses refer to acute situations that persist over a lifetime, such as heart disease consequent to infarct; degenerative processes, such as arthritis, diabetes, and hypertension; and injuries that cannot be totally rehabilitated, particularly traumas to the central nervous system.

Using Parson's typologies to describe the rights and obligations of the chronically ill, we can see that patients are exempt from

The Data: The Facts of Death

the responsibilities of their usual social roles but only insofar as they are impaired. Unlike acutely ill patients, the chronically ill have no time limit placed on their impairments. But the patients do have the obligation to will to be rehabilitated as soon as possible.

In order to obtain rehabilitative services, the patient has right of access to both appropriate information and therapy. In turn the patient is obligated to maintain rehabilitative regimes. It is not enough for a patient to be fitted with a prosthesis; he must use it. It is not enough for the diabetic to lose weight through some therapeutic process; she must maintain weight control.

Like the acutely ill, the person with chronic illness has a right to be cared for when disabled, particularly by the family. But unlike the acutely ill, the person with chronic illness must avoid dependence so as not to be any more of a burden on the care giver and society than the disability necessitates. Necessary dependency will be tolerated; evidence of independence will be rewarded.

The primary institution providing care for the chronically ill in North American society is the nursing home. As hospitals were being forced into the more narrow definitions of authority and responsibility for caring for the acutely ill, so too were nursing homes being forced to be defined and limited to chronic care. Hospitals could and can be accredited without rehabilitative services. However, many states now refuse to accredit a nursing home that cannot offer such services. And the staffs of nursing home and convalescence facilities are trained and evaluated on their abilities to provide the kind of care that the chronically ill have a right to expect.

Nursing home facilities even more than hospitals have failed to meet the needs of the terminally ill despite the fact that 30 percent of patients in nursing homes in the United States die every year. With accountability based on meeting definitions of chronic care, it is perhaps understandable if no less regrettable that nursing home personnel are not trained to meet the needs of the terminally ill except insofar as they risk their *defined competence* by assuming unique roles of caring for the terminally ill.

The governmental and accrediting definitions of institutional authority then account in part for the scenes of terminally ill patients being transferred back and forth between hospital and nursing home because "this patient doesn't belong here." The reason such facilities as Calvary Hospital exist at all is to provide patients and their families options of care that otherwise are not available to them. It is by design, not by accident, that some of the private hospitals in Manhattan and the Bronx in New York City can claim that no patient has died in their facilities. When the patient's diagnosis changes from that of acute or chronic illness, the patient is "referred out." When a patient appears about to die, it is not an uncommon practice for nursing homes to rush the person to an acute care center's intensive care facility because, in words used so frequently as to be a cliché, "we're not equipped to handle this emergency here."

Russell Noyes and John Clancy (3), psychiatrists at the University of Iowa, have used Parson's typologies to explore the unique roles of the terminally ill. They note that, like the acutely ill, the terminally ill patient is time limited; only now rather than being limited by restoration to health, death limits time. Even so, the terminally ill are under the obligation to desire to live as long as possible so that they are without responsibility for their approaching death.

Being without responsibility affords the terminally ill patient the right to be taken care of, particularly by the family. But the patient is in turn obligated to take advantage of all supports necessary for sustaining life and to cooperate with those giving the support, so as not to be any more of a burden than necessary. Recognizing what a burden terminal illness is, Noyes and Clancy believe, is the reason society relieves most of the physician's obligation to the patient, except for overseeing supportive and palliative treatments, when a patient's role changes from being sick (acute or chronic) to dying. "Society reserves the physician's role for the more important restorative function and, in so doing, jealously guards against inroads upon the physician's time and energy" (p. 42).

To be terminally ill is to be exempt from social roles of responsibility and commitments, but the patient is under the obligation to transfer to others, in orderly ways, property and authority. Unlike the acutely ill, the person terminally ill is expected to maintain as much independence as his or her declining resources will permit. And having done so, that person has the right to be given continuing respect and status despite the loss of health and life.

The typology of roles of the sick is useful for understanding why, in contrast to our grandfather's era, care of the dying has become less humane. By definition, both hospitals and nursing homes function to provide care for the acutely and chronically ill, not for the terminally ill. Contrary to popular opinion there is little evidence to suggest that awareness about the needs of the dying has changed institutional mandates or staff protocols. The hospice movement is an attempt to effect, institutionally, better care for the terminally ill.

Models of Hospice Care

Thus far, hospice care programs in North America have been designed following one of four models: 1) hospital-based palliative

care units, 2) home care services, 3) free-standing institutions, and
4) wholly voluntary programs.

Hospital-based Units

Examples of hospital-based units are the Palliative Care Unit of
Royal Victoria Hospital in Montreal; with the hospice programs of
St. Luke's Hospital, New York, and Victoria General Hospital in
Halifax, as variations. Despite recent educational efforts to make
hospital staff aware of the needs of terminally ill patients and their
families, there remains the basic problem of whether the hospital's
objectives and the staff's roles can extend beyond efforts at curing
and prolonging life. For terminally ill patients these objectives and
roles are irrelevant. Only quality of life is an appropriate objective
for them. To provide expertise in the area of terminal care, a separate
unit in a hospital has the following advantages (4):

1. It avoids having to build new facilities.
2. The close proximity of both palliative and acute-care units
   tends to stimulate improved care in both.
3. It permits use of existing hospital resources, such as radiation
   therapy, when needed for the patient's comfort.
4. It enables the hospital to provide a wider spectrum of care for
   meeting the patients' needs.

The Palliative Care Unit of Royal Victoria Hospital opened in
January 1975 after 15 months of planning. Staff is trained for four
services: inpatient care on the unit, home care, consultation, and
bereavement follow-up for families and staff of the deceased.

The in-patient unit admits only persons for whom cure and prolongation of life are no longer appropriate goals. After a request
from the patient's physician, the unit physician and head nurse
decide whether the Unit is the appropriate place for the patient.
Priority is given to those patients whose physical symptoms are
difficult to control in other hospital departments; patients in the
home care program needing admission; and patients with difficult
psychosocial conditions. Care is provided by an interdisciplinary
team made up of physicians, nurses, nursing aides, social workers,
ward clerk, dietician, physiotherapist, chaplains, recreational therapist, music therapist, and volunteers.

The home care staff consists of four nurses and a physician.
They cover patient responsibilities on a 24-hour basis. In addition,
volunteers, the physiotherapist, and the social worker make home
visits.

Consultation is provided by the physician and consultation nurse
who help regular hospital personnel develop a comprehensive plan
of care for the patient. Since the unit cannot care for all terminally
ill patients in the hospital, a key priority for the consultation staff

is to teach philosophy and skills of palliative care to other hospital personnel.

Bereavement follow-up is provided, particularly for the primary carer and key family members who are assessed prospectively as having some risk of impairment of health and psychosocial adjustment. Follow-up includes telephone contact approximately 2 weeks after the death, a visit by a staff member in about 1 month, and a letter of encouragement on the anniversary of the death. More extensive follow-up is available when indicated.

A variation of this model is used at St. Luke's and Victoria General, which have no identified unit for hospice care. Using procedures developed in liaison nursing, the hospice team circulates throughout the facility to the place where the patient has been treated for acute or chronic conditions. The hospice team includes nurses, a social worker, chaplain, and consulting physician. The program at St. Luke's has been operating since April 1975, and the one at Halifax has been operating since late 1977. When finances and space become available, the programs will include a hospice unit.

Home care services

Examples of home care services are Hospice, Inc., in New Haven, Connecticut, which began in 1974, and Hospice of Marin, in California, which began in 1976. Leaders of both programs have indicated that, had resources been available, they would have preferred to start their hospice services with a free-standing, autonomous facility. Both politics and finances have thwarted their efforts. To get a program organized, they focused on home care.

Writing about the program of Hospice, Inc., Dr. Sylvia Lack (5), medical director, reports the following services:

1. *Coordinated home care.* Because inpatient beds under autonomous hospice administration were not available, home care teams were organized that included at least a physician and nurse. Assessing the program after its first 3 years, she found that 65 percent of hospice patients were able to die at home, in contrast to the national average of 70 percent dying in hospitals or nursing homes. Visiting nurse associations and volunteers were part of coordinated services.

2. *Skilled symptom control.* The physicians and nurses used a problem-oriented approach to medical intervention for a patient's pain rather than the generalized pharmacological prescription or "standing orders," which does not account for individual variation or needs.

3. *Physician directed services.* Unlike Drs. Noyes and Clancy

who see society excusing the physician from most of his obligations to the terminally ill patient, Dr. Lack (5) believes that "it is vital to the psychological and physical well-being of the patient with terminal illness that the physician is a key figure in the care received" (p. 45), and the patient's desires are part of society's expectations. Rather than giving in to fears of abandonment by a physician because of terminal illness, the patient can be assured of continuing physician care to the point of death under hospice management. Another factor of vital importance is that by providing physician-directed services, the hospice is more likely to be acceptable to the medical community.

Other services are: care by an interdisciplinary team; availability of service round-the-clock; and care of the family before and after death of the patient. On the basis of follow-up evaluation, the staff of Hospice, Inc. has found that the primary carer or family member primarily carrying the burden of care "suffers more anxiety, depression, and social malfunctioning than the patients themselves" (5, pp. 47–48). This finding applied to both hospice and nonhospice groups in Dr. Lack's study.

Dr. Lack identifies various disadvantages of the second model. There are no easily coordinated inpatient services to which a patient can be admitted, and consequently there is a deficiency in the kind of intensive personal care that could be provided. Patients may die at home with symptoms that could have been controlled in a hospice facility. Some patient needs throw too great a strain on the family responsible for home care.

Free-standing institutions

A third model of care is the free-standing or autonomous hospice. Several religious orders in the United States and Canada have for years provided comprehensive services to members of their own group. In 1977 the first autonomous hospice to offer comprehensive services to a community, Hillhaven Hospice, opened in Tucson.

Licensed by the state of Arizona, Hillhaven Hospice has the goal "to provide patients and their families with as tranquil, supportive, and dignified an experience as possible" (6, p. 64).

Major services are: inpatient facilities providing round-the-clock care, with a 39-bed capacity; day care for patients who can be cared for at home at night by relatives or friends; home care, coordinated with the inpatient staff and using hospice nurses and visiting nurse assistance; counseling and bereavement follow-up for families; consultation services from any of the hospice staff; and "supportive services." This last includes the skills of a physical therapist, social worker, occupational therapist, dietician, chaplain, clinical pharmacist, and volunteers.

Like the other hospice programs, Hillhaven has found volunteers with unusually high educational backgrounds to assist patients and families. Trying to use whatever skill can be offered, the hospice organizes volunteers into three areas for assisting: administrative, activities, and direct patient care.

Financing has been the major impediment of other hospice programs trying to duplicate the offerings of Hillhaven. At considerable risk, the Hillhaven Corporation of Tacoma, Washington, a large nursing home chain, provided initial backing for Hillhaven Foundation to establish the hospice. Until third-party payers, either private or governmental insurance companies, recognize funding of terminal care as part of their mandates, or until some other funding option becomes available, it is unlikely that many communities can support a hospice program of Hillhaven's breadth.

Wholly voluntary programs

The voluntary programs of hospice care have developed precisely because financial backing has not been available. Interested citizens have organized self-help groups such as Syracuse's Alethea (7). Some self-help groups have evolved into voluntary agencies such as Haven of Northern Virginia, Inc. (8).

Headquartered in Annandale, Haven is a volunteer-staffed, nonprofit organization for the purpose of helping people facing life-threatening illnesses and their families. Established in September 1976, 170 volunteers helped more than 200 families in the first year alone. Funded solely by donations from the community, all work is accomplished by volunteers who undergo an initial 30 hours of training and orientation. An apprenticeship and regularly scheduled inservice training programs are provided for the volunteers' continuing education.

Haven lists the following occasions for its services: when persons who are facing imminent death alone need someone to care for them, when persons need help communicating with their families, when families need assistance in finding financial or legal aid, when parents of a child with a serious disease have no established support group, or when parents or a spouse lose someone suddenly, when younger members of a family need help coping with illness or death of a parent or sibling, or when a family or patient prefers at-home care. Haven receives referrals from hospitals, mental health groups, physicians, nurses, and public and private agencies, as well as from friends of people experiencing problems.

PROBLEMS THE HOSPICE IS
DESIGNED TO CORRECT

Abandonment

Death is not a patient's major problem. While the patient's dying may make onlookers (either relatives or staff) focus on their own fears of death, most patients have other priorities. In 1969 I directed a study at the University of Chicago to see what a majority of terminally ill patients would rank as their major problem. The overwhelming majority ranked "abandonment" as their major problem, with "loss of self-management" and "intractable pain" as their second and third greatest problems. "Fear of death" ranked ninth.

Many studies (9–12) confirm patients' fears of being abandoned. Persons entering a health care center are faced with a double burden: (a) wrestling with survival and (b) struggling to learn new expectations of those on whom they must rely for their needs. Abandonment may take overt and crass forms, such as the many well-meaning friends and relatives who say that they no longer visit a loved one in the hospital or nursing home because: "I want to remember her the way she was," or "He doesn't even remember my name," or "Everything that can be done is being taken care of by the nurses," or "Everyone has to die alone."

But there are also subtle and covert forms of abandonment, such as the physician (4, 13, 14) who rather than lingering a few minutes to answer a patient's question may pop into the room and ask a few rhetorical questions such as, "You're looking better today, aren't you?" and leave, appearing too busy to listen to intimate fears; or a member of the clergy may call on a parishioner, say a few words of good cheer, offer a formalized prayer, and leave without ever knowing what is really troubling the patient. Or nurses (15) may place dying patients in dark corners of a ward, stop at the bedside only long enough to check vital signs, or make only mandatory visits. Friends and relatives, too, may breeze into the patient's room, inform her how she ought to be feeling, promise to stop by the next day, and never return.

Or again, abandonment may take the form of ostracism in which the patient is treated as though the disease or accident has turned him into a nonperson. This is particularly noticeable when relatives begin to talk about the patient in front of him as though he weren't there anymore.

Perhaps the most obvious form of abandonment identified by patients is ignoring or rejecting the cues the patient tries to give when she wants to talk about her interpretation of what is going on. When she says, "I think I'm going to die soon," and the onlookers respond, "Nonsense, you're going to be around for years," the patient is made to feel as though no one cares for her feelings. Abandonment is the most effective short-term defense mechanism onlookers have when troubled by fears of their own death or when they are so shocked by the implications of the patient's dying that they can only separate themselves in some way to protect their own ego. This is what I call the "abandonment syndrome" (11, pp. 23–25).

It is very easy to suggest that the abandonment syndrome is a characteristic of hospitals and nursing homes. Similarly it is facile to suggest simply, "Let the patient return home to die." For some patients this may be an appropriate suggestion but not for all. We need to remember that close friends and relatives are as susceptible to the temptation to abandon the patient as are hospital personnel. The recurring statement "I'm so thankful to be here in the hospital, now maybe I can get some peace" is a grim reminder that patients are often in conflict with well-meaning relatives whose own needs do not accommodate themselves easily to the needs of the patient.

The hospice philosophy supports the value of *autonomy* by recognizing that patients need to learn how to protect themselves from abandonment through the process of addressing their personal fears consciously, keeping communication open and honest, and guarding against health concerns becoming obsessive, thereby excluding other important dimensions of living. Similarly, the philosophy calls for appropriate modeling and supervising of relatives and hospice staff to lower the need for defending one's own ego by abandonment.

Autonomy is supported by emphasis on self-management. This emphasis is not unique to hospices, although protocols and policies of hospitals and nursing homes may discourage it. On the short term, custodial care may be seen as more efficient. For example, rather than letting patients wash themselves even when confined to beds, nursing home staffs may find it is more efficient to have all patients washed by staff. Similarly, it may save staff time for a nurses aide to button all clothing rather than wait for a patient with trembling hands to coordinate fine motor skills. But such procedures soon undermine a patient's self-confidence and motivation for self-care. And, from the patient's perspective, it may take too much energy to challenge health care staff and relatives' protocols of care.

For many terminally ill patients, home is the appropriate place to spend their last days. Hospice programs, through the use of both trained and volunteer staff, help the patient learn new ways to handle such basic problems as diet, cleanliness, exercise regimes designed to foster maximum mobility, and creativity. A "primary

The Data: The Facts of Death

carer"—a relative or friend—is also trained in ways to support the patient at home as long as possible. For example, a spouse may have been cooking for 40 years the kind of food the patient likes, but because of a malignancy or medical treatment the patient ought not or cannot digest that diet. Hospices help the primary carer provide new menus. Other hospices provide day care for patients whose primary carer must continue outside employment. While the patients can be at home in the evenings and at night, they can receive basic care at the hospice during the day. Almost all hospice programs provide a regular home visitation team service. Some hospice programs provide a 24-hour "hotline" which permits the patient or primary carer to have immediate contact with trained personnel.

Uncontrolled or Intractable Pain

As noted above, uncontrolled or intractable pain is one of the most feared problems for critically and terminally ill patients. Dr. Saunders reports that in 1959 it was her experience that only 90 percent of patients could obtain some relief from severe suffering. The remaining 10 percent suffered from intractable vomiting, dysphagia, and dyspnoea more often than pain. After 17 years, however, she now reports that no patient has pain that is impossible to suppress because of pharmacological progress and sound training. "Those who complain of incomplete relief of distress in such centers as St. Christopher's are now well below the figure of 10%" (14, p. 9).

Dr. Saunders uses the term *polypharmacy* to stand for the emphasis on pain alleviation based on symptom manifestation rather than underlying pathologic characteristics addressed in acute care. Both in Britain and the United States polypharmacy is being adopted as the preferred treatment for the terminally ill. Rather than subjecting the patient to the further pain of injection, oral medication is preferred. Rather than keeping the patient dependent on staff recognition of pain or discomfort, the patient is usually given a regular 4-hour administration of a series of medicines known popularly as Brompton Mixture, or Hospice Mix, that uses a morphine base. Other medications (such as Dexanethasone for brain metastases) have been identified for problems with pain and suffering in the terminally ill.

When a patient is admitted to a hospice, the drug regimen the patient has been on before admission is not suddenly discontinued. The first 12 to 24 hours of admission are used for adjustment to the new environment, often bringing about spontaneous relief of symptoms. The staff uses these hours to evaluate the individual needs of the patient.

The object of the polypharmacy approach is to maintain an integrated functioning individual who is neither in pain nor symptomatic in any other areas and who, if able, is alert to his surroundings and to the people around him (16, p. 1048). Contrary to popular belief, even among some physicians, there is no fear of inducing addiction in the dying patient. With pain under control, hospice staff can avoid unnecessary laboratory studies, radiological scans, infusion, and intubations, except for urinary catheters when needed.

Family Separation and Estrangement

Health care staff have long recognized the difficulty of maintaining good relationships between patients and their families. As health care institutions have become larger and staff roles more specialized and restricted, patients are frequently subjected to the horrendous task of remaining oriented in strange contexts, where they are served by authority figures unknown to them, by sophisticated equipment that looks like it comes from another world. As James J. Lynch (10) noted in his book *The broken heart: The medical consequences of loneliness*, human relationships are the most important single factor in life yet are excluded from medical consideration of patient care. To be cut off from relationships of affection and trust is to be subjected to the disorientation that is commonly referred to as "craziness." Patients may become delirious, depressed, and paranoid when, fighting for survival, they cannot gain access to the persons with whom they have been oriented prior to the health crisis.

The hospice philosophy not only supports the value of relationships but seeks to incorporate the family and close friends into patterns of primary care. When relatives and friends are not a part of primary care, they seem to be cut off from the most useful means of adapting to the impending loss of their loved ones and there can develop what I call the "waiting vulture syndrome" (17). The syndrome appears when relatives have been cut off from being "useful" to the patient and begin to process their sense of loss as though the patient were already dead. Physical symptoms may be drooped head, shoulders falling forward, and general exhaustion. The emotional symptoms are despondent affect along with a general sense of "there is nothing more we can do." Sometimes there is evidence of guilt: "We're ready for him to die too soon." Some relatives appear startled by how quickly they have accepted the reality of a patient's dying and have accommodated themselves to their anticipated loss.

Relatives who have assumed the role of primary carer, particularly spouses, may need the help of hospice volunteers to give them a chance to run important errands outside of the home or have periods of undisturbed rest. A common observation of health care staff with terminally ill patients is that relatives have a harder time dealing with the patient's needs the more exhausted the relatives become. Respecting the relatives' own needs, St. Christopher's Hospice, the Palliative Care Unit in Montreal, and Hillhaven Hospice in Tucson declare a rest day when, except when the patient appears near death, relatives are excused to attend to their own needs.

Mourning Process Not Understood

Several years ago a prominent midwestern newspaper conducted a poll of the "man on the street," asking the question "How long is it normal to mourn the loss of a loved one?" The overwhelming majority reported that it is "normal" for 48 hours to 2 weeks. If there is any accuracy to this poll it illustrates that, as a people, we recognize the first characteristics that mourning takes at the time we lose a loved one but do not understand what mourning looks like later. Even among our grandfathers the emotion grief and the process mourning were not understood as being "normal" and serving a function. Despite earlier systematic studies (18), it is not until the mid-1960s that we find in medical literature the question "Is grief a pathological or an adaptive symptom?" It was widely assumed in the population and among health care disciplines that grief was a symptom of pathology. Largely through insights gained from the disciplines of psychology and pediatrics, by examining what is normal in growth and development, mourning is understood today as an emotion that not only appears at the loss of a loved one but is necessary for health if we are to adapt to the change. The hospice philosophy recognizes this change in understanding not only for the patient but also for the family and staff.

With every event that signals a basic change in how a member of a family relates to others (think for example of baptism and naming-and-blessing ceremonies, confirmation and other initiation rites, and marriage services) the central figure is an active participant. At death, however, the central figure is absent. Only the body and the artifacts of that person's life remain. We all know how reassuring it is to receive affirmative responses to our gift giving. At the funeral and at the cemetery, in acts of giving, there are no responses from the deceased except what individuals can imagine the person would have related were he still alive. The acts of relating to the deceased are unlike all other ways of relating to human beings we have learned in our normal growth and development. Consequently, the ending of our relating to one who has died is played over and over again in the scenarios of our mind until we are finally able to grasp not only the reality of our loss but how, as a result, we are able to relate to our world. This is the unique psychodynamic resolving conflicts that are imposed on us by death. If we do not resolve the conflict, we remain disoriented in those aspects of our life where the loved one was a part of orienting stimuli. And a mourner's risks for morbidity and mortality are raised even higher (10).

The process of resolving conflicts imposed on us by death is called *mourning*. The dominant emotion is *grief*. Rather than mourning being characterized only by stunned feelings and emotional outbursts, John Bowlby of Harvard and C. Murray Parkes (9) of St. Christopher's Hospice have given us four helpful descriptions of the mourning process: shock and numbness, yearning and searching, disorientation and disorganization, and resolution and reorganization.

All four dimensions of the mourning process are usually present as soon as the mourner is confronted by loss. But as the mourner begins to resolve conflicts of the event, feelings of shock and numbness pass, there is less need for yearning and searching, disorientation and disorganization appear less frequently and for shorter periods, and the mourner begins to rediscover how to best relate to society.

Shock and numbness is that dimension of mourning marked by feeling stunned and may be interrupted by outbursts of extremely intense panic, distress, or anger. Functioning is impeded, judgment-making difficult. Even for those families who have anticipated the patient's death and who view death as bringing merciful relief, the change is a shock. The patient's presence, the responsibilities for caring for the patient, the worries and conflicts, all of which were orienting cues to the way life was to be lived before death, are now gone. The basic conflict of this tension between the reality of the immediate past and imposed present is characterized by resistance to stimuli.

Yearning and searching is marked by feelings of restlessness, anger, and ambiguity. Unlike rejection of stimuli when we are in shock, we become acutely aware of stimuli when we yearn for the presence of the loved one, particularly as we search for familiar sounds, smells, and sights associated with the deceased. The search for the deceased is our attempt to test reality and is characterized by the questions: "How can this be?" "What does it mean?" "Who is responsible?" It is not enough for a person to have a philosophical and theological framework in which to interpret the basic changes of life. It is also necessary to the adaptive process, it seems, to go through a reexamining process.

Disorganization occurs when the mourner shifts from testing what is real to awareness of reality. Feelings of depression, guilt, and disorientation are frequent. Reality and roles are confused. Disorganization for some will last for months, for others, years.

As painful as disorganization is, healthy reorganization—when the mourner is able to resolve his major conflicts—seems impossible without it. I sometimes see mourners in the clinic who either pretend that they never related significantly to the deceased friend or family member or that death of that person has not affected their orientation in any real way. Their feelings are repressed and their behavior, when measured with the reality of the world, is organized around fantasy. The significance of this is that when their conflicts are resolved only in their imaginations, they become emotionally more frustrated and frustrating to be around.

More and more reorganization occurs as conflicts are resolved. When the mourner begins to function at home and at work with a sense of confidence, reorganization has become the dominant dimension of his adaptation to loss. Perspectives about reality are congruent with reality, and the mourner has the ability to cope with new challenges.

In order to better identify how to support mourners, the author used the Bowlby and Parkes descriptions to test what 1200 mourners had experienced over a 24-month period. This study has taken 10 years to complete.

Intensity was determined by the individual's self-assessment on a scale of 1 to 7, with 7 representing the behavioral and affective characteristics in their extreme. The characteristics of shock and numbness seem to be most intense in the first 2-week period (see Figure 1),

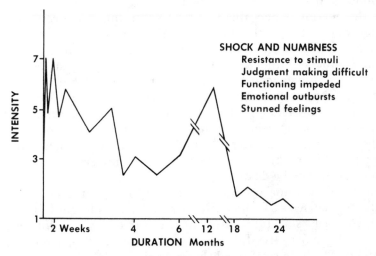

FIGURE 1 *Intensity of the characteristics of shock and numbness during the 2 years following the death of a loved one.*

the mourning period recognized by the "man on the street." Duration of the characteristics are broken momentarily when plans for the funeral or financial decisions must be addressed, but attention spans are short. Shock and numbness peak again on the anniversary of the patient's death.

Just as the familiar stimuli of home may have been the most orienting context for the patient when dealing with the terminal diagnosis, so most mourners find the home the most comforting and the context in which they can themselves best control intrusion of unwanted stimuli. It speaks to the health of society that, at least in rural areas, friends and neighbors provide food for the mourner immediately following the death and for several weeks thereafter. With functioning impeded, judgment making difficult, many mourners neglect basic nutritional needs. When the home care team from the hospice sees that the mourner doesn't feel like eating, priority can be given to caring for the mourner's survival needs.

Characteristics of searching and yearning are most acute among mourners who have suffered unexpected change or loss. But even for mourners who have anticipated the death of their loved one, an overwhelming majority report that they are very sensitive to stimuli, particularly those stimuli associated with the loved one that had served as orienting cues. The mourner may fear that he is becoming "crazy" because of bizarre episodes in which he may sense the return of the deceased. A widow, for example, may believe that her husband has returned from the dead at five o'clock in the evening because she heard sounds like those she associated with his returning from work and unlocking the door.

In this period when the mourner seems most concerned with testing what is real, the hospice staff can provide considerable comfort by encouraging the mourner to carry through with the searching process rather than trying to repress it as unreal or psychotic. It is unbalanced behavior, but recovery of balance cannot occur until the mourner has tested his feelings of responsibility and feels that he understands what has happened. For the average adult in my study, searching and yearning was most intense from, approximately, the 2nd week after the loss of the loved one until the 4th month (see Figure 2). The feeling occurred intensely again around the anniversary of the death.

Nearly all individuals report that bereavement is the most painful of all life's changes. Thomas Holmes and his colleagues (19) have shown by their "social readjustment scale" that out of 43 life events, death is the most stressful. Smith (12), Brown (20), Paykel (21), and Myers (22) have confirmed that observation.

The period when the average adult seems most vulnerable in maintaining his own health occurs between the 4th and 6th month

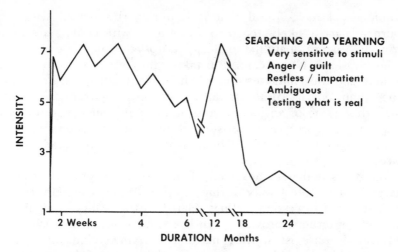

FIGURE 2 *Intensity of the characteristics of searching and yearning during the 2 years following the death of a loved one.*

when the characteristics of disorientation are most intense (see Figure 3). Because the man on the street does not seem to understand that this phase is expected or normal, the mourner may experience considerable ostracism. It is the point when the mourner most needs the support of people around him. A large number of mourners turn to the "sick role" in order to make their feelings legitimate. Gerber (23) found that mourners will return to a physician as patients for cold or flu symptoms or even more serious

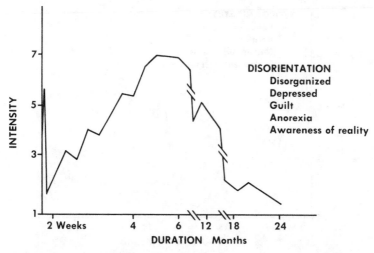

FIGURE 3 *Intensity of disorientation during the 2 years following the death of a loved one.*

Hospice Care for the Dying

pathologies. I have found that it is during this period when the mourner is most likely to go to a physician with complaints about having no energy, inability to sleep, and psychosomatic complaints. If the physician is not careful in taking the patient's history, he or she may see the characteristics of the patient as clinical depression rather than as part of the mourning process. Contrary to popular belief, the taking of antidepressants and tranquilizers will not relieve the person of these characteristics. Rather, the characteristics seem to be part of that "work" which is necessary in the readaptation process.

Volunteers and paid hospice staff members can provide effective intervention for the family during this period; they can help reorient the family by processing feelings related to the reality of their loss. For some mourners, providing gentle encouragement for basic nutrition and exercise is all they need. The trained clinician may be needed to identify other needs during this period. What makes the period of disorientation particularly difficult is that both physical and functional disorders that the mourner may have had before the loved one died tend to become worse, and it is sometimes difficult to assess whether the disorder is associated directly to the loss of the loved one or to a preexisting problem.

The four criteria for reorganization are: 1) a sense of release from the loss of the loved one, 2) renewed bursts of energy that can be confirmed by onlookers, 3) greater ease in making judgments and ability to handle more complex problems, confirmed by onlookers such as hospice staff or employer, and 4) a return to eating and

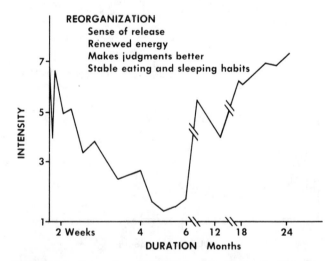

FIGURE 4   *Intensity of reorganization during the 2 years following the death of a loved one.*

The Data: The Facts of Death

sleeping habits the mourner had before the death of the loved one. These indicate that the mourner has adapted to the loss of a loved one even though the intensity of the loss is still great and the memories associated with the deceased are still present. For the average adult, it seems to take between 18 and 24 months before these four characteristics dominate (Figure 4).

Perhaps no greater service is done by the hospice staff than educating the mourner to the reality that mourning is work and that it will dominate his or her life for a much longer period of time than is commonly believed.

CONCLUSION

The hospice movement seeks to provide compassionate care for terminally ill patients and their families, care that affirms their autonomy and dignity. Such affirmation is not easily available in hospitals committed to the cure of disease or nursing homes organized to provide convalescence and rehabilitation of impairment because the needs of the terminally ill patient require a kind of care not often part of therapies for cure.

How ironic that common usage of *care* and *cure* assumes a distinction rather than a similarity. They have a common root best expressed by the word *solicitude*. *Solicitude* implies great concern or lamentation about another's condition and connotes either thoughtful or hovering attentiveness to the sufferer's needs.

Even more ironic is the distinction in popular usage between *hospital* and *hospice*. As noted above, both terms were synonyms in Western history for a place where the pilgrim/patient could find compassion and shelter. It is only in our time that health care services have been defined more precisely and separate institutions have been provided for acute and chronic care, and now a third distinction, terminal care. Even as recently as the early 1950s many hospitals in the United States and Canada provided, to the best of their resources and abilities, all three levels of service.

However, with the development of technological sophistication, the rise of the medical specialties, and the implementation of third-party payers—all designed to correct major problems in health services—the functions of health care institutions became more restricted and staff roles more uniform. The primary focus for intervention in health crises shifted from the patient suffering to the clinician diagnosing. It is the development in the history of ideas that Michel Foucault (24) calls "the clinical gaze" or perspective.

Hospice, in its modern usage, is meant to distinguish a kind of care an institution can provide and the kind of patient needs its staff will tolerate. It is meant to be a contrast to acute care (hospitals) and chronic care (nursing homes) institutions. But to define the unique services of three kinds of health-related institutions does not identify the major challenge to the staff of all three. That challenge is: Can *competence* be synonymous with *care* as well as with *cure*?

Malpractice controversies, an international phenomenon that has been a prominent part of recent health care, is at least a reflection of society's demand for professional accountability in the health fields. They must be seen as part of the same historical and sociopolitical context in which we understand the changing functions of health care institutions. Professional accountability, or competence, is possible only if roles of the professions can be knowledgeably reviewed and tested. Health care training then has emphasized standards, health care institutions have functioned according to protocols, and health care staff tend to behave according to standards of accountability. Patients are expected to behave according to patterns compatible with standards of accountability. For acute care institutions, the persuasive outcome that standards are designed to foster and against which evaluations are measured is cure. For chronic care institutions, the outcome is rehabilitation. Staff performance that leads to cure or rehabilitation is, by definition, competent.

In reaction to the objective, scientific, and fragmented competencies of modern health care, of which abandonment or mistreatment of the terminally ill are but parts, there are efforts to make hospice care fully humane. But what is the definition of competence for being "fully humane"? Certainly as a corrective to historical developments in health care institutions, and as a complement to services already available, the hospice movement is making a distinct contribution. But it will be tolerated by society only if it provides competent alternatives. What will define competence for the people serving in hospice programs? Will it be behavior that will foster a specific style of dying? Will it be behavior that will foster a specific style of living? Or will it provide a new understanding of competence, based not on "the clinical gaze" but on the patient's own sense of values? If this last, then the answers for how to assist the terminally ill with their needs may lie more with the arts and theology than has yet been identified. Compassionate care is not glibly defined nor easily practiced.

REFERENCES

1. Thompson, J. D., & Goldin, G. *The hospital: A social and architectural history.* New Haven: Yale University Press, 1975.

2. Parsons, T. *The social system.* New York: Free Press, 1951.
3. Noyes, R., Jr., & Clancy, J. The dying role: Its relevance to improved patient care. *Psychiatry,* 1977, *40,* 41–47.
4. Wilson, D. C., Ajemian, I., & Mount, B. Montreal (1975)—The Royal Victoria Hospital palliative care service. In G. W. Davidson (Ed.), *The hospice: Development and administration.* Washington, D.C.: Hemisphere, 1978.
5. Lack, S. A. New Haven (1971)—Characteristics of a Hospice program of care. In G. W. Davidson (Ed.), *The hospice: Development and administration.* Washington, D.C.: Hemisphere, 1978.
6. Hackley, J. A., Farr, W. C., & McIntier, Sr. T. M. Tucson (1977)—Hillhaven Hospice. In G. W. Davidson (Ed.), *The hospice: Development and administration.* Washington, D.C.: Hemisphere, 1978.
7. *Alethea: Caring services counselor handbook.* Syracuse, NY: Alethea, The Center on Death and Dying, 1977.
8. Haven of Northern Virginia, Inc., personal communication and pamphlet. September 1977.
9. Bowlby, J., & Parkes, C. M. Separation and loss within the family. In E. J. Anthony & C. Koupernik (Eds.), *The child in his family.* New York: Wiley, 1970.
10. Lynch, J. J. *The broken heart: The medical consequences of loneliness.* New York: Basic Books, 1977.
11. Davidson, G. W. *Living with dying.* Minneapolis: Augsburg, 1975.
12. Smith, W. G. Critical life-events and prevention strategies in mental health. *Archives of General Psychiatry,* 1971, *25,* 103–109.
13. Feifel, H. Is death's sting sharper for the doctor? *Medical World News,* October 6, 1967, *8,* 77.
14. Saunders, C. *Care of the dying.* (A Nursing Times Publication, 2nd edition.) London: Macmillan, 1976.
15. Padilla, G., Baker, V., & Dolan, V. *Interacting with dying patients.* Duarte, Calif.: City of Hope National Medical Center, 1975.
16. Liegner, L. M. St. Christopher's Hospice, 1974. *Journal of the American Medical Association,* 1975, *234,* 1047–1048.
17. Davidson, G. W. The waiting vulture syndrome. In B. Schoenberg et al., *Bereavement: Its psychosocial aspects.* New York: Columbia University Press, 1975.
18. Lindemann, E. Psychiatric factors in the treatment of ulcerative colitis. *Archives of Neurology and Psychiatry,* 1945, *53,* 322–324.
19. Holmes, T. H., & Rahe, R. H. The social readjustment rating scale. *Journal of Psychosomatic Research,* 1967, *11,* 213–218.
20. Brown, G. W., & Birley, J. L. T. Crises and life changes and the onset of schizophrenia. *Journal of Health and Social Behavior,* 1969, *9,* 203–214.
21. Paykel, E. S., Prusoff, B. A., & Uhlenhuth, E. H. Scaling of life events. *Archives of General Psychiatry,* 1971, *25,* 340–347.
22. Myers, J. K., Lindenthal, J. J., Pepper, M. P., & Ostrander, D. R. Life events and mental status: A longitudinal study. *Journal of Health and Social Behavior,* 1972, *13,* 398–406.
23. Gerber, I., Wiener, A., Battin, D., & Arkin, A. M. Brief therapy to the aged bereaved. In B. Schoenberg et al., *Bereavement: Its psychosocial aspects,* New York: Columbia University Press, 1975.
24. Foucault, M. *The birth of the clinic.* (A. M. Sheridan Smith, trans. First American Ed.) New York: Pantheon, 1973.

CHAPTER SEVEN

Death and the Elderly

HANNELORE WASS

INTRODUCTION

Throughout history, human beings of all ages have sought to understand the meaning of their existence. Different cultures and civilizations have produced different ideas about life and death. Marcuse (1) gives us a glance into the wide variety of theories about death in the

▬▬▬▬▬▬▬▬▬

The elderly are conspicuously absent from most books on death and dying, but we are including them because they have a right to be. There is a great deal of reluctance on the part of adults in general to discuss dying with their aging parents, and health care personnel in hospitals and nursing homes often go to great lengths to avoid the fact of dying. This is ironic, since old persons are nearing the end of their life cycle and their dying is imminent. Wass reports evidence that contrary to common belief, most elderly persons do not get upset when death is discussed openly.

The problems discussed in Chapters Four and Five are amplified for the elderly. For them, dying is often lonelier and far less dignified. As survivors, old people experience "bereavement overload," which often leads to feelings of abandonment and depression long before death. Wass pleads for honest discussions about death with old persons, including practical information exchange in matters such as the will, the right to die naturally, and funeral practices.

The Data: The Facts of Death

course of Western thought alone when he states: "The interpretation of death has run the gamut from the notion of a mere natural fact, pertaining to man as organic matter, to the idea of death as the *telos* of life, the distinguishing feature of human existence" (p. 64). Every life-death theory, whether it is formulated in the context of a religious belief system or a system of philosophic thought, is in the final analysis an attempt to derive a sense of order and comfort in the face of one's mortality. Each of us, regardless of our commitment to, negation of, or indifference to institutionalized religious thinking or the cultural Zeitgeist or milieu, has to conceptualize and confront our own death and derive our own personal meaning. Herman Feifel (2), the famous psychiatrist, philosopher, and pioneer in the field of death and dying, has suggested in the introduction to his book *The Meaning of Death* that the critical existential question "is not the sham dichotomy of life and death but rather how each of us relates to the knowledge that death is certain" (p. xi). Many philosophers have proposed that our identity as unique individuals becomes meaningful only as we realize that we are finite. It is the recognition of this fact that makes life precious. The psychologist Erik Erikson (3-5), in his theory of human development and particularly in his formulations about the final stage of man (discussed later), comes to similar conclusions.

Perhaps this is the fundamental factor in the human tragedy: On the one hand, we grow to learn the pride of achievement and of our ability to look back into the past and transcend our present to envision the future; thus we are able to escape our bodies with soaring dreams and imagination and are able to develop our sense of power and uniqueness. On the other hand, we are continually frustrated and humiliated by our ultimate finiteness and our impotence in the face of death, and we are possessed by a deep anxiety over our eventual fate. To come to accept this fate in the twentieth century Western world is no mean task, and its accomplishment is a great victory. Erikson has developed a theory about the obstacles we must overcome to achieve this victory.

THE FINAL STAGE OF LIFE: INTEGRITY VERSUS DESPAIR

Erik Erikson's (3-5) theory of human development asserts that there are eight stages through which a person has to pass in moving through the life cycle from infancy to old age. Each stage of development presents a crisis in one's understanding of oneself, of one's

A portion of this chapter has been published under the title "Dying as the Final Stage of Growth: Issues and Challenges" by H. Wass in *Introduction to Educational Gerontology*, R. H. Sherron, & D. B. Lumsden (Eds.). Washington, D.C.: Hemisphere, 1978.

purposes, and of one's relationships with others. One may not be consciously aware of these crises, as in the early stages, but they exist nevertheless. The developmental task at each stage is to resolve the crisis successfully; only then can the person progress to the next stage of maturity. Erikson (4, pp. 55-100) identified the eight stages and crises as follows: 1) infancy: trust versus mistrust, 2) early childhood: autonomy versus shame and doubt, 3) play age: initiative versus guilt, 4) school age: industry versus inferiority, 5) adolescence: identity versus identity diffusion, 6) young adulthood: intimacy versus isolation, 7) adulthood: generativity versus self-absorption, and 8) senescence: integrity versus despair. Although this discussion is concerned with the last stage of development, it is important to note that, according to Erikson, a person must have been successful, at least to some degree, in solving the seven crises that come before in order to be able to resolve the crisis of the final stage. It is also important to recognize that senescence is the final stage and, unlike the others, is not a stepping stone to a more mature level of development. Erikson (5) states: "Each individual, to become a mature adult, must to a sufficient degree develop all the ego qualities of the previous stages, so that a wise Indian, a true gentleman, and a mature peasant share and recognize in one another the final stage of integrity" (p. 268).

The task of the final stage of life is to achieve integrity. By Erikson's own admission, integrity has no clear definition. What he appears to mean by integrity is the achievement of a state of mind at the end of life that is a conviction that one's life has meaning and purpose, that having lived has made a difference. It is an understanding that—despite the struggles and defeats one has experienced in growing up and as a parent, mate, friend, and co-worker—one's life in its culminating phase is positive, and one's humanity has been fulfilled. More than that, one comes to comprehend that one's life is a link between past and future generations and has its place in the flow of history (3). Other psychologists have formulated similar concepts, such as Abraham Maslow's (6) *self-actualization*, Gordon Allport's (7) *self-objectification*, James Birren's (8) *reconciliation*, and Robert Peck's (9) *ego-transcendence*.

This mental state is illustrated in a religious context by Paul when he writes about his understanding of the meaning of his life in a letter from his final imprisonment in Rome to his young apprentice Timothy: "As for me already my life is being poured out on the altar, and the hour for my departure is upon me. I have run the great race, I have finished the course, I have kept faith" (2 Tim. 4:7). In the last eight lines of his poem "Terminus," Ralph Waldo Emerson expresses a similar attitude and the view that the termination of life is exultant:

The Data: The Facts of Death

> *As the bird trims her to the gale,*
> *I trim myself to the storm of time,*
> *I man the rudder, reef the sail,*
> *Obey the voice at eve obeyed at prime:*
> *"Lowly faithful, banish fear,*
> *Right onward drive unharmed;*
> *The port, well worth the cruise, is near,*
> *And every wave is charmed."*

A similar expression is found in the form of a sculpture that stands in front of the Faculty of Medicine at the University of Madrid. A young man on horseback, poised to take off on a race, reaches back to take a scroll extended by an aged man almost prostrate on the ground. The expression on the old man's face is one of serenity, as if in his final moments he sees himself as an effective, meaningful link in the continuing human chain. As Erikson (5) puts it: "He knows that for him all human integrity stands and falls with the one style of integrity of which he partakes. The style of integrity developed by his culture or civilization then becomes the 'patrimony of the soul,' the seal of his moral paternity of himself. In such final consolidation, death loses its sting" (p. 140). An excellent illustration of this attitude is in the statements of the 63-year-old Reverend Bryant in the moving film documentary *Dying* produced by Roemer (10). After the physician told Reverend Bryant that he had cancer of the liver and there was nothing that could be done, he replied: "Well, I've never had it told to me before, but it's all right; we're going on forward," and in a later scene he said, "I can say right now that I'm living some of the greatest moments in life.... The doctors told me that I don't have much longer to live, but I'm not upset. I want to live as long as I can, but I'm not going to die on account of death."

But pity the person who does not attain this final integrity. According to Erikson, this person experiences a deep fear of death and cannot accept the one and only life cycle as the ultimate life. Despair is overwhelming at the realization that time is short, too short to start another life, to find alternate ways of living and achieving integrity. Such despair, in Erikson's view, is difficult to overcome. It is the final identity crisis and the final loss of one's sense of worth. Erikson's views are very pessimistic, however. There are many instances in which an old, dying person, although not accepting life, may come to accept death, particularly when the person is either deeply religious or given understanding and love in his or her final moments. As Charles Mayo (11), retired surgeon of the Mayo Clinic, put it: "I hope that when I die, it will be quick. But if there is some delay, then I hope I'll have somebody I love with me—somebody to hold my hand" (p. 95). Mayo's wish is probably shared by most, but when deep faith is absent and no loved ones are around, help may still be rendered. Lawrence Roose (12) of the Department of Psychiatry at Mount Sinai Hospital in New York, in his article "To Die Alone," pleads with eloquence that hospitals make psychological and psychiatric service available to help non-psychiatric physicians better understand and help dying patients, particularly those who are desperate, terrified, and alone. This plea is made by others as well (13–15).

THE LIFE REVIEW

Erikson discusses the crisis at the final stage and gives us a good understanding of the mental state of integrity versus despair, but he does not discuss how one reaches this state. An answer is found in the process by which an old person redefines his or her life to obtain a new and more mature meaning, a process that is accomplished by the *life review*, a concept advanced by R. N. Butler (16). Although Butler never related his notions to Erikson's, it is apparent that the two are in close harmony. Whereas Erikson outlines the substance of the crisis at the final stage of development and its consequences of solution and failure, Butler postulates the process necessary to resolve the crisis. Butler, however, goes beyond merely asserting the life review as a natural and universal process characteristic of old people; he also postulates a purpose. According to Butler, the life review is triggered by the realization that one has reached the end of life and that death is near. The life review serves to prepare a person for dying, and it may decrease the fear of death.

Old people are known to reminisce a great deal and are often accused of living in the past. Frequently they try the patience of the listener, who tends to view this reminiscing as excessive or even as a psychological disorder. According to Butler, however, such reminiscing has an important function; it is nothing less than the attempt to revive past experiences, reevaluate them, sum them up, and integrate them into a new understanding. Obviously this task can be helped or hindered by those around the old person. Because self-esteem is centrally involved and reviewing of the past reaches into the present, the attitudes and behavior of old people's relatives, friends, or care givers can affect their success or failure in accepting their deaths. Nurturing and empathic people can help the aged a great deal. A chilling example of a hostile environment and its effect is found in Simone de Beauvoir's (17) book *A Very Easy Death*, in which she describes with moving frankness and self-analysis her own inability to give emotional support to her dying mother and the incredible indifference and coldness of the hospital staff.

Regardless of the environment, however, the life review, according

The Data: The Facts of Death

to Butler, does not always lead to well-integrated serenity. When unresolved conflicts arise from the past and unrealized ambitions and missed opportunities come crowding into the mind at a time when it is too late to do anything about it, a deep depression often sets in which may lead to disturbance or even suicide. Even if the life review leads in the end to an acceptance of death, the process may involve anguish and terror. An outstanding example is the experience of Ivan Ilych in Leo Tolstoy's (18) classic short story "The Death of Ivan Ilych." Ivan Ilych knew with certainty that he was dying, even though his physician and his family pretended that it was not so. Ivan began his internal dialogue and traveled back through his life:

> He began to recall the best moments of his pleasant life. But strange to say none of those best moments of his pleasant life now seemed at all what they had seemed—none of them except the first recollections of childhood. There, in childhood, there had been something pleasant with which it would be possible to live if it could return. But the child who had experienced that happiness existed no longer, it was a reminiscence of somebody else. As soon as the period began which had produced the present Ivan Ilych, all that had then seemed joys now melted before his sight and returned into something trivial and often nasty. And the further he departed from childhood and the nearer he came to the present the more worthless and doubtful were the joys. (p. 147)

As Ivan Ilych reminisced about his career as a government official, about his marriage and early disenchantment, his hypocrisy and the emptiness of his life, he said to himself, "Maybe I did not live as I ought to have done" (p. 148). Over the next 2 weeks, he suffered the agonies of physical pain from his cancer and the even greater agonies of mental pain over the loss of his life, and he suffered the anguish and the urgent need to understand what life was all about. Then the question began to torment him: "What if my whole life has really been wrong?" (p. 152). It was after Ivan admitted having lived with falsehood and deception, hiding life and death, that he began to scream, and his screaming continued for 3 days. He became quiet 2 hours before his death with the realization that "it was not right . . . but that's no matter. . . ." Then Ivan caught sight of the life, "and it was revealed to him that though his life had been wrong, it could still be rectified. . . . And he felt sorry for his son and for his wife. His fear of death vanished. In its place he felt there was light. 'So that's what it is,' he suddenly exclaimed. 'What joy!'" (pp. 155-156). Ivan Ilych found his meaning very late but not too late. It was his final understanding that made his dying dignified, serene, and even joyful.

Many people are spared such agonies and are deprived of such opportunities for grasping their final truths because they die in accidents, in their sleep, under heavy sedation, or in a comatose state. Others who die with conscious awareness do not achieve or strive for the state of serenity and peace that Ivan Ilych did. Many people die screaming and fighting to their last breaths and that may be the best they can do; and in terms of who they were in life, that may be appropriate and even dignified. But in our culture and the Judeo-Christian tradition, the ideal is that dying be accomplished in reconciliation, peace, and serenity. The American poet William Cullen Bryant expresses this in the final lines of his poem "Thanatopsis."

> *So live, that when thy summons comes to join*
> *The innumerable caravan, which moves*
> *To that mysterious realm, where each shall take*
> *His chamber in the silent halls of death,*
> *Thou go not, like a quarry-slave at night,*
> *Scourged to his dungeon, but, sustained and soothed*
> *By an unfaltering trust approach thy grave*
> *Like one who wraps the drapery of his couch*
> *About him, and lies down to pleasant dreams.*

Yet, although this is the ideal the attitudes and practices of our culture make it a very difficult one to achieve.

YOUTH CULT

Growing old in the United States is difficult to accomplish and is often painful to experience. Members of this society worship youth and trim, firm bodies. It is made particularly hard for women to accept their aging. Somehow in this society physical attractiveness and sexual attractiveness are made synonymous, and sociologists tell women they lose their sex appeal around the age of 35. This perception is not confined to the United States; Simone de Beauvoir (19) has harshly criticized European societies as well for their negative attitudes toward the mature and older woman.

The United States' cosmetics industry makes millions of dollars annually from promoting consumers' frantic need to appear young. Television commercials promote age-denying by telling the viewer, at least implicitly, that "young is beautiful" and "old is ugly." Advertisements tell us that using the "right" brand of detergent will make a mother's hands look just like her daughter's; that soaps have the power to wash away wrinkles and make the female skin velvety smooth. Encouraging such self-deception is not helpful for the aging person. This author has traveled in other countries and found no society in which so many older women copy the fashions of the young, wear bright colors, and go miniskirted and bikinied, with hair bleached, cheeks rouged, and faces surgically lifted. It is sad to observe such futile attempts at hiding the facts of aging; nothing is quite so pathetic as an old person trying to look young. Physical aging is less of a problem for men because, with the double standard still much in practice, an older man, graying at the temples, dressed expensively in the carefully designed casualness of the tailored leisure suit, is often found quite attractive in a variety of ways by women of all ages. But men are also prone to adopting the trappings of the youth cult, manifested in dyed hair, toupees, and so forth.

It is said that "beauty is in the eyes of the beholder," but it is equally true that concepts of beauty are adopted wholesale from the mass media and the film industry. It takes time, open minds and hearts, and some guidance to learn to appreciate the beauty of old age. Old faces have excited painters and sculptors for centuries. There can be much beauty in an old face in which the wrinkles tell the story of a rich life filled with hardships, successes, sorrows, and joys. There is beauty in a face that shows wisdom and serenity. Appreciation of old age is an attitude that is learned. It needs to be learned from childhood on. It needs to be learned by the aged themselves.

In recent years, as scientists have studied aging from various perspectives, new knowledge has emerged that needs to be learned and accepted. One of the misconceptions about the elderly, for example, is that they have lost their sexual capacities and inclinations. The old cliché "finished at 40" is still in the minds of people, and if not at forty then definitely at 50. Many adult sons and daughters find it inappropriate when an elderly single parent becomes romantic, dates, remarries, or even "lives in sin." Yet it is now clearly established that old people can and do engage in sexual activities into their 70s, 80s, and in some instances their 90s (20–23). Aside from sex, most psychologists agree that love, intimacy, and companionship are universal needs that people of all ages have. Ashley Montagu (24) has pointed out that of all senses the sense of touch is most pronounced, and that touching and being touched is one of the most basic and pervasive human needs from the moment of birth to old age and death. Old persons are not often touched by their adult children or by care givers. Being a grandparent and able to hold, hug, and sometimes care for a grandchild fills a need not only for the grandchild but for the grandparent as well. Very often the old and the young are attracted to one another and feel close and comfortable with each other. When the elderly do not have their own grandchildren nearby they can adopt one, or a child can adopt a grandparent. Esstoya Whitley (25), a grade school teacher, has carried out her own "Adopted Grandparent Program" for 10 years. Her 7- and 8-year-old charges each year adopt a grandparent in a nearby nursing home. They visit daily, and much hugging and handholding is observed.

Many dying persons report that people who know that they are dying keep at a distance or instinctively recoil when the dying approach, as if dying were a contagious disease that one does not want to catch. This must be an unhappy experience that only adds to the problems the dying have in adjusting to their terminality. Leviton (26) has pointed to the needs for love and intimacy on the part of dying patients and proposes that such needs be met. When people are *old* and dying, their problem is compounded. Their need for gentle touch and tenderness is frequently unfulfilled. One need only visit nursing homes and geriatric hospitals or wards to observe this. In our society a person's entry into the world is greeted with much cuddling, hugging, and touching, but precious little is done by way of loving when people exit, particularly when they are old.

DEATH TABOO AND THE ELDERLY

In a country that worships youth as much as ours, there is little room for concern about death. Even though the subject has rapidly become more acceptable for open discussion, and even though the book and media market are becoming flooded with materials on death, this swift movement is already perceived by noted thanatologists as yet another form of death denial. Robert Kastenbaum (27) has pointed this out in his article "We Covered Death Today," and Michael Simpson makes the point in Chapter Four. The fact is that the death taboo is still in practice with respect to the elderly. It is amazing that there is such reluctance to talk about death with old persons. After all, they are nearing the end of their life cycle and dying is closer than at any other time, and dying is the natural final process. Yet the death taboo with the elderly is pronounced. Even the experts on aging largely avoid the subject. In a recent survey Wass and Scott (28) discovered that 90 percent of the scholarly and textual books on aging examined devote less than 5 percent of their space to discussions of death, about 65 percent of the books give less than 1 percent space to death and dying, and nearly 20 percent of the books with a total of 3475 pages (an average of 386 pages per book) make no mention of death whatsoever.

There is speculation as to why death is avoided with the elderly. Some believe that younger adults avoid the topic because it reminds them too chillingly of their own eventual demise. Others believe the subject is avoided so as not to upset an old person unduly and cause additional anxiety. Some think that death is not brought up with elders because of some kind of embarrassment, particularly when an inheritance is involved. Even old persons sometimes adopt death-denying attitudes. Muriel Spark (29) has brilliantly illustrated this death-denial (death is obscene) in her novel *Memento Mori*:

> Dame Lettie telephoned to the Assistant Inspector as she had been requested to do. "It has occurred again," she said.
> "I see. Did you notice the time?"
> "It was only a moment ago."
> "The same thing?"
> "Yes," she said, "the same. Surely you have some means of tracing—"
> "Yes, Dame Lettie, we will get him of course."
> A few moments later Dame Lettie telephoned to her brother Godfrey. "Godfrey, it has happened again!"
> "I'll come and fetch you, Lettie," he said. "You must spend the night with us."
> "Nonsense. There is no danger. It is merely a disturbance."
> "What did he say?"
> "The same thing. And quite matter-of-fact, not really threatening. Of course the man's mad. I don't know what the police are thinking of, they must be sleeping. It's been going on for six weeks now."
> "Just those words?"
> "Just the same words 'Remember you must die'—nothing more."
> "He must be a maniac," said Godfrey.[1]

How pervasive is death denial among the elderly? Do they indeed become more anxious and upset when death is openly discussed with them or in their presence? Do they indeed avoid talking about death among themselves and with others? Do they have great fears about dying and death? Answers to some of these questions are found in a number of studies.

In 1968 Riley (30) surveyed a national sample of 1500 adults and found that the majority of older people report that they think and talk about death. This author (31, 32) asked over 400 old persons either by interviews or through questionnaires a number of personal questions about death and found that almost all of them were willing to answer, many of them apparently eager, and only a very small fraction was reluctant or actually upset. Old people close to death in a geriatric hospital were found to make frequent references to death according to Kastenbaum (33). Furthermore, these references were more positive than negative or neutral by a ratio of seven to one. On the other hand, Kimsey and his associates (34) reported that 35 percent of nursing home residents they studied said they almost never think and talk about death, and Roberts and his associate (35) in their study of nursing home residents found that 50 percent avoided the topic. But then Matse (36) asked nursing home staff whether or not death was talked about among residents. His findings show that death is a frequently discussed topic when residents are among themselves. Similarly Saul and Saul (37), in

[1] From *Memento Mori* p. 8 by Muriel Spark. Copyright © 1959 by Muriel Spark.

their article "Old People Talk About Death," present transcripts of taped discussions about death by a group of nursing home residents.

We can conclude from these studies that whether or not old persons talk about death depends to a large extent on the kind of environment they find themselves in. Environments can be restrictive or permissive. In a restrictive environment (whether the family, the community, a hospital, or a nursing home) there can be an implicit but nevertheless strict rule that says: "Death not talked about here." The typical nursing home is such an environment and often so is the geriatric hospital. Luckily there are exceptions. A hospice or similar setting is an example of a permissive environment, one that encourages and facilitates openness and honesty. A detailed discussion of the hospice is found in Chapter Six. As people become more accepting of death as a reality of life and a matter that concerns every person, it will become easier to talk about the topic with others including the elderly.

FEAR OF DEATH AND CORRELATES

Psychologists agree that facing up to death or denying it is closely related to one's fear of death. The general consensus among experts is that it is the fear of death that is largely responsible in bringing about the death denial in the first place. Numerous studies on the fear of death have been conducted in an attempt to give us a better understanding and insight into its dynamics.

Age Differences in the Fear of Death

Several studies have compared old people's fear of death with that of other age groups. The results of these studies show clearly that the elderly as a group have less fear of death than the younger groups (38-40). However, it must be stressed that the elderly are by no means a homogeneous group. Old people have certain characteristics in common, most important among them the facts that they are in the final phase of their lives and that death is imminent. There is variation, however, in the manner in which old people cope with these facts, and there is variation in the environmental circumstances in which old people exist. This variability becomes particularly apparent when studying the fear of death. There is no uniformity concerning the fear of death among old people as there is no single, common attitude toward death.

Sex Differences

It is commonly reported that women have greater fear of death than men in studies that are carried out primarily with college students (41-45). In only a few studies have sex differences in the fear of death among the elderly been examined. This early research shows no sex differences in noninstitutionalized, in institutionalized, and in acute geriatric patients (46-48). A recent study by Wass and Sisler (49) in which noninstitutionalized older persons were examined showed significant sex differences that indicated that women have more fear of death than males. Further study is needed to determine the generality of this finding.

Physical and Mental Health

All relevant studies show that fear of death is closely related to old persons' observed and self-reported physical and mental health status. High fear of death in aging persons goes hand in hand with poor physical and mental health (48-50). It has also been found that emotionally disturbed elderly persons have a more intense fear of death than do normal old persons (51-53).

Institutionalized versus Noninstitutionalized Elderly

In a number of studies the fears of aged, institutionalized persons were compared with those living in the community. Kimsey and his associates (34) discovered that 50 percent of the elderly living in nursing homes were very fearful of death whereas only 16 percent of the elderly living in the community were. Shrut (54) compared the fears of death of aged, female residents in the apartment section of a home for aged and infirm Hebrews with those who lived in the more institutionalized central house of the same home. He discovered that those living in the apartments show less fear than those in the more institutionalized setting. In a study by Lieberman and Coplan (55) it is reported that elderly people who are near death and living in the community are less anxious than dying, aged people waiting to be admitted to a nursing home or those who have recently been admitted.

Demographic Factors

Early studies (48, 51) seem to indicate that demographic factors have little or nothing to do with old persons' fear of death. Recent study by Wass and Sisler (49), however, shows that demographic factors are very important. In addition to the sex differences reported above showing older women more fearful of death than older men, the results show that rural elderly have significantly greater fear of death than either small-town or urban elderly. Those who are widowed are more fearful of death than are those elderly who are married or remarried. Persons living alone have greater fear of death than those living with family. Education and income also are significant factors. Elderly with a grade school education have a greater fear of death than do those elderly persons who are college graduates. Likewise, those having an annual income of $5000 or less exhibit a greater fear of death than those with annual incomes exceeding $15,000.

Fear of Death and Belief in Life after Death

Early studies (56, 57) showed that fear of death and religiosity are highly correlated among the elderly, that is, the religious old person is less fearful of death than the nonreligious person. However, in later studies Moberg (59) and Kalish (40) report that only the most conservative and "true" believers showed little fear of death, and two other recent studies (59, 60) discovered no relationship whatsoever between fear of death and belief in afterlife. In fact, Feifel (61, 62) and Wass and Sisler (49) found that fear of death is greater among religious than nonreligious old people. The latter finding is rather puzzling. One can speculate that believers are more worried about going to hell than they are hopeful of going to heaven, whereas a nonbeliever has no hell to be afraid of.

One of the problems of all these studies lies in the difficulty of finding a valid and reliable means of assessing fear of death. Different researchers use different assessment devices, and this makes comparisons between studies difficult. Given the limitations inherent in studies of such sensitive a matter as fear of death, the picture that emerges from these various findings is that old persons' fear of death is affected by numerous factors—physical, psychological, and social. We see that physical health affects the fear of death and so does psychological health, marital status, living arrangement, residence community, education, and income. We see that old people's fear of death is lower for those living with family than for those living alone, and, more powerfully, the fear is much lower for those living in the community than for those who are institutionalized.

The "fear of death" is not a simple and single feeling. Marshall (63) has suggested that the elderly may not fear death as much as they fear the process of dying; that is, they may be more concerned about the expected pain or about isolation and abandonment (physical and emotional) than about death itself. The fear of death is complex. Michael Simpson in Chapter Four identifies four components of death fear: 1) fear of dying, including the biological and social processes of pain, dependency, loss of functions, control, and consciousness, among others; 2) the fear of death, that is, of being dead or nonbeing; 3) the fear of consequences or results, such as what will happen to surviving loved ones, plans, property, also afterlife judgment, and punishment; and 4) fear of the dying or death of others, that is, the fear of separation and loss of loved ones.

Not only is fear of death a multifaceted emotion, but we must consider that there are wide variations in the degree and intensity of death fear, and that this variation not only results from personality characteristics but also from environmental factors. Most of the studies cited here then are simplistic, and the development of assessment devices for fear of death that reflect this complexity are needed.

EUTHANASIA OR THE RIGHT TO DIE

How often is an old person "sentenced to life" or, as Cicely Saunders (64) puts it, how often are we, in our medical care, "prolonging dying" rather than living? (p. 52). The issue of euthanasia is discussed in a later chapter. Here we shall deal with it only briefly and as it pertains to the elderly. *Euthanasia*, derived from the Greek, literally means "good death." Distinctions are made between "active" and "passive" euthanasia. For example, a doctor prescribing an overdose of morphine deliberately is practicing active euthanasia whereas withholding of a life-prolonging drug, treatment, or technical device would be an example of passive euthanasia. The key issues, particularly when considering the dying old person, is whether or not to use extraordinary means and devices to keep life systems functioning in cases in which there is no reasonable hope for recovery and who is responsible or accountable for making this decision.

The Living Will

A living will, that is, a statement of a person's wishes in the event that a terminal illness does occur would certainly help families and physicians in making the difficult decision about prolonging or shortening life when the dying old person is unconscious, conscious but unable to communicate, or comatose. A living will written by an older person prior to his or her life-threatening illness would lessen considerably the mental anguish associated with such decisions. Although a number of states in the United States have recently passed "natural death" or "right to die" legislation, most states in the country have not yet made such provision, and in these states a living will is not legally binding. Nevertheless, it probably has considerable influence in the sense that it may be morally binding.

How Old Persons Feel about the Right to Die

A number of surveys have been conducted to find out how old persons feel about euthanasia, the right to die, or "death with dignity" as it is sometimes called. In a survey of 171 rural and urban elderly people in Florida conducted by the author (31), an adaptation of Edwin Shneidman's (65) death questionnaire was used to determine the views and opinions of old people concerning death. Two of the questions dealt with the timing of death. To the question "If your physician knew that you had a terminal disease and a limited time to live, would you want him to tell you?" 87 percent of the elderly responded yes. To the question "What efforts do you believe ought to be made to keep the seriously ill person alive?" 73 percent responded that a person ought to be permitted to die a natural death, and none felt that a person should be kept alive by artificial means. Similar results have been reported by Mathieu and Peterson (66) in a survey of 183 elderly people in California. Of their respondents, 80 percent said they would want their physicians to tell them if they were terminally ill, and only 4 percent were in favor of keeping a person alive at all cost.

Feifel (67) commented that the temporal nearness or distance of death is an important factor in determining one's attitude toward death. Could it be, then, that attitudes of aging people toward euthanasia change as death becomes imminent? This question has been answered. There is today enough evidence from clinical studies with aging, terminal patients to show that their attitudes are the same as those of people not in the terminal stage. Kübler-Ross (68), Weisman (69), Hinton (70, 71), and Saunders (72, 73) have all found that many terminally ill geriatric patients quietly accept their death and often wait for or actually look forward to dying. Many nurses and physicians have told the author how old patients time and again plead with the doctor or with God, "Please let me go" or "How much longer will it be? I am waiting." As has been pointed out, acceptance of one's death is quite common among certain aged persons, a phenomenon that is often difficult for younger people to understand. Younger people do not readily comprehend the possibility that someone may not only passively accept but actually yearn and pray for death because he or she is tired of living, is depleted of physical strength and vital energies, wishes to be released from pain, has no goals to strive toward, or simply feels that life has been fully lived, but there is much evidence to attest to the fact that quite a few old, seriously ill and even not so seriously ill people have such feelings.

ATTITUDES TOWARD FUNERAL PRACTICES

The French sociologist Ariès (74) believes that Americans are satisfied with their funeral customs. This may have been true some decades ago, but it is no longer true today. For some time now the American funeral industry has come under severe scrutiny by federal agencies and citizens' groups, mostly for the high prices of caskets and the high prices for the packaging of services. American attitudes toward funeral practices are changing. Shneidman (75), in a survey of readers of the journal *Psychology Today*, received 30,000 responses to his death questions. Among other findings, he discovered that 70 percent of the respondents disapproved or strongly disapproved of lying in state and 80 percent considered funerals in the United States much overpriced. Shneidman concluded from his analysis of the responses of his predominantly young and highly educated national sample that this may be "a critical minority which may reveal where the rest of society is heading."

Indeed, using Shneidman's questionnaire, a survey (31) of 171 elderly people showed that almost the same percentage (78 percent) considered funeral prices too high. Of lying in state, 48 percent of the elderly disapproved or strongly disapproved, whereas 40 percent did not care one way or the other. A recent survey (76) showed that 41 percent of a sample of highly educated urban elderly persons preferred cremation, while 74 percent of a rural group with little formal education preferred earth burial. While approximately half of the rural elderly did not have any feelings one way or another about lying in state in an open casket, 72 percent of their urban counterparts disapproved or strongly disapproved of this practice. Another survey (32) of 366 people, ranging in age from 15 to 76 years, revealed that almost 50 percent of both the youngest age group (15 to 18 years) and the oldest age group (65 years or older) reported they disapproved or strongly disapproved of lying in state. The majority in all age groups considered funeral prices to be much too high. The range of this response was from 60 to 76 percent across the various age groups. These findings make clear that attitudes toward funeral practices are changing and that this change can be found at all the different age levels from adolescence to old age.

DYING OLD IN AN INSTITUTION

The Hospital

Most people young or old want to die at home in their own beds, but only a small percentage do so. Most people today die in a hospital.

At regional, metropolitan, or geriatric hospitals it has been found that family visits are minimal either because family members live too far away or because they have already abandoned their loved ones. This is particularly true when the patient is old and the process of dying prolonged (77). In addition, modern efficiency and routinization of events in the hospital all too frequently result in the dehumanization of dying (68, 78, 79). Again, the elderly are more affected by this phenomenon than younger terminal patients. The death of an old patient does not create any fuss on the ward (77). Robert Kastenbaum (80) asked nurses to list priorities for saving lives when time and energy were limited, giving as choices a 21-year-old patient, an 80-year-old patient, and a pet dog. He discovered that the ratio of importance of the 21-year-old to the 80-year-old was greater than that of the 80-year-old to the dog. This lack of concern can be attributed to a number of factors. The elderly are no longer breadwinners and are not valued as advice givers (81), but whatever the specific reasons may be, it demonstrates negative attitudes toward aging and the aged in our society. David Sudnow's (78) description of dying in a public hospital is disturbing, and his illustrations of how one county hospital copes with dying patients are appalling. One can only hope that there are not many such hospitals in operation. It would be unfair to end discussion of hospitals at this point, however. Mention must be made of pioneering efforts on the part of many health professionals and hospital administrators, federal agencies, and citizens' groups to provide quality care not only with respect to the medical needs but the emotional–social and spiritual needs of patients as well.

Nursing Homes

Commercial nursing homes have been described as "houses of death," "places where they go to die," and "halfway houses between society and the cemetery" that are peopled by "the forgotten ones." Unhappily, the typical commercial nursing home in the United States is deficient in major ways. R. N. Butler (82) and others (83, 84) charge that fundamental minimum standards for safety, hygiene, and food are unmet and uncontrolled, that nursing home staffs are untrained and underpaid (typically, a staff member draws an annual wage of about $5000), and little is done by way of rehabilitation. In Chapter Five Jeanne Quint Benoliel says nursing homes are custodial institutions that have become places for the prolonged dying of old persons with low (attributed) social value. Butler (82) states that commercial nursing homes now provide care for 80 percent of the institutionalized elderly or almost a million and angrily illustrates how these "houses of death are a lively business."

From time to time probes into the nursing home situation are conducted. The reports usually contain long lists of deficiencies, severe reprimands by the investigating committee for these deficiencies and for cases of patient abuse that contribute to dying (84), and a long list of urgent recommendations to state health officials for alleviating deficiencies and abuse. The press usually publicizes these reports, telling about the stench of urine, the filth, the disarray of medication, the poor food, and so on. The public becomes irate for a time but nothing happens, and the typical nursing home stays the same. Even though there are excellent long-term care facilities available, with trained staff and outstanding rehabilitative, recreational, social, and educational programs, the average old person cannot financially afford to go to such places. Fortunately, only about 5 percent of the nation's elderly do reside in nursing homes, and efforts are currently being made to provide more health care in the community and at home. Such efforts are probably welcomed most by the elderly themselves. The large majority of old people detest the idea of a nursing home, fearing that they might never get out alive. This fear is not unjustified. Studies have shown a substantial mortality increase in old people after being relocated (85-87). It is sad and depressing to have to leave neighbors, friends, family, and possessions and to exchange one's homestead for a room in a place to be shared with others similarly uprooted. In addition, frequently the family is of no help. In a local nursing home 90 percent of the residents literally have been abandoned by their families in that their families never visit, never write, and never even make inquiries to the nursing home staff as to the health status and general well-being of their aged relatives. Fortunately, there are many dedicated volunteers, church or civic groups, and students in the public schools and at the universities who do visit and "adopt" abandoned people in nursing homes and alleviate some of their loneliness.

OLD PEOPLE AS SURVIVORS

The average life expectancy for United States citizens was 47 years in 1900 and had increased to 71 by 1970. There are now over 20 million people of age 65 and older living in the United States. Half of these are over 73 years of age, 1 million are over 85, and more than 100,000 are 100 or older (82, p. 16). One man in six age 65 or over is widowed. Marital bereavement is much more prominent in women. By 65 years of age 50 percent of women have lost their spouses and by the age of 75 two-thirds have experienced this loss (88, p. 40). These statistics present an unescapable fact: old people are survivors. The subject of bereavement and grief is discussed in a later chapter, but it is essential that it be mentioned here. Only recently have we learned that grieving takes much longer than was believed (89) and that among the grief reactions we find are psychological and physical illness and even death (89–91). This is particularly so in later life. Kastenbaum (88) states: "The longer one lives, the more intimate companions one also outlives" (p. 41). Not only do the elderly have to cope with the death of a spouse and other significant others in their life, they also witness the death of relatives, friends, and acquaintances, many of whom are cohorts and some of whom may be considerably younger. Old people experience "bereavement overload" (92), that is, the phenomenon of not having had the time to successfully work through the grieving of one loss before another occurs. Kastenbaum (92) questions whether the death of a loved one can ever be truly "worked through" (p. 41). Grief, then, may be a constant companion in old age. Whereas several gerontologists (93) conclude from their studies that old persons take losses in stride and adapt quite well, this tends to be true only when the bereaved old are supported by deep religious faith (94) or a stable social network (95). Often the accumulation of losses through death, combined with forced retirement, financial problems, the loss of social status and decision making power, the loss of self-esteem, and physical deterioration, give elderly persons a grim burden to carry through their last years of life.

DEATH EDUCATION FOR ELDERLY PERSONS

One inevitable conclusion from the foregoing discussion is that many people in this society must obtain more knowledge and change negative attitudes concerning aging and dying. To change perceptions, concepts, misperceptions, negative feelings, and denial mechanisms of a society is no simple matter. It takes time and concerted efforts and a long-range view on the part of educators and educational agencies and institutions. Fortunately, articulate and dedicated leaders have already begun this task. However, in order to bring about changes in attitudes and to provide information about aging processes and dying, death education must occur at various levels of society, at all ages, and through a variety of means. Children and adolescents, parents, teachers, counselors, nurses, nursing home staff, physicians, and even the aged can benefit from education about aging and death.

Open Discussions about Death

Over the last decade or two the issues of aging in the United States have been brought to the foreground, and, through concerted efforts of government and private funding agencies and senior citizens' organizations, health, nutrition, social, recreational, and educational programs for old people have sprung up throughout the country. This development is most encouraging. It offers old people basic care as well as opportunities to stay active and involved. Educational programs span a wide range from defensive driving to ceramics. Along with these activity programs, catchy slogans have come into being, such as "the golden oldies," "on top of the world," "you are not getting older; you are getting better," and "add years to your life and life to your years." New concepts such as *recycling* and *career retraining* for senior citizens have added respectability to many programs and so has the rediscovered concept of *lifelong learning.*

Despite the wealth of programs now in full swing, the author has not found one that deals with the subject of death and dying. It seems there is a light-headed triviality about some of these programs and a false innocence and pretense that actually promote the denial of death with old people. Therefore, in addition to basic health, nutrition, and other educational programs, and in addition to shuffleboard and sing-alongs, there should be opportunities for serious discussions about death and dying conducted by qualified people.

Open discussion about death when old people want it is important in nursing homes and geriatric facilities. There everybody pretends that death is a bad rumor not to be talked about, yet it is on almost everyone's mind. From findings reported on the previous pages, the effect of such discussions would, in most instances, not lead to depression as is generally believed. On the contrary, by allowing for open expression of the thoughts and feelings old people experience near the end of their lives and by fostering the sharing of feelings, fear, and dread concerning death will actually be reduced. Open and honest talk sessions about death would put other activities in proper perspective. The author is convinced that it would make daily living more meaningful for old people.

Practical Information Programs

A will

The practical matter of preparing a will is often complicated, and the need for legal advice and assistance should be emphasized. For example, many people may not be familiar with changes in tax laws affecting them directly. The importance of estate planning to provide for survivors is discussed at length in Chapter Eleven. In this chapter, Barton Bernstein, an attorney, states that a person who dies without a will "provides a bonanza for lawyers, bonding companies, probate courts, and un-deserving relatives." Bernstein also points to the need for periodic review of a last will and testament to reconsider insurances, birth of grandchildren, change of residence, and other matters.

Body disposal and funeral costs
Old and young can benefit from knowledge of the legal aspects of body or body parts donations, and donations for live organ transplants, as well as the laws with respect to body disposal. Such laws vary from state to state. Persons who have strong preferences for a certain type of funeral should know that their wishes may be totally disregarded because after death a person becomes the property of the next of kin. Therefore, it is important that one discusses one's wishes with the family and hopefully achieves agreement. According to the survey results reported earlier in this chapter, many old persons have definite and firm wishes with respect to funeral arrangements and prices. Information about these matters may be particularly important to them.

Legal aspects
All elderly persons should become informed about the issues of euthanasia or the right to die without the use of heroic measures or artificial means. In states that have "natural death" laws, the elderly should know this. A number of states are considering such legislation, and it would be important for all, including the elderly, not only to know of the status of such bills but to be able to provide input into the dialogue involved in their consideration. In states that do not have legislation about the right to die, old persons should be informed about the "living will," what it does and does not do (see earlier in this chapter, also Chapter Thirteen).

Life-review therapy
From findings discussed earlier in this and other chapters it is apparent that old persons, even normal ones, are often in need of counseling. R. N. Butler (82) recommends *life-review therapy* as an effective means for counseling fearful and depressed old persons. Included in such therapy is taking an autobiography from the old person in writing or with tape recordings, using albums, scrapbooks, even searching out genealogies. Such activities and the reminiscing shared with the therapist, according to Butler, can bring about resolution of unresolved conflicts and reconciliation of family relationships (p. 413), can result in creating more positive views and valuation of the old person's self, and is thought to make the prospect of dying less fearful.

Life-review therapy does not necessarily require a psychotherapist with highly sophisticated, long-term career training unless the person is severely depressed. Nor does this kind of therapy have to be conducted in an office or hospital. Therapy can, for example, be carried out in the home, at Older Americans Centers, in the park, or in a nursing home. What is required on the part of the counselor is a great deal of empathy, basic human relations skills (particularly the skill of active genuine listening), in addition to basic knowledge of aging processes and unique problems.

Grief counseling

Similarly, persons with relatively little training can provide grief counseling. In addition to the skills and knowledge listed above, a grief counselor would need to acquire basic knowledge about grief stages and grief reactions. Such knowledge and skills can be learned fairly quickly, particularly by those who have the motivation to choose the human service fields as a profession or as volunteers. It appears that programs in operation such as widow-to-widow programs, peer grief counseling, and other emotional support programs by volunteers are successful in reducing feelings of abandonment, isolation, and a sense of worthlessness.

In this chapter an attempt has been made to discuss death and the elderly from the point of view of Erikson's theory of senescence and Butler's concept of the life review in a social context of youth cult and death taboo. We have examined special problems many elderly dying persons face. We have also reported studies dealing with the fear of death and its complexity and correlates. Old people have been described as survivors. We have proposed death education and counseling for elderly persons.

The final phase of living and dying can be tranquil or fearful for the elderly depending upon many factors, important among them the fundamental attitudes of society toward aging and dying. As we become more knowledgeable about and sensitive to the unique problems and needs of old persons in their terminal period, and to the degree that we view the aged like other members of our society as worthy and valuable, they will not have to do their dying unnoticed and alone but with humane care and dignity.

REFERENCES

1. Marcuse, H. The ideology of death. In H. Feifel (Ed.), *The meaning of death*. New York: McGraw-Hill, 1959.
2. Feifel, H. (Ed.). *The meaning of death*. New York: McGraw-Hill, 1959.
3. Erikson, E. H. Growth and crises of the healthy personality. In *Symposium on the healthy personality*. New York: Josiah Macy, Jr. Foundation, 1950.

4. Erikson, E. H. Identity and the life cycle: Selected Papers. *Psychological Issues*, 1959, *1*, 1–171.
5. Erikson, E. H. *Childhood and society* (2nd ed.). New York: Norton, 1963.
6. Maslow, A. *Toward a psychology of being* (2nd ed.). Princeton, NJ: Van Nostrand, 1968.
7. Allport, G. W. *Pattern and growth in personality*. New York: Holt, Rinehart & Winston, 1961.
8. Birren, J. E. *The psychology of aging*. Englewood Cliffs, NJ: Prentice-Hall, 1964.
9. Peck, R. Psychological development in the second half of life. In J. E. Anderson (Ed.), *Psychological aspects of aging*. Washington, DC: American Psychological Association, 1956.
10. Roemer, M. Producer of *Dying*, Documentary Film. WGBH, Boston, aired by PBS-TV, May 1976.
11. Mayo, C. In Thanatology, *Time magazine*, Nov. 20, 1964, p. 95.
12. Roose, L. J. To die alone. *Mental Hygiene*, 1969, *53*, 321–326.
13. Oesterreich, K. *Psychiatrie des Alterns*. Heidelberg: Quelle & Meyer, 1975.
14. Rosin, A. J., Wallach, L., & Assael, M. The feelings of terminal patients in relation to their symptoms. Paper read at the International Symposium on the Dying Human, Tel Aviv, Israel, January 1978.
15. Tropper, M. S. A psychogeriatric approach to the dying human. Paper read at the International Symposium on the Dying Human, Tel Aviv, Israel, January 1978.
16. Butler, R. N. The life review: An interpretation of reminiscence in the aged. *Psychiatry*, 1963, *26*(1), 65–76.
17. de Beauvoir, S. *A very easy death*. New York: Warner, 1973.
18. Tolstoy, L. *The death of Ivan Ilych and other stories*. New York: New American Library, 1960.
19. de Beauvoir, S. *The coming of age*. New York: Warner, 1973.
20. Masters, W. H., & Johnson, V. E. *Human response*. Boston: Little, Brown, 1966.
21. Pfeiffer, E., Verwoerdt, A., & Wang, H. S. Sexual behavior in aged men and women. I: Observations on 254 community volunteers. *Archives Genetic Psychiatry*, 1968, *19*, 753–758.
22. Weinberg, J. Sexual expression in late life. *American Journal of Psychiatry*, 1969, *126*, 713–716.
23. Verwoerdt, A., Pfeiffer, E., & Wang, H. S. Sexual behavior in senescence. *Geriatrics*, 1969, *24*, 137–154.
24. Montagu, A. *Touching: The human significance of the skin*. New York: Columbia University Press, 1971.
25. Whitley, E. Grandma—She died. *Childhood Education*, Nov./Dec. 1976, pp. 77–79.
26. Leviton, D. The intimacy/sexual needs of the terminally ill and the widowed. *Death Education*, 1978, *2*, 261–280.
27. Kastenbaum, R. We covered death today. *Death Education*, 1977, *1*, 85–92.
28. Wass, H., & Scott, M. Aging without death? *The Gerontologist*, August 1977, *17*, 377–390.
29. Spark, M. *Memento mori*. New York: Avon, 1959.
30. Riley, J. W. Attitudes toward death. Cited in M. W. Riley, A. Foner, & Associates, *Aging and society. Vol. I: An inventory of research findings*. New York: Russell Sage Foundation, 1968.
31. Wass, H. Views and opinions of elderly persons concerning death. *Educational Gerontology*, 1977, *2*, 15–26.

The Data: The Facts of Death

32. Wass, H. Public opinion concerning funeral practices. *Florida Funeral Director*, May 1976, *42*(3), 6-10.
33. Kastenbaum, R. The mental life of dying geriatric patients. *The Gerontologist*, June 1967, Pt. I, 97-100.
34. Kimsey, L., Roberts, J. L., & Logan, D. L. Death, dying and denial in the aged. *American Journal of Psychiatry*, 1972, *129*(2), 161-166.
35. Roberts, J., Kimsey, L., Logan, D., & Shaw, G. How aged in nursing homes view death and dying. *Geriatrics*, April 1970, *25*, 115-119.
36. Matse, J. Reactions to death in residential homes for the aged. *Omega*, 1975, *6*, 1, 21-32.
37. Saul, S. R., & Saul, S. Old people talk about death. *Omega*, 1973, *4*(1), 27-35.
38. Kastenbaum, R. Death and bereavement in later life. In A. H. Kutscher (Ed.), *Death and bereavement*. Springfield, IL: Thomas, 1969.
39. Lewell, W. Attitudes toward death and toward the future of aged and young adults. Dissertation, Michigan State University, 1976.
40. Kalish, R. A., & Reynolds, D. K. *Death and ethnicity: A psycho-cultural investigation*. Los Angeles: University of Southern California Press, 1976.
41. Collett, L. J., & Lester, D. The fear of death and the fear of dying. *Journal of Psychology*, 1969, *72*, 179-181.
42. Templer, D. Death anxiety as related to depression and health of retired persons. *Journal of Gerontology*, 1971, *26*, 521-523.
43. Templer, D. I., & Ruff, C. F. Death anxiety scale means, standard deviations, embedding. *Psychological Reports*, 1971, *29*, 173-174.
44. Lester, D. Studies in death attitudes: Part II. *Psychological Reports*, 1972, *30*, 440.
45. Bengston, V. L., Cuellar, J. B., & Ragan, P. K. Stratum contrasts and similarities in attitudes toward death. *Journal of Gerontology*, 1977, *32*, 76-88.
46. Swenson, W. M. Attitudes toward death in an aged population. *Journal of Gerontology*, 1961, *16*(1), 49-52.
47. Kastenbaum, R., & Aisenberg, R. B. *The psychology of death*. New York: Springer, 1972.
48. Rhudick, P. J., & Dibner, A. S. Age, personality, and health correlates of death concern in normal aged individuals. *Journal of Gerontology*, 1961, *16*(11), 44-49.
49. Wass, H., & Sisler, H. Death concern and views on various aspects of dying among elderly persons. Presented at the International Symposium on the Dying Human, Tel Aviv, Israel, January 1978.
50. Richardson, A. H., & Freeman, H. E. Attitudes toward death. In M. W. Riley & A. Foner (Eds.), *Aging and society. Vol. I: An inventory of research findings*. New York: Russell Sage Foundation, 1968.
51. Christ, P. E. Attitudes toward death among a group of acute geriatric psychiatric patients. *Journal of Gerontology*, 1961, *16*, 56-59.
52. Wolff, K. The problem of death and dying in the geriatric patient. *Journal of the American Geriatrics Society*, 1970, *18*, 954-961.
53. Templer, D. I., Ruff, C., & Frank, C. Death anxiety: Age, sex, and parental resemblance in diverse populations. *Developmental Psychology*, 1971b, *4*, 198.
54. Shrut, S. D. Attitudes toward old age and death. *Mental Hygiene*, 1958, *42*, 259-266.
55. Lieberman, M. A., & Coplan, A. S. Distance from death as a variable in the study of aging. *Developmental Psychology*, 1969, *2*(1), 71-84.
56. Jeffers, F., Nichols, C., & Eisdorfer, C. Attitudes of older persons toward death. *Journal of Gerontology*, 1961, *16*, 53-56.

Death and the Elderly

57. Faunce, W. A., & Fulton, R. L. The sociology of death: A neglected area of research. *Social Forces*, 1958, *36*, 205–209.
58. Moberg, O. O. Religiosity in old age. *Gerontologist*, 1965, *5*, 78–87.
59. Kurlychek, R. T. Level of belief in afterlife and four categories of fear of death in a sample of 60+ year-olds. *Psychological Reports*, 1976, *38*, 228.
60. Templer, D. I., & Dotson, E. Religious correlates of death anxiety. *Psychological Reports*, 1970, *26*, 895–897.
61. Feifel, H. Attitudes toward death in some normal and mentally ill populations. In H. Feifel (Ed.), *The meaning of death*. New York: McGraw-Hill, 1959.
62. Feifel, H., & Branscomb, A. B. Who's afraid of death? *Journal of Abnormal Psychology*, 1973, *81*, 282–288.
63. Marshall, J. R. The geriatric patient's fears about death. *Postgraduate Medicine*, 1975, *57*(4), 144–149.
64. Saunders, C. The moment of truth: Care of the dying person. In L. Pearson (Ed.), *Death and dying. Current issues in the treatment of the dying person.* Cleveland: The Press of Case Western Reserve University, 1969, 49–78.
65. Shneidman, E. S. You and death. *Psychology Today*, August 1970, pp. 67–72.
66. Mathieu, J., & Peterson, J. A. Some social psychological dimensions of aging. *Paper read at the 23rd Annual Meeting of the Gerontological Society*, Ontario, Canada, October 21–24, 1970.
67. Feifel, H. Attitudes toward death in older persons: A symposium. *Journal of Gerontology*, 1961, *16*, 64–66.
68. Kübler-Ross, E. *On death and dying*. New York: Macmillan, 1969.
69. Weisman, A. *On dying and denying*. New York: Behavior Publications, 1972.
70. Hinton, J. M. Facing death. *Journal of Psychosomatic Research*, 1966, *10*, 22–28.
71. Hinton, J. *Dying*. Baltimore: Penguin, 1967.
72. Saunders, C. The last stages of life. In M. H. Browning et al., (Eds.), *The dying patient: A nursing perspective.* New York: The American Journal of Nursing Co., 1972, 247–256.
73. Saunders, C. St. Christopher's Hospice. In E. Shneidman (Ed.), *Death: Current perspectives.* Palo Alto: Mayfield, 1976, 516–523.
74. Ariès, P. *Western attitudes toward death.* Baltimore: Johns Hopkins University Press, 1974.
75. Shneidman, E. S. You and death. *Psychology Today*, June 1971, 43ff.
76. Wass, H., Christian, M., Myers, J., & Murphey, M. Similarities and dissimilarities in attitudes toward death in a population of older persons. *Omega*, 1978–9, *9*, 337–354.
77. Glaser, B. G., & Strauss, A. L. *Time for dying.* Chicago: Aldine, 1968.
78. Sudnow, D. Dying in a public hospital. In O. G. Brim, H. E. Freeman, S. Levine, & N. A. Scotch (Eds.), *The dying patient.* New York: Russell Sage Foundation, 1970.
79. Levine, S., & Scotch, N. A. Dying as an emerging social problem. In O. G. Brim, H. E. Freeman, S. Levine, & N. A. Scotch (Eds.), *The dying patient.* New York: Russell Sage Foundation, 1970.
80. Kastenbaum, R. *The interpersonal context of death in geriatric institutions.* Paper presented at the 17th Annual Meeting of the Gerontological Society, Minneapolis, October 29–31, 1964.
81. Kalish, R. A. The effects of death upon the family. In L. Pearson (Ed.), *Death and dying: Current issues in the treatment of the dying person.* Cleveland: The Press of Case Western Reserve University, 1969, 79–107.

The Data: The Facts of Death

82. Butler, R. N. *Why survive? Being old in America.* New York: Harper & Row, 1975.

83. Toward a national policy on aging. *Proceedings of the 1971 White House Conference on Aging, Final Report, Vol. II.* Washington, D.C.

84. Garvin, R. M., & Burger, R. E. *Where they go to die: The tragedy of America's aged.* New York: Delacorte, 1968.

85. Aldrich, C., & Mendkoff, E. Relocation of the aged and disabled: A mortality study. *Journal of the American Geriatric Society*, 1963, *11*, 185-194.

86. Liebermann, M. A. Relationship of mortality rates to entrance to a home for the aged. *Geriatrics*, 1961, *16*, 515-519.

87. Novick, L. J. Easing the stress of moving day. *Hospitals*, 1967, *41*, 64-74.

88. Kastenbaum, R. Death and development through the lifespan. In H. Feifel (Ed.), *New meanings of death.* New York: McGraw-Hill, 1977.

89. Parkes, C. M. The first year of bereavement—A longitudinal study of the reaction of London widows to the death of their husbands. *Psychiatry*, November 1970, *33*(4), 444-467.

90. Kay, D. W. K., Garside, R. F., & Roth, M. Old age disorders in Newcastle-Upon-Tyne. *The British Journal of Psychiatry*, October 1965, *111*, 939-946.

91. Maddison, D. Bereavement. *Mental Health in Australia.* January 1972, *5*, 30-32.

92. Kastenbaum, R. Death and bereavement in later life. In A. H. Kutscher (Ed.), *Death and bereavement.* Springfield, IL: Thomas, 1969.

93. Cummings, E., & Henry, W. E. *Growing old.* New York: Basic Books, 1961.

94. Skelskie, B. An exploratory study of grief in old age. *Smith College Studies in Social Work*, February 1975, *45*(2), 159-182.

95. Heyman, D. K., & Gianturco, D. T. Long term adaptation by the elderly to bereavement. *Journal of Gerontology*, July 1973, *28*, 359-362.

CHAPTER EIGHT

Children and Death

JUDITH STILLION and HANNELORE WASS

INTRODUCTION

Children and *death*—the two words seem contradictory. Children symbolize life and growth whereas death marks decay, the end of growing and being. Why, then, when the subject is so foreign to the

███████████████

Children, like the elderly, are also neglected in discussions on death. This chapter deals with terminally ill as well as healthy children rather than confining the discussion to just one or the other. The terminally ill child poses a special hardship. His or her death is most difficult for everyone to reconcile. The authors discuss the reactions of terminally ill children to their own terminality. They offer helpful guidelines for care givers and the family. Special attention is focused on the phenomenon of anticipatory mourning by parents.

A review of studies concerning the healthy child's views of death considers developmental factors as well as environmental influences. The authors plead eloquently for open discussions of death with the young child to assist in developing a realistic understanding. Children's books can be excellent sources of information and comfort. The authors provide a list of 12 classics in which death is imbedded in the main theme, and an annotated bibliography of 26 books (by age levels) in which death is the main theme.

The Data: The Facts of Death

nature of children should we try to educate them about the inevitability of death? In the twentieth century the answer of U.S. culture to this question has been, we should not. Many well-intentioned adults fear that facing the facts of death straightforwardly with children will rob them of their essential innocence and, therefore, of their childhood. Some adults go so far as to believe that children, confronted with the concept of death, will become so terrified that they will not be able to face living in a courageous way. A third reason that adults fail to face the question of death with children relates to the adult's own needs for denial and repression of the inevitability of death. Finally, many adults feel that since death is an unknown it is unrealistic to try to teach anyone to prepare for it.

HISTORICAL PERSPECTIVE

That death and children have not always been so foreign to each other is evident in children's games, prayers, and chants that have been passed on from generation to generation. Peek-a-boo, a game that delights infants, is said to be derived from an old English word meaning "dead" or "alive" (1). It teaches babies their first lessons in object permanence. One of the first games children learn, ring-around-the-rosie, with its chant, "ashes, ashes, all fall down," grew out of children's reaction to death during the great plague of the Middle Ages (2). Even today children very commonly learn as their first prayer, "now I lay me down to sleep, I pray the Lord my soul to keep. If I should die before I wake, I pray the Lord my soul to take." Public awareness of death anxiety has caused the latter line to be changed by many teaching agents. However, its original form serves as a reminder that in earlier days children were supposed to recognize life as transient and death as a constant possibility at a very young age. A rope-skipping chant familiar to many children contains the lines, "Doctor, Doctor, will I die? Yes, my dear, but do not cry," or a variation of this rhyme, "Doctor, Doctor, will I die? Yes, my child, and so will I." Many other games, including hide-and-seek and many tag games, have been offered as evidence of children's lasting tendency to explore the contradictory nature of life and death (2, 3).

Until this century children were common witnesses to death. Infant mortality was high, and it was a rare firstborn who did not experience the death of a younger sibling. Similarly, life expectancy was significantly shorter. According to Lerner (4), life expectancy in 1900 in the United States was 47.3 years. Children often attended the funerals of their parents as well as of siblings before they reached adulthood. In earlier days death occurred most often at home and children were aware of it in all its aspects.

They helped care for the sick family member, were often present at the moment of death, and were included in the planning of the funeral and attended it. In short, children lived continuously with the fact of death from infancy through adulthood.

As medicine became more specialized and sophisticated, as infectious diseases and others were conquered, death became more and more remote. The past two generations are the first in known history in which many middle-aged adults have not experienced the death of an immediate family member.

ADULTS' DEATH DENIAL AND THE CHILD

Death has come to be viewed as an unwelcome stranger rather than an expected companion, and many adults refuse to discuss it or even think about it. Their denial of death has extended to their children. In a survey by Wass 144 high school seniors were asked, among other questions: "When you were a child how was death handled in your family?" Death was never talked about responded 39 percent. An additional 26 percent said that death was talked about only when absolutely necessary, and even then only briefly. The majority of students reported that this death taboo in the family was true for the present time as well. It is safe to say that in the United States parents, as a rule, do not discuss the topic of death with their children. This avoidance of death stems largely from the adults' own discomfort and anxiety concerning dying and death. It is difficult, for example, for the mother of a 4-year-old to provide a calm and well-deliberated answer to the child's totally unexpected question "Mommy, do I have to die?" What mother is not horrified at the prospect of her child's death? Even if she manages a straightforward answer such as "Yes, everybody has to die sometime, but we hope you will not die for a long long time, not for many many years," she is likely to communicate a great deal of anxiety to the questioning child. Such transmission of anxiety from adults to children may be unavoidable, and the best we can strive for is to keep the amount of anxiety at a manageable level. In addition to anxiety, adults frequently feel frustrated and sometimes angry about these death questions, and when these feelings are communicated the child may come to feel guilty as well as anxious.

Avoidance of the topic of death on the part of parents is well intentioned. Most parents have a great need to shield their children from the harsh realities of death. In fact, until recently adults generally believed that children are not concerned about death and that those who are need psychiatric help. The fact, however, as shown in many studies and supported by the authors' experiences is that children are very much concerned. This interest in death is

210   *The Data: The Facts of Death*

a normal part of human development. The question of life and death is an existential question and an expression of the child's basic curiosity and search for meaning. Children, like other people, seek to understand themselves, their relationship with others, and the world in which they find themselves. Even very young children ask existential questions such as: Where do babies come from? Where was I before I was born? Do I have to die? Who deaded Grandpa? And in their everyday world, children experience death by coming in contact with dead insects, birds, and other animals. With their all-encompassing curiosity, children try to understand the difference between the warmth, motion, and vitality that marks life and the cold, pallor, and silence that marks death. All too often when they broach their questions to adults they are met with not only evasive but often incomplete answers or disapproving silence. In this way a child learns that death is a taboo subject, and a child may well come to believe that death must be a horrifying, terrible thing, too awful even to mention.

Attempting to protect the child from the facts of death is a futile exercise. In addition to their real life experiences with dead animals, children observe death on television news and inordinate amounts of fictional death in movies and television plays. Much of the death portrayed by the media creates a totally unrealistic picture in the mind of child viewers. For example, Wiley Coyote on "Road Runner" is smashed, mashed, blown up, dropped into ravines, shot, stabbed, and run over, and yet he emerges with nothing worse than a frazzled coat and a new determination to catch the Road Runner.

In the human television world, children frequently see a central character on a soap opera die a drawn-out death only to appear on a different soap opera within a week or two. On "cops and robbers" shows characters die violently every night but are seen on other shows the next day or week. Perhaps even more disturbing, actors such as Freddie Prinze die and their deaths are publicized, but they continue to appear on reruns and syndications for years following their deaths. What impression of the nature of death can a child glean from such exposure? While realistic attempts to deal with death, bereavement, and grief are not widespread in our media, at least one notable exception is that of the Emmy award-winning show produced by Family Communications, in which death and grief were both explored at a level preschool children could understand and to which they could relate (5).

CHILDREN'S VIEWS OF DEATH

In order to answer children's questions concerning death, an adult must be aware of the child's age, experience, and prior understanding. In general, children's understandings of death seem to follow the cognitive developmental model rather closely. This model, developed by the acclaimed Swiss psychologist Jean Piaget, states that a child's level of reasoning is dependent upon both maturation and learning. Children pass through certain cognitive stages as their mental structures mature and as they interact with the world around them (6). Thus a child of 3 confronted with the death of a parent will not react or understand in the same manner as will a child of 12, even if he or she is given the same explanations and treatment.

Developmental Stages in Understanding Death

Nagy (7), in the now classical study done with Hungarian children between the ages of 3 and 10 years of age, concluded that there are three stages in children's understanding of death and that these three stages are age-related. The *first stage* in understanding death encompasses the age ranges of 3 to 5 years and is similar to what Piaget calls the preoperational stage (6) in that it reflects the egocentric mind of the preschool child. Because children know that they need to eat and breathe, they cannot imagine a human body without those characteristics. Therefore, they describe death either as a kind of sleep or as a gradual or temporary state. While there is a recognition that death differs from life (for example, most young children know that dead people are buried in the ground [8]), there is an incomplete and almost wistful tone to the child's understanding. Nagy (9) illustrates this point by recording a preschool child's remarks:

> Child: It can't move because it's in the coffin.
> Adult: If it weren't in the coffin, could it?
> Child: It can eat and drink. (p. 274)

Similarly, a small child may urge a parent to take a dead puppy to the doctor to make it well.

This stage in the child's cognitive development is also characterized by magical thinking. The lines between fact and fantasy are often blurred, and for small children many things are possible. A small child believes that flowers whisper and that mountains open up if you tell them to, and that princes can turn into frogs and vice versa. Fairy tales support the child's unrealistic concept of death: The beautiful princess sleeps for a hundred years and then a prince awakens her with a kiss (10). While young children are saddened by death, they do not yet grasp the finality and irreversibility of death at this first stage.

The *second stage*, beginning around age 5 or 6 and lasting through age 8, is comparable to the stage of concrete operations in Piagetian theory. Piaget describes this stage as the age of the scientist. During this period, children are consumed with questions concerning the workings of the world around them. They are sorting out impressions, classifying objects, and discovering laws of cause and effect (6). Their understanding of death reflects the growing awareness of the way the world operates. They now recognize that death is final. Nagy's children frequently personified death as a skeleton or powerful monster, perhaps in an attempt to bring the topic into a more easily understandable cause–effect relationship. Death personified comes to get you, but if you are fast enough or clever enough you may get away. At this stage, children worry about the mutilation of the body brought about by the death monster. This is well illustrated in poems written by children (11). Obviously the 6- to 8-year-old child, while recognizing that death is final, also sees it as capricious. The child has not yet incorporated the ideas that death is inevitable, natural, and universal. A typical conversation with one of Nagy's (9) children reveals this lack of understanding:

> Adult: Do you often think of death?
> Child: I often do. But such things as when I fight with death and hit him on the head and death doesn't die. (p. 273)

Nagy described the *third stage* of death as that of mature understanding. In Piaget's theory this stage reflects the complex integration of the formal operational stage of cognitive development. Nagy's study indicates that this stage may begin as early as 9 years of age. Children who have reached this level of reasoning realize that death is inescapable and universal; "Death is the termination of life. Death is destiny. Then we finish our earthly life. Death is the end of life on earth" (9, p. 273). In addition, children view death as personal. It is no longer something done to people from the outside (except in the case of accident) but rather the result of a natural, internal destruction process that will happen to everyone including themselves. Childers and Wimmer (12) conducted a study of the awareness of two aspects of death, universality and irrevocability, in children from ages 4 to 10. Of the 4-year-olds, 11 percent recognized that death is universal, but by the age of 9, 100 percent recognized death as universal. Of the 10-year-olds, 63 percent as compared to 33 percent of 4-year-olds recognized death as irrevocable.

However, even strict Piagetian theorists do not maintain that very young children have no concept of death. Being and nonbeing seems to be one of the first differences to which a child attends and tries to understand. Kastenbaum (13) tells the story of a 16-month-old boy who is engrossed in watching a caterpillar moving along a path. When the foot of a passing adult crushes the cater-pillar, the child looks to his father and says, "No more." Kastenbaum maintains that the solemnity of the tone and the facial expression of the child are powerful indications that the child comprehends (at least at a preconceptual level) the state of death. Such every-day experiences with death can provide the impetus for an informal death education program within the home.

The Influence of Life Experiences in Understanding Death

Children vary by age in their understanding of death, but their views are also shaped by their life experiences. For example, two 15-year-olds sharing similar backgrounds and IQs can vary greatly in understanding depending upon their religious background and their firsthand dealings with death or lack of them. One 15-year-old might have learned at a young age that talking about death made the adults in his family uncomfortable. By circumstance he may not have confronted death among family or close friends. He may even have trained himself to deny curiosity about the subject. When contrasted with a 15-year-old who has had to cope with the death of a parent, sibling, or friend, there may be as much difference in comprehension of the topic as we would expect to find between the 5- and the 9-year-old of Nagy's study. A replica-tion of Nagy's study (14) showed that children in the United States, in contrast to the Hungarian children of nearly 30 years ago, ex-press concepts of death that could be classified into four categories:

1. Relative ignorance of the meaning of death (ages 0–4).
2. Death as a temporary state. Death is not irreversible and the dead have feelings and biological functions (ages 4–7).
3. Death is final and irreversible but the dead have biological functioning (ages 5–10).
4. Death is final. It is the cessation of all biological functioning (ages 6 and beyond).

Other attempts to replicate Nagy's findings in this country (12, 14–16) have generally found a relationship between age and breadth of death awareness but have not found the personification of death among 6- to 9-year-olds that Nagy found. This may lend support to the idea that cultural beliefs and experiences also shape con-cepts of death. Nagy's children were all firsthand witnesses of a terrifying, bloody war in which death could be delivered from the skies unexpectedly. Most of them undoubtedly knew families who had lost loved ones during the war. Perhaps it was more natural for those children to try to make the concept of death more under-standable by personifying it. However, their words may also reflect a personification tendency more prevalent in Europe than in the United States.

Family and Social Class Influences

The importance of the family in the development of ideas and feelings about death was also demonstrated in a study by Wass and Scott (17). They found that children aged 11 to 12 whose fathers were college educated theorize and verbalize more about death than do children whose fathers only completed high school. Interesting also was the wide variability found in the sample concerning concepts of death. They ranged from an "immature" belief that death is a long rest to a "mature" belief that death is a natural, irreversible, and universal event. It is important to note that the need to discuss death and dying should be viewed as a sign of normal, healthy development rather than as an indication of morbid preoccupation with abnormal material. Older children in particular welcome the chance to discuss their views of death and dying. The protocols that follow are typical of responses made by 11- and 12-year-olds who were invited to tell what they thought and felt about what happens when one dies.

> Girl age 12: I would like to die of old age. Just go to sleep and never wake up, a nice quiet way to go. I would like to be buried. Then whatever the spirits wanted to do with me they could do.
>
> Boy 11 years: I think if death came slowly I would just fade out. But if it was instant, I would suddenly be gone. I believe that after you die, you have another life and you might come back from anything like a cockroach to a royalty.
>
> Girl 11 years: I think when someone knows they are going to die, they are very scared. I would be. I think after someone dies they just lie there forever and disintegrate. I hope I never die.
>
> Girl 12 years: When you die, you lay there wondering if you will go to Heaven or Hell. I get scared and don't want to die. Whenever I think about it, I get all spooked out. I don't know about you, but I am going to Heaven.
>
> Girl 12 years: When I die, some people will probably come and put me in a coffin with cobwebs in it; and they'll put me in a dark hearse, and the spiders will probably eat me before they get me in the ground. Next they'll put the coffin in a real deep hole and let me rot!
>
> Girl 12 years: I think you would be surrounded by darkness. You would be absolutely without movement. You couldn't talk or see or use any of your senses. You would be that way forever. It's like taking a very long rest.
>
> Boy 12 years: Well, to me death is a natural thing. Everybody has to die sometime. Nobody can live forever. I know that my mother and father will die sometime. I just hope it's not soon. Then, later, I myself will be threatened by this natural thing called death (17).

Children and Death

A 1974 study (18) supported the impact of the environment in children's conceptualization of death. These authors studied 199 children between the ages of 3 and 9. They grouped the children by age according to socioeconomic class. The results showed that lower class children, whose environment is more violent, tend to be more aware of death at younger ages. They concluded that "The lower class children's fantasy content indicates that they are attempting to deal in a realistic, sensible manner with their environment" (p. 19).

In summary, whereas there is ample support for the cognitive-developmental approach to children's concepts of death, it should be remembered that development involves more than maturation; it results from an interaction of biological readiness with environmental factors. Life experiences, intelligence levels, family attitudes and values, self-concepts, and many other as yet unexamined factors all seem to play a part in each child's individual attainment of meaning for death.

LOSS, ANXIETY, AND DEATH IN CHILDREN

Children begin to experience loss at a very young age. Birth itself might be regarded as a form of loss as it involves giving up one state of being (the protective womb) to enter another (the world, which requires many adaptations). Weaning represents the loss of the major source of comfort, security, and pleasure in an infant's life. Toilet training also is a milestone away from the comfortable dependency of babyhood. Each loss might be thought of as representing a "small death" to the child and each loss brings with it anxiety. The toddler moves out of the soft security of his mother's lap in an uncertain, vaguely worried way. The 5-year-old worries over the loss of her first tooth until the adult mollifies her by assuring that the "tooth fairy" will pay for the loss. The early teen watches with anxiety as the well-known, compact child body begins to assume new proportions.

The process of growing is intimately tied in with loss; and loss produces anxiety. The very young child, from infancy through preschool, manifests this anxiety over separation. The need for mother is almost equivalent to the need for survival and so to be separated arouses a form of death anxiety in the infant. The child between 5 and 9 years old, who is rapidly gaining a strong self-image, shows mutilation anxiety (fear of destruction of some part of his or her body) but is not yet able to verbalize death anxiety per se. It is the adolescents, with their newly acquired ability to think symbolically, who can torture themselves with the concept of nonbeing.

Even strong adults cannot regard nonbeing with equanimity. As children become more mature in their view of death, it is reasonable to suppose that they also become more anxious. Wahl (19) has suggested that many of his child patients' "anxieties, obsessions and other neurotic symptom formations are genetically related to the fear of death or its symbolic equivalents . . ." (p. 27). Von Hug (20) found support for Wahl's suggestion when he obtained a curvilinear relationship between age and death anxiety in normal children but a linear relationship with neurotic children. However, there is evidence that supports the environmental point of view, namely that a child's death anxiety is also largely influenced by the environment. Wass and Scott (17) found that children with college-educated fathers theorized more about death than those whose fathers only completed high school. And children who theorized showed less death anxiety than those who did not theorize.

Positive self-regard is generally viewed as a sign of mental health. Bluebond-Langner (21) suggested that the self-concept may be an important factor in children's concepts of death. It may relate importantly to children's management of death anxiety. This hypothesis is supported in the Wass and Scott study (17) in which it was found that the self-concepts of 11- and 12-year-olds were inversely related to their death anxieties, that is, the higher their self-concepts the lower their death anxiety.

It seems possible that healthy children can grow toward low death anxiety, especially if they are provided with adult models who have worked through their own attitudes toward death and who encourage children to express their fears rather than repress or deny them. Neurotic children, on the other hand, tend to grow more anxious as their concept of death matures.

Implications for Parents

During the early years, parents can help most by merely being available to children and assuring the child that he or she is loved and will not be abandoned (22). Children need honest answers no matter how unpleasant, offensive, or seemingly morbid their questions may be, Grollman (23) points out that parents should answer their children's questions factually and uncompromisingly and at a level they can understand. To tell fairy tales about death to children is not only misleading but may create serious problems in trust between the parents and the child as the child grows older. One of the problems with parental answers is that they are frequently spiritual answers to children's physical–chemical questions. Children want to know what happens after a person has died, but they are equally curious about the physical aspects of dying, particularly in the middle years. They ask questions such as: Why do people die with their eyes open? Why does the blood turn blue? Do people get buried alive? Could a doctor say a person is dead when he really isn't? How long does it take for the body to disintegrate? If parents do not know the answers to such questions it is all right to admit to ignorance. It would be wise to consult a physician or books. Evasiveness or refusal to answer children's questions may also lead to heightened anxiety (22).

Adolescents may clothe themselves in an illusion of invulnerability in order to deny anxiety brought about by their mature understanding of death (24). Kastenbaum (25) has reported that about 75 percent of the adolescents he studied shut the idea of death out of their minds. They were interested in living fully in the present, seeking their identity in the here and now. Adults working with teenagers may find invitations to discuss death go unanswered. However, meaningful dialogues on grief and life after death are also possible if and when the adolescent seeks them out.

Terminally Ill Children

How they view death

Since children's firsthand knowledge of death is a powerful environmental influence for learning about death, it would follow that the terminally ill child should have a far different conception of death than would a healthy child of the same age and intelligence. At least one researcher, Bluebond-Langner (21), makes a case for the idea that terminally ill children not only become aware that they are dying but also understand death as adults do. She discusses five stages in the process of the acquisition of information that are progressive and lead to concomitant changes in self-concept. These changes are dependent upon significant cumulative events occurring throughout the course of the illness but follow the sequence as outlined below:

Information acquisition	Self-concept changes
Diagnosis	Well
"It" is a serious illness	Seriously ill
Names of drugs and side effects	Seriously ill, but will get better
Purposes of treatment and procedures	Always ill, but will get better
Disease as a series of relapses and remissions minus death	Always ill, and will never get better
Disease as a series of relapses and remissions plus death	Dying

Death anxiety

Other researchers working with terminally ill children have found support for Bluebond-Langner's view (21) that many know of the

The Data: The Facts of Death

seriousness of their illness. Waechter (26) reported that anxiety scores of a group of fatally ill children were twice as high as those of other hospitalized children. She suggested that the fatal nature of a child's illness is communicated to the child by the changed way that persons react to him or her after the diagnosis is made. She stated that it is meaningless to argue about whether a child should be told that his or her illness is fatal. Rather, "the questions and concerns which are conscious to the child should be dealt with in such a way that the child does not feel further isolated and alienated from his parents and other meaningful adults" (26, p. 172). Her study reported a significant relationship between children's projective anxiety scores and the degree to which the child has been allowed to discuss his fears and prognosis. She concluded that accepting and permitting dying children to discuss any aspect of their illness may decrease feelings of isolation, alienation, and the sense that the illness is too horrible to discuss completely. Her final plea is that helping professionals not allow the existence of "a curtain of silence around the child's most intense fears" (p. 171).

In another supporting study (27) fatally ill children between the ages of 6 and 10 who were treated as outpatients were compared to a group of chronically but not fatally ill outpatient children. The dying children told stories that revealed significantly more preoccupation with threats to body function and body integrity as well as significantly higher general anxiety than the stories of the less severely ill children.

Most of the studies examining the attitudes of fatally ill children have included storytelling or the use of projective techniques in order to circumvent the child's initial reluctance to discuss death. Vernick and Karon (28) state that "the initiative for talking about death must come from the adult who is in possession of more emotional strength" (p. 395). These authors are representative of many health workers who feel that fatally ill children know more than they feel safe in saying. Yudkin (29) points out that children signal deep anxiety about the possibility of death in many unspoken ways: "Depression out of keeping with the effects of the illness itself; unspoken anger and resentment toward his doctors; resentment toward his parents of a child old enough not to be affected by mere separation in the hospital. These all suggest anxiety about death" (p. 39).

In children under 5 years of age, death awareness often takes the form of separation anxiety. Natterson and Knudson (30) define death awareness as the "individual's consciousness of the finiteness of his personal existence" (p. 457). Young children, totally dependent on their parents for physical and emotional comfort, often equate separation of parents to physical death. Such separation fear is not dependent upon strong ego and intellectual development. Separation anxiety is most commonly seen in children who have not yet attained language skills but may be the most prevalent fear up to 5 years of age (31). Terminally ill children between the ages of 6 and 10 often display mutilation fear. Children during this period are still working to develop a concept of death but they have well-developed body images. Threats to that image, whether from medical intervention or from the disease itself, cause severe anxiety. The third and final maturational step in death awareness is death anxiety per se. When death is certain, death anxiety must be regarded as a rational fear rather than as a neurotic symptom.

Viewpoints for working with terminally ill children

The medical profession in the past decade has begun to address itself to caring for the psychological health of dying children as well as their physical health. Many health practitioners (32-35) are advocating open honesty in dealing with dying children. Certainly, if it is true that a child may well understand that he is going to die long before he can say it (31), it would seem productive to open lines of communication as fully as possible so as to prevent loneliness, depression, and inward anger in the dying child.

However, the stance of total honesty is not shared by all health professionals. Evans and Edin (34) reflect the more widespread practice of attempting to shield the dying child from death and the fears involved in dying. They believe that this approach is advisable for the following reasons: a) the fear of death is real and cannot be dissipated by discussion; b) suppression and rejection cannot be used as mechanisms for dealing with fear if open discussion is encouraged; and c) children need the support of their parents during terminal illness and parents frequently cannot cope with their children's awareness of imminent death. Evans and Edin appear to favor a less direct method of dealing with children rather than encouraging them to meet the fears head on.

There is a midway position between total honesty and encouraging denial, which is reflected by Green (36). He encourages doctors to remain open to children's questions and to plan for time to talk with their parents. Basically three questions are generally asked by the child between the ages of 6 and 12. The first is: "Am I safe?" The second is: "Will there be a trusted person to keep me from feeling helpless, alone, and to overcome pain?" and the third is: "Will you make me feel alright?" (p. 496). Successfully dealing with these three questions may be enough to allow the child to explore his own potential for growth in the time remaining. Even young children need an atmosphere of psychological safety in which to express themselves. Green relates a story of a 4-year-old who, though sheltered from the prognosis of his terminal illness, nevertheless told the doctor that he was afraid to die. Allowing the child to express that fear is an important part of total care for the dying child as it results in direct comfort to the child and in freeing up of energy that the child can then use to fight the illness or to engage in intensive living in the time remaining.

Care giving and the dying child
In caring for a dying child the natural core conflict of compassion and nurturance for one in pain versus repulsion against impending shock of separation and loss is heightened (37). Somehow death of a child evokes depths of anger, guilt, and frustration that adult deaths do not raise. Perhaps the child's death awakens one of our deepest fears: death before fulfillment (36). Furthermore, patients' failure to get well often leads to feelings of frustration on the part of the health care workers, since one of their primary goals and needs is to restore health. Frustration may lead to feeling angry toward the dying one, which in turn leads to guilt feelings. Since one of the reactions to grief is to become angry at those who invoked the guilt feelings, "a self-sustaining emotional chain reaction" may ensue (37, p. 509). This reaction may be fully conscious, partially conscious, or unconscious to the care giver, but it affects treatment of the dying child, perhaps leading to overprotection and overindulgence or to isolating the child emotionally and caring only for his or her physical needs.

Helping parents
How much more pronounced these feelings must be in the caring parents of the dying child! One father, in a letter to a friend, expressed his anguish in the following way:

> As you are probably interested, Brian is quite bad. We wait each day for him to die. His discomfort and ours is now so great that I believe we now hope each day for him to die. But the human body does not die easily. We're like weeds in a garden. It's ironic, but waiting for a baby to die is quite similar to having a baby: you wait helplessly, you can't do anything to speed it up or slow it down, it's too late to change the course of things, you call home wondering what stage you're in, doctors and hospitals are involved, you wonder what you're going to do with the other kids when it happens, you have to call the grandparents, your friends are anxious, you want it to happen and you don't want it to happen, you're afraid and yet you desire relief from the long wait. So alike and yet so different. (38)

Friedman (39), in discussing care of the terminal child, points out that there is probably no other area in which "anticipatory guidance" is so helpful in promoting rapport between the physician and the patient's parents. Several authors (40, 41) have offered suggestions for working with parents of the dying child. At the base of all suggestions are the dual principles of open honesty and support. A summary of points to be covered with parents after the initial diagnosis is known includes the following:

1. Recognize the depth of shock and despair the parents must be feeling.
2. Explain the basis for the diagnosis and the nature and type of disease.
3. Explain the fatal outcome and type of therapy to be undertaken. Make every attempt to gain parental support both in the physical and emotional care of the child.
4. Assure parents that medical support will always be available in times of need.
5. Try to help parents anticipate problems involved in the initial telling of others and during the child's illness. Go over possible reactions of siblings (e.g., anger, jealousy, fear, guilt).
6. Discuss causes of the problem with emphasis on relieving possible parental guilt.
7. Emphasize any hope possible. If there is hope for remission, dwell on that. If there is not, discuss scientific research going on, if appropriate. If nothing is available, emphasize the support the child will get throughout the illness from the medical staff. While the good physician will discourage excessive optimism (42), parents must be allowed some hope, especially during the early stages of a disease.
8. Discuss anticipatory grief both as an attempt to educate parents about their own feelings in the coming days and to prepare them to recognize stages their child may be passing through.
9. Stress the importance of maintaining continuity in raising the child. It is essential that parents assume the child will live to adulthood and raise him or her consistent with their prior values and ideals. The alternative is that parents in their grief and guilt will indulge the child, who in turn will become confused and often test new limits until parents are forced to discipline him or her. This often leads to greater feelings of guilt both for the child and the parents. Children need the security of consistency in their parents' behavior.
10. Try to assess family's strengths and weaknesses and encourage building on the strengths. It is important to ask each parent how the other will accept the death, thus encouraging empathy and visualizing problems in advance.

11. Finally, there is evidence that a follow-up talk after the death of the child is often appreciated by the family in order to provide closure for the family and to permit them to express feelings after the death.

Parents are an integral part of total treatment of the dying child. Morrissey (43) showed that high-quality parent participation leads to better adjustment in hospitalized children. Not only can parents be of help to the ward staff throughout their child's illness, but also by doing this they work off some of their own anxiety, guilt, and grief before the child's death (30). In almost all cases of children who survived 4 months or more after the initial hospitalization, the caregiving parents (usually the mother) reacted with calm acceptance and some were even able to express relief at their child's death. There was a triphasic response among mothers whose children survived at least 4 months. In the first phase there was shock and denial often accompanied by anger, excessive weeping, and a tendency toward overprotection. In the second phase there was an acceptance of the situation coupled with the parent's willingness to expend energy in realistic ways that offered hope of saving the child. During this phase the psychological separation of the mother from the child often began. The third phase coincided with the terminal phase of the child's illness. Mothers directed their energy toward other sick children as well as their own. Sublimation was often evident in their desire to give physical and psychological comfort to parents of other terminally ill children. It is noteworthy that in cases where mothers reacted hysterically or clung to hope unrealistically, their child's death usually occurred less than 3 months after the fatal prognosis was given. It would appear that 4 months is the critical period for the working through of anticipatory grief (30).

CHILDREN AND GRIEF

There are at least three distinct types of grief reactions that are appropriate to examine in a discussion of children and death. The first is preparatory grief, the emotional reaction of a child becoming aware that he or she is dying. The second is bereavement as a child faces the fact of the death of a loved one. The third is anticipatory grief as the parents of the terminally ill child attempt to cope with the realization that their child is dying.

Preparatory Grief

Preparatory grief seems to be a universal aspect of the dying process if the person has adequate warning of his or her condition. It involves the following emotions: denial ("This cannot be happening to me");

anger ("How can you let this happen to me?"); resentment ("Why me? Why not you?"); fear ("What will dying be like? Will I suffer? Will I be alone? What will happen after I die?"). Sometimes guilt also is a part of preparatory grieving, as in the case of children who feel that their disease is punishment for earlier behavior. The idea of death as punishment as well as the child's assumption of parents' omnipotence is chillingly portrayed in Hailey's *Airport* (44) when the child in the crashing plane is heard to say "Mummy! Daddy! Do something! I don't want to die . . . Oh, Gentle Jesus, I've been good . . . Please, I don't want to . . ." (p. 142). If care givers can recognize the complexity of these interrelated emotions and encourage the child to verbalize them according to his needs, the child may be able to work through some of them, thus freeing up energy to be spent in more positive ways. Even if the child cannot work through the emotions, he or she will not feel so cut off and alone during the illness. Often, creation of a positive climate for communication with a dying child stems from the way the disease is presented to the child in the beginning. Foley and McCarthy (35) describe a typical physician's explanation to a leukemic child as follows:

> You have a serious blood disease, leukemia. Ten years ago, there was no treatment for leukemia and many people died. Now there are a number of drugs which can be used to treat leukemia. There are several types of leukemia and the type you have is the one for which there are the most drugs.
> Treatment to keep the leukemia cells away will last 3 years. You'll miss at least a month of school, the time needed to get the disease in control. The main problem right now is infection. If you stay free of infection you will be out of the hospital in about 5 days, if an infection occurs, you'll be hospitalized for at least 2 weeks." (pp. 1115-1116)

Allowing children to ask questions after such an explanation and making time to talk even when they have no questions creates the setting of mutual trust so necessary for growth during the final period of life.

Death as Loss

Death is above all else loss. The young child (aged 3 to 5) usually has experienced only temporary loss, as when a parent leaves for a short time. These children do not understand permanent loss but they know the discomfort of being without their caretakers. Bowlby's work (45) suggests that since preschool grieving and adult grieving are very similar in their intensity, the longing and mourning that are intrinsic to the grief process may be largely instinctive rather than cognitive. Spitz (46) described a syndrome that he called "hospitalism," in which the young child from infancy through preschool reacts to separation from his mother first with anger, then with a kind of quiet, resigned despair. Some of the children actually refused nutrition, turned their faces to the wall, and died. This was not learned behavior. Rather it was a natural response on the part of the child who had suffered an overwhelming loss.

Dying children suffer not only from physical separation from their home and parents but also from pain and loss of function as the disease progresses. Older children (6 years and beyond) begin to have the cognitive capacity to grieve over the loss of the future. They can understand that their tomorrows are numbered. It is difficult for the child as well as the adult to make sense of such an intrinsically unfair situation. However, many children have a need to discuss these feelings. If, when they first mention them, they are met with embarrassment, disapproval, or emotional outburst, the children learn that this is not a safe area for discussion. They must deny those feelings in themselves and retreat into the loneliness of their own loss without the support of those they love. Preparatory grief is real and it can become debilitating. Many health workers today agree that the final cruelty added to the already unbelievably cruel dying situation is to encourage these children to pretend they are *not* suffering the greatest loss of all. In dying the child loses everything: possessions, friends, parents, personality, and self. It is right to grieve then, if he or she realizes even a bit of this loss. Health workers can facilitate the grieving process not by silence but by being available to listen, empathize, and support the child in attempting to cope with the illness.

The Bereaved Child

Just as dying children profit from being able to communicate their feelings of grief, loss, anger, and bewilderment, so children who have lost a loved one profit from communication. The death of a parent can be particularly tragic for a child (47). Mingled with all the other negative emotions is a feeling of betrayal. It is almost as though the young child feels that if the parent had loved him or her enough, the parent would not have left. Bereavement is accompanied by physical symptoms including feelings of panic, insomnia, lack of appetite, nightmares, and others. Unresolved grief, especially in children, can lead to ongoing somatic illness as well as deep psychological problems. In one study (48) 41 percent of the population of 3216 depressed adult patients had lost a parent through death before age 15. In a later study (49) 27 percent of patients in a highly depressed group reported the loss of a parent before the age of 16 as compared with 12 percent of adults in a nondepressed group. Furthermore, an appreciably larger number of patients in the highly depressed group lost a parent before the age of 4. It appears that the loss of a parent is a traumatic psychological event for a child and that the earlier that loss occurs, the more potentially devastating the effect can be.

Parness (50), in working with preschool children who have sustained the loss of a parent or sibling, points out that "very young children have resiliency and fortitude in the face of some of the painful and unpredictable experiences life has to offer" (p. 7). However, she goes on to say that death and loss must be worked through with children. She points out that teachers and mental health workers can encourage healthy coping in children by beginning work with the assumption of loss as a universal human emotion. The adult must also be willing to share feelings of grief honestly and in a positive way that communicates faith in the children's "resources, resiliency, and power over their future lives—in spite of the unexpected" (50, p. 7).

Parental Anticipatory Mourning

The final type of grief to be considered in this chapter is parental anticipatory mourning. Futterman and Hoffman (51) defined it as "a set of processes that are directly related to the awareness of the impending loss, to its emotional impact and to the adaptive mechanisms whereby emotional attachment to the dying child is relinquished over time" (p. 130). It involves the following steps:

1. *Acknowledgment:* growing awareness of the approach of the inevitable moment of death accompanied by alternating feelings of hope and despair.
2. *Grieving:* the emotional reaction to loss that starts off as an intense undifferentiated response but gradually mellows in quality and the intensity becomes subdued.
3. *Reconciliation:* one step advanced from mere acceptance, it involves attempting to find meaning for the child's life and death and moving beyond that to a stage where the parents can be grateful for their blessings.
4. *Detachment:* this is the process whereby the parents gradually withdraw their emotional investment from the child.

One parent has described a very rapid detachment reaction in the following way: "As soon as the doctor told me that B. had neuroblastoma (a fatal form of the infantile cancer) I looked at him in the bed and felt like he was already dead. Later on, hope revived for a while with a change in medication, but as the disease progressed, I protected myself from too much feeling by viewing him as already lost to us" (38).

This process, so necessary to the mental health of the

parents, sometimes can result in the tragic condition referred to as the "living dead" (52). If parents complete the detachment process too soon or if the child has an unexpected late remission, the family may have completed the detachment process and the child may find himself dying alone or receiving an unwelcome greeting from a family that has already resolved his death.

5. The final stage in anticipatory grieving is called *memorialization*. It involves idealizing the child and results in the parents' developing a mental image of the child which will live beyond his death.

PROFESSIONALS AND THE FAMILY OF THE DYING CHILD

Professionals working with parents of terminally ill children can do little to lessen the sorrow that is the dominant emotion from the time the diagnosis is made until the child dies. They can, however, help the parents to anticipate and deal effectively with accompanying emotions such as anger, guilt, and anxiety.

Powerful feelings of anger often threaten to overcome parents of fatally ill children. The obvious unfairness of the situation coupled with their impotence to do anything to change it leads to feelings of frustration that can be destructive. The important question for helping professionals must be: How can the parents be helped to express their anger in positive ways? Sometimes, especially in cases of genetically transmitted diseases, one parent will turn his or her anger on the other one, thus adding to the stress of the situation (53). Other family members, including siblings and grandparents, may also have to bear the brunt of displaced parental anger. Other common recipients of anger include God, the doctors, nurses, and other caretakers, and even inanimate objects such as the hospital bed and machines used in treating the child. If parents turn their explosive anger inward, it can result in depression, suicidal urges, and even psychotic breakdown.

Parents need to be helped to find appropriate channels for venting anger. Such channels might include ongoing group or individual therapy, joining an organization to raise funds for medical research, forming parent support groups, and physical activities to discharge tension.

The second major emotion that parents should be helped to anticipate is guilt. Since the child's birth the parents' role has been that of protection and nurturance. When parents are not able to protect their child from a fatal disease, they may feel irrational guilt. In addition, if the parent–child relationship has been strained, the parents may feel guilt for the negative feelings they have had toward the child. As the illness proceeds, guilt may be compounded as the parents experience recurring wishes for the child to die. Guilt is also exacerbated as the parents become aware of hidden feelings of relief that it is not they who have the fatal illness. Folk tales and scattered heroic stories tell of parents who willingly give their lives for their children. However, it is the exceptional person who would willingly choose to exchange places with one who is suffering through a lingering death, even if that person is one's own child. Guilt can be tolerated better if the parent can be encouraged to express these feelings openly. The helping professional can then accept the parents' feelings of guilt and join them in attempting to understand those feelings as natural parts of most intimate relationships.

Commonly, parents of fatally ill children experience a third emotion, anxiety, which arises from at least five sources (53):

1. *Lack of mastery of the protective parental role*, resulting in the need to reorganize self-concept, self-esteem, and feelings of potency. Any major threat to the stable self-concept arouses anxiety.

2. *Inability to cope with the situation effectively*, resulting in feelings of an imminent breakdown. Whenever environmental stress threatens to overwhelm a person, the major emotion is that of anxiety. It is hard to envision a situation more stressful than having to watch your child suffer and die.

3. *Feelings of isolation and loneliness* caused by the parents' new identity as the parent of a doomed child. Parents have said that after finding out the diagnosis they did not want to see friends who had healthy children. They experienced feelings of resentment that the world continued to go on as though nothing had happened while their whole world was collapsing. In short, they felt that theirs was a unique position in the world, which no one else could understand; they were alone.

4. *Separation anxiety* as the parents anticipated the child's death and its psychological cost. Parents have reported feelings of loss so keen that it felt as though they had lost a limb or some other part of themselves.

5. *Death anxiety* as the realization of their own inevitable death hits home more acutely than ever before because of identification with the child.

Anxiety is best counteracted by action, and much of a parent's anxiety can be constructively channeled into caring for the dying child (54). However, parents need to know that sleeping and eating disturbances often accompany anxiety and that anxiety, like anger, can be displaced, resulting in irrational fears concerning their own health or the health of their other children.

The Data: The Facts of Death

Siblings and the Dying Child

Siblings of a dying child also suffer, often in lonely confusion, as they watch their brother or sister die and their parents grieve. Often parents react to grieving children in an overprotective and secretive manner. Green and Solnit (55) have coined the term "vulnerable child" syndrome to refer to such children. Studies done with adults who lost a sibling in childhood have indicated some support for this syndrome. As early as 1943, Rosenweig and Bray (56) found that patients suffering from schizophrenia had a higher than expected number of siblings who died in childhood. Perhaps the one axiom that will promote the best adjustment in the brothers and sisters of the dying child is quite simply, include them. They need to know some details about the illness if they are old enough; they need to visit the sibling in the hospital and be encouraged to express their thoughts, fears, and guilt feelings just as the parents are. Young children especially need to be reassured that no hostile thought of theirs is responsible for their brother or sister's illness, as magical thinking is still very much a part of their cognitive method of operation.

SUMMARY

Death is a natural event and it is normal for children to want to know about and understand it. Many parents have a need to protect their children from the harsh realities of life, but by doing so they contribute to misconceptions and increased anxieties.

The understanding of what death and dying means develops as the child grows older. The preschool child is believed to understand death as a temporary stage, a long sleep or departure. During the early school years, the child comes to recognize that death is final, but at the same time it is also personified, seen perhaps as a skeleton or a powerful monster who capriciously snatches people and kills them. Usually by the age of 9 the child understands that death is final but also natural and universal. A number of studies have shown that there is extreme variability with respect to the age at which a child reaches a mature understanding of death. These variations are due to cultural and subcultural factors, family background, personal encounters, and very likely a number of other as yet unidentified factors.

Children experience loss at a young age. Loss produces anxiety. As children become more aware of the reality of death, it is reasonable to assume that they become more anxious. Caring and patient adults can help alleviate a good deal of a child's death anxiety.

The terminally ill child usually becomes aware of his or her dying and experiences fears, but researchers find that these fears are often unspoken or couched in symbolic language. In the very young terminal child the fear of separation from parents is the predominant fear. Older children fear mutilation of their bodies.

Caring for the dying child is the most difficult task. The death of a child evokes depths of anger, guilt, frustration, and helplessness that are difficult to cope with. An important aspect of care of the terminal child is for physicians or other care givers to work with parents to help them cope with this impending loss and the feelings these bring about. When parents are an integral part of the total treatment of the dying child, it is found that parents are able to work off some of their own anxiety, guilt, and grief, while at the same time filling a need for closeness on the part of the dying child as well as assisting the staff.

There are at least three different identifiable types of grieving. First, preparatory grief or the emotional reaction of children who become aware of their own dying. Second is bereavement, as a child faces the loss of a loved one, and third is anticipatory grief, or the feeling that parents of the terminally ill child experience as they attempt to cope with the fact of their child's impending death.

REFERENCES

1. Crase, D. R., & Crase, D. Helping children understand death. *Young Children*, 1976 (November), 21–25.
2. Kastenbaum, R. J. *Death, society and human experience*. St. Louis: Mosby, 1977.
3. Maurer, A. Maturation of concepts of death. *British Journal of Medicine and Psychology*, 1966, *39*, 35–41.
4. Lerner, M. When, why, and where people die. In E. S. Shneidman (Ed.), *Death: Current prospectives*. Palo Alto: Mayfield Publishing, 1976, 138–162.
5. Sharapan, H. Mister Rogers' neighborhood: Dealing with death on a children's television series. *Death education: 1*, 1977, 131–136.
6. Piaget, J. *The origins of intelligence in children*. New York: Harcourt, Brace and World, 1932.
7. Nagy, M. The child's theories concerning death. *The Journal of Genetic Psychology*, 1948, *73*, 3–27.
8. Koocher, G. P. Talking with children about death. *American Journal of Orthopsychiatry*, 1974, *44*, 404–411.
9. Wilcox, S. G., & Sutton, M. *Understanding death and dying: An interdisciplinary approach*. Port Washington, NY: Alfred Publishing, 1977.
10. Wass, H. How children understand death. *Thanatos*, 1976, *1*, 4, 18–22.
11. Arnstein, F. I met death one clumsy day. *English Journal*, 1972, *61*, 6, 853–858.
12. Childers, P., & Wimmer, M. The concept of death in early childhood. *Child Development*, 1971, *42*, (4), 1299–1301.
13. Kastenbaum, R. Childhood: The kingdom where creatures die. *Journal of Clinical Child Psychology*, 1974, *3*, (2), 11–14.

14. Melear, J. D. Children's conceptions of death. *Journal of Genetic Psychology*, 1973, *123*, (2), 359-360.
15. Gartley, W., & Bernasconi, M. The concept of death in children. *The Journal of Genetic Psychology*, 1967, *110*, 71-85.
16. Hansen, Y. Development of the concept of death: Cognitive aspects. *Dissertation Abstracts International*, 1973, *34*, (2-3), 853.
17. Wass, H., & Scott, M. Middle school students' death concepts and concerns. *Middle School Journal*, 1978, *9*, (1), 10-12.
18. Tallmer, M., Formaneck, R., & Tallmer, J. Factors influencing children's concepts of death. *Journal of Clinical Child Psychology*, 1974, *3*, (2), 17-19.
19. Wahl, C. W. The fear of death. In H. Feifel (Ed.), *The meaning of death.* New York: McGraw-Hill, 1959.
20. Von Hug, H. H. The child's concept of death. *Psychoanalytic Quarterly*, 1965, *34*, 499-516.
21. Bluebond-Langner, M. Meanings of death to children. In H. Feifel (Ed.), *New meanings of death.* New York: McGraw-Hill, 1977.
22. Wass, H., & Shaak, J. Helping children understand death through literature. *Childhood Education*, 1976, (November-December), 80-85.
23. Grollman, E. A. (Ed.) *Explaining death to children.* Boston: Beacon Press, 1967.
24. McCandless, B. R. *Adolescents—Behavior and development.* Hinsdale, Ill.: Dryden Press, 1970.
25. Kastenbaum, R. Time and death in adolescence. In H. Feifel (Ed.), *The meaning of death.* New York: McGraw-Hill, 1959.
26. Waechter, E. H. Children's awareness of fatal illness. *American Journal of Nursing*, 1971, *71*, 1168-1172.
27. Spinetta, J. J., & Maloney, L. J. Death anxiety in the outpatient leukemic child. *Pediatrics*, 1975, *56*, (6), 1034-1037.
28. Vernick, J., & Karon, M. Who's afraid of death and leukemia ward? *American Journal of Diseases of Children*, 1965, *109*, 393-397.
29. Yudkin, S. Children and death. *The Lancet*, 1967, 37-41.
30. Natterson, J. M., & Knudson, A. G. Observations concerning fear of death in fatally ill children and their mothers. *Psychosomatic Medicine*, 1960, *23*, (6), 456-465.
31. Spinetta, J. J., Rigler, D., & Karon, M. Personal space as a measure of a dying child's sense of isolation. *Journal of Consulting and Clinical Psychology*, 1974, *42*, (6), 751-756.
32. Singher, L. J. The slowly dying child. *Clinical Pediatrics*, 1974, *13*, (19), 861-867.
33. Karon, M., & Vernick, J. An approach to the emotional support of fatally ill children. *Clinical Pediatrics*, 1968, 7, (5), 274-280.
34. Evans, A. E., & Edin, S. If a child must die. . . . *The New England Journal of Medicine*, 1968, *278*, (3), 138-142.
35. Foley, G. V., & McCarthy, A. M. The child with leukemia in a special hematology clinic. *American Journal of Nursing*, 1976, *76*, (7), 1115-1119.
36. Green, M. Care of the dying child. In *Care of the child with cancer.* Proceedings of a conference conducted by the Association for Ambulatory Pediatric Services in conjunction with the Children's Cancer Study Group A on November 17, 1966. Edited by A. B. Bergman, & C. J. A. Schultle, 1966, 492-497.
37. Rothenburg, M. B. Reactions of those who treat children with cancer. In Cancer. Proceedings of a conference conducted by the Association for Ambulatory Pediatric Services in conjunction with the Children's Cancer

Study Group A on November 17, 1966. Edited by A. B. Bergman, & C. J. A. Schultle, 1966.

38. Dorsel, T. Personal communication, 1976.
39. Friedman, S. B. Care of the family of the child with leukemia. Proceedings of a conference conducted by the Association for Ambulatory Pediatric Services in conjunction with the Children's Cancer Study Group A on November 17, 1966. Edited by A. B. Bergman, & C. J. A. Schultle, 1966.
40. Ablin, A. R., Binger, C. M., Stein, R. C., Kushner, J., Zoger, S., & Mikkelson, C. A conference with the family of a leukemic child. *American Journal of Disabled Child*, 1971, *122*, 362-364.
41. Friedman, S. B., Chodoff, P., Mason, J. W., & Hamburg, D. A. Behavioral observations on the parents anticipating the death of a child. *Pediatrics*, 1963, *33*, 610-625.
42. Lascari, A. D., & Stephbens, J. A. The reactions of families to childhood leukemia: An evaluation of a program of emotional management. *Clinical Pediatrics*, 1973, *12*, (4), 210-214.
43. Morrissey, J. R. Children's adaptation to fatal illness. *Social Work*, 1963, *8*, 81-88.
44. Hailey, A. *Airport*. New York: Doubleday, 1968.
45. Bowlby, J. *Attachment and loss. Vol. II: Separation anxiety and anger.* New York: Basic Books, 1960.
46. Spitz, R. A. Hospitalism: An inquiry into the genesis of psychiatric conditions in early childhood. In *The Psychoanalytic Study of the Child, Volume I.* New York: International University Press, 1945.
47. LeShan, E. *Learning to say goodbye: When a parent dies.* New York: Macmillan, 1976.
48. Brown, F. Depression and childhood bereavement. *Journal of Mental Science*, 1961, *107*, 754-777.
49. Beck, A. T., Sethi, B. B., & Tuthill, R. Childhood bereavement and adult depression. *Archives of General Psychiatry*, 1963, *9*, 129-136.
50. Parness, E. Effects of experiences with loss and death among pre-school children. *Children Today*, 1975, *4*, 2-7.
51. Futterman, E. H., & Hoffman, I. Transient school phobia in a leukemic child. *Journal of the American Academy of Child Psychiatry*, 1970, *9*, (3), 477-494.
52. Easson, W. M. *The dying child.* Springfield, Ill.: Thomas, 1970.
53. McCollum, A. T., & Schwartz, H. A. Social work and the mourning parent. *Social Work*, 1972, *17*, (1), 25-36.
54. Martinson, I. M. *Home care for the dying child: Professional and family perspectives.* New York: Appleton-Century-Crofts, 1976.
55. Green, M., & Solnit, A. J. Reactions to the threatened loss of a child. A vulnerable child syndrome. Paediatric management of the dying child. *Paediatrics*, 1964, *37*, 53-66.
56. Rosenweig, S., & Bray, D. Sibling death in anamnesis schizophrenic patients. *Archives of Neurology and Psychiatry*, 1943, *49*, (1), 71-92.

ANNOTATED BIBLIOGRAPHY

We must all face death, our own or that of a loved one or both. Preparation for facing death is not only possible but appears to be necessary in light of physical and emotional hazards that can arise from ineffectual handling of death and grief. Since children are aware of death from an early age, parents and helping professionals need only create a climate of tolerance toward the subject and direct children's natural curiosity. In addition, parents' and teachers' books can be excellent sources of information and comfort. The topic of death has concerned humankind from time immemorial, and for this reason death has been written about not only in the context of various theologies, philosophies, and recently the sciences, but also in the general literature, including children's books. There are, of course, the all-time favorites in which the subject of death is imbedded in the main theme but not specifically concentrated upon, such as the following books:

Armstrong, W. *Sounder.* New York: Harper & Row, 1969.
Buck, P. *The big wave.* New York: John Day, 1948.
Cleaver, V. *Where the lilies bloom.* Philadelphia: Lippincott, 1969.
Gipson, F. *Old yeller.* New York: Harper & Row, 1956.
Hunt, I. *Up a road slowly.* Chicago: Follett, 1966.
Lawson, R. *Rabbit hill.* New York: Viking Press, 1944.
O'Dell, S. *Island of the blue dolphins.* Cambridge: Riverside, 1960.
Rawlings, M. *The yearling.* New York: Scribners, 1939.
Salten, F. *Bambi.* New York: Grosset & Dunlap, 1929.
Speare, E. *The bronze bow.* New York: Houghton Mifflin, 1961.
Sperry, A. *Call it courage.* New York: Macmillan, 1940.
White, E. B. *Charlotte's web.* New York: Harper & Row, 1952.

Also, in recent years in particular, a number of gifted authors have chosen death as the main theme of their stories. These books can be informative as well as therapeutic not only for children but for adults as well. Wass and Shaak (22) have compiled a brief selected annotated bibliography of such books by age groups. That bibliography is reproduced below.

Preschool through Age 7

Brown, M. W. *The dead bird.* Glenview, Ill.: Scott, 1965. A group of children find a bird and feel its heart not beating. They have a funeral for it before returning to their play. Life continues.
Buck, P. *The beech tree.* New York: John Day, 1958. The metaphor of a beech tree is used by an elderly man to help explain his impending death.
De Paola, T. *Nana upstairs and nana downstairs.* New York: Putnam's, 1973. Tommy is heartbroken when his bedridden great-grandmother, with whom he has spent many happy hours, dies. He comes to realize that both the Nana that lived upstairs and the Nana that lived downstairs are "upstairs" in Heaven. The hope of life after death brings satisfaction.
Fassler, J. *My grandpa died today.* New York: Behavioral Publications, 1971. A description of Grandpa sleeping away to a peaceful death in his rocking chair is presented. Knowing his Grandpa was not afraid to die, David is able to continue "running and laughing and growing up with only fond memories of Grandpa." Written in simple story-line but with such factual detail that it could be classed as a nonfiction book.

Grollman, E. *Talking about death*. Boston: Beacon, 1970. The finality of death is presented uncompromisingly in simple direct language without softening the blow. Grollman's intent is to protect the child from destructive fantasy and a distorted view of death as well as guilt that often arises when a child is denied information.

Harris, A. *Why did he die?* Minneapolis: Lerner, 1965. A mother's heartfelt effort to speak to her child about death is portrayed. Death is likened to the leaves falling in autumn with new leaves to come in the spring, and to a worn-out motor. Emphasis is on the fact that, no matter what happens, memories of the deceased will never die.

Kantrowitz, M. *When Violet died*. New York: Parents', 1973. A story of the funeral preparations and ceremony for a dead bird, emphasizing the children's reactions, fascination and fun children get out of ceremonies, even funerals. The children are consoled in the continuity of life as shown through their pregnant cat. Life goes on!

Kuskin, K. *The bear who saw the spring*. New York: Harper & Row, 1961. A story of changing seasons and the changes living things go through as they are born, live, and die.

Miles, M. *Annie and the old one*. Boston: Little, Brown, 1971. Annie's Navajo grandmother says she will be ready to die after the new rug is woven. Annie tries to keep the rug from being finished, but her wise grandmother tells her that is wrong, that the "earth from which good things come is where all creatures finally go." Death is a part of life.

Stein, S. B. *About dying*. New York: Walker, 1974. A "shared" and open story about everyday dying, the kind every child meets early in his own life—the death of a pet and a grandparent. Actual photographs accompany the text of death, funeral, and mourning of Snow, a pet bird, and the Grandpa who had given him to the children. The accompanying adult text serves as a resource for handling the questions and discussion arising from the child's natural curiosity. The book explains reality, guiding a child toward the truth even if it is painful, and gives the children the inner strength to deal with things as they are. Preventive mental health!

Tresselt, A. *The dead tree*. New York: Parents', 1972. The life cycle of a tall oak tree is poetically described, showing that in nature nothing is ever wasted or completely dies.

Viorst, J. *The tenth good thing about Barney*. New York: Atheneum, 1971. The rituals of burial and mourning are observed for Barney, a pet cat. The child is led to understand that dying is as usual as living. Death is a part of life. Some readers may question whether young children will be able to comprehend the abstract idea of Barney's future role as fertilizer.

Warburg, S. S. *Growing time*. Boston: Houghton Mifflin, 1969. Jamie learns to accept the reality and meaning of the death of his dog with the help of his sympathetic and understanding family. He finds out that "death is not easy to bear." Something you love never dies; it lives in your heart.

Zolotow, C. *My grandson Lew*. New York: Harper & Row, 1974. The shared remembrances between a mother and a small child of a sadly missed grandfather keep both mother and son from being lonely. Memories keep the deceased alive in your mind.

Ages 8 through 11

Cleaver, V. *Grover*. Philadelphia: Lippincott, 1970. Ten-year-old Grover is forced to handle the changes that the suicide of his ailing mother brought about in his own groping ways, as his father is too grief-stricken to help. He finds out that there is no formula for overcoming grief other than time, friends, and maturity.

Cohen, B. *Thank you, Jackie Robinson.* New York: Lothrop, 1974. The story of the slowly deepening friendship between 12-year-old Sam Greene and the elderly black cook in Mrs. Greene's restaurant. After following their "main man"—Jackie Robinson—Sam is bereft when Davy suffers a fatal heart attack. Because their relationship seems solid, readers too will mourn Davy's death and sympathize with an honestly grieving Sam.

Lee, V. *The magic moth.* New York: Seabury, 1972. A very supportive family bravely copes with 10-year-old Maryanne's illness and death from a heart defect. A moth bursting from its cocoon as Maryanne dies and seed sprouting just after her funeral symbolize that "life never ends—it just changes."

Orgel, D. *Mulberry music.* New York: Harper & Row, 1971. The efforts of a young girl's parents to protect her from the knowledge of her adored grandmother's impending death result in turmoil, both within the girl and around her, when in her rash and rebellious actions the girl searches for her beloved grandmother. Keeping the truth of an impending death from a child can cause misunderstanding and fear.

Smith, D. B. *A taste of blackberries.* New York: Crowell, 1973. Jamie dies of a bee sting. His best friend is confronted with grief at the loss and comes to terms with a guilty feeling that somehow he might have saved Jamie. After a period of grief, life goes on.

Zim, H., & Bleeker, S. *Life and death.* New York: Morrow, 1970. This is an answer book for questions young people have about death. The physical facts, customs, and attitudes surrounding life and death are discussed. Death is described as a part of living.

Age 12 and Over

Corburn, J. *Anne and the sand dobbies.* New York: Seabury, 1967. Danny's father tries to answer questions about the death of Danny's sister.

Gunther, J. *Death be not proud.* New York: Harper & Row, 1949. The author writes of the courage of his 17-year-old son while facing death. The book is a celebration of life. It is more difficult for his parents than for Johnnie to accept his death.

Hunter, M. *A sound of chariots.* New York: Harper & Row, 1972. Bridie McShane's happy early childhood during World War I in Scotland is interrupted by the death of her beloved father whose favorite child she was. As she matures, her life is marred by her sorrow, leading her to morbid reflections on time and death, which she finally learns to deal with through her desire to write poetry.

Klein, S. *The final mystery.* New York: Doubleday, 1974. The meaning of death is explored and how people of different religions have coped with it. The on-going war against death is discussed.

Rhodin, E. *The good greenwood.* Philadelphia: Westminister, 1971. A tense and moving story of Mike who lost his good friend, Louie. After time and grief pass, Mike came to realize that Louie was really dead and was not going to reappear around the next corner. He came to remember Louie for the clown and dreamer that he was and for the good times they had together. He was not building another Louie as the grownups were, one that was almost perfect.

CHAPTER NINE

Death and the Funeral in Contemporary Society

ROBERT FULTON

THE DRAMATURGY OF DEATH

Burial of the dead is an ancient practice among humans. From paleo-lithic times to the present, human beings have responded to the death of their fellow humans with solemnity and ceremony. Not

Humans dispose of their dead with ritual. Fulton emphasizes the functions of funeral ceremonies not only for the surviving individual but also for the social system. Using a historical perspective, the eminent sociologist distinguishes between manifest functions such as disposal of the body and assistance to the bereaved, and latent functions such as reminders of economic and reciprocal social obligation, demonstration of family cohesion and affirmation of the kinship system, and affirmation of the belief in the immortality of human existence. Changing mortality factors, economy, family patterns, as well as changing religious, moral, and social values are reflected in recent criticism and attacks of traditional funeral practices and have, according to the author, led to the advocacy of inexpensive, immediate disposal with no public ceremony. Fulton stresses the role of the funeral as a rite of integration of survivors and of separation of the deceased. Many people disagree with his position on the importance of the traditional funeral and the viewing of the remains.

The Data: The Facts of Death

only has the event of death evoked a religious awe, but its threat to the survival of communal life has engendered fear, and its disruption of family life has aroused sorrow. The vehicle through which these reactions to death have been expressed has been the *funeral*. The funeral has traditionally served as a ceremony acknowledging a death, a religious rite, an occasion to reassure and reestablish the social group, a commemoration of a life, and a ritual of disposal.

The dramaturgical celebration of death and its significance for the individual and society has long attracted the interest of scholars. Van Gennep, Radcliffe-Brown, Malinowski, Durkheim, Evans-Pritchard, Hertz, Goody, Mandelbaum, and others (1) have emphasized the function of ritualized behavior in promoting and maintaining the emotional well-being of the individual as well as the social cohesion and structural integration of the group.

Malinowski (2), for instance, viewed ceremonies associated with death as a part of the institution of religion that bestowed upon individual men and women the gift of mental integrity, a function he believed was also fulfilled with regard to the whole group. He saw funerary customs as powerful counteractions to the centrifugal forces of fear, dismay, and demoralization. He believed they possessed the potential for providing the most powerful means of re-integrating a group's weakened solidarity and reestablishing its shaken morale.

Radcliffe-Brown (1) and Durkheim (3) emphasized the role of ritualized behavior in promoting and maintaining social forms. Durkheim, for example, spoke of ceremony as being a collective expression of sentiment and interpreted certain attitudes and rituals as "objectified sentiments." On the other hand, Van Gennep (1) assigned the greatest importance to the rituals associated with death because he found that funeral rites that had as their express purpose the incorporation of the deceased into the "world of the dead" were characteristically the most extensively elaborate.

More recently, Mandelbaum (1) has examined death rites in five widely separated cultures. His research has not only contributed new insights into our understanding of the role of ritual and ceremony before the fact of death but it also permits us to comprehend more clearly its place and meaning in our changing world. Mandelbaum concludes that funeral customs serve "manifest" as well as "latent" functions. Manifest functions refer to those activities associated with mortuary rites that are most readily apparent, such as the disposal of the body, assistance to the bereaved, the public acknowledgment of the death, and assertions of the continued viability of the group.

Less readily perceived or understood but nonetheless important, however, are the latent functions that funeral practices serve. Among such functions Mandelbaum cites the economic and reciprocal social obligations that are remembered and reinacted at the time of a death. In this way, he observes, the role taken by a participant in a funeral not only reflects his or her position in society but also reaffirms the social order. He notes that a second latent function is found in the obligations and restrictions placed upon all members of the deceased's family with regard to such things as dress, demeanor, food, and social intercourse. Such observances serve to identify as well as to demonstrate family cohesion. A third latent function of the funeral is the acknowledgment and affirmation of the extended kinship system. Members of the larger family console the survivors and frequently share in the expenses of the ceremony.

Mandelbaum argues that participation in the funeral ceremony, the procession, the partaking of food and other social exchanges, as well as the mourning and keening, all add to the sense of being a part of a larger social whole, just as the order of precedence in the conduct of the ceremony reminds one that there is structure and order in the social system. Finally, he regards the funeral as a "rite of passage." It not only marks the completion of a life and separation of the dead from the world, but it also reaffirms the belief in the immortal character of human existence.

CEREMONY:
FUNCTIONAL AND DYSFUNCTIONAL

The question for us, however, is whether or not the funeral (as described by Mandelbaum and others and based on non-Western or preindustrial societies, as their analyses have been) is relevant for modern society. Is the funeral a functional ceremony today? Does it meet the needs of our citizens? These are not new questions, yet they are still being asked. Indeed, they still need to be asked— perhaps now more than at any time in our history.

Ritual can be dysfunctional. Geertz (4), for example, cites the case of a funeral in Java in which the insistence on traditional practices served to disrupt rather than restore the sense of community. He reports the traditional rites that were suited to an agricultural village folk milieu served to be inappropriate and caused much dissension and confusion among villagers transplanted to town life, where the economic, social, and political orientations were different from those of the village.

Mandelbaum (1) too gives us the example of the Kota, for whom the traditional funeral ceremony actually aggravates the sorrow of the mourner and serves to provoke social discord. At one stage of the Kota funeral, at what is termed the "dry funeral," there is a juncture when all Kotas present at the ceremony come forward one by one to give a parting bow of respect to the relics of the deceased. This

The Data: The Facts of Death

becomes a time of great tension and conflict. Mandelbaum (1) describes the situation as follows:

> Around this gesture of social unity, violent quarrels often rage. When kinsmen of a deceased Kota are fervent supporters of one of the two opposing factions in Kota society, they may try to prevent a person of the other faction from making this gesture of respect and solidarity. This is tantamount to declaring that those of the other faction are not Kotas at all—a declaration which neither side will quietly accept. Thus a ritual action which symbolized concord has frequently triggered a good deal of discord. Yet among the Kotas, as in other societies, neutral people try to bring about a compromise— the ceremony is somehow completed with as much show of social unity as can be managed—especially for funerals of the great men of the tribe. (p. 213)

In this instance, however, Kota mourning ceremonies appear to be "rituals of rebellion" rather than an illustration of ritually inspired discord and disunity per se (5).

There is still a further point to consider: the level of social organization under analysis. We have come to learn that what may be operative and functional at one level of social life (for example, the family or community) may not be functional for or congruent with the aims and purposes of the broader social system.

Let me illustrate. In 1969 the Minister of Defense for Kenya, Tom Mboya, was assassinated. His death resulted in the subsequent deaths of more than a dozen fellow citizens among the Luo and Kikuyu tribes of that nation and the destruction of hundreds of thousands of dollars worth of property. The English journal *The Economist* reported at the time that never in the history of Nairobi had there been such disturbance and loss of life as that which followed the memorial service that was held in Mr. Mboya's honor in Nairobi.[1]

In Kenya it is a family obligation to see that the deceased is returned to his or her village and buried on the father's land with only members of the tribal community in attendance. Mr. Mboya was killed by a member of the Kikuyu tribe. The Kikuyu were excluded from taking part in his funeral not only by virtue of the fact that they had been held responsible for his death, but also because it is traditional for the tribes to exclude all but their own. Therefore, there is the possibility that when Jomo Kenyatta, the present prime minister of Kenya, dies, there will be civil strife in Kenya—

---

[1] *The Economist*, in both the July 12 and August 9th issues (1969), also expressed concern over the assassination of Mr. Mboya by a Kikuyu member from the Kenya African National Union youth movement. It reported that the rioting that followed the Requiem Mass that was said for Mr. Mboya was the worst that Nairobi had ever seen. *The Economist* observed that his death provoked a return to tribal politics as the Luo, convinced that the murder was a political ploy, showed signs of forming a united tribal front against Kikuyu domination of the government and its agencies. In return, it was reported that President Kenyatta moved to reinforce old tribal alliances with the Kalenjin and Kamba in order to forestall any attempt to isolate the Kikuyu.

strife of such magnitude that the national aspirations of Kenya may well be threatened. Mr. Kenyatta is a Kikuyu. It is highly possible that his mourners will exclude the Luo (who represent the second strongest political party as well as the second largest tribal group in Kenya) from participation in the ceremonies. Indeed they may hold the Luo responsible for the death itself. If the national state of Kenya survives his death, it will only be because the Kikuyu and the Luo recognize that the state must take precedence over tribal ambitions and traditions if it is to endure.[2]

By way of contrast, let me recall to mind our own society's experience with death in recent years. The sudden and unexpected deaths by assassination of President John F. Kennedy, Senator Robert Kennedy, and Dr. Martin Luther King came as successive shocks to the American body politic and were sorely felt.

To review the events following the assassination of President Kennedy is to recall a period of social and political turmoil unparalleled in this country since the assassination of President Lincoln a century earlier. At that time the country bordered on panic, as rumors of conspiracy and intrigue swept through Washington and across the nation. The attempted assassination of other members of Lincoln's cabinet gave substance to those fears and placed Washington on a war emergency alert.

A sequel to that episode in our history was reenacted in the hours and days following President Kennedy's death. At the same time that the nation was plunged into grief and mourned his death, it was alive to reports and rumors of conspiracies both from the political left and right. The murder of Lee Harvey Oswald, President Kennedy's alleged assassin, by Jack Ruby before a nationwide television audience only aggravated the anxiety and compounded the fears of the entire nation as it added to the sense of tragedy.

The state funeral that was held for President Kennedy was the most widely viewed ceremony in history. It is estimated that one-half billion people throughout the world watched the funeral and its proceedings on television (6). In attendance were, in addition to President Kennedy's immediate family, personal friends, and colleagues, dignitaries from all branches of the government, representatives from the various political parties, and the heads of state or their personal representatives of all nonbelligerent countries.

A montage of images of that funeral continues to have the power to stir the emotions and to remind us again of that tragic time: Mrs. Jacqueline Kennedy kneeling at the side of her husband's flag-draped

---

[2] Since this writing, Prime Minister Kenyatta has died. His funeral took place amid great mourning, but without incident. This was mainly due to the fact that precautions were taken to make his funeral as public and as symbolic of the nation as possible. The British government helped to arrange the funeral and provided the use of Winston Churchill's funeral carriage in order to emphasize the international significance of the event.

casket with her daughter Caroline; John, the President's son, standing in brave salute; the solemn procession down Pennsylvania Avenue; the heavy casket borne gracefully and respectfully by both black and white members of the Armed Services; a spirited black horse following a casket-laden caisson, pulled by six matched greys. President Kennedy's funeral served to declare not only that he was dead but also that order had been restored to the country and that the nation was secure in its relations with most other nations of the world.

The state funeral of President Kennedy was followed in quick succession by the funeral of his brother, Senator Robert Kennedy, and that of Dr. Martin Luther King. As before, their deaths threatened social and political disruption throughout the nation. As one of the leading spokesmen for the peaceful integration of white and black America, Dr. King's sudden and violent death, particularly, was little short of cataclysmic in its import. It precipitated racial disturbances across the country resulting in the deaths of more than a score of citizens, both black and white, as well as the destruction of millions of dollars worth of property (7).

Dr. King's death removed the strongest voice of moderation from our racially antagonistic society. Despite this fact, however, and the fact that his assassin was a white man, his funeral included many prominent political and social leaders from the white community. In effect, his funeral announced to the nation as well as to the world that, regardless of his death and the friction between the black and white races in America, the followers of Dr. King were determined to remain true to his philosophy of nonviolence and to his dream of a nation free from bigotry.

Death evokes powerful emotions within us that need to be vented or calmed. This was made evident with the assassinations of President Kennedy, his brother Robert, and Dr. King. The country grieved their deaths; the nation mourned openly not only as solitary citizens but also together as a society. As a society it observed public as well as private expressions of grief; it participated in three funerals to which the whole world paid heed.

Public evidence of the private reactions to President Kennedy's death is available. At least 39 different surveys (8) were conducted at varying intervals following his assassination. While the studies were manifestly different in design and intent, certain common reactions were discernible. These reactions are best shown by the study of the National Opinion Research Center in Chicago (9) which polled a representative national sample of 1400 adults within a week of the assassination. The study showed the following results:

1. Preoccupation with the death was almost total.
2. Nine out of ten people reported experiencing one or more physical symptoms such as headache, upset stomach, tiredness, dizziness, or loss of appetite.

3. Two-thirds of the respondents felt very nervous and tense during the 4 days.
4. A majority of the respondents confessed to feeling dazed and numb.
5. Most people—men and women—cried at some period during this time.
6. The event was compared most often to the death of a parent or close friend or relative.
7. There was a tendency to react to the assassination in terms of personal grief and loss rather than in terms of political or ideological concern or anxiety about the future.

As the researchers described it, reactions of the American people during the 4 days after the death of President Kennedy appeared to follow a well-defined pattern of grief familiar to medical practice. The funeral of the President channeled that grief and gave it poignant expression.

Moreover, the relatively peaceful association of white and black in this country is to some extent made possible today by virtue of the fact that in his funeral Dr. King's survivors saw an opportunity to bind the wound that his death had caused to the body politic. The funerals of President Kennedy, Senator Kennedy, and Dr. King were functional in that they served the formal structural needs of our society and, at the same time, provided a vehicle for the utterance of private grief.

A funeral, then, is a functional or a dysfunctional set of activities depending upon place and circumstance. I am tempted to predict that in the case of Kenya, the funeral of President Kenyatta has the potential to do the state profound injury, given Kikuyu philosophy and tribal tradition. But for the United States, I would contend that the recent national funerals have been functional with respect to the social order.

But what of the "average" American funeral, the funeral of the ordinary man or woman? Is it also beneficial? The question is more than an academic one in view of the fact that in the past few years criticism of funeral practices and funeral directors has become increasingly strident and extensive. The funeral has been charged with being pagan in origin and ostentatious in practice, while the funeral director has been characterized as one who exploits the dead at the expense of the living (10).

FUNERAL PRACTICES AND ATTITUDES

Over the past 15 years I have conducted three nationwide surveys (11–13) dealing with the issues surrounding mortality in America. Let me highlight the major findings from these studies.

The first study (11), conducted in 1959, surveyed the attitudes of the clergy toward funerals and funeral directors in the United States. It showed that clerical criticism of funeral directors and funeral practices was both widespread and intensive. Among the different reasons the clergy gave for their negative appraisal, two stand out. First, funeral directors were charged with dramatizing the presence of the body while ignoring spiritual matters, and, second, they were charged with taking undue advantage of the bereaved. A third factor should be noted that was left unstated but was nevertheless implicit in the clergy's criticism: Funeral directors make their services available to people of different faiths. By such a relative attitude toward the religious aspects of funeral rites, funeral directors appear to leave themselves open to the charge of paganism.

Specifically the study showed that the Protestant clergy, more so than their Catholic colleagues, were troubled by contemporary funeral rites and practices and by the emerging role of the funeral director in connection with these rites and practices. Inasmuch as the religious service for Protestants is most often held in the "chapel" of the funeral home, the relative change of function of the Protestant clergyman vis-à-vis the funeral director appears to be troublesome for many clerics, both professionally and personally.

These factors, as well as others, have led members of the clergy to charge the contemporary funeral with paganism and to view the expense associated with it as conspicuous waste. Such concern has also led to active promotion of what is called the "simplified" funeral, the advocacy of cremation, and the recommendation that monies normally spent on funerals be diverted to scientific research and public charities.

The second study (12), conducted in 1962, surveyed the attitudes of the American public toward death, funerals, and funeral directors. Included in the study was a cross-section of those persons who were members of the funeral reform or memorial society movement. As with the clergy study, the survey showed that negative and critical attitudes toward contemporary funeral rites and practices are held by some segments of the public. However, the survey showed that these attitudes are not shared equally by the public, but rather that criticism of the contemporary funeral varies by geographical region as well as by religious affiliation, education, occupation, and income.

It was found that a majority of the American public surveyed was favorably disposed toward present-day funeral practices and the funeral director. The majority of respondents also viewed the funeral as providing a meaningful emotional experience for survivors. Moreover, more than half of the respondents viewed the funeral director as a professional person or as one who combined a professional service with a business function.

Members of the memorial societies, however, expressed views strongly divergent from those of the general public. They believed the funeral director was primarily a businessman offering the public no professional service whatsoever. The majority of them expressed an unfavorable opinion of funeral costs, and funeral directors. In addition, a majority of these respondents did not believe that the purposes of the funeral were in fact served by the funeral ceremony. Only 25 percent of the memorial society respondents believed that the funeral served the emotional needs of the family in any way, while 16 percent perceived the traditional funeral as performing no useful function at all. Consistent with these findings the study further showed that the memorial society members were the strongest advocates for cremation, for the donation of the body to medical programs or scientific research, and for recommending that the ritual and ceremony of the funeral be simplified or avoided.

Of interest here is the social profile of the average memorial group. The study showed that the members of a memorial society group reported educational attainments significantly higher than nongroup members as well as the highest percentage of professional occupations and an average annual income twice that of the typical U.S. family. On the other hand, they reported the lowest percentage of traditional religious affiliation.

As a whole the study showed that favorable responses toward funerals and funeral directors varied with religious affiliation. Religious affiliation or its absence was the pivotal factor around which the various attitudes expressed in the study revolved. Simply stated, Catholics most often reported being favorably disposed toward the funeral and the funeral director, followed by Protestants, Jews, nonaffiliated respondents, and Unitarians. The order was reversed with respect to critical attitudes. The Unitarians were the most critical, followed by Jews, nonaffiliated, Protestants, and finally Catholics. Regionally, the most favorable attitudes toward the funeral and the funeral director were expressed by residents from central sections of the country, while the least favorable views were expressed by respondents residing along the Atlantic and Pacific coasts.

In the third study (13), it was sought to determine the character of contemporary funeral practices in the United States. A questionnaire was prepared and mailed to the entire 1967 membership of the National Funeral Directors Association as well as to the membership of the Jewish Funeral Directors Association. In all, 14,144 questionnaires were mailed. One out of every four (24.6 percent) of the funeral directors polled returned their questionnaires for a total of 3474 replies.

In many important aspects, the results of the third study complimented the findings of the two previous studies. The 1967 study, however, went beyond mere confirmation. It showed that according to funeral directors the funeral in contemporary America is a different thing to different people: While what might be called the "traditional" funeral (a public service with a public viewing and a public committal service) is almost totally characteristic of the great central portion of the United States and the predominant mode of behavior everywhere else, it is nevertheless subject to modification and change. New rites and practices for coping with death and for disposing of the dead are emerging. Emergent variability is a fact in funeral dramaturgy as it is a fact throughout all of society. Change is at work not only in the mode of disposal of the dead but in every sphere of funeralization as well—from the type of funeral establishment constructed, to the emotional climate in which the funeral is conducted, to the "meaning" imputed to death.

In order to grasp the significance and implications of the findings of the third study, as well as the two that preceded it, they must be placed within the larger context of U.S. culture. A funeral does not take place in a vacuum. Rather these three studies can be understood to mirror, albeit in a small way, what society as a whole has been experiencing by way of shift in its beliefs and values as they relate to death and dying since at least the time of World War I.

Cultural Baseline

First let us be reminded of a cultural baseline, as it were. According to religious doctrine we are creatures of God and have been formed in His image. Due to our fall from grace, however, we are born in sin and therefore spiritually flawed. Death is the consequence of that sin and is a necessary experience for each one of us if we are to be restored to our prior state of perfection. In our society the funeral has been the instrument of such a theology and its ritual has dramatized such beliefs for the living at the same time that it effected a liturgy for the dead.

However, this sacerdotal image of humans is not shared by everyone in the U.S. today. Rather, the idea being entertained by a growing number of persons is that death is not the wages of sin nor need it be as certain as taxes. And also it is no longer an unquestioned belief that life is the gift of God. The Papal encyclical on birth control in 1968, *humanae vitae*, created a storm of continuing debate in the U.S. that has had almost no precedent (14). Protests, petitions, and pronouncements by clergy and laity of all religious faiths strongly questioned or opposed the papal edict. Moreover, the same year saw the first successful heart transplant in the United States, the continued progress toward kidney and other organ transplants, and increased speculation regarding the unlimited possibilities being opened by medical science technology. The religious, moral, and legal arguments surrounding such operations and their future implications are only now beginning to take definite form. One thing appears increasingly clear: humankind persists in its refusal to accept the inevitability of death, and, with death as well as with birth, seeks to be the final judge.

Demographic Factors

A second point to consider is the demographic one. This year approximately 1 percent of the U.S. population, or almost 2 million persons, will die (15). Of these deaths, 67 percent will occur among persons 65 years of age or older. In excess of 70 percent of these deaths will take place outside the home, either in hospitals or in a nursing home.[3] The number of persons over the age of 65 is now over 23 million, or 10 percent of the population (16). In contrast, 54 million (25 percent of the population) are children under 15 years of age (16). However, children account for only 5 percent of all deaths (15). This is a dramatic reversal in mortality statistics as compared to the 1920s when the mortality rate was highest for children (17). As a matter of fact, contemporary U.S. youths could be called the first "death-free" generation in the history of the world. That is, statistically, a family in the United States can expect not to have a death occur among its immediate members for 20 years, or one generation. The implications of these statistics cannot be overlooked. Our conception of death as well as our view of what constitutes an appropriate response to it are colored by these basic demographic facts.

Inflationary Economy

A third factor that must be considered among the myriad of social and cultural changes that could be mentioned is the seemingly relentless inflationary character of the U.S. economy. The inflationary spiral seriously threatens the private household economies of literally millions of U.S. families. Over 10 million households today are headed by a widow who, in the majority of cases, lives on a fixed income consisting of Social Security or other retirement benefits (18). Regardless of the provisions made beforehand, death expenses are a source of anxiety and concern to them. Moreover, such concern is deepened by a fourth factor: the changing character of the U.S. family.

[3] This figure is an extrapolation of data gathered from indirect and diverse sources. See the following for the most direct reference to place of death in the United States: "Vital Statistics of the United States, 1958," Vol. 2, Public Health Service, Washington, D.C.: U.S. Government Printing Office, 1960, Table 67.

The Data: The Facts of Death

Changing Family

Over the past several generations the U.S. family has been transformed from a large, extended family into a small, nuclear group.
It is more mobile, socially as well as geographically, than ever
before. It is child oriented rather than adult oriented; it is more
individualized than integrated. The young, contemporary family is
less a part of a rural community or a neighborhood-enclosed group
than before, while increasingly it tends toward being singular in an
anonymous urban environment. As it has been pointed out, death
is increasingly an experience of the aged, most of whom are retired
from work, free of parental obligations, and frequently outside of
or absent from the main current of family life. The extension of
medical service and the advances in medical science research,
moreover, make possible not only the prolonging of life of the
elderly but often cause those hospitalized to be further separated
from their families. Familial and friendship commitments are
decreased by such separations, and emotional and societal bonds
are often loosened by time and distance. Not the least consequence
of this development is the fact that great numbers of the elderly
must not only live alone but, as a recent survey of ours shows,
they die alone as well (19). Therefore, the disengagement of the
aged from society prior to their deaths means that their dying has
little effect on the round of life.

As we have noted, the death of a leader such as President
Kennedy, Senator Kennedy, or Dr. King can seriously disrupt the
functioning of modern society. The vacuum they left in the social
and political life of the United States has been sorely felt. For the
common man or woman and for the average family, it is the death
of someone either in the middle productive years of life or
someone young and unfulfilled that will have a comparable effect
upon the social or familial group. Because the elderly are less
relevant to the functioning of our modern secular society, their
deaths do not compel such attention. Like the late General
MacArthur's "old soldier," they do not die but seemingly "fade
away."

Change in Values

Changing attitudes toward the funeral as a meaningful rite for the
dead have led to criticism and attacks on it in recent years. In a
society where only half the population is church-affiliated and the
social and spacial mobility of its citizens is one of its more
remarkable characteristics, the religious, emotional, and economic
obligations that a funeral has traditionally imposed on a family are

often seen today as inappropriate. Increasingly, the funeral is for that member of the family who is least functionally relevant to it. He or she has been, as I have suggested, often physically and socially removed from the family, perhaps by a long confinement. In our society, which has a strong bent toward the youth generation as well as a need to economize, in an era of inflation in expenses of the funeral are perceived as high.

Advocacy of memorial services with the body absent and cremation are attempts within the context of emerging contemporary values to resolve the different problems associated with the traditional disposal of the dead.

What of the funeral, then, in the face of these trends and developments? Over 60,000 years ago, as recent archeological discoveries at Shanidar, Iraq show, people buried their dead with ceremony (20). They did so in a particular way and presumably for very specific ideological or religious reasons, given the manner of burial recorded. We must ask ourselves if the practices that pre-Neanderthal man saw fit to observe following a death some 600 centuries ago are still relevant and functional for contemporary humans.

While entombment is not universal, it has been practiced in many different societies far back into archeological time and has served to express the idea of immortality through the symbolism of the funeral as a rite of incorporation. The concept of immortality implies another world, a world in which the "dead" live. As Van Gennep (1) observed, this corollary belief has meant that historically, a primary focus of the funeral has been the physical incorporation of the dead with all their attributes, possessions, and effects into the next world.

Today such beliefs and practices are contrary to the religious, philosophical, and ideological commitment of many people in American society. They do not believe in a "world of the dead," and they do not believe that it is necessary or felicitous to consume the resources of the living for the doubtful benefit it may have for the dead. For some, the most desirable procedure is also the simplest—one that involves as little material expense as possible and few people in attendance at the funeral. For a growing number of persons this means immediate disposition of the body with no public ceremony (13).

But as we have noted, anthropologists have recognized that there are important aspects of the funeral other than the symbolic expression of a theological belief in immortality or the dramaturgical incorporation of the dead into an afterlife. I think it is important for us to consider what these aspects are and what their place and function may be for our contemporary world.

THE FUNERAL AS A RITE
OF INTEGRATION AND SEPARATION

Besides being a rite of incorporation (i.e., burial or entombment for reasons of resurrection or rebirth), the funeral is a rite of separation and integration. The funerals of President Kennedy, Dr. King, and Senator Kennedy, as well as that of Mr. Mboya, were rites of integration. The dramaturgy of those funerals declared that the world goes on; that we, the survivors, still live; that the social order prevails; and that we continue to have faith in the justice and mercy of God. But the funeral is a drama that tells us that we have lost someone through death. As such, it also focuses attention on the survivors and to the degree that it does so is a rite of separation as well.

Psychologically, the loss of a significant other person by death is a crisis situation. Medical and behavioral science experts have taught us in recent years that such loss evokes powerful emotions that need to be given proper expression (21). Erich Lindemann, Elisabeth Kübler-Ross, Avery Weismann, and other investigators (22) inform us, however, that the acceptance of separation or permanent loss is an exceedingly difficult task to achieve. Many persons never do recover from permanent loss or ever wholly accept, or indeed ever admit to, the death of a loved one. How do we get people to accept permanent loss? is the question.

Two leading British psychiatrists, John Bowlby and C. Murray Parkes (23), have pointed out that a major element in acute grief is the denial that the death or the separation has occurred. As they describe it:

> There is a restless searching for the lost person, a constant wandering from room to room as if seeking for the loved individual, often calling his or her name. The necessary tasks and rituals, whether they are religious or not, which surround death serve, however, to bring home gradually to the bereaved person the reality of the loss they have sustained and the knowledge that life will never be quite the same again. Drawing the blinds, viewing the body, attending the funeral service, lowering the coffin into the grave all serve to emphasize the finality and the absoluteness of death, and make denial more difficult.

When it is responsive to the psychological needs of the survivors, the ritual of the funeral can aid in the ventilation of profound emotions and help facilitate the normal dissolution of grief. According to a number of psychologists, viewing the dead potentially allows this dissolution to take place.

It is true, as critics charge, that there are elements of disguise in the preparation of the body for the funeral. But such disguise is no more the basis of the funeral ceremony than the use of cosmetics or a veil is the basis for the wedding. I am led to propose that slight disguise of death is functional because it helps to move the grieving survivors along from a shocked denial of the death to a final acceptance of it.

The events leading up to the actual interment or cremation of the body are those in which the survivors are invited to gather together, acknowledge the death, share in the grief, participate in the mourning rites, and witness the final disposition of the body. The funeral must be understood in terms of this dramaturgical denouement: the deceased has been removed forever from the living community.

Stigma and Callousness

The recent work of Geoffrey Gorer (24) shows that the problems of the recently bereaved are not limited to the United States. Gorer indicates that there is the same denial of death and stigmatization of the bereaved in Great Britain as in America. He hypothesizes a link between this stigmatization and public callousness. It is his contention that the present preoccupation with death and cruelty, coupled as it is with an excessive squeamishness concerning it, displays the modern irrational attitude toward this inevitable event. Gorer argues that such an attitude toward death makes it something obscene or pornographic and ultimately invites the maladaptive and neurotic behavior observed in his study.

In this regard it is my belief that the observation he made several years ago regarding the denigration of grief and mourning in Great Britain now finds its counterpart emerging in this country. Such movies as *Cat Ballou* and *The Loved One*, which commanded some attention several years ago, were mild precursors of poor taste compared to the gross assault on our sensibilities that is presented by some mass media "entertainments" today.

Is the Funeral Beneficial?

The question before us still is: If the funeral is a rite of integration and separation, is it beneficial? The answer to that question is a contingent one. Ultimately it is one that depends upon the individual survivor and the circumstances surrounding a death. For some survivors the loss of an elderly relative is an occasion for the barest acknowledgment of the death and the most expeditious disposal of the body. In such an instance, of what could be described as a "low grief" death, loss can be slight and grief muted. The sudden unexpected death of a child or of a young husband on the other hand may be perceived as premature and unjust and/or denied or resented by the survivors. Such a death could be termed a "high grief" loss.

The social and emotional needs of family, friends, and community in such instances are infinitely greater and the potential problems of the survivors more extensive than in the case of what has been termed a "low grief" loss. On the other hand, "no grief" may be felt by a relative who is privately relieved or pleased at the death while "improper grief" may be experienced by a person who is not allowed to publicly mourn. Care has to be taken, therefore, not to define too narrowly what funeral rites or behaviors are appropriate for the bereaved. Insensitivity and poor social management of the intensity or absence of grief and the social expectations of the bereaved can only intensify their difficulties. For instance, when members of the clergy perceive the funeral as a rite of passage only and describe death as a joyful spiritual victory, they ignore the fact that death is also separation (of, say, a husband from a wife or a father from a daughter) and, as with any irrevocable separation, the survivors may experience a profound sense of loss.

Mourning is the intersection of grief (a psychological drama) and bereavement (a social drama), where loss through death may find harmonious expression. The proper orchestration of this human event can permit social therapy to take place or at least begin so that private grief may be expressed and the process of mourning facilitated.

The funeral provides a setting in which private sorrow as well as public loss can both be expressed and shared. It is a ceremony that can facilitate the mourner's expression of grief. It is Fulcomer's (25) conclusion, based on his case studies of 72 bereaved subjects, that there is a definite indication that the bereaved person's responses are positively affected if he or she realizes or imagines that other persons are also mourning. In other words, "Sorrows tend to be diminished by the knowledge that another sorrows with us" (26). Likewise it is the conclusion of Glick, Weiss, and Parkes (27), following their recent 4-year case analysis of 68 bereaved persons, that even though the survivor is frequently mixed in his or her feelings the tasks and activities associated with the ceremonies of leave taking meet profound human needs. The funeral not only provides an orderly and proper way of dealing with and disposing of the body but it also acknowledges that a life has been lived. It was their observation, however, that many survivors found it difficult to view the corpse. But as they and Elisabeth Kübler-Ross (28) and others have observed, viewing is a way for many to confront the death of their loved one. Glick et al. (27) quote one widow who remarked, "I didn't believe he was dead until I saw him in the casket" (p. 110).

Loss through death can be a crisis situation. Studies show, however, that survivors display a wide range of responses and demonstrate varying capacities to adjust to a death. Prolonged maladjustment, however, as characterized by mental and physical ailments as well as the increased consumption of alcohol and sedatives, is all too common. Preliminary findings from a study at the University of Minnesota (19) on the other hand, as well as the results from the studies of Mole (29) and Glick et al. (27), show that apart from family and friends relatively few health care persons are in contact with a survivor following a death. Yet the evidence strongly suggests that many persons are in need of much more than the good will and concern of their closest family members or friends. The Minnesota study shows, for example, that only 15 percent of the survivors out of a sample of 568 widows and widowers reported professional health care contact or support following the death of the spouse.

The funeral, as a rite of separation and integration, requires of funeral directors that they too be cognizant of and sensitive to the social and emotional needs of the families that they serve. They must believe (as must the survivors) that the funerals they conduct and in which they participate are something more than commercial transactions.

In this connection it is important to note that in addition to this author's own previously cited work, both the study by Binger (30) and his colleagues at Langley-Porter Institute and the Harvard Bereavement Study conducted by Glick, Weiss, and Parkes (27), found the funeral director played a valuable social role in the discharge of responsibilities. Binger et al. reported, for instance, that 15 of the 20 families interviewed "expressed positive feelings toward the mortician or funeral director." They observed that "experience with grief reactions makes them skilled in offering solace to grieving families" (p. 417).

Of course our citizens must not only be competently and adequately served; they must also be protected from malpractice. They must have freedom of choice as well. Ultimately, a client's relationship with the funeral director must be based on trust.

There is increasing scholarly evidence today that can stand beside social custom for the belief that a funeral is a ceremony of value for the mourner, just as skilled funeral directors can be and are of assistance to the bereaved—socially and emotionally.

Our society is experiencing rapid social change, particularly with regard to death and death customs. We are presently in the process of defining and redefining grief, bereavement, and loss to say nothing of death itself. Comparable issues face us with respect to the elderly and the dying. The role of the funeral director is an emergent one. I think it would be beneficial if the funeral director would come to be seen as a participant in a community's mental health network. This view would not only support those practices that historically have served human needs but it would strengthen the movement within funeral service itself to play a positive part in helping with the burdens of bereavement. Perhaps, most of all, by treating funeral service people as one would normally treat other professional and paraprofessional health care givers, trust in the good intentions of others is expressed. To do so might be to remove the admonition *caveat emptore* (let the buyer beware) that has been held over the funeral director's head. I would hope to see that warning replaced by the historical medical directive *primum non nocere* (above all do no harm)—an admonition to which we might all pay more heed.

The ceremonialization of death compels the recognition that a death has occurred. In a society in which there is a strong tendency for many to respond to the death of another by turning away, the funeral is a vehicle through which recovery from the crisis of bereavement is initiated. The funeral is also a ceremony that recognizes the integral worth and dignity of human beings. It is not only a sociological statement that a death has occurred, it is also a declaration that a life has been lived.

REFERENCES

1. Van Gennep, A. *The rites of passage*, (Trans. M. B. Vizedom & G. L. Caffee. Chicago: The University of Chicago Press, 1961; Radcliffe-Brown, A. R., Taboo. In *Structure and function in primitive society*. London: Cohen and West, 1952; Evans-Pritchard, E. E., *Theories of primitive religion*. Oxford: Clarendon Press, 1965; Hertz, R., *Death and the right hand*, (Trans. R. Needham & C. Needham, (Glenco, IL: The Free Press, 1960; Goody, J. *Death, property and the ancestors: A study of the mortuary customs of the Lo Dagaa of West Africa*. Palo Alto, CA: Stanford University Press, 1962; Goody, J. Religion and ritual: The definitional problem. *British Journal of Sociology*, 1961, *12*, 142-164; Mandelbaum, D. Social uses of funeral rites. In H. Feifel (Ed.), *The meaning of death*. New York: McGraw-Hill, 1959; Habenstein, R. W., & Lamers, W. M. *Funeral customs the world over*. Milwaukee: Bulfin, 1963; Puckle, B. S. *Funeral customs: Their origin and development*. London: T. W. Laurie, 1926; Bendann, E. *Death customs: An analytical study of burial rites*. New York: Knopf, 1930.
2. Malinowski, B. Death and the reintegration of the group. In *Magic, science, and religion and other essays*. New York: Doubleday, 1954.
3. Durkheim, E. *The elementary forms of religious life*. (Trans. J. W. Swaine) London: Allen and Unwin, 1954.
4. Geertz, C. Ritual and social change: A Javanese example. *American Anthropologist*, 1957, *59*, 32-54.
5. Gluckman, M. Rituals of rebellion in South-East Africa. In M. Gluckman (Ed.), *Essays on the ritual of social relations*. New York: The Humanities Press, 1962.
6. Kennedy is laid to rest on an open slope in Arlington National Cemetery. *New York Times*, November 26, 1963, p. 2.
7. They came to mourn. *Time*, April 19, 1968, 18-19.
8. Wolfenstein, M., & Kliman, G. (Eds.) *Children and the death of a president*. Garden City, NY: Doubleday, 1965; Greenberg, B. S., & Parker, E. B.

(Eds.), *The Kennedy assassination and the American public: Social communication in crisis.* Stanford, Calif.: Stanford University Press, 1965; Bureau of Social Science Research, *Studies of Kennedy's assassination.* Washington, D.C.: Bureau of Social Science Research, 1966.

9. Sheatsley, P. B., & Feldman, J. J. The assassination of President Kennedy: A preliminary report on public reactions and behavior. *Public Opinion Quarterly,* 1964, *28*, 189–215.

10. Mitford, J. *The American way of death,* New York: Simon and Schuster, 1963; Harmer, R. M. Funerals, fantasy, and flight. *Omega,* 1971, *2*, 127–135; Bowman, L. E. *The American funeral: A study in guilt, extravagance and sublimity.* Washington: Public Affairs Press, 1959.

11. Fulton, R. The clergyman and the funeral director: A study in role conflict. *Social Forces,* 1961, *39*, 317–323.

12. Fulton, R. The sacred and the secular. In R. Fulton (Ed.), *Death and identity.* New York: Wiley, 1965, 89–105. *A compilation of studies of attitudes toward death, funerals and funeral directors.* Minneapolis: Center for Death Education and Research, University of Minnesota, 1971.

13. Fulton, R. Contemporary funeral practices. In H. C. Raether (Ed.), *Successful funeral service practice.* New York: Prentice-Hall, 1971, 216–235.

14. Humanae vitae, *New York Times,* July 30, 1968, p. 1, 20–; Pope speaks on birth control. *Time,* August 2, 1968, p. 54; see particularly the criticism reported in the following issues: August 9, 1968, p. 40, October 4, 1968, p. 57.

15. *Monthly vital statistics report.* U.S. Dept. of Health, Education, and Welfare, Public Health Service, National Center for Health Statistics, Vol. 23, No. 3, May 30, 1975, p. 20.

16. *Statistical abstracts of the United States—1975.* U.S. Dept. of Commerce, Bureau of the Census, p. 6.

17. *Historical statistics of the United States, colonial times to 1957,* U.S. Bureau of the Census, Washington, D.C.: U.S. Government Printing Office, 1960, p. 29.

18. Berardo, F. Widowhood status in the United States: Perspectives on a neglected aspect of the family life cycle. *The Family Coordinator,* 1968, *17*, 191–203.

19. Fulton, R., & Gupta, V. Psychological adjustment to loss. Minneapolis: Center for Death Education and Research, University of Minnesota, 1974 (Unpublished).

20. Solecki, R. S. *Shanidar.* New York: Knopf, 1971.

21. Illustrative of the growing literature on grief are the following: Ciocco, A. On the mortality in husbands and wives. *Human Biology,* 1940, *12*, 508–531; Cox, P., & Ford, J. R. The mortality of widows shortly after widowhood. *The Lancet,* 1964, *1*, 163–164; Frederick, J. F. The physiology of grief. *Dodge Magazine,* 1971, *63*, 8–10; Holmes, T. H., & Rahe, R. H. The social readjustment rating scale. *Journal of Psychosomatic Research,* 1967, *11*, 213–218; Kraus, A., & Lilienfeld, A. Some epidemiologic aspects of the high mortality rate in the young widowed group. *Journal of Chronic Diseases,* 1959, *10*, 207–217; Parkes, C. M. Bereavement and mental illness, Part I. A clinical study of the grief of bereaved psychiatric patients. *British Journal of Medical Psychology,* 1965, *38*, 1–12; Parkes, C. M. Bereavement and mental illness, Part II. A classification of bereavement reactions. *British Journal of Medical Psychology,* 1965, *38*, 13–26; Parkes, C. M. Effects of bereavement on physical and mental health—A study of the medical records of widows. *British Medical Journal,* 1964, *2*, 274–279; Rahe, R., Mckean, J., & Arthur, R. J. A longitudinal study of life-change and illness patterns.

Journal of Psychosomatic Research, 1967, *10*, 365; Rahe, R., Meyer, M. et al., Social stress and illness onset. *Journal of Psychosomatic Research*, 1964, *8*, 35–43; Rees, D. W., & Lutkins, S. Mortality of bereavement. *British Medical Journal*, 1967, *4*, 13–26; Stern, Winokur, et al. Alterations in physiological measures during experimentally induced attitudes. *Journal of Psychosomatic Research*, 1961, *5*, 73–82; Wretmark, G. A study of grief reactions. *Acta psychiatrica neurologica Scandinavica*, 1959 (Supplement 136), p. 292; Fulton, R. (Ed.), *Bibliography on death, grief and bereavement (1845-1973), 3rd Ed.*, Minneapolis: Center for Death Education and Research, University of Minnesota, 1973.

22. Lindemann, E. Symptomatology and management of acute grief. *American Journal of Psychiatry*, 1944, *101*, 141–148; Weisman, A. *On dying and denying.* New York: Behavioral Publications, 1972; Kübler-Ross, E. *On death and dying.* New York: Macmillan, 1969; Bowlby, J. Childhood mourning and its implications for psychiatry. *American Journal of Psychiatry*, 1961, *118*, 481–498; Bowlby, J. Pathological mourning and childhood mourning. *Journal of the American Psychoanalytic Association*, 1963, *11*, 500–541; Bowlby, J. Some pathological processes engendered by early mother-child separation. *British Journal of Psychiatry*, 1953, *99*, 265–272; Young, M. et al. The mortality of widowers. *The Lancet*, 1963, *2*, 254–256.

23. Bowlby, J., & Parkes, C. M. Separation and loss. In Anthony, E. J., & Koupernik, C., *The child in his family.* New York: Wiley, 1970, 198.

24. Gorer, G. *Death, grief and mourning.* New York: Doubleday, 1965.

25. Fulcomer, D. M. The adjustive behavior of some recently bereaved spouses: A psycho-sociological study. Unpublished doctoral dissertation, Northwestern University, 1942, p. 182.

26. Shand, A. F. *The foundations of character.* London: MacMillan, 1914, p. 342.

27. Glick, I. O., Weiss, R. S., & Parkes, C. M., *The first year of bereavement.* New York: Wiley, 1974, pp. 97–117.

28. Mole, R. L. Next of kin: A study of bereavement, grief and mourning. Unpublished doctoral dissertation, Howard University, 1974.

29. Binger, C. M. et al. Childhood leukemia: Emotional impact on patient and family. *The New England Journal of Medicine*, 1969, p. 417.

CHAPTER TEN

Bereavement and Grief

EDGAR N. JACKSON

*While the last chapter dealt mainly with the funeral as a social cus-
tom, this chapter deals with the emotional reactions and behaviors
brought about by the death of a loved one. Jackson defines bereavement as "the perception of death by those who suffer this loss." Bereavement is always a social as well as a personal experience. Its impact upon people is different depending upon a number of factors
including personality, the "appropriateness" of the loss (an aged person, a criminal, a child), and religious and philosophical perspectives
of the bereaved. Grief is "the emotional responses to a loss." It is a
process, that aside from physiological reactions, includes withdrawal
of emotional investment, a period of compulsive searching, and restoration of emotional balance when the process has been successfully
completed. A long-time, widely respected grief counselor and minister, Jackson draws upon his own experiences to illustrate the impact
and management of grief with clinical cases and anecdotes. Reviewing recent studies on grief, Jackson suggests that a broader frame of
reference be used to consider grief, including transpersonal insights.
He charges that current study is often plagued by fragmentation,
superficial generalization, and popularization.*

The Data: The Facts of Death

Terms applied to the experience of death and its concomitant human responses are often used without precision. So at the beginning we will try to sharpen up the usage for the terminology we will be employing.

The words *death* and *bereavement* may be interchangeable. Death describes an event in someone's personal history. Bereavement describes the perception of the event by those who suffer the loss. So with both terms, *death* and *bereavement*, we are talking about an event in personal history.

The word *grief* describes the emotional response to the event. Death may occur without emotional response. It may merely be noted as an event in the news. It takes some form of personal involvement emotionally to produce the response to grief.

Another word is used to describe the process by which grief is managed or resolved. That is the word *mourning*. In the context in which we are using it, there cannot be grief without bereavement first. Nor can there be resolution of the grief through mourning until the basic emotions that are triggered by death are experienced by an individual.

THE NATURE OF BEREAVEMENT

Social

Bereavement is always a social experience because it involves human relationships. The event is characterized by a breaking of ties, changes in the social context of living, and employs rites of passage as appropriate means of coping with the loss. Rites of passage are always social events shared by a number of persons engaged in formal or informal rituals or ceremonies.

The social significance of these rites of passage tends to give structure to the community and establish both group values and group methods of response to changes in the nature of the group. It may be as simple as the family response to a death of one of its members, or it may be as elaborate a response as the national ceremonies surrounding the loss of a national leader in the midst of administrative responsibilities.

Historical

The experience of loss in a national context may actually change the course of empire and set the mood of national policy for years to come. Three illustrations may be sufficient to establish the point.

When tragic and untimely death came to Lincoln at the crest of the Civil War, the grief that was steeped in anger changed the mood of the country so that the Reconstruction became a nightmare of retribution that deepened the scars Lincoln sought to heal. The loss of creative national leadership at a crucial time in history sowed seeds of conflict that lasted a century and gave a completely different direction to national life. What was became so different from what might have been.

When death claimed the Prince Consort of Queen Victoria the bereavement event conditioned the life of England. For 40 years the Queen reacted to the loss of her lover taken in the full vigor of life. She would make no decision of state without going into seclusion to commune with his spirit. Decisions she made were tempered with such great emotion that the national life responded accordingly. Each city tried to win favor by creating a more magnificent memorial to Albert. The empire was flooded with Albert Gardens, Albert Halls, and Albertas of one kind or another. Appeals to her sensitivity at the point of her loss were the major manipulative devices to curry favor with the bereft sovereign. Her preoccupation with her grief might well have been the seedground from which grew the dissolution of the empire she served.

When John F. Kennedy was assassinated, deep feelings emerged in national life. Sorrow, dismay, and guilt motivated major national legislation and propelled others with the same name into national prominence. The Kennedy mystique gained so much emotional significance that logical processes seemed to take second place. Colleges, high schools, and boulevards here and abroad were given the Kennedy name. The emotional impact of this tragic loss continues to be a factor in our national life today.

Other events, such as the death of Anne Frank, the death of Joan of Arc, and the central theme of the Gospel stories of the New Testament, have in their various ways had immense historical impact. An examination of these events gives some idea of the influence of acute loss on group life as history reflects it.

Anthropological

The study of primitive life as well as of our contemporary ancestors and present-day responses to emotional crises adds another dimension to our understanding of the nature of bereavement. Remnants of ceremonial processes at the time of death in ancient Persia reflect attitudes that existed 60,000 years ago. Loss stimulated concepts of survival so that the bereaved tried to supply the needs of the dead in some afterlife. Clumps of grain and heaps of pollen survived under the protection of elks' shoulder blades where bodily remains were crudely protected. These are the oldest indications of ceremonial life among primitive people and they reflect the contemporary attitudes toward loss by death.

The research in many tribal cultures indicates that the ceremonies surrounding loss by death had a special significance in the life of the tribe. Marcea Eliade in *Myth and Reality* (1) defines the common practice of using ceremonies of death and resurrection to cope with death anxiety as a function of group life.

Geoffrey Gorer (2) as a cultural anthropologist interprets contemporary group behavior in England. He finds that the loss of significant group processes has a disastrous impact on personal and group life.

> I think my material illustrates the hypothesis that this lack of accepted ritual and guidance is accomplished by a very considerable amount of "maladaptive behavior" from the triviality of meaningless "busyness" through the private rituals of what I have called mummification, to the apathy of despair. To the best of my knowledge, there is no analogue from either the records of past societies or the description of present societies outside the Judeo-Christian tradition to this situation in which the majority of the population lacks common patterns or rituals to deal with the crises inherent in man's biological nature. (p. 127)

Further studies of American Indians by Erik Erikson and Ruth Benedict, of primitive tribes by Frazer and Malinowski, and of contemporary cultures by Margaret Mead as well as Goeffrey Gorer underline the importance of group values and group methods of supportive management of feelings for personal and social health in coping with the impact of loss by death.

William Gladstone, the astute English leader once remarked, "Show me the manner in which a nation or a community cares for its dead, and I will measure with mathematical exactness the character of its people, their respect for the laws of the land, and their loyalty to high ideals." In Hitler-dominated Germany, when respect for human life was severely damaged by his racial theories, all values suffered and Hitler's career ended without any form of ceremonial process to recognize his life or his death. In contemporary American society, with the trend toward loss of significant ritualized behavior to aid in coping with loss through death, we find increased retreat from reality and the social and emotional reactions that Gorer has so well characterized in the earlier quotation.

Psychological

At the level of individual response, the psychological manifestations may be most significant. In a later section we will deal with the emotional aspects of grief more fully. Here it is sufficient to point out and illustrate the effect of loss as it is manifest most acutely in psychological processes.

Erich Lindemann (3), pioneer researcher in the psychological aspects of grief, after speaking of some of the values of religious comfort adds,

> While these measures have helped countless mourners, comfort alone does not provide adequate assistance in the patient's grief work. He has to review his relationships with the deceased, and has to become acquainted with the alterations of his own modes of emotional reaction. His fear of insanity, his fear of accepting the surprising changes in his feelings, especially the overflow of hostility, have to be worked through. . . . He will have to find an acceptable formulation of his future relationships to the deceased. He will have to verbalize his feelings of guilt, and he will have to find persons around him whom he can use as "primers" for the acquisition of new patterns of conduct. (p. 127)

Managing these psychological processes that are a response to acute loss is also part of the nature of the human response to bereavement. The experience of loss manifests itself in varied forms and one does not really confront the meaning of loss until the full spectrum of these responses are brought into focus.

THE IMPACT OF BEREAVEMENT

The human response to loss varies considerably according to the personality structure of the person who is bereaved, the social concomitants that are a part of the experience, and the psychological conditioning that the individual brings into the encounter with loss.

Types of Personality

The vulnerability of the person who experiences loss may vary considerably depending on the personality structure that has become a part of the personality's development.

The response to bereavement is dependent upon the capacity to establish an identity relationship with another person. The sociopath or the psychopath who has a limited capacity for relationships will not be apt to experience a significant response to loss. The person who is highly dependent and whose inner being needs the support of others will suffer severely from loss. Also, the person who has made intense investment of self in the life of another will feel severely reduced by loss.

Because the nature of human relationships is always individual

The Data: The Facts of Death

and personal, so the response to loss will always be measured by these personal qualities. No two persons experience loss in the same way. All that has gone into the development of the person will be drawn upon when bereavement is experienced. So the strong may be strengthened and the weak disorganized. The borderline personality may be fractured and the paranoid turn against the forces of cosmic injustice. The depressive may be plummeted into deeper despair while the drug dependent may become completely addicted.

Social Concomitants of Loss

Not all loss is the same; social factors may contribute to the meaning of the event. A martyr may grow in stature through death. A suicide may lay a heavy burden on those who survive. The death that is heroic has a different meaning from that of a criminal who is executed for crimes committed. Death during wartime may be quite different from other death because the meaning of the death has social acceptance and even approval. Cause–effect factors may weigh heavily in assessing the meaning of a death for the survivor.

So also the appropriateness or inappropriateness of death may modify its impact on the bereft. The death of the aged and senile has a minimum of the tragic about it, whereas the death of a child or youth seems out of keeping with our concept of valid life process.

Medical advancement has changed the context within which we encounter death. In 1900 more than half of all deaths were among children. Now child death has been reduced to less than 6 percent. In 1900 the average life span was 46 years. Now it is more than 70 years. So the control of infectious disease has added a generation to life expectancy in less than a century. This has a bearing on how we experience death. Now more than 65 percent of deaths are among a social group who have had a chance to live a long life. Their death lacks the element of the inappropriate. When death is foreseen and expected, when it is timely and relevant to our larger perspective of the meaning and value of life, our emotional response to it is quite properly different than that of the invalid and tragic.

Also, religious and philosophical perspectives can modify the impact of death. When life is cheap and the individual's existence is relatively meaningless there will be limited impact of loss. In *Roots* (4) the deaths of enslaved blacks were discounted except in economic terms. Philippe Ariès (5), in his historical study of Western attitudes toward death, points out that the contemporary perception of the meaning and value of life conditions the responses toward death through 2000 years of the history of Christendom. When life was valuable death had significance. When life was steeped in despair and futility, death was of little consequence.

Psychological Conditioning

Of course, the impact of death is always personal. Those who survive are the vulnerable victims. But there are psychological factors that condition the vulnerability.

When a person has developed adequate coping skills they modify the impact of acute deprivation experiences. However, when the psychological resources of the individual are under-developed or impaired, there is the strong possibility that the repressed emotions will be detoured into organic acting out usually referred to as disease. Dr. Willard Parker (6), after 53 years of experience with cancer surgery, said, "It is a fact that grief is especially associated with disease." Dr. Charles Anderson (7) has reported in the *International Journal of Psychoanalysis* that 9 percent of the patients in one English hospital were described as requiring treatment for "morbid grief reactions." Dr. Erich Lindemann (8) writes,

> For many years psychiatrists and those interested in nervous breakdowns have talked about anxiety and about conflict as things that make people sick. It is only recently that we realize that depression, sorrow and loss of those who belong to the supportive human environment can be equally severe hazards in a person's life . . . In the wards of mental hospitals the patient's mental disease had very frequently broken out when some dear person had departed from his life. (p. 48)

In more recent studies of spontaneous regressions, Dr. Lawrence LeShan (9) reports that in the cases of malignancy he studied there was a "loss of cathexis" preceding the first appearance of the neoplastic tissue. The emotional impact of the loss that adversely affected the body chemistry usually had a gestation period of from 6 months to 2 years with an occasional case where the time factor was more extended.

With children the grief reaction may be acted out directly against objects that are considered symbols of authority and cosmic injustice. Dr. Mervyn Shoor (10), psychiatrist in charge of the guidance clinic of Santa Clara's county juvenile probation department says,

> These are not children who hated. These are children who mourned. . . . Delinquent behavior by children and adolescents is sometimes a substitute grief reaction. These children were unable to release their feelings in socially acceptable ways when confronted with the impact of loss and death. They could not mourn normally, instead they masked their grief in delinquent behavior. Their mourning, then, was pathological.

Dr. Shoor's findings are supported by those of Rollo May (11) in *The Meaning of Anxiety* and of Geoffrey Gorer (2) in *Death, Grief and Mourning*.

So it becomes clear that well-developed skills for the management of emotional crises may make it possible for a person to move through the event of loss with perspective and intrapsychic balance, whereas the lack of these skills may produce physical, social, and personal forms of pathological response.

THE NATURE OF GRIEF

We have looked at the event of loss or bereavement to assess its nature and impact. We have indicated indirectly that there is considerable emotional impact to the event. Now it is important for us to look more closely at the emotion that is triggered by the event. Grief may have a tremendous emotional impact on the bereft person in a variety of ways. Because the total person is involved, it is impossible for us to discuss any aspect of grief without being aware of the interaction of mind, emotion, society, and even politics. But as a matter of convenience we will try to bring various aspects of the human response into focus, clearly aware of the fact that what we are doing is for the purpose of convenience and not for precise definition.

Physiological

The great weight of research in recent years brings into sharp focus the impact of acute grief on the physical structure of the individual. Every system of the body is involved. The glandular system, the cardiovascular system, the sensory system, the muscular and skeletal system, the digestive system, and the respiratory system are all implicated in the emotional responses of acute grief.

In the normal course of grief work the physical symptoms are usually worked through in a relatively brief span of time. Difficulties arise when the grief work is inadequately or unwisely done, and a chronic disorganization of the body's functioning produces a prolonged imbalance of body chemistry with the concomitant reduction of resistance to viral developments and abnormal cell division. Then grief can become a problem of major proportions.

The publication of the Rees and Lutkins study (12) in 1967 on the mortality of grief showed that individuals undergoing the impact of acute loss had a mortality rate that was seven times that of nongrieving persons. These findings support the statistics of two other studies, one in Cambridge, Massachusetts and the other in Wales. Similar studies in a general hospital show that admissions are 600 percent higher among the acutely bereft as compared to the general community. More than half of the parents of children who die of leukemia at Langley Porter Hospital are in psychotherapy before a year is past. So the impact of the emotion of acute grief on the total organism seems to be well established (10).

We could go into great detail about the symptoms that are reflected by each of the body systems, but that has been done adequately elsewhere. Reference is made to the work of Lindemann (3) and Jackson (13) *Understanding Grief, Its Roots, Dynamics and Treatment.* The relationship of grief and its physical metaphors seems to be accepted without argument.

Psychological

As grief is an emotion it would be in the realm of emotional responses that the central problem of response would be expected. The degree of the grief seems to be closely identified with two conditions: the intensity of the emotional relationship and the stability of the intrapsychic balance of the individual.

As all death is not the same, so all grief is not manifest in equal degrees. This is illustrated by the response of the average person to the two centers of death in the average community. Two institutions deal directly and exclusively with death. One is a place of sadness, the funeral home. The other, the butcher shop, is a center of anticipated pleasure, even elaborate ceremonials of family enjoyment. What explains the difference of mood between these two centers of death activity?

Quite obviously it is the emotional factors that are operative in each. We enjoy eating. When we want to enjoy a convivial occasion we plan a special meal or a banquet. The national holiday of Thanksgiving is centered about the carcass of a turkey. The carver serves the role of the high priest for the occasion. All the trimmings and other extras of a ceremonial occasion bring the family together for moments of joy and fulfillment. This is possible because there is no real emotional involvement with the turkey. It is viewed in impersonal terms emotionally. The values have to do with weight, tenderness, and the chance to get a favorite slice of the meat. When a person looks at a lobster swimming lazily in a tank or a juicy steak ready to be sliced, the emotions that are involved do not have to do with sympathy for the source of the meat. Rather it is the anticipation of the pleasure of ingesting it. We say, "Do I only love lobster" or "I can't wait to sink my teeth in that chateaubriand." The emotions are far from sad because the relations to the creature making the supreme sacrifice are remote and impersonal.

The funeral home on the other hand copes with quite a different set of feelings. We may approach it with sadness, apprehension, and in a quiet and reverent state. At the human level someone who has been closely identified with the meaning of life has died, and the emotional amputation has a profound effect on the inner being. We feel reduced. Our security system is disturbed. Our emotions overflow. The experience of life is painful, yet under the pain there are ambivalent feelings for we know that the pain we feel is an evidence of life, and if death is bad then life is good and our feelings of hurt verify our capacity to have other feelings. So we go on into life trying to adjust the burden of grief to the prospects for life in the future. At first it may seem to be too burdensome a task to confront. But time serves its useful purpose and the momentum of life moves us slowly into the healing future.

But during this period of slow adjustment there are many basic psychological processes at work. We will mention three as illustrations: 1) there is a process of searching, 2) a withdrawal of emotional investment, and 3) a struggle for intrapsychic balance.

If kittens are taken away from the mother cat we observe several days of almost constant searching. Something comparable is observed among humans. It may be expressed verbally. It may show up in some ritualized behavior as when a person relentlessly moves from room to room as if the lost love object were in hiding. It may be in symbolic acts such as mending the garments of the deceased as if in preparation for a return. It may be in setting an extra place at the table as if old habits were verifying an expected return. The funeral process, with its quiet and dignified sense of finality at the graveside, can help to release a person from this compulsive searching.

The withdrawal of emotional investment may vary according to the age and personality dynamics of the individual. For some the process may be so slow that they are unaware of it, and others may find that life reorients itself quite rapidly as they invest themselves in things and people who are still important in their lives. Usually it is a living testimony to the forward moving momentum of life itself. In normal circumstances one cannot live in the past for long. The present and the future make their insistent demands and grief is resolved in the process. This explains why so many persons say, "I just have to keep busy. That is the only thing that helps me."

With acute grief there is usually a struggle to restore intrapsychic balance. This may be manifest in a series of stages. At first the person may try to assure a freedom from mental illness. The inner turbulence may produce such remarks as "I think I'm losing my mind," and in the context in which it is uttered there is usually a quest for reassurance. Then there may come a time of turbulent and distressing dreams. The restoration of balance may be reflected in the changing quality of the dreams from the more distressing to the less distressing and finally comfortable perspectives on the relationship of the dead person. These processes are often reflected in counseling procedures. The final stage of restoration is apparent when the deceased can be recalled without emotional pain.

Normally these processes and others comparable to them will be experienced in the disease that heals itself. It is when the normal processes are interfered with by unwise grief management that special help may be required.

Social

The study of grief responses and their resolution reveals that the support of social groups is of singular importance in the working through of the deep feelings.

Most social groups have well-established ways for meeting life crises. Within ethnic groups there are traditions that are set in motion immediately upon the death of one of the group. The total group engages in supportive behavior that is quickly and easily understood by both the grieving and those who surround them. The activities become part of the social movement that catches up those who are bereft and starts the process of moving them into the future. When depression might overcome the individual and immobilize forward motion, the group process supplies the energy and the direction for the disabled individual.

Problems occur when people are separated from the established patterns for acting out their feelings. In his book *Future Shock* Toffler (14) defines how uprootedness may become critical for people in times of crisis. When established ways of moving through turbulent experience are lost or forgotten, and are not replaced by other forms of group behavior that are equally significant, the individual feels isolated and abandoned when the needs for social support are most acute. This tends to produce not only a reduction in healthful means for externalizing strong feelings but may even compound the emotional problems by adding injury to injury.

Political

We have learned in recent years that the nature of grief can have strong political ramifications. National identification with idealized leadership can give direction to political activity. The leader represents hope and security. Tragic loss may precipitate disorganization, insecurity, and even self-destructive behavior. When a leader who gave hope to a minority group was slain the immediate impact was rioting and the nonrational behavior that was a sign of helpless and hopeless protest.

Personal symbols with charismatic appeal have an important influence on national cohesion. Creative leaders may leave a power

The Data: The Facts of Death

vacuum if they are killed. Inversely, the death of a dictator may produce a new birth of freedom among those who have been oppressed. In either case the loss by death may have far reaching implications.

THE IMPACT OF GRIEF

We have looked at the nature of grief in terms of its broader implications. Now let us personalize the human aspects of this powerful emotion as it would be reflected in clinical case and anecdotal material.

The Vulnerable Victim

John and Mary had been married for more than 50 years. They had no children and no immediate family. They found meaning for life in each other. They had wealth and social status so there was little struggle in their lives. Their major emotional investment was in each other. Mary died rather suddenly from a heart failure. John was so overwrought that he had great difficulty moving through the funeral process. A week later he was admitted to the hospital with no specific ailment but a generalized state of debilitation. His will to live seemed to have evaporated. Before the month was over he was dead of unspecified ailments. Heart failure was listed on the death certificate but it was merely the last event in a process of rapid disintegration of organic function. The will to die seemed to have been realized organically.

Rachel was a pediatrician. She was known far and wide for her skill in treating the ailments of children. She was a consultant for several social agencies serving the needs of children. She was self-assured, dynamic, and, in all the ways one would usually measure life, a most successful person. Her marriage seemed healthy and secure. Her two children seemed physically robust and socially promising. Then her 11-year-old boy became listless and lost weight. Diagnosis indicated a virulent form of leukemia. Within a few months he was dead. Rachel carried on her work with a stoic attitude and people looked at her as a worthy example of maturity and self-control. Within a year she became pale and lost weight, showed signs of weakness, and curtailed her professional activities. A few months later she entered a hospital for the treatment of an ailment much like that which caused her son's death. She gave orders that there were to be no visitors but her husband. She shut herself off from her many friends and quietly turned her back on life. Within 2 months she too was dead.

Jennifer's marriage fell in ruins. She was beautiful, intelligent, and an accomplished musician. She became depressed and brooded over her condition as if she had experienced the ultimate form of rejection and abandonment. She had counseling for her depression but was unresponsive. Eight months later she detected a lump in her breast and after a biopsy was diagnosed as having a malignancy.

A radical mastectomy was performed, and she experienced a change in her emotional state. In counseling she said that this now solved all her problems. She would never again be appealing to a man. She spoke of her surgery always as her "disfigurement." She changed her life style, the circle of her friends and acquaintances. In effect she killed one self-image and gave birth to another that would never again threaten her with the experience of acute loss that she had found to be emotionally intolerable.

In grief responses to death or the death of an important relationship, a person may act out deep feelings so vigorously that the response is lethal or devastating. When death occurs or acute deprivation is experienced, it is not the person who dies who is the victim as much as it is the person who may be obliged to cope with the crisis when motivation or skills are underdeveloped and inadequate.

Personality Manifestations

Often under the hammer blows of acute grief a person may change completely.

Richard was a successful writer. His column appeared in papers all over the country. When his wife died after a long illness he became restless. His brilliant writing was affected. Soon the number of papers carrying his column decreased. He tried self-applied psychotherapy. He had never been more than an occasional drinker, but now he turned to alcohol in immoderate doses. He could not function dependably and was reduced to doing occasional hack work and freelance editorial revisions of other people's work. Within 5 years of his wife's death he was also dead, but during those 5 years his personality had changed and he had disintegrated into a pathetic and nonfunctional human being.

Willard was a highly placed politician. He wielded considerable power in the national capitol. He had always seemed to enjoy life and power and had a large circle of powerful friends with whom he lived a convivial existence. After the death of his wife, Willard changed. He became a single-minded crusader for the rights of the underprivileged. The energy of his emotions of grief seemed to be directed toward all others who suffered deprivation and abandonment. For the rest of his term of office he was serious, intense, and completely devoted to his newly assumed role as the champion of other humans who suffered grievously. When he retired from office he left a monument of social legislation that appeared to be the creative acting out of his grief.

Andrew was seven when his father died of a heart attack while many miles from home on a business trip. Family members whisked him away to the home of some relatives who cared for him for a week. He was confused by the unusual set of circumstances that surrounded him. When he returned home his mother was distraught and often crying. In response to his questions he was told it was nothing to concern him. In response to direct questions about his father he was told that his father was on a trip and would not be back for a long time. Andrew's schoolwork deteriorated and he was often dreamily looking out of the window with thoughts far away. Finally he was referred to a child guidance clinic by the school psychologist. Here he communicated that he felt he had done something so bad that his father had decided to stay away. His guilt was too heavy a burden for a small child. In therapy it was worked through, and he proved that he could cope with death more adequately than with a fabric of deceit that let loose a fertile imagination.

When improperly managed the impact of grief can disrupt the personality. Fears, loneliness, or guilt can destroy normal functioning. Or new dedication can make it possible for a person to try to live for two and find a new energy and direction for living.

Psychological Distortions

One of the hazards of unwisely managed grief may be the distortion of reality. A person may become unreasonably judgmental of self, so magnify inconsequentials that they dominate life and fill the mind and emotions with self-deceit. These distortions of normal perception may grow to the place where they dominate life and threaten its existence.

On a dark and rainy night Clement ran into a pedestrian, killing her instantly. He brooded over the accident. He sold his car and used public transportation. He modified his life style considerably. He went to confession regularly. He had some counseling that was recommended. Still he could not seem to escape from his guilt. He made contributions to the care of the victim's children. He referred to himself as a murderer. On the anniversary of the accident he killed himself. He became his own executioner for a crime that was primarily existent in his own mind. His grief, heavily burdened with guilt, so distorted his perception of reality that he was unable to manage his self-punishing impulse therapeutically and worked it out with an act of self-destruction.

Clara cared for her aged father. She mixed her resentment with resignation. She envied other members of the family who lived their own lives. She hated some of the chores that went with the care of an incontinent and senile old man who was so paranoid that he gave accusation rather than appreciation for Clara's ministrations to his needs. Often she entertained hostile and hateful thoughts and prayed for the day when she would be free of her burden. However, when her father died Clara became withdrawn, self-judging, and depressed. Not only did she miss the rigid routine that had structured her life, but she reexamined her attitudes saying in effect, "Why couldn't I have been more patient and loving for a poor old man who couldn't help what he was?" Her answers were always judgmental of herself, and she never seemed to get beyond the inclination to punish and hate herself for quite a natural human response to circumstance.

Larry had been married nearly 20 years when his wife died of a rapidly developing malignancy. At first he seemed disoriented and depressed but soon moved into a manic state, bought a racy sports car, farmed his children out to relatives, and spent much time in sexual acting out with women half his age. However, the more frenzied and obtuse his behavior became, the less inner peace he seemed to find. After more than a year of this activity he suffered a general form of collapse, physically and emotionally. He asked his counselor, "Whatever has happened to me? How could I be like this? Can I ever straighten myself out?" An effort was made to understand his behavior as a form of grief work and then go back and manage the grief in a more normal and valid way. Because of added guilt and embarrassment it was a difficult process, but it was possible in time to manage the psychological distortions and establish a more valid form for emotional expression.

In a culture that discourages the direct expression of deep feelings the distortions tend to appear quite often. The professional counselor and the other members of caregiving professions have to be prepared to interpret this distorted behavior and direct the emotional energy toward more normal forms of expression.

We have looked at the vulnerability of the surviving victim who still has the problem of coping with deep feelings, we have looked at some of the personality manifestations that occur, and we have illustrated some of the distortions of the feelings that are apt to appear. We have used case studies because they make it possible for the grieving person to come to life for us. But it is reassuring that many persons move through their grief with more normal responses.

THE MANAGEMENT OF GRIEF

We are prepared now to examine more closely some of the positive resources that may be employed in coping with grief. Each individual has some resources to draw upon, and society generally provides some supportive resources. We may examine these in more depth to know what it is we have to work with constructively.

Acting Out

Since Lawrence Abt (15) published his book *Acting Out* in 1965 there has been a renewed interest in the therapeutic significance of rites, rituals, and ceremonies. In its broadest sense, acting out is the process of translating impulses into action. When the impulses are hostile, angry, and sick they produce vandalism, delinquency, and the sociopathic stance against what are thought to symbolize sources of pain and injury. The problem with much acting out is that people "tend to change their environment rather than themselves, and whereas their behavior seems appropriate to them, it seems implausible and inappropriate to others" (16).

Acting out can have therapeutically valid uses as well as effects causing problems for individuals and society. Every well-developed society has surrounded the crisis events of life with ceremonies that make it possible for the person to find healthful ways to express his emotional drives before they become repressed and seek self-destructive and socially unacceptable forms of expression.

The acting out process is particularly valuable for it gives the total person a chance for organized expression. The ceremonial act usually is socially oriented and employs intellectual, emotional, and psychic activity as well as large-muscle expression. It becomes the healthful channel for powerful emotions that might well be directed against the self and society.

Gorer (2) in his study of funeral practices in England finds that the more elaborate the acting out process at the time of the emotional crisis the more quickly the bereaved persons are restored to normal. Such findings bring into focus a trend in this country that could have unhealthy implications. Partly because of uprootedness, partly for economic reasons, and partly due to a tendency to try to intellectualize emotions, those acting out processes at the time of death have been increasingly curtailed. In the name of simplification people have been denying themselves the acting out processes they need most at the time when it would be most valid, when the feelings are most intense.

It seems important for the wise management of grief to make a fresh study of the processes that afford healthful acting out so that they can be elaborated with intellectually valid perceptions, adequate emotional support, a healthful confrontation of reality (rather than the fostering of illusion), and a respect for deep feelings (rather than an unhealthful effort to deny or escape from them).

Incorporation

In the sense in which we use the term, *incorporation* means to take within or embody something that may not have been so embodied previously. This phenomenon may be observed among the grief-stricken as one of the processes for management of the emotion (17).

Incorporation can have healthful as well as unhealthful manifestations. Let us look at the unhealthy ones first. A grieving person may incorporate the disease that caused the death of the one mourned. This may well be quite a common experience. The bereft may incorporate the manner, attitudes, and behavior of the deceased. A person may take on the dislikes of the lost loved one and experience changes in personality. Because these changes usually tend to make a person less responsive to sound judgment and are conditioned by emotions that are examined with difficulty, the end result may well be an unfortunate change in the mourner.

Healthful incorporation shows up in the more dedicated and purposeful living of the survivor. A well-known case is that of Russell H. Conwell, whose life was saved by the intervention of a youth in the Civil War. Conwell was so moved by this self-sacrificing act that for the rest of his life he seemed to live with double purpose and doubled energy. His dedicated action produced Temple University, Good Samaritan Hospital, and other notable institutions in Philadelphia and elsewhere. The power of his life seemed doubled because he was determined to live not only for himself but for another. This process is verified in many ways and statistics show that those who live for others are less prone to disease and usually live longer (18).

How does one develop a skill in managing grief through incorporation? Most grief has a strong selfish quality about it and leads people to feel sorry for themselves and dwell upon their inner misery. An act of will that can change the focus of thought and action can move the concern from self to others, from selfishness to self-lessness. One of the goals for the wise management of grief may be the development of this outer focus and a strengthening of the will to live creatively in spite of pain and loneliness.

Identification

Not unrelated to incorporation the processes of identification have positive and negative manifestations. *Identification* is the psychological term for love or interrelationship with another emotionally. The loss of the object of the love starts in motion powerful feelings that can make or break a person depending on how the feelings are used.

It is unfortunate when the bonds of identification enslave a person and prevent the open and honest facing of reality. When we identify with another we tend to feel with them. When something good happens to them we feel pleased. When something unfortunate happens to them we feel the injury. When something devastating happens we can feel devastated. Then it is but a short step to acting out the feelings of fractured selfhood. We can take on the illness of the object of our mourning. We can lose our emotional balance and our social poise. In fact, we can allow our grief to damage or destroy us through the nonrational forms of our identification.

On the other hand, these deep feelings can be put to work creatively. Many memorials are focal points for identity with the dead

The Data: The Facts of Death

person. We can endow a scholarship, give a building to a university, or place a book in a library. We take a diffused feeling and bring it into a focus that makes it possible for us or the object we give to project the relationship into the future. It becomes a healthful form of acting out for the mourner as well as a benefit to others.

Substitution

As the word *substitution* implies, we can put something else in the place of our grief. We may be able to transform it into something good, or we may set up some form of behavior that uses the energy of grief to make life more difficult.

> Wendell took one part of his grief and made of it a way of life. He became God's angry man. He seemed to reject every soft and gracious feeling and instead acted out his hostility and aggression. People tried to understand but he made it so difficult that they gradually withdrew leaving him more alone with more cause for anger. When there was no one to pour his anger out on he directed it in upon himself and became increasingly depressed and nonfunctional. Life became more contracted and increasingly miserable until he acted out his own anger in his own self-destruction.

> Della was a college professor's wife with one daughter who died tragically. Della reached out with her strong mothering impulse and became a surrogate mother for many students away from home who were lonely and uncared for. Her home became a haven for a long line of grateful students through the years. She made something beautiful and good out of her grief and helped herself in the process by creating a family that reached all over the country and even into some foreign lands. She substituted other youths for the empty spot left by her daughter's death.

Each person has some freedom to decide what will be done with grief. The wise management of it can often be determined by the planning ahead that people do when they look at life and seek to find its most valid meaning. But whether it be acting out, incorporation, identification, or substitution, there can be healthful or unhealthful ways of managing it, and the ultimate choice seems to be in the hands of those who grieve and those who care for them through the painful process.

RESEARCH ON GRIEF

Recent years have produced a wealth of research and writing on the subject of grief and its wise management. When my book *Understanding Grief, Its Roots, Dynamics and Treatment* (13) came out just a little more than a score of years ago, it was the only clinically oriented study on this major emotion. Since that time hundreds of books have been published relating to the subject. They fall into three classes, generally speaking: there is original and useful research, derivative material that may be valid but less useful, and finally a large amount of writing that is personal, emotional, and largely uninformed. The latter is probably more useful to the writer than the reader in most instances. Nearly a score of books in these three groups are added to publishers' lists each month.

Psychosomatic Medicine

The more dramatic findings concerning the impact of grief and suggestions for its wise management have come from physicians seeking to discover the etiology of disease processes. Often acute grief that has been poorly managed appears in the recent history of the patient. The list of studies is too long for a comprehensive recording of them here, but basic have been the contributions of Lindemann (3, 8), LeShan (9), Dunbar (18), and Frederick (19). All imply that the emotional shock to the system of the acutely bereaved may produce a chronic disturbance of the body chemistry that reduces resistance to viral developments and neoplastic tissue or cellular developments. These studies have probably been most explicit in defining the vulnerability of the bereft.

Sociological Findings

Those who study demographic patterns of the behavior of cohorts make it clear that we are experiencing death in this period in history as it has never been encountered before. As we noted earlier, the control of infectious diseases has reduced the incidence of child death from more than 56 percent of all deaths in 1900 to less than 6 percent today. At the same time the life expectancy has increased from 46 years to over 70. Most dying now is done by those who have lived a normal life span, so the element of the tragic and untimely is reduced. Among these people death is the end result of deteriative diseases and is expected and often hoped for as a helpful release from infirmity or senility. The second highest time of death is in the age group from 17 to 24 years, with much drug overdose, accidents, and military action as primary causes. Here the tragic and untimely is a powerful emotional factor. So when and how we meet death is quite different from what it was in 1900, and quite obviously the emotional impact varies considerably. Also, social experience tends to deprive persons of skills needed for facing the reality of death, and discomfort with deep feelings has led to the loss of supportive social action at the same time that people are acting out their death anxiety by escape into denial and illusion.

　　　　　　　　　　　　The Data: The Facts of Death

Transpersonal Insights

A major change in the psychological climate is affecting the way people look at death. This may change the quality of grief and the acting out processes that accompany it. When mechanistic attitudes dominated educational and experimental psychology, there was little thought about the psyche or its survival of bodily death. However, with the development of humanistic psychology there has been a renewed interest in every aspect of human behavior. The transpersonal mood has even entered into medical studies such as those of Moody (20) and Kübler-Ross (21). Here the effort is to examine the state of consciousness of those who have had a brief and carefully observed experience of cessation of body function. After restoration of life processes there is a report of psychic experience that includes feelings of euphoria and visions rich in symbolism. From this it seems to be extrapolated that real death is comparable to clinical death, though in reality there seems to be no basis for comparison, for the experiences reported may be duplicated under drugs, anesthetics, or other forms of temporary interruption of normal processes of consciousness.

However, the mood of researchers in the personality sciences seems to be far more open to speculation of transpersonal phenomena than was the case a few years ago. This is reflected in the title of some recent books. A sociologist, Peter Berger (22), has written *Rumor of Angels: The Rediscovery of the Supernatural*, and a psychologist and psychiatrist write about dream telepathy (23). Many persons are having their attitudes toward death and grief influenced by either valid research or pseudoscientific theories concerning reincarnation, spiritualism, or psychic phenomena. The mood that now exists may well stimulate the forms of valid research that can change the focus of serious students from the materialistic emphasis of the past century toward a more open response to paranormal phenomena that may be incorporated into acceptable philosophies of life.

PROBLEMS AND PROSPECTS

The contemporary preoccupation with death and the emotions that are related to it are producing mixed results. Some research is valid and useful, yet some of the emphasis may lead toward the morbid and disorganized perceptions about life and its meaning.

Fragmentation and Fracturing of the Person

When more and more people focus on an area of research it often follows that the preoccupation with smaller and smaller aspects of the subject lead to fragmentation. Many of the more recent studies are clinical studies of small groups of widows, widowers, blacks, Indians, or other groups that can be isolated for detailed study. This tends to lead the research into small pockets of interest, and the large view of the human condition may be lost in this fracturing process. It was with this thought in mind that the author tried to reverse the trend in his most recent book. Aware of the fact that the grieving person was being lost in the specialization that was exerting a significant influence on research, the author tried to bring into focus the person who grieves and the feelings that are paramount in the experience of personal loss. So *The Many Faces of Grief* (24) is deliberate in its concentration on the broad aspects of the personal experience and carefully avoids statistics, footnotes, and research projects, though at every point it is willing to recognize the contributions such research has made. But unless analysis can lead to a synthesis that is humanly useful, the human condition may not be improved.

Superficial Generalizations

Much of the research and writing in the field of grief has emerged from personal experience and so is apt to have a large measure of the subjective about it. It is acknowledged that all grief is personal, but that is why the hazard of the subjective exists. It may so easily lead to the generalizations that are a projection of the individual experience upon the broader sweep of humanity. Literature on bereavement and grief needs to be carefully evaluated to assess its validity, for too often the sweeping generalizations can be misleading.

Popularized Treatments

The increased interest in grief and its management has led to a plethora of articles in the mass media that suggest procedures that are not only unwise but may be emotionally damaging. Some of these suggestions deal with minifunerals, body donations, and grief counseling by untrained and uninformed amateurs.

The valid research indicates that it is unwise to assume that grief can be reduced by reducing the chances for therapeutic acting out at the time of death. The process of body donation is more complicated than most people realize and should be done with careful planning in advance in cooperation with the institution receiving the donation. Also there is need for a clear distinction between giving of bodies for replacement parts such as kidneys and corneas and the giving of a body for use by students of anatomy. So many bodies are available and so few are needed that some medical schools have become highly selective and will take only unmutilated, undiseased, unobese and young bodies, and those where death occurs near the medical school. This can compound the emotional problems of a family that offers a body and then is confronted with rejection at the time when their emotions are highly sensitive. While much useful talking out of feelings can be done with friends and neighbors, it is unfortunate when well-meaning but misguided people move into a counseling role with bad advice and damaging counsel. Anything as important as wise grief management should be approached with caution, discipline, and skill.

False Hopes

The airwaves and institutions that present other programs of pseudo-religious insight may make it more difficult for people to confront the feelings that are a part of the grief syndrome. The large number of TV and radio programs that give simplistic answers to basic life questions and invite a retreat from reality may well be providing the starting point for mental and emotional illness. Even meditation programs that seek to reduce the content of consciousness to a minimum may be creating a vacuum that is filled with potential hazard. To focus the powerful resources of consciousness on the ultimately meaningless can lead to dissociation. Rather, it is wise to fill consciousness with the most meaningful insight so that the mind and emotions have something firm to build on, especially in times of acute crisis. Any retreat from reality into the domain of unexamined shortcuts or quick and easy methods for managing personal crises should be suspect. Nothing is more cruel than to promise what cannot be delivered or to encourage what is unwise and possibly damaging at the time of greatest vulnerability. Such false hopes may well compound the problems of moving toward true health of mind and emotion.

PERSONAL, SOCIAL, AND PROFESSIONAL RESPONSIBILITY

In view of some of the hazards just enumerated it is important for us to set some standards for those who seek to be care givers in times of bereavement and grief. What are the obligations? What are the responsibilities? And what are the resources available to those who would want to be helpful in times of crisis?

Personal

Much valuable therapeutic intervention may be produced by friends, relatives, and neighbors of the bereaved. However, there are some simple guidelines that may be proposed. Feelings are highly individualized and should be accepted rather than manipulated. To tell someone that "they should not feel that way" seems to be strangely irrelevant when the feelings exist. Rather, it seems wise to be patient, accepting, and understanding. It is important to be there, to provide warmth and support to the person who is struggling with powerful emotions. This is a time for listening rather than talking, and those who are suffering acute loss should be freed from stress rather than having it added by advice and counsel that may not be relevant. The dimension of touching may be added to other forms of communication; the warm embrace and the supportive contact may be more helpful than words. Anxiety seems to be contagious so it is important even while being accepting to be as calm and stable as possible.

Social

Anthropological and sociological studies verify the significance of the social processes involved in managing grief. However, in recent years social mobility and the acting out of death anxiety have tended to curtail the social resources available for confronting grief. While change is inevitable, it is important to develop new and valid ways for meeting social needs of individuals in crisis. The research and writing of Robert Fulton (25) provide some of the best insights and resources for this purpose. Through the Center for Death Education and Research at the University of Minnesota a series of tapes (26) provide information and training for those who would understand the needs of various groups of the bereft, from the sudden infant crib death parent to the special needs of the aged.

Professional

The generation of raw research data relating to bereavement and grief has been so extensive in recent years that it has been difficult to digest or organize it into programs useful to the professionals involved with the crises of acute loss. Efforts to upgrade the education of funeral service personnel has been encouraging but has been limited by state law and traditional practice. It is important for the professional qualifications of these trainees that they be kept abreast of the important research on the care of the grieving. But equally important, it is essential that physicians, nurses, clergymen, counselors, and lawyers be provided with a sound basis for their professional intervention with the bereft. It is important that the care givers in our culture be able to see and understand the whole person in grief, for dealing with parts of the person in professional specializations tends to fracture the person when integrity of being is essential. Constant efforts must be made to upgrade the training of professional persons who care for the grief-stricken so that the benefits of research will be made available to those who need it as quickly as possible.

PHILOSOPHICAL AND THEOLOGICAL PERSPECTIVES

Humans have always struggled with the burden of their mortality and have tried to find some cosmic perspectives on the problems of life and death. Our day with its special needs has developed insights that may be useful for the wiser management of grief.

Philosophy has sought to resolve the body–mind dichotomy in ways that are compatible with contemporary psychology and cosmology. The nature of consciousness has been explored to discover what it is of the person that is more than mechanical, chemical, and organic responses. Physicists have observed that the sixth dimension is called the "eternity dimension." It seems that death as we know it is a physiological phenomenon and that aspects of consciousness are able to persist independent of the measurements of space and time that are the boundaries of the physiological. This would inevitably have an influence on how one would perceive both life and death.

The main purpose of theological study is to find meaning for the human experience. This specialized form of philosophical exploration often seeks to attribute meaning to the apparently meaningless. This usually leads to an expansion of perspectives, so the bereaved person is able to look beyond the individualized experience of death that is emotionally painful to the more generalized idea of death as being cosmically valid and essential to the processes of birth, growth, and entropy. When persons are able to move beyond the personal perspective to the larger dimensions of the experience of loss, intrapsychic balance may be restored and a person can then move into the future with inner balance and emotional acceptance.

CRISIS PSYCHOLOGY AND GRIEF MANAGEMENT

The rapid development in recent years of the psychological perspectives that emerge from psychosomatic research has led to the development of more adequate understanding of the nature, impact, and management of emotional crises. This research provides useful

insights and skills in crisis management that are of special importance to the professional person working with the bereaved. A basic
introductory text that takes a comprehensive view of the subject
is the author's book *Coping with the Crises in Your Life* (27). Other
books have dealt more specifically with the crises of childhood,
middle age, the aged, and the problems of the handicapped and the
addicted. The combined insights of these various studies clarify the
nature of human crises and define more adequately the role of the
teacher and the therapist in working with the bereft.

CONCLUSION

We have tried to define the nature of the grief experience and assess
its impact and manifestations as the individual griever or the professional person would encounter it. We have tried to bring into focus
some of the resources that could help in the wiser management of
the crisis. Incident to that we have shown some of the problems
that exist and some of the unfinished work that needs to be done
in research and therapy. We trust that this exploration will be useful
in moving toward a more helpful program for meeting the emotional
needs of the griever at this unique time in our history and culture.

REFERENCES

1. Eliade, M. *Myth and reality.* New York: Harper & Row, 1963.
2. Gorer, G. *Death, grief and mourning.* Garden City, NY: Doubleday, 1965.
3. Lindemann, E. Symptomology and management of acute grief. *American Journal of Psychiatry*, 1944, *101*, 147.
4. Haley, A. *Roots.* New York: Doubleday, 1976.
5. Ariès, P. *Western attitudes toward death.* Baltimore: Johns Hopkins University Press, 1973.
6. Parker, W. Quoted by L. LeShan in, Personality states as factors in the development of malignant disease: A critical review. *Journal of the National Cancer Institute*, 1959, *22*, 1-18.
7. Anderson, C. Aspects of pathological grief and mourning. *International Journal of Psychoanalysis*, 1949, *30*, 48-55.
8. Lindemann, E. Neuropsychiatric observations after the Cocoanut Grove fire. *Annals of Surgery*, 1943, *117*, p. 48.
9. LeShan, L. *You can fight for your life.* New York: Evans, 1977.
10. Shoor, M. Death, delinquency and the mourning process. *The Psychiatric Quarterly*, 1963, *37*.
11. May, R. *The meaning of anxiety.* New York: Roland Press, 1950.
12. Rees, W., & Lutkins, S. The mortality of bereavement. *British Medical Journal*, 1967, *4*, 13-16.
13. Jackson, E. *Understanding grief, its roots, dynamics and treatment.* Nashville: Abingdon, 1957.
14. Toffler, A. *Future shock.* New York: Random House, 1970.
15. Abt, L. *Acting out.* New York: Grune and Stratton, 1965.

16. Weiss, E., & English, C. S. *Psychosomatic Medicine*. Philadelphia: Saunders, 1943.
17. Weiss, E. *Loneliness*. Cambridge, MA: MIT Press, 1973.
18. Dunbar, F. *Emotions and bodily changes*. (4th Ed.) New York: Columbia University Press, 1954.
19. Frederick, J. Grief as a disease; The physiology of grief. *The Dodge Magazine*, 1972, *64*, 1.
20. Moody, R. *Life after life*. New York: Bantam Books, 1976.
21. Kübler-Ross, E. *Death: The final stage of growth*. Englewood Cliffs, NJ: Prentice-Hall, 1975.
22. Berger, P. *Rumor of angels: The rediscovery of the supernatural*. New York: Doubleday, 1969.
23. Krippner, S. et al. *Scientific experiments in the supernatural*. New York: Macmillan, 1973.
24. Jackson, E. *The many faces of grief*. Nashville: Abingdon, 1977.
25. Fulton, R. *Death and identity*. New York: Wiley, 1965.
26. Cassette Series, *Death, grief and bereavement* (12 tapes). Minneapolis: Center for Death Education and Research, University of Minnesota, 1972.
27. Jackson, E. *Coping with the crises in your life*. New York: Hawthorn Books. (New Edition) New York: Jason Aronson, 1978.

CHAPTER ELEVEN

Death and the Law

BARTON E. BERNSTEIN

*Bernstein, a practicing attorney, presents the facts of death in rela-
tion to our legal system. He approaches the subject in a down-to-
earth manner, and his advice is practical and valuable. He points at
the importance not only of having a last will and testament but also
of having it reviewed periodically to adjust for changes in tax laws or
family circumstances. He reminds the reader that regardless of our
wishes about the disposal of our body (including body and organ donation), in the end it is all up to the family since after death, according to the law, a person becomes the property of the next of kin.
Those who feel strongly about how they want to be disposed of
should discuss this matter with their family. Of great importance,
though still largely unsettled, is the question of the right to die. California's "Natural Death Act," like similar legislation in several other
states, offers a solution to the problem of a personal right to die
naturally, that is, without the use of artificial means. Taking steps to
take care of the legal matters discussed in this chapter demonstrates
acknowledgment of one's personal death as a reality. It also greatly
benefits the loved ones left behind at death.*

The Data: The Facts of Death

Lawyer, individual, and mental health professional interface
ing pre- and postdeath legal problems.

Death affects not only the dying; it also affects the livin
has long-established traditions and spells out procedural ,
stantive rights that allow the living to determine and contro
own destiny (as this affects accumulated wealth) and to name t.
natural or whimsical objects of their bounty upon death. Occasionally the sophisticated person dies with every "i" dotted and every
"t" crossed. Such planning is a welcome phenomenon. Generally,
however, bits and pieces of an estate may have been effectively
arranged, but an overall estate plan that includes all possible alternatives has not been established.

Although chaos will not necessarily result from the lack of proper
prior consideration of death's legal and financial implications, such
negligence and lack of concern is an open invitation to calamity
at a time when one's family is emotionally vulnerable and least
able to deal with critical decisions. It is rank foolishness to waive
the right to determine the plan for supporting one's loved ones
and instead to abandon personal desires to the impersonal machinations of the cold, slow, rigid, and expensive whims of the state probate system. In a society that refutes and denies death, the ultimate
selfishness is to leave a family as if it died with the decedent and
needed no help in arranging for the organized transfer of the accumu-
lations of the decedent's life.

What are prime considerations to be evaluated by individuals
and helping professionals, and what are some of the problems to be
solved and available tools for their solution? Prior to death one
may make arrangements for one's own peace of mind. These include
a will as a basic minimum, and then lists and inventories of assets,
perhaps a trust, a systematic review of all insurance policies and
profit-sharing plans, and an organization of assets in a way that will
serve the ends for which they were accumulated. Also an individual
might have desires concerning the disposition of his or her body
or its donation in toto or in parts such as eyes, ears, heart, or kidneys
to a medical school. Some other specific document or procedure
such as a power of attorney or guardianship could neatly meet the
individual's needs. None of these arrangements happen automatically nor do they occur without effort. Time must be invested in
order to provide the legal instruments that implement desires.

Following death a myriad of complex arrangements must be
made. The funeral has to be arranged or the body must be delivered.
Little items may be either divided, appropriated, or misplaced
during the immediate postdeath confusion if not carefully inven-
toried and secured. The will has to be probated and details such as
the recovery of insurance benefits must be handled. Social Security,

veteran's benefits, and private or public pension and profit-sharing plans that inure to the benefit of the deceased must be assembled, and then debts must be paid and the assets cataloged and earmarked for distribution. Uncle Sam holds out his friendly, but somewhat sticky, hand as he and the state require federal and state estate tax returns.

HOW CAN THE LIVING PREPARE FOR DEATH SO AS TO PROTECT THEMSELVES AND THEIR SURVIVORS?

Basic Minimum: A Will

A couple visited concerning an estate plan. Although they had been aware of estate planning for many years, it took a parent's death *intestate* (without a will) to provide the immediate incentive to call for an appointment. They were still in shock. Without a will, hundreds of dollars in lawyers' fees and countless hours of their time would be wasted by the estate in determining the rights regarding intestate succession and the ultimate disposition of a complex estate. A simple will would have been sufficient, but one had never been prepared or executed.

As the interview progressed, certain facts emerged. The husband had two children of a previous marriage, and this couple had one young child. Both sides of the family had natural expectations for a substantial portion of the inheritance. They were not poor people. The wife had little financial experience, and most of the family's monetary planning was handled by the husband, who was terminally ill. He had been informed that he had cancer, and the doctors indicated that although miracles do happen, he had an estimated 3 years to live. After being informed of the illness, he was referred to a counseling therapist. With the counselor's compassion and understanding, the husband and family came to realistically understand the diagnosis, prognosis, and treatment plan. Husband and wife faced the future bravely, savoring each moment together.

This family had sought the help of a counselor in an effort to understand and solve the real and imagined problems facing them. Yet at no time did the therapist ever inquire into their legal, financial, or estate planning needs. Nor did he ever refer them to an attorney who might draft the document or documents necessary to tie the estate into a neat legal bundle, guaranteeing that when the husband died his wife and all children would be sensibly provided for. Indeed, though the husband would still face medical problems that would gradually worsen, he could at least have the peace of mind that comes from knowing that his wishes would be honored and his loved ones protected.

Clearly, waiting so long had restricted his options, but the individual nevertheless retained a considerable degree of flexibility.

The Tax Reform Act of 1976 has altered the old section on gifts made in contemplation of death by providing an irrevocable presumption (i.e., one which cannot be rebutted) that all gifts made within 3 years of death are in contemplation of death and must be included in the decedent's estate for estate tax purposes. Nonetheless, the $3000 per person per year exemption from gift tax obligations could work to reduce the size of the taxable estate. More important however, in a circumstance such as this, is the present ability to transfer sufficient assets to assure the surviving wife of funds for support while the estate is probated. The husband might even desire to make a gift to his wife and/or children either outright or in trust including everything he owns and thus avoid the probate process entirely. (Caveat—both wife and children may have rights that could defeat the gift if it were adjudged a fraud upon their interests depending on the local jurisdiction. Therefore consultation with an attorney is not only advisable but necessary.)

Perhaps the counselor was personally naive concerning finances or was unaware of estate planning or perhaps he or she felt that an inquiry into legal and monetary matters might be overstepping the bounds of a therapeutic relationship. Any of these reasons or others would be inadequate; they would not satisfy the client's needs. Any person with any property at all needs a will. This is axiomatic. A person who dies without a will provides a bonanza for lawyers, bonding companies, probate courts, and nondeserving relatives. The difficulties are enormous.

How Can a Comprehensive Estate Plan
Provide Peace of Mind?

A properly drafted and current will, trust, or combination of both, coupled with insurance planning, does the following:

1. It provides for the naming of a guardian upon the death of a parent or both parents.
2. It allows present planning with future flexibility as circumstances change. Every person with an estate has a right to determine its disposition.
3. It provides the wife or husband with:
   a. Immediate funds to meet expenses during the period prior to settling the estate.
   b. A home, and clears the title.
   c. Security of income insofar as funds are available.
   d. Business management of property.
   e. A structure that enables either party to realistically provide for their family.

  f. A document that can guard against improvidence.

  g. Freedom to manage personal affairs with professional management of the trust corpus, where a bank or competent party is named trustee.

  h. Funds for an existing business.

  i. Funds for going into business, yet with a screening procedure.

  j. Protection that guards either spouse against the dangers of incapacity through old age, illness, or a bad subsequent marriage.

4. It provides the children with:

  a. Funds for an education.

  b. Protection for life or at least until certain age levels are reached.

  c. Protection against a designing or incompetent spouse (at least one of every three marriages in the United States ends in divorce).

  d. Business or personal financing, including education.

  e. Professional management of property.

  f. Restrictions against unfettered disposition of properties.

  g. A significant income supplement.

  h. A preselected guardian during minority, unfettered by the needless bureaucratic restrictions under which a court-appointed guardian operates.

Estate planning is not just for the rich. The probate of a will is not a society page item, and a trust is not a status symbol. Clearly not everyone will dedicate all the time and expense required to achieve the ultimate in tax-savings devices; however, the inordinate delay, frustration, and expense of intestacy (court management of the assets, formal adjudication of all major transactions, inflexibility in meeting rapid changes in individual needs, etc.) can be avoided. This is only one of the purposes of an estate plan. The limitations of an estate plan are very few.

Although state laws vary, wills, trusts, insurance policies and plans, and property ownership are basically contractual obligations that the lawyer can tailor to the needs and capacities of any particular client. In this way the individual characteristics of each family member can be considered as well as family needs and requirements. Provisions of all kinds can be inserted, including protection for spendthrift or handicapped children and clauses providing protection in the event of a child's divorce, as well as designated funds for support, health, and education. In short, there are few family financial problems that cannot be solved by careful planning and draftsmanship. Of course there are some obvious limitations, such as the size of the estate to be accumulated and the relative insurability of the parties. These are limitations easily taken into account.

ESTATE PLANNING:
THE INTERDISCIPLINARY TEAM

Many families have estate plans. When the plan is current and has been recently reviewed by an attorney, there is no further requirement. In absence of a later change requiring an amendment or codicil, the basic requirements have been met. However, where there is no will and there is property or insurance or a combination of both, a referral must be made either to the family attorney or to an attorney known by the counselor to be competent in sensitive areas. Indeed it behooves every mental health professional to develop colleagues in the law who can be relied upon to furnish quick and accurate service to all clients.

The term *mental health professional* in this context is considerably broadened to include all professionals who impact on the family and each of its members: the physician, nurse, psychiatrist, psychologist, minister or pastoral counselor, hospital chaplain, conceivably a well-trained hospital volunteer, the hospital social worker, or just about any helping professional who deals with and wishes to alleviate the trauma that is sure to occur if the estate plan is not in order.

Unfortunately, most institutions that train helping professionals have not yet broadened their scope to include courses in the legal aspects of death, nor do they encourage or sponsor in-depth seminars and training programs that bring into focus actual and potential legal problems. Indeed, there is even some resistance in this area, implying that legal problems are beyond the scope of the helping professional.

What are the minimum requirements? Every health professional should be aware of the broad scope of services offered by attorneys in wills and estate planning and of the interrelationship of legal and insurance programs. The degree of sophistication can depend on the level of the student. It is more important to know the questions to be asked (1) and the issues to be raised than it is to know substantive rules of law. The law changes daily as statutes are amended, repealed, or reinterpreted by court decisions. The issues and questions will always remain to be answered and considered. Where courses are not available, workshops and seminars can be organized. Professional legal, banking, insurance, and financial expertise is available in every area. These are professional public people. They will deliver a guest lecture, conduct a workshop, address a class, or participate in a roundtable dialogue at the drop of an invitation. Such individuals are available resources to be used in every community and indeed they should be with ever increasing regularity. Education may be formalized in an institutional setting as a foundation. Where a legal framework is involved, only continuing education can keep one's knowledge current. Obsolete concepts of law are worse than no concepts at all. The periodic workshop or seminar provides a convenient, quasisocial, pleasant framework for bringing the latest specialized legal happenings to the mental health community.

Preparation: Prior to the Visit
with the Lawyer

Much time can be saved if the counselor assists the client when deeply personal matters are involved. Who should be guardian of the children in the event of a simultaneous death? A brother, sister, or parents? How can one be selected without consulting the others? Do they want the child or children? Who should be executor and collect and distribute the assets? Is the wife or husband or family competent? Interested? Without guidance the resolution of these issues can be heartbreaking. With help they can be resolved in a way that is comfortable for all concerned.

Are the views of the heirs on religion, education, and lifestyle consistent with the lifestyle visualized by the testator or testatrix? While a lawyer might be available in this area, a mental health professional is better prepared to delve into the wishes and desires of the parties by rendering assistance in selecting the persons most likely to serve in any given capacity. The counselor can further resolve the conflicts that usually arise when individuals pull toward their own families or own children by a prior marriage. Certainly it is better for clients to be secure in these decisions prior to visiting the lawyer's office.

The interdisciplinary team serves the same purposes as any group of specialized professionals. Certain problems can be assigned to the lawyer and others to the counselor. Then the totality of advice is related to the client's capacity and inclination, and a series of decisions are jointly reached and implemented.

Financial Questionnaire

Few people prepare documents that illustrate their financial status at a glance. Generally, individuals keep sufficient records to prepare income tax returns and handle day-to-day problems. Millions of dollars in forgotten bank accounts *escheat* (pass as unclaimed property) to the state each year because passbooks are lost, misplaced, and forgotten. A basic minimum is the will fact sheet shown in

Appendix A, as it requires thinking about property, often causing people to recall the grammar school bankbook or the stock certificate used as a bookmark. Every lawyer will have a personal method for collecting data. This is primarily a review that would enable the client to have an overview of his finances prior to the interview and then establish general areas of concern.

The financial questionnaire, although laborious and detailed, should be completed over several days and delivered to the attorney along with any other relevant financial documents that clarify the monetary situation of the parties. Likewise, lists of specific areas of concern should be prepared in advance to assist in the planning process and serve as an agenda for discussion. Why? Because lawyers charge $40 to $50 *plus* per hour. Abraham Lincoln did not visualize such charges when he coined his oft-quoted (by lawyers) phrase, "A lawyer's time and advice are his stock in trade." Thus the time of the lawyer can best be used in advising, in exploring the issues, and then in making the client comfortable with decisions. Time spent by an attorney in merely gathering information that can easily be assembled and provided in advance is time misspent. True, the lawyer will have many questions that will augment the information furnished, but much essential data will already have been provided, and the immediate focus can be on the real issues at hand for that particular individual.

To the counselor the financial data provide necessary input concerning the coordination of wishes, whims, and abilities. Net worth plus insurance proceeds must be related to practical long- and short-term goals and desires.

Collateral Considerations

Earning capacity of survivor

The lawyer and counselor realistically review the survivor's potential position in relation to the funds available. Just as important and worthy of in-depth counseling is the issue of the survivor's capacity to earn, projected lifestyle, and willingness to be employed. A surviving mother or father with ample funds may seek to devote full time to children or charitable pursuits. With only modest funds available, a survivor may choose to work full or parttime to augment income and provide the luxuries that the estate cannot make available.

Many survivors are forced to work out of necessity. This is especially true when income plus estate proceeds are inadequate to provide a standard of living acceptable to the survivor. Here the counselor can be most helpful in anticipating future problems by present planning. When the survivor is elderly, there are local, state, and national governmental benefits including Social Security. There are also organizations that assist senior citizens in gaining employment suitable to their capacity. Often the legwork necessary to cut through the bureaucracy involved is mind boggling. Preparation now can assist in quick benefits later. When a party is terminally ill and the time frame can be estimated, paperwork can be assembled and prepared for undelayed execution and filing when needed.

When the survivor is young, the problem may be to develop a marketable skill or profession. If the spouse is terminally ill, the parties must explore all educational and employment opportunities for the survivor in the locality and seek out and prepare for employment. This can be through a junior or 4-year college, home study, correspondence courses, a trade school, a parttime job to update skills, the preparation of a current resume or any other plan that recognizes the uncertainty as well as frailty of human life and the need for advance planning and preparation.

The form an estate takes depends on the objectives it is to fulfill. A classic estate planning device is a trust utilizing estate funds to provide management and a steady cash flow to someone perhaps inexperienced in dealing with securities or too pressed for time to provide the day-to-day management needed. If other sufficient income is available it might be preferable to have a trust invested largely in growth stock (i.e., stocks paying low dividends but appreciating rapidly). In this way a large yield will result at some future date when the securities are sold (and taxed only at the lower long-term capital gains rate). This, for example, could provide extra funds for a child's college education. On the other hand, where little outside support can be expected and the problem is more immediate, higher dividend investments are desirable. If the surviving spouse is elderly, his or her needs are probably better served by providing present income for present enjoyment. A younger survivor with a major fraction of his or her financial needs met may prefer growth investments. Since a trust may pay income tax on earned but undistributed income, it is preferable to increase the trust's value by appreciation of holdings rather than by accumulating income. To the extent a person's condition and needs change, periodic updates should be made in the estate plan.

Emotional support

Estate plans are complex. For an involved family with grandparents, "your, my, and our" children, and perhaps handicapped or retarded children, such a plan can run into 30 pages, especially when a bank or trust company is involved. Much of the language is tailored to the specific needs of the individuals involved, but some is "boiler plate," that is, language common to almost all documents that

The Data: The Facts of Death

comply with the technical requirements of the law. Some clients will wade through the legal jargon. Others will just have the witnesses assemble and then ask, "Where do I sign?" Either way there is a certain finality as this last earthly chapter is written.

Lawyer and counselor serve clients well if the will is simplified in diagram form for purposes of explanation. With the counselor and lawyer, separately or together, the client can review the basic will and estate provisions and ultimately fully understand that the will can provide for intimate personal concerns as well as financial planning. Where doubts become apparent the counselor and client consult further and advise the lawyer of needed changes. In this way the final document together with ancillary arrangements provides the client with the basis for true peace of mind.

Furthermore, the clients may understand the multiplier effect of inflation for the first time and make other remedial changes (that is, increasing fire or life insurance on their home and furnishings). Knowing the way the estate is going to pass will alert them to seek more advice when projected significant changes arise and, conversely, avoid unnecessary reviews.

Age and possibility of relocation
and remarriage

In our mobile society distance means little. When death is imminent certain preparations should be considered that are not factors otherwise. Vultures hover over distressed properties. If assets are nonliquid such as real estate, which has considerable value but is often difficult to dispose of, an earnest review is needed. Present planning is necessary to insure that, on the death of one party, funds are available at once for the survivor to relocate if that is known to be the survivor's desire, or liquidity is arranged for taxes or to wind up a business. Likewise the instruments must provide clauses that secure the survivor from a bad second marriage.

In this sense the interdisciplinary team is expanded. The totality of the estate is viewed from all aspects. Insurance specialists explain the various options available under each insurance policy. Investment counselors review the stock portfolio in order to determine needs: appreciation, income, safety, flexibility, or a combination of all. A certified public accountant would advise concerning record keeping so that all available supporting data would avoid unnecessary taxes or insure that individual properties are segregated in the event of a second marriage. When should the team be assembled? Now. Before death takes one of the parties, man or woman. When family input can include the collective desires of both spouses who can interrelate with each other. Few people can function this objectively when the hour of bereavement arrives. Experience has indicated that a widow or widower who inherits a substantial amount of money tends to dissipate the inheritance quickly and unwisely. Prior planning can protect a survivor against him- or herself as well as others.

Suggested Sequence

In sum then, the events of estate planning and execution might proceed as follows:
1. Determination: Client has at least a minimal estate and no will.
2. Counselor determines appropriate therapy and consults concerning current estate plan.
3. If there is no current plan, the counselor reviews personal wishes with parties: What does each party wish for the survivor, and what does the survivor wish for himself or herself?
4. Counselor suggests completion of financial data sheet and consultation with attorney.
5. Attorney coordinates wishes with capacity and drafts initial rough draft of will and trust if appropriate, together with indepth advice regarding totality of the legal processes involved in dying.
6. Attorney and counselor as an interdisciplinary team review wishes, capacity, and instruments with client.
7. Instruments executed.
8. Postexecution followup: Lawyer and counselor consult informally every 6 months or so to provide financial and emotional update, and indicate to the survivor that there is a continued availability of the interdisciplinary team.

An Itemized List

Dr. G. recently died in Dallas at 80 years of age, leaving three sons and a daughter surviving. He was a widower. When his wife died several years previously, her will assigned all her possessions to him. Thus he paid his taxes and continued living in the home, elegantly surrounded by a lifetime accumulation of beautiful artifacts, with all property and a physical and financial lifestyle relatively intact. When he died the result was chaos. Why? Because although he was ready to die and was at peace with himself concerning death he had not thought out the ramifications that would affect his children. He had fulfilled the minimum requirements. He had a simple will.

Dr. G. had been a missionary in China and later in Japan. Upon his return to the United States he became a college professor. His homestead had greatly appreciated in value and was paid in full. He had collected artifacts throughout his life: vases from China

292   *The Data: The Facts of Death*

and Japan, chests of lacquer and inlaid woods and ivory, as well as statuary of wood, brass, and ivory. What happened upon his death? The house would be sold and the sum received divided among the children. Likewise cash, insurance, and other marketable properties would be sold and an allocation made to each child.

Where did the problem lie? In the personal property. It was priceless in a sense and yet not readily divisible in any way that would enable the children to be satisfied. There were sets and collections; items that could be divided in kind but that should not be separated or sold; hundreds of objects of art all with particular sentimental as well as market value and strong personal attachments.

Imagine the scene. Four children, four in-laws, and perhaps 11 grandchildren descend on the house from various parts of the state and nation. Funeral arrangements are made and the burial is complete. Guests and well-meaning visitors extend their condolences. Then the reality of the situation appears as the children make plans to return to their respective homes, arms filled with inheritances. What shall each child take? How can a division in kind be made, and who gets what? What has Dr. G. promised over the years to individual children, sons and daughters-in-law, grandchildren, and in this case a great-grandchild? As the enormity of the task becomes obvious, tensions appear. Although civility is the cornerstone of the relationship, fractures and fissures indicate weaknesses in the bonds that once united all the family members. Decisions must be made and the estate settled in an amicable manner that accomplishes an equal division yet preserves the closeness and integrity of the family. How could these difficult problems have been avoided during Dr. G.'s life so he could pass on with a sad yet cohesive family remaining?

Dr. G. had a will and his insurance was properly endorsed. Insofar as these details were important they were suitably handled. What had escaped Dr. G.'s mind was the difficulty of dividing the accumulation of a lifetime among family members at a time of bereavement. Were he alive and time were not a problem, the household items might have been allocated by Dr. G. in a manner acceptable to all, and the division made without hard feelings or difficulty. Cool heads would prevail and piece by piece the estate would be earmarked for one person or the other. The presence of a list would have encouraged and facilitated discussion among the family members so that particular preferences could have been accommodated. Dr. G.'s wishes would insure that everyone was satisfied and that treasured pieces would receive the care and appreciation they deserved.

What Dr. G. needed was an *itemized inventory* of his household. He would have divided the list into four relatively equal parts, each specifically earmarked for the child, an in-law, or a grandchild. Although a list such as this would not be binding in law, it would have been an accepted moral obligation. It is extremely doubtful that any child would have filed a will contest, or would have insisted that he or she receive something on another child's list. All the chaos could have been avoided. The children would walk into the house, pick up their lists, take possession of the property, and harmony would have prevailed. There are few families without some accumulation of meaningful items. Insofar as these items have particular intrinsic value, each individual owes a duty to the survivors to divide the small items of personal property in a way that will be fair, equitable, and satisfactory to all.

Periodic Review

In law there is no final solution, no time when the estate has been organized so that it need never be changed or altered. Documents are not set in concrete; neither are laws. Rather, estate plans are flexible arrangements, which must at any given time be maintained current so as to reflect the wishes of the parties. The instruments must be reviewed and updated to provide a current reflection of the parties' wishes. The list that follows contains barometers of concern; when occasions such as these arise the helping professional, the attorney, accountant, and insurance agent (or perhaps all four) should be consulted to see if the will or insurance should be revised.

1. *Marriage.* Marriage, like a business partnership, automatically brings about legal relationships that may conflict with the terms of a will made prior to marriage.
2. *Birth of a child.* There are statutes that safeguard the rights of children born subsequent to the execution of a will.
3. *Adoption of a child.* Many a person has been astounded to learn that the adoption of a child in effect changes the will drawn previous to the adoption.
4. *Change of residence.* State laws differ so much that one should immediately consult an attorney should one change residence from one state to another. While a will drawn in another state may still be valid, a new will may nevertheless be advisable.
5. *Acquisition of property in another state.* Whenever one acquires real property in another state, an attorney should review the will to make sure that it can be made operative in that state.
6. *Improved business status.* When one's financial status is improving one is less likely to consider possible difficulties ahead. Here is a common occurrence: A man's business enters

The Data: The Facts of Death

a period of marked improvement. The value of his stock interest in it advances sharply. But there may be no real market for any considerable amount of the company's stock. Obviously, in the event of his death at that particular time, his estate would face a greatly increased tax liability. Question: Would the estate be able to raise the necessary cash to meet taxes without sacrificing valuable assets?

7. *Change in business interests.* The death of a partner may seriously affect a partnership and end in the liquidation of the deceased partner's interest. If the surviving partner is to become sole owner of the business and continue it without interruption, and if the widow or widower of the deceased partner is to get cash for her or his interest in the business, proper arrangements must be made beforehand.

A similar situation can arise in the case of a closely held corporation. Here again, not only may the death of a key person be costly to the company through the loss of services, but also the question of disposing of his or her stock in the company *at the right price to the right person or persons* will also be important.

The sole or principal owner of a business should also be alert to the problems that will arise in continuing or liquidating the business after his or her death without severe losses.

In every instance a plan or formula for death tax valuation of a business interest is essential.

8. *Drastic shrinkage in securities values.* In the flush of prosperity, a person with large holdings of securities may readily make a will arranging for large gifts and bequests outright in cash, *after which* the family is to divide the remainder of the estate. However, experience has shown that drastic shrinkages in securities values can occur not once but very frequently during a person's lifetime. Should that happen when there is a will that has not been revised in line with changes in a person's financial circumstances, the family can virtually be disinherited because there may be little or no remainder after prior gifts and bequests have been paid.

9. *When a son comes of age or marries.* Wills made when children are still minors frequently contain trust provisions that parents will obviously wish to alter when children come of age. For example, at what age should a son receive his share of an estate outright? Should his share be structured to pass to his wife automatically, or only if they have children? What provisions should be made for his yet unborn children?

10. *When a daughter marries or comes of age.* Parents with daughters will readily realize the effect that the marriage of

a daughter may have on estate plans and wills. Trusts that have been set up to give a daughter an independent income for life may no longer be necessary—or may appear more necessary than ever. Perhaps sons and daughters should always be treated equally, perhaps not. Each family has its own individual preference.

11. *Birth of grandchildren.* The birth of grandchildren may also make will revision advisable in order to make them the ultimate beneficiaries.

12. *Changed status of a beneficiary.* In the course of time the personal or financial status of beneficiaries can so markedly change as to make revision of one's will highly desirable.

13. *Approaching retirement.* When one retires, he or she may decide to sell or convert certain assets, alter investment programs and otherwise rearrange personal property. All this can have a real impact on considerations that should be dealt with in the will.

14. *Changes in the tax laws.* A few generations ago taxes were a negligible item in estate settlement; now they are a major source of shrinkage, particularly in the case of large estates. Every general revision of tax laws should be followed by a review of one's will.

THE BODY AND ITS PARTS

For very practical reasons people do not own their bodies after death. The will, trust, insurance, and other financial instruments dispose of the estate and the accumulated assets. The body, however, belongs to a person's next of kin according to their degree of kinship. Many people have provided in their wills or in donative instruments instructions for their bodies to be delivered to science or to a local medical school. Others live in states that provide a donor's certificate. This might typically read as follows:

> I, the undersigned, being of sound mind and over 18 donate my [heart, eyes, ears, kidneys, body] as an anatomical gift at the time of my death under the provisions of Article 6687.6, Vernon's Civil Statutes (the Texas Statutes) and in conformity with Article 4590.2, Vernon's Civil Statutes. [Signatures of the donor and two witnesses are required.]

While this does state donative intent, complies with the law and appears legal, it does not bind the next of kin. They may honor the request or they may refuse and make a personal determination concerning the ultimate disposal of the remains. As a practical matter, the body has value for the purpose of organ transplants for a very

The Data: The Facts of Death

limited period of time. Within hours or even minutes after technical death has occurred, organs must be removed and preserved. No medical organization would want to commence litigation to enforce its rights. Within a short time the question would be moot and the organs valueless; likewise with the body. It is inconceivable that a lawsuit would be undertaken to remove a body from the possession of the next of kin. Where even a hint of a dispute might arise, the medical facility would certainly take the position that the wishes of the next of kin prevail.

Why can an individual not contract away or donate the body and have this binding on the heirs, or the executor, or even binding at once as a contract that can be enforced in a court of equity using the remedy of specific performance? The reasons are many. First of all, public policy would militate against poor people selling their bodies before death to institutions or individuals. One can only imagine cadaver-short hospitals offering cash premiums for bodies or parts of bodies prior to death. The same logic would follow with frantic families needing a matching kidney or other body part and a poor person struggling in despair to feed his or her family and perhaps near suicide. What kind of an arrangement could be made to provide dignity and a rational justification for suicide? A pact. Donate the organ in exchange for financial relief or perhaps a college education for the children. Or perhaps worse, a person could sell the same parts to multiple potential recipients and then let them fight it out after death.

Secondly, assuming one is donating his or her body parts, who has the right to make the first incision and when? The first to arrive at the scene? The kidney bank? The eye bank? The cadaver keeper? The practical problems are enormous and limitless. Chaos would result if no central identifiable person were designated to determine the wishes of the deceased along with the feelings of the survivors. The cause of death and the individuals' condition likewise make it impractical to involve third parties in the dissection of a body instantly. Only the immediate next of kin, after being informed of the death, can view the body, consider the family needs and perhaps the psychological overtones, and then make a rational decision. And even a choice at this particular time may be clouded in haste or affected by profound emotion.

Where practical the individual does have a duty or at least an obligation. In clear and certain terms donors should execute all instruments necessary for disposal of their remains and make the contents and location of these instruments and the donors' intent known to their heirs and next of kin in unequivocal terms. Donors must also comply with the technicalities of rapidly changing state statutes. This is a developing area in law and current requirements must be checked. When death does occur, the wishes of the deceased can be honored with a minimum of confusion and a maximum of consideration for both the deceased and the survivors. Both the desires of the deceased and the community needs are then satisfied.

Fresh organs are required for transplant or organ bank purposes, while age is less of a factor when used for dissection or for teaching purposes. Fresh skin is needed for transplants, while slightly older skin may be used for a covering as this skin is ultimately shed. Only a fresh cornea, kidneys, or bones are valuable for implantation, and blood is valueless shortly after death. For practical purposes, a medical team is helpful and often essential at the moment of death. From that point on the value of the body to medical science and waiting patients gradually diminishes.

Wills are not probated until days or even months after a person dies. Thus verbiage in the will that refers to bodily remains is effective as a statement of desire only. It is not technically binding on the heirs and is respected only insofar as it is consistent with the wishes of the next of kin who, incidentally, may or may not be heirs.

Fortunately, all 51 jurisdictions, the 50 states, and Washington, D.C. have adopted some form of the Uniform Anatomical Gifts Act. Some states have approved forms such as donor cards to be carried by an individual demonstrating his or her intent to donate the body or its parts and streamlining the process considerably. In Texas it is possible for a relative to make the donation, provided it is known that the donor has no objections and that no close relative objects (Texas Revised Civil Statutes, Article 4590-2, Section 3(6)). Another important point in the Texas statute, as in most others, is a specific charge that upon removal of organs, the body cannot be mutilated. This prevents the psychological burden at the funeral from becoming more onerous.

UNSETTLED QUESTIONS AND PROBLEMS

When Does Death Occur?

The question of when death occurs is in and of itself a technical and somewhat changing area. Modern medicine has created distinctions that cloud the traditional concept that death occurs when the heart stops beating. Does death occur when the brain ceases to function as measured by sophisticated equipment? Bodily organs cease their functions at different times. Should one wait until the last organ has no measurable sign of life before determining that death has occurred? Scientists and medical doctors are still seeking a workable and practical definition of death and the time it occurs.

The law does look to the medical profession for guidance in this area. As "brain death" gains more widespread support as the "right" definition, dissatisfaction with the present heart failure concept will grow. Law tends to look toward precedent and tradition as the basis for decisions. Change can come either through judges expanding, interpreting, and applying past cases to new situations or through legislatures enacting new statutory provisions. Both groups fear alienating the people by making bold decisions accepting the latest fad on so sensitive a point as the definition of death.

Generally doctors have tended to adopt the standards of the *ad hoc* committee of the Harvard Medical School in defining the brain death syndrome. There are four basic tests which indicate that brain death has occurred:

(1) Unreceptivity and Unresponsivity.—There is a total unawareness to externally applied stimuli and inner need and complete unresponsiveness—our definition of irreversible coma. Even the most intensely painful stimuli evoke no vocal or other response, not even a groan, withdrawal of a limb, or quickening of respiration.

(2) No Movements or Breathing.—Observations covering a period of at least one hour by physicians is adequate to satisfy the criteria of no spontaneous muscular movements or spontaneous respiration or response to stimuli such as pain, touch, sound, or light. After the patient is on a mechanical respirator, the total absence of spontaneous breathing may be established by turning off the respirator for three minutes and observing whether there is any effort on the part of the subject to breathe spontaneously. (The respirator may be turned off for this time provided that at the start of the trial period the patient's carbon dioxide tension is within the normal range, and provided also that the patient had been breathing room air at least ten minutes prior to the trial.)

(3) No Reflexes.—Irreversible coma with abolition of central nervous system activity is evidenced in part by the absence of elicitable reflexes. The pupil will be fixed and dilated and will not respond to a direct source of bright light. Since the establishment of a fixed, dilated pupil is clearcut in clinical practice, there should be no uncertainty as to its presence. Ocular movement (to head turning and to irritation of the ears with ice water) and blinking are absent. There is no evidence of postural activity (deliberate or other). Swallowing, yawning, vocalization are in abeyance. Corneal and pharyngeal reflexes are absent. . . .

(4) Flat Electroencephalogram.—Of great confirmatory value is the flat or isoteric EEG. . . . We consider it prudent to have one channel of the apparatus used for an electrocardiogram. This channel will monitor the ECG so that, if it appears in the electroencephalographic leads because of high resistance, it can be readily identified. It also establishes the presence of the active heart in the absence of the EEG. . . . The apparatus should be run at standard gains 10v/mm, 50 v/5 mm. Also it should be isoteric at double this standard gain which is 5 v/mm or 25 v/5 mm. At least ten full minutes of recording are desirable, but twice that would be better. . . .

All of the above tests shall be repeated at least 24 hours later
with no change.

Irreversible cessation of cerebral function, irreversible cerebral
function and brain death for purposes of this paper denote the same
condition. The causes of such a condition can be varied, but they all
indicate that the individual has no discernible central nervous system
activity. They are able to be sustained on rescusitative devices which
keep the body functioning performing the function of the brain. (2,
pp. 337–340)

The Karen Quinlan case has brought due focus to the issue, and
modernization of the legal definition of death approaches inexorably
down both avenues of change.

Judges have made their move toward accepting the brain death
definition, notably in *People* v. *Lyons*, a California Supreme Court
case heard in 1974. In that case a man was shot in the head. Although his bodily functions continued, doctors determined that he
had an irreversible cessation of brain function and removed his
heart for transplant purposes. In the murder trial against the trans-
planting physician, the Court held as follows:

As jurors, it is your exclusive duty to decide all questions of fact
submitted to you.

On the basis of the evidence introduced in the case, the question
of the proximate cause of the death of the victim, . . . is not an issue
of fact, but is a matter of law.

Death is the cessation of life. A person may be pronounced dead
if, based on usual and customary standards of medical practice, it is
determined that the person has suffered an irreversible cessation of
brain function.

The usual and customary standards of medical practice involving
determination of life and death, in the light of developments in the
medical knowledge acquired by experiment, research, clinical practice and surgery in the past approximate 20 years, was the subject of
testimony of pre-eminent medical experts in the field of cardiology,
neurosurgery, cardiac surgery and electroencephalography. All of the
experts were in agreement as to such standards.

The testimony of all experts was that the proximate cause of, the
time of the death of the victim, was determined and established
under such usual and customary standards of medical practice; there
was not a scintilla of evidence to the contrary. Thus as applied to the
case before this Court, there remains no issue of fact.

You are instructed, as a matter of law, that at eight o'clock in the
morning of September 12, 1973, the victim, . . . had an irreversible
cessation of brain function, proximately caused by gunshot wound;
that at that time death had occurred.

You are further instructed, as a matter of law, the victim, . . .
was legally dead, before the removal of the organs from his body. (3)

Understandably, courts have more freedom to make the first move
in this area than the legislatures. It is likely that the first legislative
move in this area will be along permissive lines; the right to die and

the living will will be established possibly similar to the California Natural Death Act.

Euthanasia

When to pull the plug is perhaps the most sensitive and heartbreaking issue ever considered by loving relatives. Modern medicine is both blessed and cursed. Thousands of life-maintaining machines have been developed, including kidney dialysis machines, respirators, and others. The question of when or whether to cease operation of a life-sustaining device has been the subject of philosophical discussions for many years. There are safeguards (panels of medical doctors who make the final decision) and procedures (court orders and hearings) that provide some relief. They ameliorate the problem but do not solve it. As long as humans are in a position to decide the fate of others, the problem will remain.

The issue is in a particular state of flux at present, especially along legal lines. The celebrated case of Karen Quinlan (70 N.J. 10, 355 A.2d 64 F [1976] rev'g 137 N.J. Super. 227, 348 A.2d 801 [ch. 1975]) has led to increased legal literature on the subject. While Karen had mentioned that she would not want extraordinary life support to keep her body alive after "mental" death, the court gave little significance to those earlier statements because they did not show that she was aware of the magnitude of her decision. An outline has been proposed (4) for a voluntary *euthanasia* or *antidysthanasia* statute (the former term means "happy death" or the deliberate easing into death of an individual, while the latter term refers to the cessation of use of extraordinary life-support devices to prolong the life of an incurable patient), which would require:

1. Establishment of a highly formalized, witnessed and memorialized document clearly manifesting the signor's intent (a "living will," functional equivalent of a testamentary disposition with similar formalities).
2. A general statement of the operative circumstances in which the document will be legally effective, terminology to be definite but sufficiently flexible to accommodate medical advances.
3. Prior judicial permission to implement the will (functional equivalent of probate).
4. Maximum flexibility in revocation, either oral or written.
5. Limited effective duration with stringent renewal requirements (annual renewals recommended).
6. Removal of criminal and civil liabilities for participation.
7. Provision for effects on property rights, life insurance, etc.

8. Imposition of criminal and civil liabilities for fraud or negligence.

As mentioned previously, California has established the first legislative response to the problem. The Natural Death Act was passed in 1976, allowing the individual to assume the burden of this final decision. The act includes all safeguards proposed by the various legal scholars who have addressed the issue. An important aspect of the act specifically declares that life insurance policies cannot be invalidated by the exercise of this right. Without such a stipulation, the act could have been a vacuous gesture impaired by financial necessity. The act is an important step toward individual dignity and freedom in our ultimate decision. On the other hand, the day is upon us when we may have to face up to an uncomfortable issue. As always, the granting of a new right is accompanied by a new responsibility, both for the individual and the surrounding family.

DEATH INTESTATE

Each state has specific laws concerning intestate (without a will) succession. When individuals do not have a will properly executed, the state in effect drafts one in the sense that the law provides how the estate shall be divided. A will allows the testator to choose his or her heirs and provide for them. To die intestate is to fail to fulfill a last obligation to one's family.

The problems created by intestate death can be horrendous. They may include:

1. Unnecessary expenditures of time and money in determining heirship.
2. Family disputes that revolve around general percentages of interest as well as the disposition of particular items of property.
3. Obscure areas of authority in which the more assertive and often least competent person generally prevails.
4. Practical problems when the estate includes a business that must be run or perishable commodities that must be disposed of.
5. Continued court supervision of the estate at a major cost in time, frustration, and money.
6. Inflexibility in shaping the estate's makeup making it difficult to take advantage of promising investments or to meet an expected family need.
7. Dictated dispositive scheme by operation of law, which can be diametrically opposed to the desires of the decedent and the needs of the family.

The list is endless. No one should die without a professionally drawn and properly executed will.

The power of attorney is a written and notarized or witnessed instrument that authorizes another to act in one's behalf. It can be a general power of attorney that authorizes another to act fully in behalf of the grantor, or a specific power of attorney that limits the grantee to certain acts, such as the selling of a house or automobile, or managing a piece of property in the absence of the grantor. The power of attorney may also be limited as to time and may be drafted so as to terminate either on the happening of an event or after a particular date. It may also be terminated at any time by the grantor. Further, the power of attorney may provide that "this instrument and the powers given thereunder shall not terminate on the mental or physical incapacity of the grantor." Thus this becomes an irrevocable power of attorney should mental illness or senility occur. When recorded, anyone dealing with the grantee has the right to rely on the recorded instrument. Likewise, when a revocation is filed, the power of attorney is null and void.

A power of attorney can be especially vital for an active business executive. Mental or physical incapacity can leave securities unattended as they take precipitous falls in value. Partnerships, sole proprietorships, and privately held corporations may languish without guidance. A business partner who worked well while under a partner's observation may prove less than trustworthy alone. More than once a partner has stripped an incapacitated associate of a small fortune while the family was powerless to act, and it may be that by the time legal action can be taken, the business, its assets, and the partner have simultaneously disappeared. A power of attorney would enable a designated person to step in at once and preserve the business and the rights of the parties.

The power of attorney is a useful legal tool when something has to be done and some problem exists concerning the ability to perform. Another can be appointed to perform the task. The danger occurs when the power is carelessly given to an undeserving or unqualified person. The power is vast and the grantor is liable for all the acts of the grantee.

THE FIDUCIARIES
(GUARDIANSHIP, CONSERVATORSHIP, TRUSTEESHIP)

Fiduciaries serve a broad and vital role in financial assistance on many occasions within our society. Their use extends beyond death-related functions and can be helpful in any planning situation. When a person has an estate that must be protected, the court may, upon application and order, or the parties may by written instrument establish a guardianship, conservatorship, or trusteeship. These procedures separate the person from his estate and allow a friend, relative, or financial institution to manage the estate of and for the individual. They act in a fiduciary, or trust, capacity and must exercise scrupulous good faith in their dealings on behalf of the individual. Fiduciaries are thus accorded great latitude in their handling of the estate. As in the power of attorney, the protection afforded can maintain the estate productive and intact. It can also, in the hands of a scheming relation or incompetent professional, portend the beginning of the end of a lifetime of accumulation. Fiduciaries are useful tools and when appropriate provide continuity, professional management, and conservation but should be carefully chosen so that the trust will not be violated.

FOLLOWING DEATH

Following death the body belongs to the next of kin. The body can be disposed of in accordance with the terms of the will or the wishes of the deceased, including the distribution of organs or the delivery of the body to a science foundation. When a relative takes possession of the body and then makes funeral arrangements, one must keep in mind that although the will may provide for the payment of expenses, one who signs a contract for burial and interment is likewise responsible under the terms of the contract. Funeral expenses are always a debt of the estate and are paid out of the assets. However, when there are insufficient assets, the individual making the contract is likewise responsible for their payment.

Insurance proceeds are paid to designated beneficiaries. Thus a person can die leaving insurance policy proceeds to various individuals and yet have an estate with insufficient assets to pay debts including funeral expenses.

The executor or administrator, if the person dies without a will, immediately enters onto the scene for the conservation and preservation of assets. By definition and function the administrator resembles an executor but, being court-appointed, must give security or post bond for the proper administration of the estate. The administrator has only limited authority: collecting assets, paying debts, and distributing the residue to the beneficiaries. As with any court-appointed fiduciary, the individual or corporate entity must operate in a tangle of statutory red tape and with an eye to meeting legal obligations rather than the personal needs of the deceased's family. Unfortunately, the cost for these services runs higher than for an executor.

Also included would be the hiring of a lawyer. This is a most sensitive area because the lawyer is normally engaged at a time when people are unaware of all their legal rights and obligations. An attorney should be sought out who has experience in the area of wills, trusts, and estates, and who is known to have an excellent professional reputation. Consultation with the attorney prior to death is preferable for several reasons. The family members who will have to deal with the attorney will be able to express any doubts or difficulties they may feel they might have with that individual, possibly allowing a timely end to the relationship and search for a new attorney. The attorney will have the same opportunity and will also be able to assemble essential data before the pressures accompanying bereavement set in. In this way, a good working relationship will be established to handle the situation.

A fee should be clearly discussed, and all parties should know whether or not the fee is on an hourly basis, a percentage of the estate, or some combination of the two. Inasmuch as a layperson might not appreciate the complexity of the services, the executor and administrator must be satisfied he or she has made a sensible agreement at its initiation rather than letting doubts erode the working relationship with the attorney at some future date.

The Executor

The executor is the person appointed by the testator (author of the will) to carry out the directions and requests in the will and to dispose of the property according to the testamentary provisions after the individual's death.

The executor collects all assets, which include bank accounts, real and personal property, insurance, patent and copyright interests, and so forth. The executor, having marshaled the assets, then pays all outstanding debts, and will file the tax returns for the estate and see that the taxes are paid. The executor will ascertain the individual bequests set forth in the will and distribute particular items of personal property as is appropriate. Following this, the remainder will be divided among the heirs either in accordance with the wishes of the testator under the will or in accordance with the laws of intestate succession in the particular jurisdiction.

There is always the chance that the selected executor may not serve or may become unable or unwilling to continue after having served for awhile. For such an eventuality, there should be named an alternate or substitute executor—another individual or a corporate entity such as a bank. The advantage to naming a bank as an alternate trustee is continuity; security in knowing that the bank will actually be there when necessary and that the estate will not require court appointment and supervision of a trustee or administrator.

The executor may be allowed to serve without bond and without the filing of frequent accountings to the court. This permits greater ease of action at lesser expense and cost to the estate. Again, this underscores the importance of selecting the proper executor. Needless to say, the testator can also include extra safeguards restricting or augmenting the executor's actions.

WHY GET PROFESSIONAL HELP?

The mechanics involved in handling contemporary estates can be highly complex. The 50 states and the District of Columbia each have their own laws. Federal law, with reference to income, estate, and gift taxes if nowhere else, must be considered. With a society as mobile as ours (5 percent of the population moves across state boundaries each year) it is imperative that a flexible plan be made. While it is the attorney's duty to see that the will and trust drafted will be valid in every jurisdiction, certain considerations are of special significance. The devise of real property must meet all the particular formalities of the jurisdiction within which it is situate, whereas personal property usually must meet only the requirements of the testator's domicile. There are eight community property jurisdictions in the United States, in which half of all assets accumulated during the marriage are attributed to the other spouse. But even among these states, there are wide variances (California treats all income from separate property during marriage as separate property whereas Texas treats the same income as community property). Each state places estate and inheritance taxes on property, real and personal, within its jurisdiction. Different states require different formalities for probate shortcuts (e.g., self-proving wills), but these formalities may not be sufficient for passing real property. In all, there are myriads of problems that might cause the average person to drown in the details, let alone effectuate his or her desires without the assistance of an attorney.

The interdisciplinary team can shape the estate to best suit the individual's needs. There are options such as intervivos (living) trusts, either revocable or irrevocable, testamentary (established by the will) trusts. Frequently used is the insurance pour-over trust where the proceeds of the policy go into the trust set up according to the testator's wishes. Many people employ the generation-skipping trust, where the income is paid to one individual (e.g., the surviving spouse) and the corpus is paid at that individual's death to the *remaindermen*, those surviving after the death of the surviving spouse or the primary beneficiary. Remaindermen receive the property after a spouse receives a life interest in the income. Remaindermen may also receive the property after a spouse receives a life estate, such remaindermen to receive their property on the death of the surviving spouse.

Sometimes the testator feels that the future is too distant to make properly the division of a trust at present. In that case a power of appointment, where a person other than the testator can determine to whom the trust should be paid, either general (anyone can be ultimate recipient) or specific (persons with the power cannot exercise in favor of themselves, their estates, or their creditors). The relative merits of life insurance should be investigated. While proper investment can be cheaper than life insurance, it does not always act as a forced savings technique. The Tax Reform Act of 1976 has further muddied the water with extensive revisions in the estate, gift, and income tax sections. An example of the importance of tax planning is the appropriate use of the marital deduction (the greater of $250,000 or one-half of the estate, with various limitations). A combination of attorney, counselor, trust officer or banker, and stock broker can work together to formulate the best plan for each individual. Obviously a complete review of the tax law would be an exercise in futility. By the time of publication, the law can change. Tax law is a sophisticated specialty.

APPENDIX A

Sample Will Fact Sheet
(Please Print)

Social Security No. _____ Date _____

Your
Name _____
       (First)   (Middle)   (Last)

Home   Home
Address _____ Telephone _____
     (Street) (City) (State) (Zip Code)

Date of Birth _____ Place of Birth _____

Employer _____ Position _____

Business   Business
Address _____ Telephone _____
     (Street) (City) (State) (Zip Code)

If presently holding more than
one job, additional employer(s)_____

Military Service_____ Branch_____Serial No._____
          (Yes or No)

Date of Service_____ to_____ Reserve Status_____

Your   Social Security
Wife's Name_____ No._____
      (First) (Middle) (Maiden) (Last)

Date of Birth_____ Place of Birth_____

Has wife worked since marriage? Yes_____ No_____

Wife's present
Employer_____ Position_____

Business   Business
Address_____ Telephone_____
     (Street) (City)   (State)   (Zip Code)

Date of Marriage_____ Place of Marriage_____

    If either you or your wife has been married before, please furnish the following information as to each prior marriage below: (1) name of former spouse, (2) time and place of the marriage, (3) place, date, and cause (death, divorce, etc.) of termination of the marriage. (Use the reverse side of sheet if necessary.)

Children:
                             Date of   Place of
1. Name_____ Birth_____ Birth_____
     (First)   (Middle)   (Last)

If married, name of husband or wife_____
                           (First)   (Middle)   (Last)

Present address, if
different from yours_____
             (Street)   (City)   (State)   (Zip Code)

How many children (your Grandchildren)_____

                             Date of   Place of
2. Name_____ Birth_____ Birth_____
     (First)   (Middle)   (Last)

If married, name of husband or wife_____
                           (First)   (Middle)   (Last)

Present address, if
different from yours _____
     (Street) (City) (State) (Zip Code)

How many children (your Grandchildren)_____

             Date of   Place of
3. Name_____ Birth_____ Birth_____
  (First) (Middle) (Last)

If married, name of husband or wife _____
         (First)   (Middle)   (Last)

Present address, if
different from yours _____
     (Street) (City) (State) (Zip Code)

How many children (your Grandchildren)_____

             Date of   Place of
4. Name_____ Birth_____ Birth_____
  (First) (Middle) (Last)

If married, name of husband or wife _____
         (First)   (Middle)   (Last)

Present address, if
different from yours _____
     (Street) (City) (State) (Zip Code)

How many children (your Grandchildren)_____

(If additional space is needed, please list the same information for each child on the reverse side of this sheet.)

(If any child listed is not a child of your present marriage, please place an asterisk [*] beside such child's name, and furnish any additional information on the reverse side of this sheet.)

(If there are any deceased children, please list the name, date of birth, etc. of any children [your grandchildren] of deceased children.)

(Please specify if any of the above listed children or grandchildren have any special problems such as physical or mental infirmities.)

FINANCIAL INFORMATION:

ASSETS

 1. Average cash balance (including savings) $_____

 2. Bonds $_____

 3. Stocks $_____

 4. Business Interests (describe under "Remarks") $_____

 5. Residence   Value $_____

      Less Mortgage _____ Real Equity $_____

6. Other Real Estate (describe)

_____ Value $_____

_____ Less Mortgage _____

_____ Real Equity $_____

_____

_____ Value $_____

_____ Less Mortgage _____

_____ Real Equity $_____

_____

7. Autos, Boats or Planes

_____ Value $_____

_____ Less Mortgage _____

_____ Real Equity $_____

_____ Value $_____

_____ Less Mortgage _____

_____ Real Equity $_____

_____

8. Livestock $_____

9. Benefits (see below for detail) $_____

10. Other assets, including furnishings of
    house, antiques, collector's items, etc. $_____

_____ _____

_____ _____

_____ _____

_____ _____

$_____

(Place an asterisk [*] by any debt or mortgage which is
covered by credit life insurance.)

11. (a) Life Insurance on your life (Place an asterisk [*] by any
        insurance on your life which is owned by your wife.)

Insurance Company	Type & No. of Policy	Face Amount of Policy	Cash Surrender Value, If Any	Date of Issue	Present Beneficiary Primary Contingent	Amount of Accidental Death Provisions

(b) Life Insurance on your wife's life (Place an asterisk [*] by any insurance on your wife's life which is owned by you.)

LIABILITIES

1. Average accounts payable (including monthly bills) $ _____

2. Any loans or debts other than those mortgages shown above—(describe)

_____ $ _____

_____   _____

_____   _____

(Place an asterisk [*] by any debt or mortgage which is covered by credit life insurance.)

INCOME

Your salary $ _____ /year

Your wife's salary $ _____ /year

Any income in excess of your and your wife's salaries—(describe sources)

_____ $ _____

_____   _____

_____   _____

List any benefits to which you or your wife are entitled or will be entitled. Mark yours "H" and mark your wife's "W". (Examples: Pension Plan, Thrift Plan, etc.)

Value, if known

_____Pension Plan $_____

_____Thrift Plan   _____

_____Profit-Sharing Plan   _____

_____Social Security   _____ .

_____Other (describe)—such as Government Disability, Retirement Pay, Teacher's Retirement, etc.

____ _____   _____

____ _____   _____ $_____

Do you own any property located outside of Texas? _____ If so, describe:
(Yes or No)

_____

_____

Have either you or your wife inherited or do you expect to inherit any property?_____ If so, describe and give approximate values. $_____

_____

_____

Have you always lived in Texas?_____ If not, when did you move to Texas?_____
(Year)

Do you have a safe deposit box?_____ If so, what bank?_____

_____

List below the name, age, relationship and address of the person (or the name and address of the bank) that you and your wife wish to have serve in the capacities indicated:

Your Will

Executor_____

Alternate Executor(s)_____

_____

Trustee_____

_____

Alternate Trustee_____

_____

Guardian _____

Alternate Guardian _____

Your Wife's Will

Executor _____

Alternate Executor(s) _____

Trustee _____

Alternate Trustee _____

Guardian _____

Alternate Guardian _____

List below the name, age, relationship and address of any person who has not been mentioned above in this Will Fact Sheet but is to receive property under your Will or your wife's Will.

_____

_____

_____

_____

DISPOSITION OF PROPERTY

In your own words, describe the way you want your property to pass under your Will: (Use back of sheet if necessary.)

(a) If your wife survives you.

(b) If your wife does not survive you.

In your own words, describe the way your wife wants her property to pass under her Will: (Use back of sheet if necessary.)

(a) If you survive her.

(b) If you do not survive her.

Are all of the persons whose names appear on this form citizens of the U.S.?_____

List below the name, address and telephone number of:

(a) Your insurance agent_____

_____

(b) The accountant or other person who prepares your income tax return:

_____

Remarks: (Use back of sheet if necessary.)

_____
Signature of Client

_____
Client's Spouse

_____
Date

APPENDIX B

Questions to Be Asked when an Individual
Enters an Institution

When an individual is left with an institution the most pressing problem is to get the person safely and commodiously settled. Without in any way detracting from the importance of a peaceful adjustment, this time presents an excellent opportunity to ask either of the individual or of the family certain lay questions of legal health. The counselor should inquire:

1. Does the individual have a will?
2. Is its location known?
3. Is the will up to date and satisfactory? (With an affirmative response here, no further questions are necessary.)
4. Have any significant legal events occurred since the making of the will?
5. Has the individual ever been married, and, if so, how many times and with what offspring?
6. Has the individual ever adopted any children?
7. What is the status and location of all relatives of the individual?
8. To what extent have all been treated in the will?
9. Does the individual have a safety deposit box, and with what possessions?
10. Has disposition been made of any and all insurance policies, securities, bank deposits, and royalty payments?
11. Does the individual wish to donate parts of his body to science?
12. Are the specific bequests to be given to specific people?

While these questions only scratch the surface, they should immediately alert the individual or relatives as to whether legal and financial planning help should be sought.

REFERENCES

1. Bernstein, B. E. Lawyer and social worker as collaborators in the medical setting. *Health & Social Work*, 1977, *2*, p. 148.
2. Ad Hoc Committee of the Harvard Medical School to Examine the Definition of Brain Death. A definition of irreversible coma. *Journal of the American Medical Association*, 1968, *205*, 337–340.
3. *People* v. *Lyons*, No. 56072, California Supreme Court, 1974.
4. Hyland, W. F., & Baime, D. S. In Re Quinlan: A synthesis of law and medical technology. 8 *Rutgers-Camden, Law Journal*, 37 at 54, n 110 (1976).

BIBLIOGRAPHY

Bailey, E. W. *Texas law of wills.* Kansas City, MO: Vernon Law Book Co., 1968.

Callahan, P. J. T. *How to make a will, How to use trusts.* Dobbs Ferry, NY: Oceana, 1975.

First National Bank of Dallas, Trust Department. *Texas will manual service,* looseleaf, current. (In most large cities at least one bank will keep a current will and trust service, largely for the use of attorneys. While this may be somewhat difficult for a layman, with proper background reading it could aid in grasping some of the changes being made in the field.)

Grange, W. J., Staub, W., & Blackford, E. *Wills, executors and trustees: A practical work on the law, administration and accounting of estates and trusts.* New York: Ronald Press, 1950.

Haskel, P. *Preface to the law of trusts.* Mineola, NY: Foundation Press, 1975.

Lynn, R. *An introduction to estate planning.* St. Paul, MN: West Publishing, 1975.

Republic National Bank of Dallas. *Family financial planning library* (pamphlet series). "Investment Supervision," "Life Insurance," "The Living Trust," "Making Your Estate Last," "Your Trust Officer," "Your Will." (The Trust Departments of most banks have similar series of publications, generally free of charge, providing a general understanding of family financial planning and the particular areas in the field.)

State Bar of Texas, Real Estate, Probate, and Trust Sections. *How to live and die with Texas probate; Here's a comprehensive treatment of how every Texan can save money, time and taxes.* C. A. Saunder (Ed.), Houston: Gulf Publishing, 1968. (State and local bar associations usually have similar publications and can aid in finding more material on point. Bar associations usually also have some kind of referral service to identify the specialists in particular areas of the law.)

Cantor, N. L. A patient's decision to decline life-saving medical treatment: Bodily integrity v. the preservation of life. 26 *Rutgers Law Review,* 228 (1973).

Shattuch, J. E. How to do it: Donation of bodies or body parts under the Texas Anatomical Gifts Act. 27 *Baylor Law Review* 141 (1975).

When are you really dead?, *Newsweek,* December 18, 1967, p. 87.

Snider, A. J. When is a person dead?, *Science Digest,* October 1967, p. 71.

Cable, K. R. The tell-tale heart. 27 *Baylor Law Review* 157 (1975).

Gaylin. Harvesting the dead. 249 *Harpers* 24 (September 1974).

Bernstein, B. E. Lawyer and counselor as an interdisciplinary team: Interfacing for the terminally ill. *Death Education,* 1977, *1,* 277–291.

Further direction in locating source material is possible through local law schools and law libraries. Often, the introductory chapters of case books can be helpful (e.g., J. Ritchie, H. Alford, Jr., & R. Effland, *Cases and materials on decedents' estates and trusts,* (5th ed.) Mineola, NY: Foundation Press, 1977. Legal clinics are also likely to have introductory materials available.

The Challenge:
Meeting
the Issues
of Death

P art Three consists of four "closing" chapters. Although they
appear at the end of this volume, their aim is not to provide closure
and their substance concerns open matters. It concerns major issues
and controversies about dying and death that are unresolved. These
issues challenge us as members of society as well as individuals.

Modern medical science and technology can keep a human being
from dying naturally. "Live" organ transplants raise ethical issues
with respect to the time of death of the donor. When physicians have
to form committees and debate criteria for determining death, and
when courts of law rule about whether physicians are correct, then
we must admit we have an issue of enormous proportion. We are
forced to reexamine and redefine fundamental human values and the
meaning and quality of life. A new definition of death is needed, one
not confined to medical-technical aspects but embracing ethical,
moral, personal, and social aspects as well. New medical technology
also brings to the fore the complex issue of euthanasia and the right
to die. As Carson suggests, we have come to fear the technological
trappings as much as death itself. Such fear leads naturally to the
questions: What is life worth? and Under what circumstances do I
wish my life to be terminated? Two of the chapters in Part Three discuss these issues, explore possibilities for solutions, offer a proposal,
or offer not answers but more challenging questions.

Issues about death arise also from half a century of silence and suppression of the subject. The problem of educating an entire society about death and dying provides a critical challenge to that society. Can it be done? Indeed should it be done? What are we to teach and who are the teachers? How can we avoid superficiality? This issue is considered, guidelines are offered, and predictions are made.

A practical problem and hotly debated controversy concerns the U.S. funeral industry, the high cost of funerals in general, the packaging of services in particular, and a number of other related issues. This problem is addressed, and projections for solution are offered.

These final chapters of the book are intended to provoke thought and action and, hopefully, assist the reader to achieve his or her own resolutions of the problems associated with death and dying.

CHAPTER TWELVE

Defining Death Anew

ROBERT M. VEATCH

TECHNICAL AND ETHICAL PROBLEMS
OF DEFINING DEATH ANEW

On May 24, 1968, a black laborer named Bruce Tucker fell and suffered a massive head injury. He was rushed by ambulance to the
emergency room of the Medical College of Virginia Hospital where

███████████████████

*It would be difficult to find a person better qualified than Veatch to
address this complex issue. As senior associate of The Hastings
Center, Institute of Society, Ethics and The Life Sciences, he has the
background in both theology and science to enable him to critically analyze the problem of redefining death in light of new medical
technology. While the issue of a new definition of death was briefly
mentioned in chapter eleven, Veatch examines step by step the various concepts of death, the loci of death and the criteria by which to
determine death. He identifies four concepts of death and then looks
at the empirical data to see what the corresponding loci and criteria
are. He finds the major difficulty lies in integrating and matching
these dimensions to derive a consistent definition of death.*

*The critical question is which concepts, locus, and criteria should
be used in pronouncing a person dead. In response to this question
Veatch outlines various policy options available for a new definition
of death. This writing is demanding but its subject matter concerns
everyone.*

The Challenge: Meeting the Issues of Death

he was found to have a skull fracture, a subdural hematoma, and a brain stem contusion. At eleven o'clock that evening an operation was performed (described as "a right temporoparietal craniotomy and right parietal bur hole" in a later court record of the case), opening the skull to relieve the strain on the brain. A tracheostomy was also done to help his labored breathing. By the next morning Tucker was being fed intravenously, had been given medication, and was attached to a respirator. According to the court record, he was "mechanically alive"; the treating physician noted, his "prognosis for recovery is nil and death is imminent."

In cases like Tucker's, the patient has frequently stopped breathing by the time he arrives at the hospital, and his heart may have gone into fibrillation. However, the rapid application of an electrical shock can cajole the heart back into a normal rhythm, while a respirator forces the breath of life from the tube of the machine into the tube of the patient's trachea. Thus technology can arrest the process of dying.

The Medical College of Virginia, where Tucker was taken, is the hospital of David M. Hume who, until his own recent accidental death, headed one of the eminent heart transplant teams of the world. At the time Tucker was brought in, there was a patient on the ward named Joseph Klett who was an ideal recipient. Bruce Tucker, with irreversible loss of brain function from a period of oxygen starvation in the brain and an otherwise healthy body, was an ideal heart donor.

Early in the afternoon a neurologist obtained an electroencephalogram (EEG) to determine the state of Tucker's brain activity. He saw that the electrical tracing was a flat line "with occasional artifact." Assuming the artifacts were the kind normally found from extraneous causes, this meant there was no evidence of cortical activity at that time. If the flat line on the EEG is not caused by drug overdose or low body temperature and is found again in repeated tests over several hours, most neurologists would take it to mean that consciousness would never return. Nevertheless, the respirator continued pumping oxygen into Tucker's lungs and, according to the judge's later summary, "his body temperature, pulse, and blood pressure were all normal for a patient in his condition."

In August of the same year a prestigious committee from the Harvard Medical School published more rigorous criteria for irreversible coma. Drafts of the report were circulating among professionals early in the year, but there is no evidence that the physicians in Virginia had access to it. Their use of their own judgment about criteria for diagnosing irreversible coma is still the subject of controversy.

Adapted from *Death, Dying, and the Biological Revolution*, chapters 1 and 2, New Haven, Conn.: Yale University Press, 1976.

At 2:45 that afternoon Tucker was taken back into the operating room to be prepared for the removal of his heart and both kidneys. Oxygen was given to preserve the viability of these organs. According to the court record, "he maintained, for the most part, normal body temperature, normal blood pressure and normal rate of respiration," but, in spite of the presence of these vital signs, at 3:30 the respirator was cut off. Five minutes later the patient was pronounced dead and the mechanical support was resumed to preserve the organs, and his heart was removed and transplanted to Joseph Klett. According to the record, Tucker's vital signs continued to be normal until 4:30, soon before the heart was removed.

The heart was removed although it had continued functioning while the respirator continued to pump. It was removed without any attempt to get the permission of relatives although Tucker's wallet contained his brother's business card with a phone number and an address only fifteen blocks away. The brother was in his place of business that day and a close friend had made unsuccessful inquiries at three information desks in the hospital. The heart was removed although Virginia law, according to the interpretation of the judge in the subsequent trial, defines death as total cessation of all body functions.

William Tucker, the "donor's" brother, brought suit against the surgical team for wrongfully ending Bruce Tucker's life. During the trial, physicians testified that Tucker was "neurologically dead" several hours before the transplant and that his heart and respiratory system were being kept viable by mechanical means. To this William Tucker responded, "There's nothing they can say to make me believe they didn't kill him." (1, p. 2) Commenting on the decision in favor of the surgeons, Dr. Hume said, "This simply brings the law in line with medical opinion."

The New York Times headline read, "Virginia Jury Rules That Death Occurs When Brain Dies." Victor Cohn's Washington Post story announced, " 'Brain Death' Upheld in Heart Transplant." The medical news services were equally quick to treat this unquestioningly as a brain death case. The Internal Medicine News claimed, " 'Brain Death' Held Proof of Demise in Va. Jury Decision." Even a law review article considered the judgment to affirm that cessation of brain activity can be used in determining the time of death (2). There has been some outcry, especially in the black community, over the hasty removal of a man's heart without permission from the next of kin, but the general public seemed undisturbed by the decision. The medical community felt that one of their outstanding members had been exonerated.

Although the press, public, and some legal opinion treat this case as crucial in establishing the legitimacy of the use of brain criteria for death (thus bringing the law in line with "medical opinion"), more issues than that are at stake. The case raises basic questions about the definition of death.

The debate has become increasingly heated in the past decade, because fundamental moral and religious issues are at stake. The very meaning of the word *definition* is ambiguous. Some of the issues are indeed matters of neurobiological fact and as such are appropriate for interpretation by medical opinion. But judgments about facts made by scientists with expertise in a particular and relevant field can be called *definitions* only in an operational sense. The debate over the definition of death also takes place at philosophical, religious, and ethical levels, probing into the meaning of life and its ending. The more practical, empirical problems are an important part of the debate, but they must be separated from the philosophical issues. The philosophical question is, What is lost at the point of death that is essential to human nature? We can avoid the serious philosophical errors committed in the Virginia trial only by carefully separating the levels of the debate.

Four separate levels in the definition of death debate must be distinguished. First, there is the purely formal analysis of the term *death*, an analysis that gives the structure and specifies the framework that must be filled in with content. Second, the *concept* of death is considered, attempting to fill the content of the formal definition. At this level the question is, What is so essentially significant about life that its loss is termed *death*? Third, there is the question of the locus of death: where in the organism ought one to look to determine whether death has occurred? Fourth, one must ask the question of the criteria of death: what technical tests must be applied at the locus to determine if an individual is living or dead?

Serious mistakes have been made in slipping from one level of the debate to another and in presuming that expertise on one level necessarily implies expertise on another. For instance, the Report of the Ad Hoc Committee of the Harvard Medical School to Examine the Definition of Brain Death (3) is titled "A Definition of Irreversible Coma." The report makes clear that the committee members are simply reporting empirical measures which are criteria for predicting an irreversible coma. (I shall explore later the possibility that they made an important mistake even at this level.) Yet the name of the committee seems to point more to the question of locus, where to look for measurement of death. The committee was established to examine the death of the brain. The implication is that the empirical indications of irreversible coma are also indications of "brain death." But by the first sentence of the report the committee claims that "Our primary purpose is to define irreversible coma as a new criterion for death." They have now shifted so that they are interested in "death." They must be presuming a philosophical concept of death—that a person in irreversible coma should be considered dead—but they nowhere argue this or even state it as a presumption.

Even the composition of the Harvard committee membership signals some uncertainty of purpose. If empirical criteria were their concern, the inclusion of nonscientists on the panel was strange. If the philosophical concept of death was their concern, medically trained people were overrepresented. As it happened, the committee did not deal at all with conceptual matters. The committee and its interpreters have confused the questions at different levels. The remainder of this chapter will discuss the meaning of death at these four levels.

The Formal Definition of Death

A strictly formal definition of death might be the following:

> Death means a complete change in the status of living entity characterized by the irreversible loss of those characteristics that are essentially significant to it.

Such a definition would apply equally well to a human being, a nonhuman animal, a plant, an organ, a cell, or even metaphorically to a social phenomenon like a society or to any temporally limited entity like a research project, a sports event, or a language. To define the death of a human being, we must recognize the characteristics that are essential to humanness. It is quite inadequate to limit the discussion to the death of the heart or the brain. The direct link of a word *death* to what is "essentially significant" means that the task of defining it in this sense is first and foremost a philosophical, theological, ethical task.

Furthermore, we behave socially in a very different way when we determine that a living individual has become a corpse. This new, now appropriate behavior might be called *death behavior*. We may pronounce death, go into mourning, begin a funeral or other ritual, conduct an autopsy under certain conditions, read the will, perhaps remove organs which could not have been removed previously. Death changes the roles of others as well. Lyndon Johnson has told of the awful feeling of being elevated to the presidency upon hearing of the death of President Kennedy. We are saying that the dead person has so changed in essence that entirely different behavior is not only permitted but required. Thus important policy payoffs ride on the definition of death debate, no matter how tenuous some of the fine distinctions may seem in critical borderline cases.

It is important to realize that stopping medical treatment is not directly linked to the judgment that a person is dead. Some kinds of treatment might well be stopped long before anyone would want to call the patient dead. The question of stopping treatment on a dying but not yet dead individual is quite separate from deciding when a person is dead.

The actions of the physicians in the Tucker case are ambiguous. The physicians turned off the respirator after deciding that their patient was in an irreversible coma. They argued that their patient was "neurologically dead" for several hours before the transplant, and that his heart and respiratory system were kept functioning by artificial means merely to keep his heart and kidneys viable for transplant purposes. Yet they felt it necessary to shut off the respirator before pronouncing death—and Tucker's attorney charged that the patient's death was hastened by shutting off the mechanical support systems.

This reported sequence of events is morally as well as factually confusing. If the physicians really believed that Tucker was dead when he was in a confirmed irreversible coma, why did they feel compelled to turn off the mechanical oxygenating device? On the other hand if their purpose was to preserve the organs of the corpse for transplantation, there were physiological reasons at least for not turning off the equipment. It might be not only morally acceptable but also required to continue oxygenation of a new corpse for purposes of preserving transplantable organs. If this were the interpretation of the case it would be appropriate for the debate to center on the use of neurological criteria for death. To this one would have to add a moral argument about the practice of continued oxygenation of known corpses.

What the physicians did, however, was to turn off the mechanical respirator, wait five minutes, pronounce Tucker dead, and then start the respiration again in order to preserve the organs. Did they do this to satisfy themselves and others that the patient had died "all the way?" This sequence of events implies that the patient might be considered still living at least "part of the way." The physician who finally pronounced death had only said that death was "imminent" after the EEG had shown a flat line.

Given this sequence of events, their use of a "new definition of death" as a legal defense makes no sense, since in reality the physicians were using the same old definition—the time when the heart and lungs stop functioning. It would seem that they had available a much more substantial defense—they were continuing a practice long accepted in the tradition of law and medical ethics of allowing an inevitably dying (but not yet dead) patient to die by discontinuing the use of an extraordinary, clearly useless medical procedure.

It is clear at least that death is a dramatic change in the status of the entity. Most types of death behavior (religious ritual, will reading, succession to the presidency) either happen or they do not. A point must be established at which the individual is no longer treated as living. When short-hand terms like *brain death* or *heart death* are used, it must be clear whether the reference is simply to the death of the organ or to the event which signifies the change in status of the organism as a whole.

The Concept of Death

To ask what is essentially significant to a human being is a philosophical question—a question of ethical and other values. Many elements make human beings unique—their opposing thumbs, their possession of rational souls, their ability to form cultures and manipulate symbol systems, their upright postures, their being created in the image of God, and so on. Any concept of death will depend directly upon how one evaluates these qualities. Four choices seem to me to cover the most plausible approaches.

Irreversible loss of flow of vital fluids

At first it would appear that the irreversible cessation of heart and lung activity would represent a simple and straightforward statement of the traditional understanding of the concept of death in Western culture. Yet upon reflection this proves otherwise. If patients simply lose control of their lungs and have to be permanently supported by a mechanical respirator, they are still living persons as long as they continue to get oxygen. If modern technology produces an efficient, compact heart-lung machine capable of being carried on the back or in a pocket, people using such devices would not be considered dead, even though both heart and lungs were permanently nonfunctioning. Some might consider such a technological man an affront to human dignity; some might argue that such a device should never be connected to a human; but even they would, in all likelihood, agree that such people are alive.

What the traditional concept of death centered on was not the heart and lungs as such, but the flow of vital fluids, that is, the breath and the blood. It is not without reason that these fluids are commonly referred to as "vital." The nature of humans is seen as related to this vitality—or vital activity of fluid flow—which man shares with other animals. This fluidity, the movement of liquids and gases at the cellular and organismic level, is a remarkable biological fact. High school biology students are taught that the distinguishing characteristics of "living" things include respiration,

The Challenge: Meeting the Issues of Death

circulation of fluids, movement of fluids out of the organism, and the like. According to this view the human organism, like other living organisms, dies when there is an irreversible cessation of the flow of these fluids.

Irreversible loss of the soul from the body

There is a longstanding tradition, sometimes called vitalism, that holds the essence of man to be independent of the chemical reactions and electrical forces that account for the flow of the bodily fluids. Aristotle and the Greeks spoke of the soul as the animating principle of life. The human being, according to Aristotle, differs from other living creatures in possessing a rational soul as well as vegetative and animal souls. This idea later became especially pronounced in the dualistic philosophy of gnosticism, where salvation was seen as the escape of the enslaved soul from the body. Christianity in its Pauline and later Western forms shares the view that the soul is an essential element in the living man. While Paul and some later theologian-scholars including Erasmus and Luther sometimes held a tripartite anthropology that included spirit as well as body and soul, a central element in all their thought seems to be animation of the body by a noncorporeal force. In Christianity, however, contrasting to the gnostic tradition, the body is a crucial element—not a prison from which the soul escapes, but a significant part of the person. This will become important later in this discussion. The soul remains a central element in the concept of man in most folk religion today.

The departure of the soul might be seen by believers as occurring at about the time that the fluids stop flowing. But it would be a mistake to equate these two concepts of death, as according to the first fluid stops from natural, if unexplained, causes, and death means nothing more than that stopping of the flow which is essential to life. According to the second view, the fluid stops flowing at the time the soul departs, and it stops because the soul is no longer present. Here the essential thing is the loss of the soul, not the loss of the fluid flow.

The irreversible loss of the capacity
for bodily integration

In the debate between those who held a traditional religious notion of the animating force of the soul and those who had the more naturalistic concept of the irreversible loss of the flow of bodily fluids, the trend to secularism and empiricism made the loss of fluid flow more and more the operative concept of death in society. But human intervention in the dying process through cardiac pacemakers, respirators, intravenous medication and feeding, and extra-venous purification of the blood has forced a sharper examination of the naturalistic concept of death. It is now possible to manipulate the dying process so that some parts of the body cease to function while other parts are maintained indefinitely. This has given rise to disagreements within the naturalistic camp itself. In its report, published in 1968, the interdisciplinary Harvard Ad Hoc Committee to Examine the Definition of Brain Death gave two reasons for their undertaking. First, they argued that improvements in resuscitative and supportive measures had sometimes had only partial success, putting a great burden on "patients who suffer permanent loss of intellect, on their families, on the hospitals, and on those in need of hospital beds already occupied by these comatose patients." Second, they argued that "obsolete criteria for the definition of death can lead to controversy in obtaining organs for transplantation."

These points have proved more controversial than they may have seemed at the time. In the first place, the only consideration of the patient among the reasons given for changing the definition of death was the suggestion that a comatose patient can feel a "great burden." If the committee is right, however, in holding that the person is in fact dead despite continued respiration and circulation, then all the benefits of the change in definition will come to other individuals or to society at large. For those who hold that the primary ethical consideration in the care of the patient should be the patient's own interest, this is cause for concern.

In the second place, the introduction of transplant concerns into the discussion has attracted particular criticism. Paul Ramsey, among others, has argued against making the issue of transplant a reason for updating the definition of death: "If no person's death should *for this purpose* be hastened, then the definition of death should not *for this purpose* be updated, or the procedures for stating that a man has died be revised as a means of affording easier access to organs" (4, p. 103).

Clearly, the need for organs cannot in itself be a legitimate cause for adopting a new concept of death. The need of someone else for organs is simply not an adequate reason for changing our view about what it is in an individual that is so significant that when it has been lost the person is no longer considered alive. This does not mean that the search for a new concept of death must be abandoned or even that the need for organs is not a relevant factor. Even if the need for organs is not a legitimate reason for adopting a new concept of death, it may very well be one legitimate reason among others for taking up the tasks of searching for a new and more carefully stated concept. Henry Beecher (5) argues:

> There is indeed a life-saving potential in the new definition, for, when accepted, it will lead to greater availability than formerly of

> essential organs in viable condition, for transplantation, and thus
> countless lives now inevitably lost will be saved. (p. 1)

When he says this is one of the reasons for accepting a new definition (granted that it is only one of the reasons) he has made an ambiguous statement. If he means that it is a reason for adopting the new concept, he is making an unacceptable compromise with the value of the individual human being. If, however, he means that this is a reason for undertaking the task of philosophical examination of the meaning of death, that is something quite different. It would indeed be morally outrageous if "countless lives" were lost simply because society was too lazy to undertake the philosophical task of reexamining and clarifying its precise understanding of death.

Nevertheless, this reason for undertaking the reexamination of the concept of death must still be subordinated to the primary one. It is morally wrong to treat dead persons as if they were alive, but it is certainly morally relevant that others may benefit from a clarity of definition. This is true even without consideration of transplantation and is a legitimate reason for undertaking the reexamination. I would argue, however, that even if no one were to benefit—even if no family members would suffer psychologically and economically from the needless preservation of a corpse as if it were alive, even if no one needed the hospital bed, and even if no one needed the organs of the corpse mistakenly thought to be alive—it would still be a moral affront to the dignity of man to treat a corpse as if it were a living person.

We now must consider whether concepts of death that focus on the flow of fluids or the departure of the soul are philosophically appropriate. The reason that the question arises as a practical matter is fear of a "false positive" determination that human life is present. But there are two relevant and important moral principles at stake—preservation of an individual life and preservation of the dignity of an individual by being able to distinguish a dead person from a living one. The introduction of a moral obligation to treat the dead as dead leaves one perplexed. It creates moral pressures in each direction. The defenders of the older concepts, which may lead to false pronouncements of living, must defend their action as well. It seems to me that only when such positive moral pressure is introduced on both sides of the argument can we plausibly overcome the claim that we must take the morally safer course and consider a person alive until heart and lung functions cease. We must consider that it may be not only right to call persons dead but also wrong to call them alive.

At first it would appear that the irreversible loss of brain activity is the concept of death held by those no longer satisfied with the vitalistic concept of the departure of the soul or the animalistic concept of the irreversible cessation of fluid flow. This is why the name *brain death* is frequently given to the new proposals, but the term is unfortunate for two reasons.

.First, it is not the collection of physical tissues called the brain, but rather their functions—consciousness; motor control; sensory feeling; ability to reason; control over bodily functions including respiration and circulation; major integrating reflexes controlling blood pressure, ion levels, and pupil size; and so forth—which are given essential significance by those who advocate adoption of a new concept of death or clarification of the old one. In short they see the body's capacity for integrating its functions as the essentially significant indication of life.

Second, we are not interested in the death of particular cells, organs, or organ systems, but in the death of the person as a whole— the point at which the person as a whole undergoes a quantum change through the loss of characteristics held to be essentially significant, the point at which "death behavior" becomes appropriate. Terms such as *brain death* or *heart death* should be avoided because they tend to obscure the fact that we are searching for the meaning of the death of the person as a whole. For purposes of simplicity we shall use the phrase *the capacity for bodily integration* to refer to the total list of integrating mechanisms possessed by the body. The case for these mechanisms being the ones that are essential to humanness can indeed be made. Humans are more than the flowing of fluids. They are complex, integrated organisms with capacities for internal regulation. With and only with these integrating mechanisms is homo sapiens really a human person.

There appear to be two general aspects to this concept of what is essentially significant: first, a capacity for integrating one's internal bodily environment (which is done for the most part unconsciously through highly complex homeostatic, feedback mechanisms) and, secondly, a capacity for integrating one's self, including one's body, with the social environment through consciousness, which permits interaction with other persons. Clearly these taken together offer a more profound understanding of the nature of humanity than does the simple flow of bodily fluids. Whether or not it is a more profound concept of humanity than that which focuses simply on the presence or absence of the soul, it is clearly a very different one. The ultimate test between the two is that of meaningfulness and plausibility. For many in the modern secular society, the concept of loss of capacity for bodily integration seems much more meaningful and plausible, that is, we see it as a much more accurate description of the essential significance of humanity and of what is lost at the time of death. According to this view, when individuals lose all these "truly vital" capacities we should call them dead and behave accordingly.

At this point the debate may just about have been won by the defenders of the neurologically oriented concept. For the most part the public sees the main dispute as being between partisans of the heart and the brain. Even court cases like the Tucker suit and the major articles in the scientific and philosophical journals have for the most part confined themselves to contrasting these two rather crudely defined positions. If these were the only alternatives, the discussion probably would be nearing an end. There are, however, some critical questions that are just beginning to be asked. This new round of discussion was provoked by the recognition that it may be possible in rare cases for a person to have the higher brain centers destroyed but still retain lower brain functions including spontaneous respiration (6). This has led to the question of just what brain functions are essentially significant to human nature. A fourth major concept of death thus emerges.

The irreversible loss of the capacity
for social interaction
The fourth major alternative for a concept of death draws on the characteristics of the third concept and has often been confused with it. Henry Beecher (5) offers a summary of what he considers to be essential to human nature: "the individual's personality, his conscious life, his uniqueness, his capacity for remembering, judging, reasoning, acting, enjoying, worrying, and so on . . ." (p. 4).

Beecher goes on immediately to ask the anatomical question of locus. He concludes that these functions reside in the brain and that when the brain no longer functions, the individual is dead. We shall take up the locus question later in this chapter. What is remarkable is that Beecher's list, with the possible exception of "uniqueness," is composed entirely of functions explicitly related to consciousness and the capacity to relate to one's social environment through interaction with others. All the functions that give the capacity to integrate one's internal bodily environment through unconscious, complex, homeostatic reflex mechanisms—respiration, circulation, and major integrating reflexes—are omitted. In fact, when asked what was essentially significant to man's living, Beecher replied simply, "Consciousness."

Thus a fourth concept of death is the irreversible loss of the capacity for consciousness or social integration. This view of the nature of human beings places even more emphasis on social character. Even if a hypothetical human being with the full capacity for integration of bodily function had irreversibly lost the capacity for consciousness and social interaction, that person would have lost the essential character of humanness and, according to this definition, would be dead.

Even if one moves to the so-called higher functions and away from the mere capacity to integrate bodily functions through reflex mechanisms, it is still not clear precisely what is ultimately valued. We must have a more careful specification of "consciousness or the capacity for social integration." Are these two capacities synonymous and, if not, what is the relationship between them? Before taking up that question, we must first make clear what is meant by capacity.

Holders of this concept of death and related concepts of the essence of humanity specifically do not say that individuals must be valued by others in order to be human. This would place life at the mercy of other human beings who may well be cruel or insensitive. Nor does this concept imply that this essence is the fact of social interaction with others, as this would also place a person at the mercy of others. The infant raised in complete isolation from other human contact would still be human, provided that the child retained the mere capacity for some form of social interaction. This view of what is essentially significant to the nature of human beings makes no quantitative or qualitative judgments. It need not, and for me could not, lead to the view that those who have more capacity for social integration are more human. The concepts of life and death are essentially bipolar, threshold concepts. Either one has life or one does not. Either a paricular type of death behavior is called for or it is not. One does not pronounce death halfway or read a will halfway or become elevated from the vice-presidency to the presidency halfway.

One of the real dangers of shifting from the third concept of death to the fourth is that the fourth, in focusing exclusively on the capacity for consciousness or social interaction, lends itself much more readily to quantitative and qualitative considerations. When the focus is on the complete capacity for bodily integration, including the ability of the body to carry out spontaneous respiratory activity and major reflexes, it is quite easy to maintain that if any such integrating function is present the person is alive. But when the question begins to be, "What kinds of integrating capacity are really significant?" one finds oneself on the slippery slope of evaluating kinds of consciousness or social interaction. If consciousness is what counts, it might be asked if a long-term, catatonic schizophrenic or a patient with extreme senile dementia really has the capacity for consciousness. To position oneself for such a slide down the slope of evaluating the degree of capacity for social interaction is extremely dangerous. It seems to me morally obligatory to stay off the slopes.

The Challenge: Meeting the Issues of Death

Precisely what are the functions considered to be ultimately significant to human life according to this concept? There are several possibilities.

The capacity for rationality is one candidate. Homo sapiens is a rational animal, as suggested by the name. The human capacity for reasoning is so unique and so important that some would suggest that it is the critical element in humanity's nature. But certainly infants lack any such capacity and they are considered living human beings. Nor is possession of the potential for reasoning what is important. Including potential might resolve the problem of infants, but does not explain why those who have no potential for rationality (such as the apparently permanent back ward psychotic or the senile individual) are considered to be humanly living in a real if not full sense and to be entitled to the protection of civil and moral law.

Consciousness is a second candidate that dominates much of the medical and biological literature. If the rationalist tradition is reflected in the previous notion, then the empiricalist philosophical tradition seems to be represented in the emphasis on consciousness. What may be of central significance is the capacity for experience. This would include the infant and the individual who lack the capacity for rationality, and focuses attention on the ability for sensory activity summarized as consciousness. Yet, this is a very individualistic understanding of humanity's nature. It describes what is essentially significant to the human life without any reference to other human beings.

Social interaction is a third candidate. At least in the Western tradition, humans are seen as essentially social animals. Perhaps it is their capacity or potential for social interaction that has such ultimate significance that its loss is considered death. Is this in any sense different from the capacity for experience? Certainly it is conceptually different and places a very different emphasis on their essential role. Yet it may well be that the two functions, experience and social interaction, are completely conterminous. It is difficult to conceive a case where the two could be separated, at least if social interaction is understood in its most elementary form. While it may be important for a philosophical understanding of humanity's nature to distinguish between these two functions, it may not be necessary for deciding when a person has died. Thus, for our purposes we can say that the fourth concept of death is one in which the essential element that is lost is the capacity for consciousness or social interaction or both.

The concept presents one further problem. The Western tradition that emphasizes social interaction also emphasizes, as we have seen, the importance of the body. Consider the admittedly remote possibility that the electrical impulses of the brain could be transferred by recording devices onto magnetic computer tape. Would that tape together with some kind of minimum sensory device be a living human being and would erasure of the tape be considered murder? If the body is really essential to humans, then we might well decide that such a creature would not be a living human being.

Where does this leave us? The earlier concepts of death—the irreversible loss of the soul and the irreversible stopping of the flow of vital body fluids—strike me as quite implausible. The soul as an independent nonphysical entity that is necessary and sufficient for a person to be considered alive is a relic from the era of dichotomized anthropologies. Animalistic fluid flow is simply too base a function to be the human essence. The capacity for bodily integration is more plausible, but I suspect it is attractive primarily because it includes those higher functions that we normally take to be central—consciousness, the ability to think and feel and relate to others. When the reflex networks that regulate such things as blood pressure and respiration are separated from the higher functions, I am led to conclude that it is the higher functions that are so essential that their loss ought to be taken as the death of the person. While consciousness is certainly important, man's social nature and embodiment seem to me to be the truly essential characteristics. I therefore believe that death is most appropriately thought of as the irreversible loss of the embodied capacity for social interaction.

The Locus of Death

Thus far I have completely avoided dealing with anatomy. Whenever the temptation arose to formulate a concept of death by referring to organs or tissues such as the heart, lungs, brain, or cerebral cortex, I have carefully resisted. Now finally I must ask, "Where does one look if one wants to know whether a person is dead or alive?' This question at last leads into the field of anatomy and physiology. Each concept of death formulated in the previous section (by asking what is of essential significance to the nature of humanity) raises a corresponding question of where to look to see if death has occurred. This level of the definitional problem may be called the locus of death.

The term *locus* must be used carefully. I have stressed that we are concerned about the death of the individual as a whole, not a specific part. Nevertheless, differing concepts of death will lead us to look at different body functions and structures in order to diagnose the death of the person as a whole. This task can be undertaken only after the conceptual question is resolved, if what we

The Challenge: Meeting the Issues of Death

really want to know is where to look to determine if a person is dead rather than where to look to determine simply if the person has irreversibly lost the capacity for vital fluid flow or bodily integration or social interaction. What then are the different loci corresponding to the different concepts?

The *loci* corresponding to the irreversible loss of vital fluid flow are clearly the heart and blood vessels, the lungs and respiratory tract. At least according to our contemporary empirical knowledge of physiology and anatomy, in which we have good reason to have confidence, these are the vital organs and organ systems to which the tests should have applied to determine if a person has died. Should a new Harvey reveal evidence to the contrary, those who hold to the concept of the irreversible loss of vital fluid flow would probably be willing to change the site of their observations in diagnosing death.

The locus, or the "seat," of the soul has not been dealt with definitively since the day of Descartes. In his essay "The Passions of the Soul," Descartes (7) pursues the question of the soul's dwelling place in the body. He argues that the soul is united to all the portions of the body conjointly, but, nevertheless, he concludes:

> There is yet . . . a certain part in which it exercises its functions more particularly than in all the others; and it is usually believed that this part is the brain, or possibly the heart: the brain, because it is with it that the organs of sense are connected, and the heart because it is apparently in it that we experience the passions. But in examining the matter with care, it seems as though I had clearly ascertained that the part of the body in which the soul exercises its functions immediately is in no wise the heart, not the whole of the brain, but merely the most inward of all its parts, to wit, a certain very small gland which is situated in the middle of its substance . . . (p. 345).

Descartes was clearly asking the questions of locus. His anatomical knowledge was apparently sound, but his conclusion that the soul resides primarily and directly in the pineal body raises physiological and theological problems that most of us are unable to comprehend today. What is significant is that he seemed to hold that the irreversible loss of the soul is the critical factor in determining death, and he was asking the right kind of question about where to look to determine whether a man is dead.

The fact that the Greek term *pneuma* has the dual meaning of both breath and soul or spirit could be interpreted to imply that the presence of this animating force is closely related to (perhaps synonymous with) breath. This gives us another clue about where holders of the irreversible loss of the soul concept of death might look to determine the presence or absence of life.

The locus for loss of capacity for bodily integration is a more familiar concept today. The anatomist and physiologist would be sure that the locus of the integrating capacity is the central nervous system, as Sherrington has ingrained into the biomedical tradition. Neurophysiologists asked to find this locus might reasonably request a more specific concept, however. They are aware that the autonomic nervous system and spinal cord play a role in the integrating capacity, both as transmitters of nervous impulses and as the central analyzers for certain simple acts of integration (for example, a withdrawal reflex mediated through the spinal cord); they would have to know whether one was interested in such simple reflexes.

Beecher (5) gives us the answer quite specifically for his personal concept of death: he says spinal reflexes are to be omitted. This leaves the brain as essentially the place to look to determine whether a person is dead according to the third concept of death. The brain's highly complex circuitry provides the minimal essentials for the body's real integrating capacity. This third concept quite specifically includes unconscious homeostatic and higher reflex mechanisms such as spontaneous respiration and pupil reflexes. Thus, anatomically, according to our reading of neurophysiology, we are dealing with the whole brain, including the cerebellum, medulla, and brain stem. This is the basis for calling the third concept of death *brain death*, and we already discussed objections to this term.

Where to seek the locus for irreversible loss of the capacity for social interaction, the fourth conception of death, is quite another matter. We have eliminated unconscious reflex mechanisms. The answer is clearly not the whole brain—it is much too massive. Determining the locus of consciousness and social interaction certainly requires greater scientific understanding, but evidence points strongly to the neocortex or outer surface of the brain as the site (6). Indeed, if this is the locus of consciousness, the presence or absence of activity in the rest of the brain will be immaterial to the holder of this view.

The Criteria of Death

Having determined a concept of death, which is rooted in a philosophical analysis of the nature of humanity, and a locus of death, which links this philosophical understanding to the anatomy and physiology of the human body, we are finally ready to ask the operational question, What tests or measurements should be applied to determine if an individual is living or dead? At this point we have moved into a more technical realm in which the answer will depend primarily on the data gathered from the biomedical sciences.

Beginning with the first concept of death, irreversible loss of vital fluid flow, what criteria can be used to measure the activity of the heart and lungs, the blood vessels and respiratory tract? The methods are simple: visual observation of respiration, perhaps by the use of the classic mirror held at the nostrils; feeling the pulse; and listening for the heartbeat. More technical measures are also now available to the trained clinician: the electrocardiogram and direct measures of oxygen and carbon dioxide levels in the blood.

If Descartes' conclusion is correct that the locus of the soul is in the pineal body, the logical question would be "How does one know when the pineal body has irreversibly ceased to function?" or more precisely "How does one know when the soul has irreversibly departed from the gland?" This matter remains baffling for the modern neurophysiologist. If, however, holders of the soul-departing concept of death associate the soul with the breath, as suggested by the word *pneuma*, this might give us another clue. If respiration and specifically breath are the locus of the soul, then the techniques discussed above as applying to respiration might also be the appropriate criteria for determining the loss of the soul.

We have identified the (whole) brain as the locus associated with the third concept of death, the irreversible loss of the capacity for bodily integration. The empirical task of identifying criteria in this case is to develop accurate predictions of the complete and irreversible loss of brain activity. This search for criteria was the real task carried out by the Ad Hoc Committee to Examine the Definition of Brain Death of Harvard Medical School; the simple criteria they proposed have become the most widely recognized in the United States:

1. Unreceptivity and unresponsivity
2. No movements or breathing
3. No reflexes
4. Flat electroencephalogram

The report states that the fourth criterion is "of great confirmatory value." It also calls for the repetition of these tests 24 hours later. Two types of cases are specifically excluded: hypothemia (body temperature below 90° F) and the presence of central nervous system depressants such as barbiturates (3, see also 8).

Other criteria have been proposed to diagnose the condition of irreversible loss of brain function. James Toole (9), a neurologist at the Bowman Gray School of Medicine, has suggested that metabolic criteria such as oxygen consumption of the brain or the measure of metabolic products in the blood or cerebral spinal fluid could possibly be developed as well.

European observers (10, 11) seem to place more emphasis on

demonstrating the absence of circulation in the brain. This is measured by angiography, radioisotopes, or sonic techniques. In Europe sets of criteria analogous to the Harvard criteria have been proposed. G. P. J. Alexandre (12), a surgeon who heads a Belgian renal transplant department, reports that in addition to absence of reflexes as criteria of irreversible destruction of the brain, he uses lack of spontaneous respiration, a flat EEG, complete bilateral mydriasis, and falling blood pressure necessitating increasing amounts of vasopressive drugs. J. P. Revillard (12), a Frenchman, reportedly uses these plus angiography and absence of reaction to atropine. Even among those who agree on the types of measures, there may still be disagreement on the levels of measurement. This is especially true for the electroencephalogram, which can be recorded at varying sensitivities and for different time periods. The Harvard-proposed 24-hour period is now being questioned as too conservative.

While these alternate sets of criteria are normally described as applicable to measuring loss of brain function (or "brain death" as in the name of the Harvard committee), it appears that many of these authors, especially the earlier ones, have not necessarily meant to distinguish them from criteria for measuring the narrower loss of cerebral function.

The criteria for irreversible loss of the capacity for social interaction are far more selective. It should be clear from the above criteria that they measure loss of all brain activity, including spontaneous respiration and higher reflexes and not simply loss of consciousness. This raises a serious problem about whether the Harvard criteria really measure "irreversible coma" as the report title indicates. Exactly what is measured is an entirely empirical matter.

What then is the relationship between the more inclusive Harvard criteria and the simple use of electrocerebral silence as measured by an isoelectric or flat electroencephalogram? The former might be appropriate for those who associate death with the disappearance of any neurological function of the brain. For those who hold the narrower concept based simply on consciousness or capacity for social interaction, however, the Harvard criteria may suffer from exactly the same problem as the old heart- and lung-oriented criteria. With those criteria, every patient whose circulatory and respiratory function had ceased was indeed dead, but the criteria might be too conservative, in that some patients dead according to the "the loss of bodily integrating capacity" concept of death (for which the brain is the corresponding locus) would be found alive according to heart- and lung-oriented criteria. It might also happen that some patients who should be declared dead according to the irreversible loss of consciousness and social interaction concept would be found to be alive according to the Harvard criteria.[1] All discussions of the neurological criteria fail to consider that the criteria might be too inclusive, too conservative. The criteria might, therefore, give rise to classifying patients as dead according to the consciousness or social interaction conception, but as alive according to the full Harvard criteria.

A report in *Lancet* by the British physician J. B. Brierley and his colleagues (6, see also 13), implies this may indeed be the case. In two cases in which patients had undergone cardiac arrest resulting in brain damage, they report, "the electroencephalogram (strictly defined) was isoelectric throughout. Spontaneous respiration was resumed almost at once in case 2, but not until day 21 in case 1" (6, p. 560). They report that the first patient did not "die" until 5 months later. For the second patient they report, "The Patient died on day 153." Presumably in both cases they were using the traditional heart and lung locus and correlated criteria for death as they pronounced it. They report that subsequent detailed neuropathological analysis confirmed that the "neocortex was dead while certain brainstem and spinal centers remained intact." These intact centers specifically involved the functions of spontaneous breathing and reflexes: eye-opening, yawning, and "certain reflex activities at brainstem and spinal cord levels." As evidence that lower brain activity remained, they report that an electroretinogram (measuring electrical activity of the eye) in patient 1 was normal on day 13. After day 49 there still remained reactivity of the pupils to light in addition to spontaneous respiration.

If this evidence is sound, it strongly suggests that it is empirically as well as theoretically possible to have irreversible loss of cortical function (and therefore loss of consciousness) while lower brain functions remain intact.

This leaves us with the empirical question of the proper criteria for the irreversible loss of consciousness which is thought to have its locus in the neocortex of the cerebrum. Brierley and his colleagues (6) suggest that the EEG alone (excluding the other three criteria of the Harvard report) measures the activity of the neocortex. Presumably this test must also meet the carefully specified conditions of amplifier gain, repeat of the test after a given time period, and exclusion of the exceptional cases, if it is to be used as the criterion for death according to our fourth concept, irreversible loss of capacity for social interaction. This is a question for the neurophysiologists to resolve.

There is another problem with the use of electroencephalogram, angiography, or other techniques for measuring cerebral function

---

[1] The inclusion of absence of breathing and reflexes in the criteria suggests this, but does not necessarily lead to this. It might be that, empirically, it is necessary for lower brain reflexes and breathing to be absent for 24 hours in order to be sure that the patient not only will never regain these functions but will never regain consciousness.

as a criterion for the irreversible loss of consciousness. Once again we must face the problem of a false positive diagnosis of life. The old heart and lung criteria may provide a false positive diagnosis for a holder of the bodily integrating capacity concept, and the Harvard criteria may give false positive indications for a holder of the consciousness or social interaction concept. Could a person have electroencephalographic activity but still have no capacity for consciousness or social interaction? At least theoretically there are certainly portions of the neocortex that could be functioning and presumably be recorded on an electroencephalogram without the individual having any capacity for consciousness. For instance, what if through an accident or vascular occlusion the motor cortex remained viable but the sensory cortex did not? Even the most narrow criterion of the electroencephalogram alone may still give false positive diagnoses of living for holders of the social interaction concept.

Complexities in Matching Concepts with Loci and Criteria

It has been our method throughout this portion of the chapter to identify four major concepts of death and then to determine, primarily by examining the empirical evidence, what the corresponding loci and criteria might be. But there are good reasons why the holders of a particular concept of death might not want to adopt the corresponding criteria as the means of determining the status of a given patient. These considerations are primarily pragmatic and empirical. In the first place, as a matter of policy we would not want to have to apply the Harvard criteria before pronouncing death while standing before every clearly dead body. It is not usually necessary to use such technical measures as an EEG, whether one holds the fluid-flow concept, the loss of bodily integration concept, or the loss of social interaction concept.

Reliance on the old circulatory and respiratory criteria in cases where the individual is obviously dead may be justified in either of two ways. First, there is the option implied in the new Kansas statute (to be discussed later in the chapter) of maintaining two operating concepts of death, either of which will be satisfactory. This appears, however, to be philosophically unsound, since it means that a patient could be simultaneously dead and alive. If the philosophical arguments for either of the neurological concepts are convincing, and I think they are, we should not have to fall back on the fluid-flow concept for pronouncing death in the ordinary case.

A second way to account for the use of the heart- and lung-oriented criteria is that they do indeed correlate empirically with the neurological concepts. When there is no circulatory or respiratory activity for a sufficient time, there is invariably a loss of capacity for bodily integration or capacity for consciousness or social interaction. Using circulatory and respiratory activity as tests is crude and in some cases the presence of such activity will lead to a false positive diagnosis of life; but the prolonged absence of circulation and respiration is a definitive diagnosis of death even according to the neurologically-oriented concepts. Their use is thus an initial shortcut; if these criteria are met, one need not go on to the other criteria for the purpose of pronouncing death. This would appear to be a sound rationale for continuing the use of the old criteria of respiratory and circulatory activity.

A second practical difficulty is inherent in correlating concept and criteria. Let us examine this by asking why one might not wish at this time to adopt the EEG alone as a definitive criterion for pronouncing death. There are two possible reasons. First, quite obviously, there will be those who do not accept the correlated concept of death. They reject the irreversible loss of the capacity for consciousness or social interaction in favor of the irreversible loss of capacity for bodily integration or for fluid flow. Second, there are those who accept the concept of irreversible loss of consciousness or social interaction, but still are not convinced that the EEG unfailingly predicts this. If and when they can be convinced that the EEG alone accurately predicts irreversible loss of consciousness or social interaction without any false diagnosis of death, they will adopt it as the criterion. In the meantime they would logically continue to advocate the concept while adhering to the more conservative Harvard criteria, which appear to measure the loss of whole brain function. Since the distinction is a new one and the empirical evidence may not yet be convincing, it is to be expected that many holders of this concept will, for the time being and as a matter of policy, prefer the Harvard committee's older and more conservative criteria for determining death.

Having examined the theoretical distinctions associated with different concepts of death, as well as their related loci and the empirical criteria for determining when death has occurred according to any one of the concepts, we now may turn our attention to the critical policy question. Which concept, locus, and criteria should be used as a matter of public policy to pronounce a human being dead?

POLICY OPTIONS
FOR DEFINING DEATH ANEW

While we philosophize about the meaning of death in the age of the biological revolution, people are being pronounced dead (or alive) by physicians who choose one definition or another. The philosophical discussion becomes literally a matter of life and death. You may be pronounced dead by a randomly available physician even if you and your family believe (or have believed) you are still alive and even if you would be considered alive at another hospital down the block. Or you may be considered living by a physician who has chosen to reject the newer notions of death centered on the brain or some part of it, even if you have thought about the issue and decided in favor of a brain-oriented concept.

Doctors in the states that have not adopted specific legislation are taking it upon themselves to use a brain-oriented concept of death although the laws in these states do not authorize them to. Other doctors are reluctant to use newer concepts of death, fearing they may offend the patient's family or some district attorney. The fact is, "there is currently no way to be certain that a doctor would not be liable, criminally or civilly, if he ceased treatment of a person found to be dead according to the Harvard Committee's criteria, but not according to the 'complete cessation of all vital functions' test presently employed by the courts (14, p. 97).

Some order must be brought out of this confusion. A public policy must be developed that will enable us to know who should be treated as alive and who should be treated as dead.

If it is true that there are several levels in the definition of death debate, it may be that different public actions will be required at the different levels. It would be foolish to use a Gallup poll or a group of legislators to determine how many minutes of flat electro-encephalogram readings are necessary before we can predict confidently that a patient will not regain consciousness. The question whether to treat a person who will never regain consciousness as dead is really one of what concept of death ought to be used by society. It is, as I have argued, a philosophical question, which can be answered independent of medical training or healing skills.

Our options are more numerous than they once were. Many have argued forcefully that medical professionals should be free to use the definition of death they deem appropriate. Others, including state legislators in Kansas and Maryland, take a second position, that physicians should be required by law to pronounce death when the individual's brain is completely destroyed. This proposal seems very attractive today. A third proposal beginning to receive some consideration reflects a different concept of death; holders of this view would pronounce death when there is irreversible loss of the capacity for consciousness or social interaction, that is, when there is no longer any cerebral cortical activity in the brain. The debate among these approaches leads me to offer a fourth proposal which, although it has not yet received consideration in the public debate, may be the most reasonable and workable solution in the terribly confusing state in which we find ourselves. In a pluralistic world, different philosophical interpretations may well have to operate simultaneously. We may wish to give patients and their agents some choice in deciding the meaning of death in their individual cases. If we are dealing at the conceptual level with philosophical choices about what is essential to human living, we may have to tolerate philosophical pluralism.

Of course there is a fifth alternative: the traditional concept, locus, and criteria of death focusing on the functioning of the heart and lungs could be reaffirmed. If we are to continue to use this older concept, however, we now must choose consciously to establish it as a public policy. As yet no such choice has been made. The remainder of this chapter discusses the four new policy alternatives that offer some hope of resolving this chaotic situation.

The Medical Professional's Choice

At first it seems obvious and reasonable to let the choice of a definition of death rest in the hands of the physicians. The medical journals are filled with articles claiming that the physician is the only one with adequate experience and knowledge to make such a determination (3, 15).

This bestowing of the decision-making authority on the physician is implied in the oft-cited Black's Law Dictionary definition of death: "The cessation of life; the ceasing to exist; *defined by physicians* as a total stoppage of the circulation of the blood, and a cessation of the animal and vital functions consequent thereupon, such as respiration, pulse, etc." (italics added). The question now raised by advocates of newer notions of death is, what if physicians decide to define death otherwise? If the physicians' old view of death was accorded legal standing, why should not any new medical consensus have legal significance? A *Health Law Bulletin* (16), for instance, argues: "Thus, courts are actually free to accept new definitions by physicians and to recognize other manifesting signs of death besides respiration and pulsation (p. 3).

Other authorities are also willing to give special weight to physicians' opinions about what counts as significant for life. Pope Pius XII, at a 1957 meeting of the International Congress of Anesthesiologists, recognized that what was at stake was determining when a body no longer has its "vital functions." This the Pope distinguished from "the simple life of the organs." But then he said, "The task of determining the exact instant of death is that of the physician." It is not clear whether he was ceding to the medical community the role of determining what bodily functions are really vital or simply the more limited technical task of making empirical observations about various body functions.

A lawyer, Walter C. Ward (17), is more explicit in his willingness to leave to the physician the critical policy choices:

> There is no need for a specific legislative definition of death. Such an effort would be futile in that the use of a flexible definition is required for differing circumstances. There is also the likelihood that currently accepted medical definitions will change or expand in the future or that medical science will discover new methods of death determination. What is needed is legislative recognition that, if done without negligence, physicians may apply criteria other than cessation of respiration and circulation in death determination without fear of adverse consequences. (p. 156)[2]

According to this view all that is needed is legal protection for physicians so that they can use "criteria other than cessation of respiration and circulation," that is, so they can choose other concepts of death according to their own philosophies. It is true, of course, that medical science may someday discover new specific criteria for evaluating the functioning of a particular part of the brain or even of the functioning of the circulatory and respiratory system but this is measurement. How could medical research possibly discover that death should be pronounced when brain function rather than heart function has stopped irreversibly? Ward's proposal is really a dangerous invitation for medical professionals to exercise their philosophical judgments at the expense of nonconsenting or even unwilling patients.

Some philosophers have also expressed faith that the medical community is the appropriate body to make such decisions. Dallas High (18), for example, has written one of the best expositions on record of the essentially philosophical nature of the definition of death debate: He recognizes that "If . . . a philosopher or lawyer or theologian wants to claim that he has no professional business with the issue and that it is a purely medical or biological one, that too, I suggest, is to opt for a philosophical position concerning the concept of death, namely, that it is empirically decidable." He makes clear his belief that the question is not resolvable by the sciences of biology and medicine. It is disturbing, however, that what he sees as needed is a "medical-legal consensus" together with "the bona fides of the wider public," rather than a legislative determination. He concludes "I do not believe that further legislation is needed at this time . . ." (p. 456).

One could conceivably oppose legislation because there are other,

[2] Ian McColl Kennedy, in an article "The Kansas Statute on Death—An Appraisal," *New England Journal of Medicine* 285 (1971), p. 947, argues "If one accepts, as I do, that the matters properly within the competence of a profession should be dealt with by that profession, whose views would then be accepted if it could be shown that they were informed and objectively arrived at, the intervention of the legislature is regrettable."

more effective public mechanisms for deciding: court decisions, executive agency directives, or an informal public consensus created without overt governmental actions. But that means something much more than "the bona fides of the wider public"; it requires direct public action or the action of their agents. It may be that High simply means that the medical profession is as good at the task of philosophy and social policy choices as the rest of humanity, and that if it is left alone it will reach essentially the same decision that an informed public would have. If that is his position, however, it needs to be stated explicitly.

Let us assume for a moment that the biologist or physician may have some special skill in resolving the policy question. Would not the consensus of the profession as a whole still be more meaningful than the opinions of individual professionals? Individual members of any professional group may have biases that affect their judgment. An individual physician may have a particular attachment to the body's blood pump going because of his childhood experiences or other extraneous factors, but should he be permitted to keep a cardiac-functioning corpse pumping blood for months or years just because of personal, and perhaps outdated, philosophy?

Thus some have proposed that in a given locality a committee of physicians, a board at the local hospital, or the medical society as a group should have the authority to determine the concept of death to be used. Gunnar Biorck (19), the prominent Swedish physician, has called for a new definition but added, "This may not have to be in the form of law. Better, perhaps, would be a recommendation issued by a proper medical authority" (p. 542).

The *Health Law Bulletin* has proposed a statute specifying only that the method used for determining death shall be "one approved by the state medical society" (16, p. 4). This is too sweeping in at least two respects. If it meant only that the state medical society should determine the criteria to be used for measuring the presence or absence of functions in the organs associated with a particular concept of death, it would seem preferable to entrust this task to specialists—neurophysiologists, cardiologists, or others—depending on the tests to be made. But the proposal actually would place *all* authority in the hands of the medical society, not simply selection of criteria. This might effectively eliminate biases of individual physicians, substituting the consensus of the medical profession or some subgroup. But the question still remains: Why should I have to be pronounced dead or alive because there is a consensus of those trained in biology and medicine in favor of the philosophical concept of life that focuses upon fluid flow or integrating capacities or consciousness?

Laying the responsibility on the individual physician or the profession as a whole for deciding what the definition of death should be is the result of inadequate analysis, of failing to distinguish adequately between the levels of the debate. The medical professional undoubtedly has special skills for determining and applying the specific criteria that measure whether particular body functions have irreversibly ceased. Whether the Harvard criteria taken together accurately divide those who are in irreversible coma from those who are not is clearly an empirical question (although the important consideration of just how sure we want to be takes us once again into matters that cannot be answered scientifically). But the crucial policy question is at the conceptual level: should the individual in irreversible coma be treated as dead? No medical answers to this question are possible. If I am to be pronounced dead by the use of a philosophical or theological concept that I do not share, I at least have a right to careful due process. Physicians in the states that do not authorize brain-oriented criteria for pronouncing death who take it upon themselves to use those criteria not only run the risk of criminal or civil prosecution but, in my opinion, should be so prosecuted.

A Statutory Definition of (Whole) Brain Damage

When the Tucker case (in which the Virginia physicians defended their use of criteria for death not sanctioned by state law) reached court, it was the first case to test a *public* policy for defining death. Judge A. Christian Compton was not willing to have such a major question resolved in his court, saying, "If such a radical change is to be made in the law of Virginia, the application should be made therefore not to the courts but to the legislature wherein the basic concept of our society relating to the preservation and extension of life could be examined, and, if necessary, reevaluated" (20, p. 10).[3]

[3] The firm tone of this call for legislative action if the definition of death was to be changed was not maintained in Judge Compton's later statements. Three days after citing the Black's Law Dictionary definition and ruling that it must be followed by the jury, he said in his instructions to the jury: "In determining the time of death, as aforesaid, under the facts and circumstances of this case, you may consider the following elements, none of which should necessarily be considered controlling, although you may feel under the evidence that one or more of these conditions are controlling; the time of the total stoppage of the circulation of the blood; the time of the total cessation of the other vital functions consequent thereto, such as respiration and pulsation; the time of complete and irreversible loss of all functions of the brain; and, whether or not the aforesaid functions were spontaneous or were being maintained artificially or mechanically." Although this seems to allow the jury to use a brain-oriented concept, it may not. To say that these factors may be considered in determining the time of death, is not to say that any one or any combination of them is what we mean by death. The instruction could be interpreted to mean that loss of brain function could be seen as a contributory cause of death defined traditionally as the stoppage of all vital functions. For a fuller discussion of the case see my comments in "Brain Death: Welcome Definition or Dangerous Judgment?" *Hastings Center Report* 2, no. 5 (November 1972), pp. 10-13.

The Kansas proposal

In 1968 Kansas was the first state to pass a law permitting the procuring of organs for transplantation (21). The transplanters at the University of Kansas Medical Center were in a dilemma because a year earlier a court case had affirmed the traditional definition of death. With some overstatement of the problem, Dr. Loren Taylor noted that they were able to procure organs at the same time case law was interpreted as precluding organ transplantation.[4]

The same year Kansas passed its organ procurement statute M. M. Halley and W. F. Harvey (22) proposed a statutory definition of death initiating a debate about the proper statutory formulation. As a result of prodding from the transplanters Kansas passed the first statutory definition of death. It is reproduced below.

> A person will be considered medically and legally dead, if in the opinion of a physician, based on ordinary standards of medical practice, there is the absence of spontaneous respiratory and cardiac function and, because of the disease or condition which caused, directly or indirectly, these functions to cease, or because of the passage of time since these functions ceased, attempts at resuscitation are considered hopeless; and, in this event, death will have occurred at the time these functions ceased; or

> A person will be considered medically and legally dead if, in the opinion of a physician, based on ordinary standards of medical practice, there is the absence of spontaneous brain function; and if based on ordinary standards of medical practice, during reasonable attempts to either maintain or restore spontaneous circulatory or respiratory function in the absence of aforesaid brain function, it appears that further attempts at resuscitation or supportive maintenance will not succeed, death will have occurred at the time when these conditions coincide. Death is to be pronounced before artificial means of supporting respiratory and circulatory function are terminated and before any vital organ is removed for purpose of transplantation.

> These alternative definitions of death are to be utilized for all purposes in this state, including the trials of civil and criminal cases, any laws to the contrary notwithstanding.

Maryland next passed an almost identical bill.[5] Subsequently Alaska, California, Georgia, Illinois, Michigan, New Mexico, Oregon,

---

[4] Of course even the most rigid interpretation of the old definition of death would preclude taking organs only from donors not yet dead—not even that unless one assumes that organs can be taken only from the corpse. But Dr. Taylor can be granted his hyperbole for the purposes of the political debate.

[5] Maryland Sessions Laws ch., 693 (1972). The phrase "in the opinion of a physician" was deleted from the first paragraph and the phrase "and because of a known disease or condition" was added in the second paragraph following "ordinary standards of medical practice." It is not clear why the irreversible loss of brain function must be caused by a known disease or condition unless this is thought to be a protection against falsely diagnosing irreversibility in cases where a central nervous system depressant is present, unknown to the medical personnel.

Oklahoma, West Virginia, Tennessee, Louisiana, Iowa, Montana, Idaho, North Carolina, and Virginia passed such legislation. States now considering changes include Florida, Minnesota, and New York. Others have legislators interested in new death definitions.

These statutory proposals have not gone without opposition. Probably the best focused and most widely known criticism has come from British law professor Ian McColl Kennedy (23). "Let us have guidelines by all means. They are essential," he argues. "But let them be set down by the medical profession, not by the legislature." That the medical profession, as a profession, may have no special competence to set such guidelines is a possibility he completely misses. Like many others, he confuses medical and policy expertise. He goes on to outline six specific criticisms of the Kansas bill. Some of them seem to me more valid than others.

The first is probably the most critical and the most valid. The act, he observes, "seems to be drafted only with transplantation surgery in mind." Indeed, the bill incorporates explicit directions on this matter: "death is to be pronounced before artificial means of supporting respiratory and circulatory function are terminated and before any vital organ is removed for purpose of transplantation." As Dr. Taylor has revealed in his 1971 article, the University of Kansas Medical Center was concerned about transplants when staff members began promoting the change in the law.

The relation between a new definition of death and transplantation is complex, and Ian Kennedy's (23) first critical point identifies a major cause of worry: "To draft a statute on death inspired apparently by the desire to facilitate what must still be considered experimental surgical procedures must serve to disturb the man in the street. . . . The Act in its present form does not serve to reassure the person who may fear that during his last hours on earth his doctors will be less concerned with his condition than with the person earmarked to receive one of his vital organs" (p. 947).

Don Harper Mills (24), physician and lawyer, does not agree that the statute is so closely associated with transplant policy. He claims that it intentionally extends to questions of when the physician can terminate resuscitative efforts or discontinue artificial maintenance. Whatever the intentions of the bill's authors, both the authors and Mills may be wrong in their assumptions of what purposes such a statutory definition should serve. It is dangerous to propose a statutory definition solely for the purpose of obtaining organs, but it is equally dangerous to confuse the issue of when resuscitation should be stopped with the one of when a patient is dead. Neither considers that a statutory definition may be needed to prevent the basic indignity of treating a corpse as if it were alive—of confusing a living human with one who has lost essential humanness.

The Challenge: Meeting the Issues of Death

Kennedy is right in recognizing that the link between transplantation and the definition of death should not be as close as in the Kansas bill.

Second, Kennedy objects that the Kansas bill seems to propose two alternative definitions of death, implying a person may be simultaneously dead according to one criterion and alive according to the other. In a law review article agreeing with Kennedy on this point, Alexander Capron, law professor at the University of Pennsylvania, and Leon Kass, professor at the University of Chicago, pose a bizarre problem (14). A patient who meets the brain-oriented criteria for death and is a good tissue match with a potential organ recipient, is pronounced dead under a special "transplant definition." What would the patient's status be if the potential organ recipient dies before the donor organs are removed? The donor would be alive according to the heart and lung-oriented definitions but pronounced dead according to a definition no longer applicable. If it is the person who dies and not some organ or cells or function, then we need a single definition that can apply to all of us, independent of what someone may want to do with our parts. These two problems raised by Kennedy—the dangerous link with transplantation and the implication of alternative definitions of death—should be taken into account in any future bills dealing with a new definition of death.

Third, Kennedy senses something wrong with the requirement that death be pronounced before artificial means of supporting respiration and circulation are stopped. Here his instincts may be sounder than the reasons he uses to support them. The proposal that death be pronounced first is taken from the Harvard committee report. Kennedy seems to agree with the policy but feels it should not be written into the legislation. He writes that the dilemma faced by physicians is "more imagined than real" and declares that "doctors do this every day without legislative fiat and will continue to do so with impunity. . . ." I don't follow his reasoning. Does he mean that physicians declare death every day before turning off resuscitation equipment? The cry for legislative protection seems to contradict that. Or does he mean that physicians decide to stop supportive maintenance on dying patients every day? That is probably true, but an entirely different issue. Kennedy goes on to argue that the requirement that death be pronounced before stopping life support is "entirely redundant." He says, "Once the doctors decide that the conditions specified in the Act exist, and 'further attempts at resuscitation or supportive maintenance will not succeed,' death has already occurred." Indeed it has, according to the new definition, but to say that "death must be pronounced" is something else. If nothing more, this makes clear that the concept of death being used is radically new.

There is a more serious problem, which Kennedy does not mention. To say that death should be pronounced before supportive maintenance ceases (on a corpse) might imply to the less careful reader that it is never appropriate or legal to decide to stop life support on a dying individual. If anyone were to read that from the Kansas legislation it would be a serious problem. The question of stopping treatment of the dying is a separate issue.

Kennedy's fourth objection to the Kansas bill is that it does not require a confirmatory judgment of a second physician before pronouncing death according to brain-oriented criteria. He criticizes others who find this "commendable" (25, see also 14, pp. 116–117). Whether the requirement of a second judgment is reasonable will depend upon the purpose and context of the legislation. In the context of organ transplant practices, a second judgment may indeed control aggressive transplanters. But if Kennedy is also right that the redefinition should not be limited to the transplantation context, then a confirmatory judgment seems less crucial. Is his position that the brain criteria are so much more complicated than the older heart and lung criteria that two technically competent individual judgments are necessary? I doubt that this is true now, and surely it will become completely unlikely, as experience is gained during the life of the legislation. There seems no plausible reason to have two experts involved in the general task of pronouncing death unless the techniques used are so complex that one cannot handle them adequately.

Kennedy's fifth criticism is that the act should require the physician pronouncing death to be a different one from the transplant physician. He calls for "safeguards" to protect the patient from potential conflict of interest. This is important and valid, particularly in the context of legislation explicitly for transplantation. Even better would be a more general ban on conflict of interest as part of a more general redefinition of death. No physician who has any interest beyond the patient's own welfare should be permitted to pronounce death.

Kennedy's final criticism is the most confusing. He claims that the act implicitly incorporates "the detailed clinical procedures that serve to determine 'brain death'," and he is rightly concerned that the law is no place to spell out in great detail the technical procedures for measuring whether a death has occurred. But it is impossible to read any such specification into the act, which simply says that the diagnosis of absence of spontaneous brain function is to be "based upon ordinary standards of medical practice." These standards will vary from place to place and from time to time.

New technical innovations or empirical data will change the tests to be used or the way they are used. The length of time an electroencephalogram has to be flat may change. Virtually all others who have criticized the Kansas bill (14, 24, p. 969) have thought that it does avoid the trap of overspecificity. The problem seems to be one of confusing the levels of the definition debate. Whatever Kennedy is taking exception to, "the absence of spontaneous brain function" certainly seems a rather general term. It specifies a function or a "locus" in the body, not empirical criteria or tests.[6]

A better (whole) brain statute

Capron and Kass are not happy with the Kansas statute for some of the same reasons as Kennedy: they do not like the close link with the transplantation issue, and they are particularly distressed at the implication that there are alternative forms of death appropriate for different situations. But they are still in favor of legislation. The questions at stake, in their opinion, are crucial matters that call for public involvement. "Physicians *qua* physicians are not expert on these philosophical questions nor are they expert on the question of which physiological functions decisively identify the 'living human organism'" (14, p. 94). The legislative route, they argue, would permit the public to play a more active role in decision making. It would also dispel both lay and professional doubt and provide needed assurance for physicians and patients' families that the new definition could be used without fear of a legal suit. They propose five "principles governing the formulation of a statute."

1. The statute should concern the death of a human being, not the death of cells, tissues, or organs, and not the "death or cessation of his role as a fully functioning member of his family or community."
2. It should move incrementally, supplementing rather than replacing the older cardiopulmonary standards.

[6] In order to clarify the problem of what can and should be legislated, Capron and Kass ("A Statutory Definition," pp. 102–103) have outlined four possible levels for legislative action. These parallel to some extent those mentioned earlier in the chapter. While they also specify a purely formal definition ("the transition, however abrupt or gradual, between the state of being alive and the state of being dead"), the *basic concept* is the most general level of the four on the list. Not unlike my use of the term *concept*, they mean a philosophical specification of what it is that is the essential change in a person who is no longer considered alive. This, they argue, should not be legislated. I would agree provided it is recognized that certain assumptions at the basic conceptual level will have to be made in order to move to the next level, which they call "the general physiological standard." They mean here something like what I called the locus: an area of the body whose functioning is critical. Here, we all agree, is the prime area for legislation. The third and fourth levels outlined by Capron and Kass are the operational criteria (e.g., absence of cardiac contraction and movement of the blood) and "specific tests and procedures" (e.g., pulse, heart beat, blood pressure, etc.). All agree that there is no place in legislation for something as ephemeral as specific empirical tests. I also concur with Capron and Kass that "operational criteria" should not be incorporated into the law.

3. It should avoid serving as a special definition for a special function such as transplantation.
4. It should apply uniformly to all persons.
5. It should be flexible, leaving specific criteria to the judgment of physicians. (14, pp. 104–108)

On the basis of these guidelines they propose a new draft statute as an alternative to the laws in Kansas and Maryland:

> A person will be considered dead if in the announced opinion of a physician, based on ordinary standards of medical practice, he has experienced an irreversible cessation of spontaneous respiratory and circulatory functions. In the event that artificial means of support preclude a determination that these functions have ceased, a person will be considered dead if in the announced opinion of a physician, based on ordinary standards of medical practice, he has experienced an irreversible cessation of spontaneous brain functions. Death will have occurred at the time when the relevant functions ceased. (14, p. 111)

Capron and Kass have captured all of the virtues and none of the problems of the Kansas statute. They include the initial observation of spontaneous and respiratory activity, not because they are themselves inherently significant, but because they are normally very good predictors of the state of the brain. In cases where they would not predict the state of the brain, that is, when artificial means of support interfere with the normally good relationship, then we must shift to more direct measures. Their bill fails to meet two of Kennedy's objections—it does not require two physicians to participate in determining death and it does not provide that the death-pronouncing physician be separate from the physician interested in the potential cadaver's organs—but these requirements seem superfluous for a general public policy for determining when we are dead. Nevertheless, in holding to the principle of making the definition independent of transplantation concerns, Capron and Kass may have missed an important protection for the patient potentially dead because his brain has completely and irreversibly ceased functioning. They argue, "if particular dangers lurk in the transplantation setting, they should be dealt with in legislation on that subject, such as the Uniform Anatomical Gift Act" (14, p. 116). That is reasonable, but it is also reasonable that there be observed a general requirement that the physician pronouncing death should be free of significant conflict of interest (whether interest in a respiring "patient," research, continued treatment fees, or transplantation). That there must be no such conflict is obviously essential, whether or not it should be banned by the statute itself.

Critics of the proposals for statutes setting out new standards for determining death have either dealt with technical wording difficulties or made misguided appeals for vesting decision-making authority in physicians or medical professional groups. These, however, are not the only problems. In order to accept the Kansas statute or the preferable Capron–Kass revision, it is first necessary to accept the underlying policy judgment that irreversible destruction of the brain is indeed death—that individuals should be treated as dead when, and only when, their brains will never again be able to function.[7] Some of us continue to have doubts about that basic judgment.

A Statutory Definition of Cerebral Death

There has been great concern that statutes designed to legalize and regularize the use of brain-oriented criteria may not be sufficiently flexible to keep up with changes in this rapidly developing area. Kennedy and others who place their faith in medical discretion fear that a statute would not permit adoption of new techniques and procedures. For the most part they are wrong, since none of the proposed statutes specifies any particular criteria, techniques, or procedures. Techniques and procedures are changing rapidly; with that the proposed laws can cope. But our concepts, our philosophical sophistication, are evolving rapidly, too. Even today most people writing in the field, including competent scientists and physicians, are careless in distinguishing between the whole brain and the cerebrum and the functions of each. Here may arise a significant problem, for under even the highly generalized statutory proposals it may not be possible to make wanted distinctions between lower brain functions, such as those that control spontaneous respiration, and those giving rise to consciousness and individual personality.

If it is decided that a person without the capacities that are thought to reside in the higher brain (cerebral) centers should really be considered dead, then an amendment to the brain death statutes might be in order. The change could be a simple one: simply strike the word *brain* and replace it with *cerebral*. One further problem remains. Capron and Kass could rely on observations of respiratory and circulatory function for most death pronouncements because the loss of these functions normally correlates with loss of brain

[7] According to both the Kansas and the Capron-Kass proposals, physicians may pronounce death without actually making measurements of brain activity. The implication of the Kansas wording is that there are really two meanings for death—at the conceptual level something like either irreversible loss of vital fluid flow centering in the heart and lungs *or* irreversible loss of bodily integrating capacity centered in the whole brain. Capron and Kass seem to lean to a single concept underlying the statute: the irreversible loss of integrating capacity. That there may be two alternate *criteria* under different circumstances for accurately predicting the loss of this essential function is not shocking. I find this explanation much more plausible.

function. If we are really focusing only on cerebral function, however, we cannot specify that it is appropriate to look beyond respiratory and circulatory function "in the event that artificial means of support preclude a determination that these functions have ceased." In a small group of cases these functions may remain intact even if the cerebral function has ceased. Thus we must replace this wording by a more direct expression: "in the event there is reason to believe that cerebral function has ceased while spontaneous respiratory and circulatory functions remain, a person will be considered dead if in the announced opinion of a physician, based on ordinary standards of medical practice, he has experienced an irreversible cessation of spontaneous cerebral functions." This change in specifying the locus or the general standards for determining death may or may not have practical significance to the clinician who pronounces death. The question of criteria is an empirical one and the answer will change periodically. It may be that the only way of knowing for sure that the cerebrum has irreversibly lost its ability to function is to use exactly the same tests as for determining that the whole brain has lost its power to function, that is, the Harvard Committee criteria or something similar. But it may also be that other tests—such as EEG alone—could predict with adequate certainty when individuals have irreversibly lost cerebral function even if they retain some lower brain functions, even if, say, they are still breathing spontaneously. The question of criteria can and must be left to the neurological experts.

There may be reasons for sticking with the old-fashioned statutes based on whole-brain conceptions of death. Only a few people will be dead according to a cerebral concept but alive according to a whole-brain concept. There may be some risk of making an empirical error in applying cerebral criteria and pronouncing someone dead who could still regain some form of consciousness. Some moral doubt may remain about the legitimacy of pronouncing someone dead who retains lower brain function. But these same problems arise with the whole-brain–oriented statutes as well. Once the judgment has been made that false positive diagnoses of life are a serious problem, serious enough to overcome any empirical or moral doubts, there is a strong case for moving on from the whole brain to a cerebral focus.

A Statute for a Confused Society

There is still another option. Part of the current confusion reflects sincere and reasonable disagreements within society over which philosophical concept of death is the proper one. As with many philosophical questions, the conflict will not easily be resolved. In a democratic society, however, we have a well-established method for dealing with a diversity of religious, moral, or philosophical perspectives. It is to allow free and individual choice as long as it does not directly infringe on the freedom of others and does not radically offend the common morality.

When dealing with a philosophical conflict so basic that it is literally a matter of life and death, the best solution may be individual freedom to choose between different philosophical concepts within the range of what is tolerable to all the interests involved. There have been rare and tentative hints at this solution in the literature. In 1968 proposed by the general definition of human death Halley and Harvey had an apparent option clause:

> Death is irreversible cessation of *all* of the following: (1) total cerebral function, (2) spontaneous function of the respiratory system, and (3) spontaneous function of the circulatory system.
> Special circumstances may, however, justify the pronouncement of death when consultation consistent with established professional standards have (sic) been obtained and when valid consent to withhold or stop resuscitation measures has been given by the appropriate relative or legal guardian. (22, pp. 423–425)

They abandoned this "consent" formula, however, in later versions of their proposal (26).

Halley and Harvey have been criticized for their "mistake in making the state of being dead (rather than the acceptance of imminent death) depend on the 'consent' of a relative or guardian" (14, p. 105). It seems likely that they did indeed confuse the state of being dead with the state of being so close to death that a decision could justifiably be made by a relative or guardian to stop resuscitation. But I do not see that their perhaps naive formulation makes "the state of being dead" dependent upon consent of a relative. It makes the state of being *pronounced* dead dependent upon consent. Being dead or alive may be quite independent of the wishes of relatives, but the treatment of persons as if they were dead or alive can logically still be a matter of choice of a relative or even a prior choice of the individual. For those who believe that metaphysical states are to some extent independent of personal choice (as I do), this will mean that in some cases we shall continue to treat corpses as if they were alive or living people as if they were corpses, but we run that risk under any public policy alternative, whether or not it permits freedom of philosophical choice.

More recently Michael Sullivan (27), county probate judge in Milwaukee, had to make two critical legal decisions concerning whether patients have the right to refuse treatment. He has explained the basis of his decisions in the *New England Law Review*. He writes in his article that he does not believe legislation defining death to be advisable "in this context." Since he is discussing whether dying patients have the right to refuse treatment, this attitude is perfectly plausible. But, although it is also irrelevant to his context, he goes on to state his opinion on who should decide what definition of death should be used: "The individual should decide whether he will employ the Harvard criteria, or some other definition for his death." According to Sullivan, it is the individual, not the physician, the medical society, or the state, who should have the "right to prescribe his death style" including the person's own definition of death. This obviously raises some problems, as in the cases of individuals in irreversible coma who have not recorded an opinion while conscious and competent. Some provision will have to be made for these cases.

There are two possibilities: (1) shifting decision making to the individual (or the next of kin or other legal guardians) and (2) setting up a definition to be followed unless otherwise instructed. As a practical matter both can probably be used. The law could specify a given general standard—oriented to heart or the whole brain or the cerebrum—with the proviso that the individual has the right to leave explicit instructions to the contrary. Further, as with the Uniform Anatomical Gift Act, the law could provide that, in those cases where the individual has left no instructions while conscious and competent, the right would be exercised by the next of kin or guardian appointed for the purpose.

There is another problem, however. Has individualism run amok? Do we really want to be so antinomian, so anarchical, that any individual no matter how malicious or foolish can specify any meaning of death that the rest of society would be obliged to honor? What if Aunt Bertha says she knows Uncle Charlie's brain is completely destroyed and his heart is not beating and his lungs are not functioning, but she still thinks there is hope—she still thinks of him as her loving husband and does not want death pronounced for a few more days? Worse yet, what if a grown son who has long since abandoned his senile, mentally ill, and institutionalized father decides that his father's life has lost whatever makes it essentially human and chooses to have him called dead even though his heart, lungs, and brain continue to function? Clearly society cannot permit every individual to choose literally any concept of death. For the same reason, the shortsighted acceptance of death as meaning whatever physicians choose for it to mean is wrong. A physician agreeing with either Aunt Bertha or the coldhearted son should certainly be challenged by society and its judicial system.

There must, then, be limits on individual freedom. At this moment in history the reasonable choices for a concept of death are those focusing on respiration and circulation, on the body's integrating capacities, and on consciousness and related social interactions. Allowing individual choice among these viable alternatives, but not beyond them, may be the only way out of this social policy impasse.

To develop model legislation, we can begin with the Capron-Kass statutory proposal and make several changes to avoid the problems we have discussed. First, a cerebral locus for determining if a person is dead can be incorporated by simply changing the word *brain* to the narrower *cerebral* and making the other necessary adjustments in wording. Second, it seems to me a reasonable safeguard to insist, in general terms appropriate for a statutory definition, that there be no significant conflict of interest. Finally, wording should be added to permit freedom of choice within reasonable limits. These changes would create the following statute specifying the standards for determining that a person has died:

> A person will be considered dead if in the announced opinion of a physician, based on ordinary standards of medical practice, he has experienced an irreversible cessation of spontaneous respiratory and circulatory functions. In the event there is reason to believe that cerebral functions have ceased while spontaneous respiratory and circulatory functions remain, a person will be considered dead if in the announced opinion of a physician, based on ordinary standards of medical practice, he has experienced an irreversible cessation of spontaneous cerebral functions. Death will have occurred at the time when the relevant functions ceased.
>
> It is provided, however, that no person shall be considered dead even with the announced opinion of a physician solely on the basis of an irreversible cessation of spontaneous cerebral functions if he, while competent to make such a decision, has within the limits of reasonableness explicitly rejected the use of this standard or, if he has not expressed himself on the matter while competent, his legal guardian or next of kin explicitly expresses such rejection.
>
> It is further provided that no physician shall pronounce the death of any individual in any case where there is significant conflict of interest with his obligation to serve the patient (including commitment to any other patients, research, or teaching programs which might directly benefit from pronouncing the patient dead).

REFERENCES

1. Clear MD's in "living" donor case. *New York Post*, May 26, 1972.
2. Frederick, R. S. Medical jurisprudence—Determining the time of death of the heart transplant donor. *North Carolina Law Review*, 1972, *51*, 172-184. For another review of the case see Converse, R. But *when* did he die?: *Tucker* v. *Lower* and the brain-death concept. *San Diego Law Review*, 1975, *12*, 424-435.
3. Ad Hoc Committee of the Harvard Medical School to Examine the Definition of Brain Death. A definition of irreversible coma. *Journal of the American Medical Association*, 1968, *205*, 337-340.

4. Ramsey, P. On updating procedures for stating that a man has died. In *The patient as person*. New Haven: Yale University Press.
5. Beecher, H. K. *The new definition of death, some opposing views.* Paper presented at the meeting of the American Association for the Advancement of Science, Dec. 1970.
6. Brierley, J. B., Adams, J. A. H., Graham, D. I., & Simpson, J. A. Neocortical death after cardiac arrest. *Lancet*, September 11, 1971, 560–565.
7. Descartes, R. The passions of the soul. In *The philosophical works of Descartes*, Vol. 1. Cambridge: Cambridge University Press, 1911.
8. Mellerio, F. Clinical and EEG study of a case of acute poisoning with cerebral electrical silence, followed by recovery. *Electroencephalography Clinical Neurophysiology*, 1971, *30*, 270–271.
9. Toole, J. F. The neurologist and the concept of brain death. *Perspectives in Biology and Medicine*, Summer 1971, 602.
10. Hadjidimos, A. A., Brock, M., Baum, P., & Schurmann, K. Cessation of cerebral blood flow in total irreversible loss of brain function. In M. Brock, C. Fieschi, D. H. Ingvar, N. A. Lassen, & K. Schurmann (Eds.), *Cerebral blood flow*. Berlin: Springer-Verlag, 1969.
11. Beis, A. et al. Hemodynamic and metabolic studies in "coma depasses." In M. Brock et al. (Eds.), *Cerebral blood flow*. Berlin: Springer-Verlag, 1969.
12. Wolstenholme, G. E. W., & O'Connor, M. (Eds.) *Ethics in medical progress: With special reference to transplantation*. Boston: Little, Brown, 1966.
13. Ceballos, R., & Little, S. C. Progressive electroencephalographic changes in laminar necrosis of the brain. *Southern Medical Journal*, 1971, *64*, 1370–1376.
14. Capron, A. M., & Kass, L. R. A statutory definition of the standards for determining human death: An appraisal and a proposal. *University of Pennsylvania Law Review*, 1972, *121*.
15. What and when is death? *Journal of the American Medical Association*, 1968, *204*, 539–540; Sadler, A. et al. The Uniform Anatomical Gift Act: A model for reform. *Journal of the American Medical Association*, 1968, *204*, 2501–2506; Dukeminier, J., & Sanders, D. Organ transplantation: A proposal for routine salvaging cadaver organs. *New England Journal of Medicine*, 1968, *279*, 403–419; Report of the Special Committee on Organ Transplantation. *British Medical Journal*, 1970, *1*, 750–751; British Medical Association, The Problem of Euthanasia. London: B.M.A., 1971, p. 3.
16. Warren, D. G. Developing a new definition of death. *Health Law Bulletin*, July 1972, 35.
17. Ward, W. C. Human organ transplantation: Some medical-legal pitfalls for transplant surgeons. *University of Florida Law Review*, 1970, *23*.
18. High, D. M. Death: Its conceptual elusiveness. *Soundings*, Winter 1972.
19. Biorck, G. Thoughts on life and death. *Perspectives in Biology and Medicine*, Summer 1968. For a similar position by a lawyer see D. W. Meyers, *The human body and the law*. Chicago: Aldine, 1970.
20. *Tucker* v. *Lower*, No. 2831, Richmond, Va., Law and Equity Court, May 23, 1972.
21. Taylor, L. F. A statutory definition of death in Kansas. *Journal of the American Medical Association*, 1971, *215*, 296.
22. Halley, M. M., & Harvey, W. F. Medical vs. legal definitions of death. *Journal of the American Medical Association*, 1968, *204*, 412–415.
23. Kennedy, I. M. The Kansas statute on death—An appraisal. *New England Journal of Medicine*, 1971, *285*, 946–950.
24. Mills, D. H. The Kansas death statute: Bold and innovative. *New England Journal of Medicine*, 1971, *285*, 968–969.

25. Curran, W. J. Legal and medical death—Kansas takes the first step. *New England Journal of Medicine*, 1971, *284*, 260-261.
26. Halley, M. M., & Harvey, W. F. Law-medicine comment: The definitional dilemma of death. *Journal of the Bar Association of the State of Kansas*, 1968, *39*, 179.
27. Sullivan, M. T. The dying person—His plight and his right. *New England Law Review*, 1973, *8*, 197-216.

CHAPTER THIRTEEN

Euthanasia or the Right to Die

> *He liked to think "human" meant account-*
> *able in spite of many weaknesses—at the last*
> *moment tough enough to hold.*
> Saul Bellow (1)

> *A dying man needs to die as a sleepy man*
> *needs to sleep and there comes a time when it*
> *is wrong as well as useless to resist.*
> Stewart Alsop (2)

RONALD A. CARSON

"Under what circumstances might I prefer that my life not be pro-
longed even if the technical capability to do so is available?" Carson
points out that many pleas for humane dying are made by survivors
who experience their loved ones dying in a hospital attached to life
support systems long after "life" has gone out of them. The prob-
lems of modern dying discussed at length in Chapters Four and Five
make the issue of euthanasia timely and appropriate. The hospice
allows a natural death. However, the issue of euthanasia is not so
simple. Carson brings the problem clearly into focus and points at
the conflicts and dilemmas. He pleads against a unilateral mode of
decision making in favor of a modified consensual mode both of
which are carefully illustrated.

The reader is challenged to examine what it might mean to say
that death is "good," and what it might mean to be a "survivor." Pre-
senting three characters from Albert Camus's The Plague, *Dr. Rieux,*
Paneloux, and Tarrou as three different kinds of survivors in the face
of death, Carson provides a new perspective for the issue and com-
pels the reader to stop and reflect.

So many good and reasonable things have been written on euthanasia that one approaches the subject with some trepidation. The writing of this chapter has been guided by two obligations—the obligation, placed upon the author by the title of the volume, to inform, and the obligation to challenge the reader, as stated in the section heading of Part Three. I have chosen to meet the former obligation by reviewing several salient issues in the debate over euthanasia and by providing a selected bibliography at the end of the chapter. By way of challenge I invite the reader to explore with me some ideas and literary materials that variously address the questions implicit in the title of the chapter. What is meant by a good death or a quiet and easy death? And, perhaps even more fundamentally, how is one to live with the knowledge that one (or someone dear) has been put on notice?

FEARS OF HOSPITAL DEATH

That death has become the subject of civil discussion is probably in the main a salutary development. It appears that much of the silence and deception that once surrounded dying are being displaced by a new candor. To the extent that this candor is not confused with bluntness but rather is construed as a sensitive blending of honest feelings and plain speaking it is to be welcomed.

What has given rise to these public discussions of death? The reasons are easy to discover but difficult to deal with. Quite simply, we have come to fear the technological trappings of dying as much as the dying itself. In our wildest fantasies we fear the torment of tubes, chemicals, and machines. In search of words to describe her visual impression of her hospitalized dying husband, The Wife in Edward Albee's *All Over* (3) says indignantly, "A city seen from the air? The rail lines and the roads? Or, an octopus: the body of the beast, the tentacles electrical controls, recorders, modulators, breath and heart and brain waves, and the tubes! In either arm and in the nostrils. Where had he gone!? In all that equipment" (p. 21). Ironically, now that medicine can do so much to prolong life and ease misery, we are coming to view it, and especially the hospital, with ambivalence. It is this ambivalence that has given rise to such questions as: under what circumstances might I prefer that my life not be prolonged even if the technical capability is at hand to prolong it?

Many of the eloquent and moving pleas for humane dying that one reads these days in the professional literature and the public press are patently motivated by a survivor's unsettling experience of the death of a loved one in a hospital. We can anticipate more and more such pleas as people live longer and die attached to life support systems long after "life" has gone out of them. (By *life* here I mean something commonsensical—the ability to walk, talk, eat, recognize, and respond.) If we read between the lines of these pleas and press them for their content, they look less like indictments than like declarations of outrage. At their best they are not designed to place blame but to question the propriety of the habit we have fallen into of bringing our dying to the hospital.

Upward of 80 percent of deaths in this country occur in institutions, most of them in hospitals. Thus, a discussion of euthanasia or the right to die may fruitfully begin with a brief look at the context of dying in our society. Our current popular conception of the hospital as a place of healing that epitomizes modern medical sophistication is a conception of fairly recent origin. One need look back little more than 50 years to discover that, as George Orwell (4) once wrote:

> A hospital is popularly regarded as much the same thing as a prison, and an old-fashioned dungeon-like prison at that. A hospital is a place of filth, torture and death—a sort of ante-chamber to the tomb. If you are seriously ill and if you are too poor to be treated in your own home then you must go into hospital, and once there you must put up with harshness and discomfort. (p. 27)

This description may seem far-fetched to our ears, familiar as we are with immaculate, efficient hospitals. Recall, however, that Orwell is describing not an actual hospital, but a vague, troubling notion that many people even today carry alongside their realistic conception of what hospitals are like. For many this notion may be informed by an experience of attending a loved one who is dying.

> However great the kindness and the efficiency in every hospital death there will be some cruel, squalid detail. Something perhaps too small to be told but leaving terribly painful memories behind arising out of the haste, the crowding, the impersonality of a place where every day people are dying among strangers. (4, p. 30)

Hospitals are by and large acute care facilities designed to receive the sick, get them through an episode of illness or a surgical procedure, off sick call, and back into society. They are, in short, way stations for the afflicted—places for getting well and then getting on with it. Perhaps it is inappropriate and functionally untenable to expect an institution designed to keep the patient moving to double as a last stop for the severely debilitated and dying (but, more about this later).

ALTERNATIVES TO HOSPITAL DEATH

What then are some alternatives to dying in the hospital? For some families dying at home may be an alternative. (The very sensitively executed photographic essay *Gramp* (5) is an example of how one such family coped with the death of a grandfather at home.) Albee (3) has The Mistress defend the decision to bring the dying man home: " 'When it becomes pointless,' he said, 'have me brought back here. I want a wood fire, and a ceiling I have memorized, the knowledge of what I could walk about in *were* I to. I want to leave from someplace I have known' " (p. 22). However, for most people, separated from their families by miles and unfamiliar with death except at a distance, this option is closed. A kind of middle way between home and hospital is the hospice, a European experiment that is attracting considerable attention in this country. (Because there is a full consideration of the hospice elsewhere in this volume, I will limit myself to a few reflections on a personal experience.)

Historically a hospice was something of an amalgam of a hospital and a hotel where travelers interrupted their pilgrimages to this holy place or that for rest and sustenance. Perhaps the best known of the English hospices today is St. Christopher's on the outskirts of London. It too is a place of respite. No one is cured at St. Christopher's, but it is in no way a morbid place. It is on the contrary a positively homey place effusing a sense of safety and steadfastness.

It was a student of mine who introduced me to St. Christopher's some years ago. I was skeptical from the outset. I could not imagine that an institution for the terminally ill in which the average length of stay is 17 days could be anything but a dreary place. But I paid a visit, willing to be persuaded otherwise and found no evidence to support my skepticism.

Instead I met Dr. Cicely Saunders, a nurse–social worker–physician whose no-nonsense caring attitudes pervade St. Christopher's at every level from patient care through teaching and administration. I found open, airy rooms each with ample windows, plants and fresh flowers, brightly colored blankets, and room enough for several visitors. I discovered a well-groomed English garden with benches and walkways accessible to wheelchairs and mobile beds. I ate in the dining room where patients and visitors, staff and their children from the day care center at the hospice gather for meals. When I describe the character of this remarkable institution as homey, I do not mean sentimental. There is no sentimentality at St. Christopher's. There is caring, hard work, and attention to concrete tasks on the part of a staff dedicated to making the final days of patients proud, pain-free days. This last is accomplished by the skillful tailoring of pain medications to individual needs and by permitting patients to imbibe alcohol, if that is their custom. The overriding aim is not to bring about sedation but to control pain and acute discomfort. This artful blending of first-rate nursing care and the skillful use of drugs in a climate of trust and support communicates to patients as words might not that they will not be abandoned in their dying. This message, communicated subtly and reaffirmed many times a day by the actions of the staff, mitigates against anxiety and permits patients to live a reasonably lucid and autonomous life until they die.

Another development that shows real promise is the creation of a hospicelike unit within a hospital. A pilot study was launched recently at Methodist Hospital in Indianapolis aimed at making the incurably ill as comfortable as possible, reducing the number of heroic medical and surgical procedures, and permitting dying to become a family affair rather than an event faced in loneliness. The 11-bed unit is open to visitors around the clock, accessible to children and pets, and family members who so desire are trained to participate in the care of the patient. The program also incorporates family care after the patient's death when the bereaved are particularly vulnerable (6).

Adapting a unit or a wing of an existing facility for a special purpose is probably more likely to succeed in our society than establishing new single-purpose institutions. This approach has the advantage of gradualness and does not fly in the face of our custom of admitting our dying to the hospital. On the other hand there is no reason why a society as various as ours should adopt any single set of arrangements for the dying. Some people, given a choice, will undoubtedly prefer to die at home, some in hospitals, others in nursing homes, others still, perhaps, in hospices. To the extent that the ravages of disease can be controlled and pain and discomfort kept to a tolerable minimum, why should not all these alternatives be available to the dying?

It is imperative that we reflect on these institutional arrangements because they influence, in ways we are only beginning to glimpse, the manner of a person's dying and the character of the experience of those left behind, quite independent of treatment decisions. There are occasions when simple care is not enough, when what is wanted is deftness in intervening to retard a disease process or excise a tumor. And there are occasions when simple care is quite enough, is in fact precisely what is called for. We must learn better to distinguish the latter from the former occasions and to discern well the desires of the sick. But now let us examine some aspects of the ethics of euthanasia—of decisions to treat or not to treat the incurably, irreversibly ill.

THE ETHICS OF EUTHANASIA

Decisions to leave off aggressive treatment and to initiate supportive care for a peaceful and dignified death are of course made and carried out every day in hospitals everywhere. Such decisions may or may not be made deliberately, they may or may not be recognized for what they are, but they are made. How are they made?

Upon entering their profession, physicians assume a dual obligation: to prolong life and to ease suffering. When those obligations conflict, as they commonly do near the end of a patient's life, physicians must often choose between extending a life while increasing suffering and assuaging suffering at the risk of hastening death by, for example, increasing pain medications to near lethal levels. Such conflicts commonly precipitate discussions of the merits of active versus passive euthanasia. Arguments surrounding the distinction between killing (active) and letting die (passive) are many and complex. A few pertinent observations must suffice.

That the outcome of the two courses of action is identical—the death of the person in question—is important to acknowledge but may not be the most significant consideration. To say that taking action to hasten the dying of a person ravaged by an incurable disease and standing passively by, allowing the disease to kill, are morally equivalent postures is offensive to common sense. Outcome must be weighed against such other considerations as the condition of the dying person (is the physical pain bearable? is he or she suffering terrible mental anguish? or is the person semiconscious and apparently at rest?), the intentions of those attending the patient (do they mean well or ill? are they ambivalent in their intentions?), and, perhaps preeminently, the wishes of the patient as he or she now expresses them or has expressed them in the past regarding the manner of dying (how has the person viewed his or her life and how does he or she view it now in the face of death?).

It is possible to argue that the distinction between active and passive euthanasia is worth preserving and that neither is justifiable, or that passive euthanasia is defensible on the grounds of charity but that active euthanasia is indefensible on just those grounds (these being, of course, only two of many permutations of arguments for and against euthanasia). For my part, I find the case laid out by Philippa Foot (7) in support of active euthanasia motivated by kindness and performed with the dying person's consent and for the dying person's sake a persuasive one. Such an argument does not extend to minors or to incompetent or unconscious adults, but it will take us some considerable distance toward understanding and decent action in the presence of the dying.

This is not to say that physicians should be active in hastening the death of patients (I would categorize increasing dosages of pain-controlling medications as *passive*—allowing a person to die with some semblance of composure while running the risk of depressing respiratory activity or decreasing cardiac output). I would argue that physicians should not take active measures to end their dying patients' lives for two reasons. Patients expect their physicians to extend and prolong life. Were we, as patients, given reason to suspect the genuineness or depth of that commitment, our confidence in physicians would predictably diminish. On the other side, one must ask after the probable effects of the taking of life on members of a profession otherwise committed to the mending of broken life. We know too little to say for sure, but the suspicion is strong that one long-term consequence of the active taking of life may be the brutalization of sensibility.

To argue that physicians' traditional allegiance to the preservation and prolongation of life is worth maintaining does not mean that physicians are bound absolutely to prolong life. George Fletcher (8) has made a convincing case for the circularity of the argument that physicians are bound by an absolute duty to prolong life. Fletcher has shown that that duty is a function of a doctor's relationship with the patient; that that relationship rests most fundamentally on the patient's expectation of the kind and quality of care he or she will receive; that these expectations are, in turn, largely a function of prevailing practices; and, finally, that prevailing practices with regard to the prolongation of life are virtually equivalent to what doctors actually do. To claim that physicians are bound by an absolute duty to prolong life is to ignore the social context in which medical care for the dying takes place.

Conflicts in caring for the dying typically arise when decisions are made unilaterally. Disagreements also occur when expectations regarding who shall make or influence decisions (and to what degree) differ radically among staff or between staff and patient or family. Long-inattentive children often appear at the bedside of an institutionalized dying parent and protest that "nothing is being done" for the parent who at the parent's own request is being cared for but not treated aggressively.

Staff members, too, often question the wisdom of tacit decisions for euthanasia—tacit, because the rationale for the decision has not been communicated, only the decision itself. Consider the following example (9):

> Mrs. R, a middle-aged mother of two, suffers from multiple sclerosis. Her husband divorced her 5 years ago; her teenage daughters live with her at home. Mrs. R often appears at the local hospital for emergency treatment of acute asthma attacks. A physician has ordered a "no code" in the event Mrs. R should go into cardiac arrest during such an episode; that is, she should not be resuscitated. The nurses reading the order in Mrs. R's chart believe that the physician made the decision without consulting the patient or her family. One nurse is incensed by the decision because it offends her sense of

professional values. This nurse has been heard to describe Mrs. R's home situation as "intolerable," and she has volunteered that she, the nurse, "certainly wouldn't want to live under those circumstances." However, Mrs. R has not herself expressed such sentiments to the nurses, although she does seem invariably depressed when she arrives at the emergency room.

Putting the best possible face on this case, it may be that Mrs. R, having endured much suffering and considering her lot carefully, finds her life unbearable and has asked her physician to treat her asthma (suffocation being particularly fearful) but not, should it occur, her heart failure. Even this "benefit of the doubt" interpretation (there are, of course, others) raises a number of difficult questions about how best to square Mrs. R's wishes with her physician's obligations. But our subject here is the *effect* of the decision for euthanasia on the uninformed. At least one nurse is upset at the decision because it does not jibe with her sense of professional right and wrong. One surmises, however, that, given a sound rationale for the decision, she might find it less objectionable. In view of the fact that she and her colleagues are the ones whose job it will be to carry out the "no code" order, they may justifiably expect such a rationale from the physician who wrote the order. In requesting such a rationale the nurse may, of course, find that the physician made the decision without consulting the patient or her family.

Compare this unilateral mode of decision making to a modified consensual mode. Consider, for example, the recommendation that an Optimum Care Committee be established (in this case, at Massachusetts General Hospital) to respond to requests for consultations on how most appropriately to treat hopelessly ill patients. The committee would serve in an advisory capacity, and its mandate would be to convene all members of the care team, to serve as a sounding board for determining the best interest of the patient and the patient's family, and to clarify the treatment rationale. The chief benefits of such a consultation would be,

> clarification of misunderstanding about the patient's prognosis, reopening of communication, re-establishment of unified treatment objectives and rationale, restoration of the sense of shared responsibility for patient and family, and, above all, maximizing support for the responsible physician who makes the medical decision to intensify, maintain or limit effort at reversing the illness. (10, p. 364)

I termed this a "modified consensual mode of decision making"— modified because group decision making in this setting is undesirable (and, if a patient or family member is burdened with making an unbearable decision, may even be nontherapeutic). Some*one* must finally make the decision, but in a modified consensual mode that person (usually a physician though not always) will first consult with everyone who has a stake in the outcome.

Even if it is reached in this deliberate and "inclusive" way, can a decision for passive euthanasia be justified? It can, on the grounds of what is best for the dying person as determined by that adult, competent, conscious person. (Consideration of the special problems presented by dying children, the incompetent, and the unconscious is beyond the scope of this chapter.) As stated in a recent proposal emanating from a law and ethics study group (11) at the Harvard School of Public Health,

> The basis for a final decision or Orders Not to Resuscitate must be concern from the patient's point of view, and not that of some other person who might present what he regards as sufficient reasons for not resuscitating the patient. It is only the clinical interest of the patient that must be considered. . . . (p. 366)

The medical profession justly boasts a long and honorable tradition of preserving human life. Now that it has at its disposal means to prolong life indefinitely by artificial means, perhaps it is timely that the languished tradition of respect for a patient's "right to die," that is, the right to respectfully refuse available life-prolonging treatment, be refurbished.

A most eloquent defense of the practice of "medical euthanasia" was penned by a young German physician 150 years ago. C. F. H. Marx (12) spelled out for his colleagues at Göttingen "what can be done so the passing from life may be gentle and bearable."

> . . . the physician . . . is not expected to have a remedy for death but for skillful alleviation of suffering. . . . This is that science, called euthanasia, which checks oppressing features of illness, relieves pain, and renders the supreme and inescapable hour a most peaceful one. (p. 405)

Marx (12) writes of the importance of medications "properly and cautiously administered" for the alleviation of suffering, but he identifies the provision of "some kind of higher comfort" as the "most noble and rewarding aspect of his [the physician's] work" (p. 410). Until recently, attending the patient during dying was an integral part of the physician's calling.

More and more patients are assuming a greater share of responsibility for their own health. This is on the whole a welcome development. Thoughtful physicians have been telling us for years that medicine, for all its remarkable accomplishments, is not a panacea for all the ills that befall humankind. Assuming greater responsibility for one's health may include expressing one's wishes regarding the manner of one's dying. The chief virtue of living wills, if they come into widespread use, may well reside less in their content than in the function they serve. If they precipitate a conversation between doctor and patient or among family members or between doctors and families, conversations that might otherwise not have taken place, they will have served a valuable purpose indeed. For it is the conversation that matters, not the document. And where such conversations occur spontaneously the documents are superfluous. Death is so ominous and forbidding to us moderns not least because we seldom experience it. It is not uncommon for us at middle age to confront the death of a parent or indeed come face to face with death ourselves without a previous exposure to death. This can understandably be a terrifying experience. I do not wish to be misunderstood on this point. I am not arguing for the domestication of death. (There is an assumption barely hidden in many of the popular how-to handbooks on "managing" the dying that death can be tamed and made palatable. This is ludicrous and in any case impossible to achieve.) Death is alien whether we have lived life well or poorly. Its power to terrorize us, however, is mitigable and may to no small degree be a function of our familiarity or lack of familiarity with death. From the pinnacle of his 80-odd years Arnold Toynbee (13) wrote shortly before his death, "The key, for each one of us, to the relation, for him, between life and death is, I believe, the extent of his familiarity with death and the stage in his life at which he has become familiar with it . . ." (p. 260). In ceasing to isolate ourselves from death, by reincorporating humane dying into the rhythms of family life, we may find ourselves and our children no less bereaved at the loss of a loved one but instructed, enlightened even, and less terrorized by our or their own death.

THE MEANING OF EUTHANASIA

Now let us shift from the descriptive and literal to the suggestive and metaphoric and ask: What is meant by *euthanasia*? Aside from the sentimental, what might it mean to say that death is "good" or "easy"?

There may be, as Terrence Des Pres (14) has so forcefully argued, typical forms of response to extremity. The record of life in the death camps, Des Pres has demonstrated, is testimony to the emergence of a type of moral identity—that of the *survivor*—a powerless person fiercely unreconciled to victimhood. Survival is the moral style of one who lives in the face of death but beyond its grip. It is characterized by staying power, moral tenacity, and, to name a further characteristic distinguishing it radically from heroism, it is fundamentally social. The modern literary imagination has produced a number of such survivors, but perhaps none commands more critical interest than Albert Camus's (15) Doctor Rieux. Rieux can tell us much about dying decently and living lucidly in the presence of death.

The Plague is set in a North African coastal city in the 1940s. The narrator sets the stage for his tale by intimating to the reader that life in Oran is languid and complacent, that "doing business" is the chief activity, and that dying there is difficult. The reader is introduced early to Dr. Bernard Rieux, a man weary of the world— though he had much liking for his fellow men. (Only in the end does Dr. Rieux declare himself also to have been the teller of the tale.) Rieux begins to read the bewildering portents that signal the invasion of this docile town by the plague and to chronicle the town's reaction to the coming of death into its midst—how disbelief gave way to panic, panic to fear, and how "with fear serious reflection began" (15, p. 83). I want to elucidate the reflections of three of the story's characters—Rieux, Tarrou, and Paneloux— each of whom represents a distinctive response to the presence of death.

Toward the end of the first month of the plague, Father Paneloux, a local Jesuit scholar and popular public lecturer, was asked to preach a sermon as part of the Week of Prayer organized by the ecclesiastical authorities in (now quarantined) Oran. Paneloux is described as a man of fiery temperament, so it was no surprise to the townspeople when he launched passionately into his sermon on the plague. What he said, however, took them aback:

> Calamity has come on you my brethren and, my brethren, you de-served it. . . . If today the plague is in your midst, that is because the hour has struck for taking thought. The just man need have no fear, but the evil-doer has good cause to tremble. For plague is the flail of God and the world His threshing-floor, and implacably He will thresh out His harvest until the wheat is separated from the chaff. . . . Now you are learning your lesson. . . . Now, at last, you know the hour has struck to bend your thoughts to first and last things. (15, pp. 124–26)

About the sermon Tarrou notes in his diary: "At the beginning of a pestilence and when it ends there's always a propensity for rhetoric. In the first case, habits have not yet been lost; in the second, they're returning. It is in the thick of the calamity that one gets hardened to the truth, in other words, to silence. So—let's wait" (15, p. 137).

A certain mystery surrounds Tarrou. We know only that he is newly arrived and that he is apparently a man of private means who enjoys Oran's beaches. "Good humored, always ready with a smile, he seemed an addict of all normal pleasures without being their slave" (p. 83). "The only thing I'm interested in," he told the night porter at the large hotel where he resides, "is acquiring peace of mind" (p. 85). It is Tarrou who, as the pestilence spreads, organizes volunteer sanitary squads and invites Father Paneloux to join them. Paneloux works hard, spending long hours in the hospitals and other places where the risk of contracting the plague is great. But it is the drawn out, sordid death of the magistrate's son that most severely tests the resolve of Paneloux and Rieux, both of whose best efforts—the prayers, and the antiplague serum— fail. After a brief, heated exchange it is Paneloux who says to Rieux:

> "That sort of thing is revolting because it passes our human understanding. But perhaps we should love what we cannot understand."
>
> Rieux straightened up slowly. He gazed at Paneloux, summoning to his gaze all the strength and fervor he could muster against his weariness. Then he shook his head.
>
> "No, Father. I've a very different idea of love. And until my dying day I shall refuse to love a scheme of things in which children are put to torture. . . . But I'd rather not discuss that with you. We're working side by side for something that unites us—beyond blasphemy and prayers. And it's the only thing that matters."
>
> Paneloux sat down beside Rieux. It was obvious that he was deeply moved.
>
> "Yes, yes," he said, "you, too, are working for man's salvation."
>
> Rieux tried to smile.
>
> "Salvation's much too big a word for me. I don't aim so high. I'm concerned with man's health; and for me his health comes first."
> (15, p. 197)

The child's death changes Paneloux, so much so in fact that shortly before his own death at the hands of the plague Paneloux preaches another sermon, this one gentler in tone, less sure, and more modest in delivery. Where before he had said "you," he now says "we." He stood by what he had said on that previous occasion, he told the congregation, but what he had said then was lacking in charity.

> And, truth to tell, nothing was more important on earth than a child's suffering, the horror it inspires in us, and the reasons we must find to account for it. In other manifestations of life God made things easy for us and, thus far, our religion had no merit. But, in this respect, He put us, so to speak, with our backs to the wall. . . . My brothers, a time of testing has come for us all. We must believe everything or deny everything. And who, I ask, amongst you would dare to deny everything? . . . My brothers, . . . the love of God is a hard love. It demands total self-surrender, disdain of our human personality. And yet it alone can reconcile us to suffering and the deaths of children, it alone can justify them, since we cannot understand them, and we can only make God's will ours. That is the hard lesson I would share with you today. That is the faith, cruel in men's eyes, and crucial in God's, which we must ever strive to compass. We must aspire beyond ourselves toward that high and fearful vision. (15, pp. 200-203)

Euthanasia or the Right to Die

Just as Rieux and Paneloux had fought side by side but for different reasons, so the bond of friendship between Rieux and Tarrou grew as they made common cause against the plague. In a rare moment of respite Tarrou confides in Rieux his reasons for battling the plague. " All I maintain is that on this earth there are pestilences and there are victims, and it's up to us, so far as possible, not to join forces with the pestilences. That may sound simple to the point of childishness; I can't judge if it's simple, but I know it's true. . . . It comes to this,' Tarrou said almost casually, 'what interests me is learning how to become a saint.' " To this the doctor confesses that he feels more fellowship with the downtrodden than with the saints. " ' Heroism and sanctity don't really appeal to me, I imagine. What interests me is—being a man.' 'Yes,' Tarrou replies, 'we're both after the same thing, but I'm less ambitious' " (pp. 218-219).

From one angle of vision (there are of course many others in this rich and complex narrative) Camus's novel may be read as the struggle of three men against the plague. I have chosen this angle because of the light it throws in an oblique but instructive way on three different postures toward death.

Paneloux saw the plague as part of a larger scheme of things only partially transparent to human understanding, and he fought the plague as part of his own small contribution to working for man's salvation.

Tarrou was a troubled man for whom the complexities of living in the world distilled down to a few simple truths and some hard choices: death is the only certainty, against which one must be forever vigilant. In the struggle between pestilences and victims one must side with the victims or, at the very least, not join forces with the pestilences. And for Tarrou all this is to be done not for the sake of the salvation of mankind but for one's own peace of mind. Tarrou aspires to a kind of secular sainthood.

Rieux's reasons for fighting the plague are secular reasons. He is a doctor, and there are sick and dying people to be cared for. As he puts it on more than one occasion, "There's no question of heroism in all this. It's a matter of common decency. . . . I don't know what it means for other people. But in my case I know that it consists in doing my job" (p. 166). Paneloux and Tarrou lost their match with the plague, and Rieux was finally helpless to change the course of their disease. But as the plague departed Oran, and Rieux reflected on the ordeal he had lived through, he concluded that there was another sense in which he was a "survivor." As a doctor he had been impotent to cure, but he had known friendship and affection and these he vowed to remember. "So all a man could win in the conflict between plague and life was knowledge and memories. But Tarrou, perhaps, would have called that winning the match" (p. 239). Tarrou might also, perhaps, have counted his friend Rieux among the "true healers"—those few who devote themselves full time to practicing the hard vocation of doing battle against the plague, of saving as many as possible from "being doomed to unending separation" (p. 147).

The mythology of death can tell us much about ourselves beyond the obvious. There, in imaginative literature, for example, as I have attempted to intimate in discussing *The Plague*, one finds images of death as an enemy, a thief in the night, but also as a friend to the miserable. There are examples of people dying reluctantly, of others dying willingly, of yet others dying in their own beds or with their boots on. And there are those patients I have witnessed slipping out almost imperceptibly, not to the naked eye rebelling or acquiescing, but simply allowing death to have its way with them. There may be patterns here, but I am impressed above all with the rich variety of ways of dying. The aim of whatever changes we may initiate in our familial and institutional arrangements for the dying should be to support the autonomy of dying persons (not least by genuinely listening to them), to assist them in keeping their meaningful relationships intact until the time for leave taking comes, and to provide a setting in which death may be as individual in character as is life. The poet Rainer Maria Rilke got it just right when he wrote in his *Prayerbook:*

> Grant, O Lord, everyone a death of his own.
> A dying which proceeds from a life
> Wherein were love, meaning, and necessity.

REFERENCES

1. Bellow, S. *The victim.* London: Weidenfeld and Nicolson, 1947, p. 138.
2. Alsop, S. *Stay of execution.* Philadelphia: Lippincott, 1973, p. 299.
3. Albee, E. *All over.* New York: Atheneum, 1971.
4. Orwell, G. How the poor die. In *Shooting an elephant and other stories.* London, 1970.
5. Jury, M., & Jury, D. *Gramp.* New York: Penguin, 1976.
6. Personal communication from William Elliott, MD. See also Mount, B., "The problem of caring for the dying in a general hospital: The palliative care unit as a possible solution. *Canadian Medical Association Journal,* 1976, *115*, 119–121.
7. Foot, P. Euthanasia. *Philosophy and Public Affairs,* 1977, *6*(2), 85–112.
8. Fletcher, G. Legal aspects of the decision not to prolong life. *Journal of the American Medical Association,* 1968, *203*, 65–68.
9. Aroskar, M. The nurse and orders not to resuscitate. *Hastings Center Report,* August 1977, p. 27.
10. "Optimum care for hopelessly ill patients. *New England Journal of Medicine,* 1976, *295*, 362–364.

11. Rabkin, M. et al. Orders not to resuscitate. *New England Journal of Medicine*, 1976, *295*, 364–366.
12. Marx, C. F. H. Medical euthanasia. (Trans. and introduced by W. Cane). *Journal of the History of Medicine*, Autumn 1952, pp. 401–416.
13. Toynbee, A. The relation between life and death, living and dying. In *Man's concern with death*, New York, 1968, p. 260.
14. Des Pres, T. *The survivor*. New York: Oxford University Press, 1960.
15. *The Collected Fiction of Albert Camus*, London: Hamilton, 1960.

SELECTED BIBLIOGRAPHY
ON EUTHANASIA

Behnke, J., & Bok, S. (Eds.) *The dilemmas of euthanasia*. Garden City, NY: Anchor Books, 1975.

Bok, S. Personal directions for care at the end of life. *New England Journal of Medicine*, 1976, *295*, 367–369.

Branson, R., Casebeer, K., Levine, M. D., Oden, T. C., Ramsey, P., & Capron, A. M. The Quinlan decision: Five commentaries: Guardians, physicians, and medical technology. *Hastings Center Report*, 1976, *6*, 8–19.

Carson, R. A. Amidst children and witnesses. *Humanitas: Journal of the Institute of Man*, 1974, *10*, 9–19.

Crane, D. *The sanctity of social life: Physicians' treatment of critically ill patients*. New York: Russell Sage Foundation, 1975.

de Beauvoir, S. *A very easy death*. New York: Putnam, 1966.

De Vries, P. *The blood of the lamb*. Boston: Little, Brown, 1961.

Duff, R., & Campbell, A. G. M. On deciding the care of severely handicapped or dying persons: With particular reference to infants. *Pediatrics*, 1976, *57*, 487–492.

Hinton, J. The dying and the doctor. In A. Toynbee (Ed.), *Man's concern with death*. New York: McGraw-Hill, 1968.

Holden, C. Hospices: For the dying, relief from pain and fear. *Science*, 1976, *193*, 389–391.

Kohl, M. (Ed.) *Beneficent euthanasia*. Buffalo, NY: Prometheus Books, 1975.

Rachels, J. Active and passive euthanasia. *New England Journal of Medicine*, 1975, *292*(2), 78–80.

Ramsey, P. *Ethics at the edges of life*. New Haven, CT: Yale University Press, 1968.

Robertson, J. A., & Fost, N. Passive euthanasia of defective newborn infants: Legal considerations. *Journal of Pediatrics*, 1976, *88*, 883–889.

Smith, D. The sanctity of social life: Physicians and the critically ill. *Hastings Center Report*, 1976, *6*(3), 31–34.

Steinfels, P., & Veatch, R. (Eds.) *Death inside out: The Hastings Center Report*. New York: Harper & Row, 1975.

Swiss guidelines on care of the dying. *Hastings Center Report*, 1977, *7*(3), 30–31.

Tolstoy, L. *The death of Ivan Illych*, New York: Signet, 1960.

Wertenbaker, L. T. *Death of a man*. Boston: Beacon Press, 1957.

CHAPTER FOURTEEN

The Funeral Industry

CAROL TAYLOR

Sooner or later most of us will become dead bodies to be disposed of, and those who make decisions about what is to be done to and with our corpses will, in most cases, become instant customers of

While in Chapter Nine Fulton stresses the importance and functionality of the funeral rite for individuals and the social system, in this chapter Taylor focuses attention on contemporary funeral practices in the United States, particularly as they have become controversial. She relates some of the numerous criticisms that have been leveled at the funeral industry and at funeral directors, among them the high cost of funerals in the United States and ethically questionable procedures for acquiring possession of bodies. At the same time she also presents some of the responses of the funeral industry to these criticisms. Based on hearings conducted by the Federal Trade Commission's Bureau of Consumer Protection, Taylor predicts the establishment of federal constraints upon the funeral industry.

As an anthropologist in the medical field Taylor offers a broad perspective from which to view the issue of modern funeral practices. As a professional she deals with the issue squarely and fairly.

the funeral industry.[1] The funeral industry is a relatively recent phenomenon in U.S. society. Until the turn of the present century the laying out of the body, the making of the coffin, digging the grave, and carrying the encoffined corpse to it were neighborly acts. In isolated parts of our country neighbors and kin continue to bury each other's dead but for the most part the funeral industry has taken over the task of disposing of our dead. Amateur pallbearers recruited from among the kin and associates of the dead person serve as a reminder of these traditional arrangements. My title suggests that there is some discontent with what once was each community's mutual assistance program, and in this chapter we will examine the cultural aspects of our present funeral practices in such a way as to enable each reader to come to his or her own conclusions about the funeral industry.

CULTURAL CONSIDERATIONS

Among nomadic peoples and in societies not able to support nonproductive adult members, those who endanger the survival of the group by becoming nonproductive are expected to recognize the moment when they become a luxury the group cannot afford and to remove themselves from the group in order to await death. If, as sometimes happens, persons in this position fail to realize that they now threaten the survival of the group, ritualized ways of getting the message across have been developed. Among the polar Eskimos, for example, the personal possessions of the candidate for death are bundled and placed at the opening of the igloo.[2] In societies of this sort, subsistence societies, the body removes itself before its death, recognizing that its living presence threatens the survival of the group and that to die at home would necessitate the squandering of the group's precious resources in an attempt to placate the spirits that linger in the body after death. On the other hand, in societies with sufficient resources to sustain nonproductive adult members, funerals, and the rituals accompanying them, sometimes seem extravagant to the point of economic recklessness. The most usual explanation of this phenomenon is that the spirits of the dead are dangerous to the living and must be appeased at whatever cost. An examination of beliefs about death in prescientific societies suggests that the spirits of the dead were thought to be a threat to the living and that the dangers implicit in them can be diminished in two ways: either the

---

[1] Those lost at sea and those who fall off mountains into inaccessible crevices do not leave body disposal problems behind them. Also falling into this category are persons who donate their bodies to science.

[2] Survival as a prisoner hinges on sleeping at night, and in our prisons the guards are informed that a new cellmate is unacceptable by bundling his or her personal effects and placing them at the door of the cell.

dying person can remove the body and the evil spirits it contains to a safe distance before death or the spirits of the dead person can be placated with costly farewell rituals.[3]

In societies like our own where science is assumed to have ousted superstition, economically reckless funerals for the dead are the rule rather than the exception and the practice of paying more than can be, or should be, afforded for funerals is claimed by the morticians who dominate the funeral industry as an essential part of grief therapy. As one mortician put it: "The living are guilt ridden about their dead and one of our functions is to ease this guilt by providing opportunities to spend money for the departed." This rationalization sometimes seems spurious to those who do not have a vested interest in costly funerals.

CRITICISMS AND APPROVAL
OF THE FUNERAL INDUSTRY

Morticians are trained in the art and science of preparing dead human bodies for burial or cremation, and they are licensed as practitioners of this art and science. They also manage, and in most cases own, the funeral homes that sell coffins and cater funerals.[4] Morticians claim to be professionals and as such they assume the responsibility of policing the behavior of members of their profession. As a profession, they also are politically active in protecting their professional territory, including their business interests.

The undertaking profession has been under periodic attack since Jessica Mitford's book *The American Way of Death* was published in 1963.[5] More recently the Bureau of Consumer Protection has investigated the commercial activities of morticians and is attempting to impose legal restraints on the funeral industry. The Bureau of Consumer Protection has made it clear that these attempts are being made not because the funeral industry is more venal than other industries but because its customers are uniquely vulnerable. Funerals cannot be put off to more propitious moments, and the bereaved are rarely in an appropriate frame of mind to comparison shop. Funeral directors object to this interference by the federal government and claim that they police themselves in an adequate fashion and that they have eradicated the abuses identified by Miss Mitford.

[3] In our society Japanese Americans are most sensible about the high cost of burial. All persons attending the funeral contribute to its cost and, as a consequence, the family is not placed in economic jeopardy when one of its members dies.
[4] In earlier times the funeral home was called an "undertaking parlor," reminiscent of the practice of placing the dead person on display in the parlor at home. In those days the mortician was an undertaker.
[5] Prior to the publication of Mitford's book economic disenchantment with undertakers was voiced by physicians and the public. Their crime seemed to be that they were making a profit out of what had been a neighborly act. Interestingly enough, today's corporation hospital is under attack for a similar reason.

Morticians I have listened to compared their self-policing record favorably with that of physicians; they have asked me to compare the costs of their coffins with those of other fine pieces of furniture and explained how and why an expensive funeral was a bargain as grief therapy.

Other death-related professionals—doctors, nurses, chaplains, and the like—tended to be critical of morticians and the funeral industry although exceptions to this opinion (the "benign" mortician) were identified from time to time. In addition to the high cost of coffins and funerals, certain specific business practices indulged in by funeral directors were criticized by other professionals in the field. The two behaviors most frequently mentioned negatively were getting possession of the body and escalating the cost of its disposal. As one critic explained it to me:

> Once a funeral home has the body the customer has had it. Bodies are solicited in more or less subtle ways, including kick-back to hospital staff, and once in a funeral home a body is difficult to extricate. Hence a funeral director in possession can increase the cost of the funeral and his profit, by such tactics as mobilizing guilt, appealing to pride, playing on the emotions, and so forth. Under the circumstances surrounding death the customer tends to be putty in the hands of the mortician.

This somewhat jaundiced opinion of the mortician and the funeral industry summarizes the opinions of the other death-related professionals I listened to. However, most of those I talked with mentioned exceptions, the humane and compassionate funeral director.

The opinions of the customers varied according to the sense of bereavement being experienced at the time negotiations were conducted. In some cases the bereavement was token. Distant relatives and close kin separated by time and distance fell into this category. When the bereavement was token the funeral director seemed to recognize this circumstance by suggesting a funeral that was appropriate to the status of the deceased and did not demand heroic sacrifice on the part of the family. As one satisfied customer put it, "The funeral cost us a leg and an arm but he (the undertaker) cut corners when he could and where they didn't show." Some distanced bereaved compared physicians unfavorably with funeral directors in this respect. This comment was typical, "Arranging the funeral I was made to feel that I was being sensible and in no way disrespectful when I asked that we be as economical as possible. When I asked the doctor not to inflate the hospital bill by prolonging life unnecessarily, he (the doctor) made me feel like a criminal." When I asked this woman how the doctor had made her feel like a criminal she said, "He said, 'As a physician I put life above price.' Then he turned on his heel and walked away." At the other end of

The Challenge: Meeting the Issues of Death

this continuum, those with an acute sense of bereavement most frequently reported that they had dealt with sympathetic funeral directors who had tried to save them undue expense. The following example is typical.

> Over the burial vault he (the undertaker) said, "Having one is a cemetery requirement but there is no need to be extravagant about it. I'd suggest the least expensive." That night it rained and he telephoned me. "Hearing it rain started me thinking about you. I wouldn't want you worrying about water getting into the coffin and to your husband. You seem to me to be the sort of wife who would prefer the best vault money can buy." He mentioned a trade name and said, "It's completely waterproof and guaranteed by Good Housekeeping." He was right. I did. And wasn't it thoughtful of him, with all he's got on his mind, to think about me?

The contention by funeral directors that the high cost of their management of the disposal of our dead can be therapeutic is confirmed by some of their customers. The following comment is typical. "Her death left unfinished business between us and it comforted me to spend more than I could afford on the funeral." My impression is that many segments of our society are not too terribly dissatisfied with the services provided by the funeral industry. As one person put it, "They deserve a high profit. Theirs is the last way I'd choose to make a living."

The dissatisfactions I most frequently encountered were with the funeral itself and seemed to be the result of cultural misunderstandings. For example, the normal grieving behavior of some South American peoples is perceived as hysteria by many North Americans, and the consequent "safe" funeral sold by a North American funeral director to a bereaved South American may not satisfy the customer. One Mexican American made these complaints about the Anglo funeral he had purchased: "The coffin was open as requested but we were forced to gaze into it from a distance and they (the cemetery's employees) had erected barriers to keep us from the graveside." The custodian at the cemetery said, "They (Mexican Americans) like to crowd 'round the grave and in the frenzy of their grief they sometimes jump into it." And he explained that he kept Mexicanos and other hysteria-prone minorities at a distance from the grave to protect them from themselves.

My conversations with funeral directors suggest that the poor are buried more as a public service than for whatever profit may be in it. The owner of a chain of funeral homes summed up what other funeral directors had told me when he said, "The pauper's funeral is a thing of the past. The city pays a reasonable price for the burial of those unable to bury themselves. The poor pay far more than they can afford for funerals and, in most instances, they pay the bill however long it takes them. But the best the poor can afford and the most the city will pay is a lean profit for us (the funeral industry). We need profitable funerals to survive." In his opinion the best customer was a family that drove Fords but wanted a Cadillac for the final journey of a loved one.

PROTECTION FOR THE VULNERABLE

The Federal Trade Commission has caused studies of the funeral industry to be made and has concluded that this industry's consumers need additional protection because at the time of negotiation they are, in most cases, inexperienced at purchasing funerals and uniquely vulnerable. The Commission's contentions are valid, but my observations suggest that social pressures as well as emotional factors create purchasing climates that encourage the escalation of funeral costs. As I have suggested, vulnerability varies from consumer to consumer. To some, arranging the disposition of the deceased's body is a mere matter of business and the apparent emotion displayed is lip-service acknowledgment of social convention. These customers are not vulnerable because of bereavement although they may buy more funeral than they would have chosen to do for other reasons; in most cases they are sold the notion that the deceased's religion and social position demand the additional funeral expenditures. In some cases the emotionally bereaved already have worn off the edge of their bereavement and, as a consequence, are less vulnerable than one would have supposed. This premature easing of bereavement occurs because, in our society, dying people frequently are taken into hospitals or nursing homes and separated to a greater or lesser extent from friends and family during the last days, weeks, or months of life. Under these circumstances the about to be bereaved begin to mourn the death prematurely and when death occurs the first throes of grief have passed and the funeral industry's new instant customer has not been shocked into instant vulnerability. As one woman put it, "I was wept out and able to make sensible decisions." But many of those who must make arrangements for the disposal of the body of a loved one are vulnerable to the social pressure of the funeral director, and the Federal Trade Commission is moving to protect these vulnerable people.

The Federal Trade Commission's Bureau of Consumer Protection began to investigate the funeral industry in the early 1970s, and by the end of this decade will undoubtedly have placed restraints on the funeral industry that will protect the consumer. These restraints are considered necessary not because the funeral industry is more venal than other industries but because those

The Challenge: Meeting the Issues of Death

shopping for funerals are uniquely vulnerable. Periodically the average U.S. family buys a car and over the years becomes fairly sophisticated about this process. Periodically the average U.S. family purchases a funeral, an equivalent expenditure, but in most cases has not become so sophisticated. The reasons for this difference are obvious. When we buy cars our horse-trading senses are alert. We seek and absorb tips from those more experienced than ourselves and we do not hesitate to haggle. When we shop for funerals these protective behaviors are either muted or absent. It is deemed unseemly to compare costs with respect to the disposal of a supposedly dear deceased. It also is considered unseemly to itemize and compare the prices of services bought with other customers. Did you buy refrigeration or embalming? (Most funeral homes are not equipped to offer refrigeration, a less expensive preservation technique.) Did your funeral include viewing? (A significant component of the traditional U.S. funeral.) The bereaved rarely prepare themselves for funeral purchases by talking with others about the art and commonsense of negotiating for funerals. As one man put it, "I have bought cars, land, houses, and cattle in sensible fashion, but when it came to arranging funerals for my son and my wife I was a business moron." The Federal Trade Commission is attempting to protect the business moron in each of us by placing restraints on the funeral industry.

Morticians and funeral directors do not relish categorization of their activities as an industry. They prefer to consider themselves a profession. In support of this contention they claim that they police their members in order to prevent exploitation and other excesses. In this posture they fail to recognize a conflict of interest between the funeral director who is selling goods and services at a profit and the health helper who is facilitating the disposal of dead bodies as economically and tastefully as possible. Interestingly enough the public—you and I—seem to accept the funeral profiteer as a genuine helper probably because in all societies, including our own, dealing with the dead is an unpalatable undertaking felt to be, in some way or another, dangerous.

MEMORIAL SOCIETIES

A small group of consumers have organized to protect themselves from the excesses of the funeral industry. These people, for the most part older professionals (professors, lawyers, and so forth), have formed memorial societies in the United States and Canada to combat the high cost of disposing of their bodies after death. Through their nonprofit organizations they encourage their members to arrange dignified and economically sensible disposal ceremonies

The Funeral Industry   381

for themselves by providing them with the information that will enable them to do so. Prearranging the afterdeath procedures is the secret of success of the memorial society, and the most frequent reason for their failure is that their members do not arrange the disposal of their remains before death. One man said, "I meant to—mean to—but cannot bring myself, in cold blood, to enter a funeral home and tidy up this loose end of my life." This reaction was typical and not limited to mere members of memorial societies. Board members of some memorial societies I talked with claimed to have found making final disposal arrangements most difficult. One of them said, "I'll get round to it. I want to be an example to others but facing death is most difficult." It is difficult for persons in a youth-oriented society like our own to acknowledge that our lives are finite. The death avoidance behaviors that characterize Americans encourage us to act as if death is for other people—the disadvantaged in our own society and the disease-ridden starving members of third world countries. It is almost as if death is considered un-American.

For a modest sum, $10 to $15, memorial societies sell lifetime memberships and provide information about legal restrictions, current costs, and corners asking to be cut. Some memorial societies are purely advisory; others provide a complete array of body disposal services. One of the more enterprising memorial societies accepts and fills orders for coffins you can put together yourself. Their most popular line seems to be the oblong-ended coffin that can be used prior to death either as a blanket chest or a coffee table.[6] These societies are nonprofit, managed by volunteers (mostly retired persons), and dedicated to the notion of bringing economic common sense to the problem of disposing of the bodies of the dead. Their membership is, as yet, sparse and they have not become a significant threat to the funeral industry. But the funeral industry is overplanted, there are too many funeral homes, and it fights the growth of memorial societies as well as other attempts to cut into its profits.

This commonsense approach to the problem of disposing of our dead is not accepted as enthusiastically as one might expect it to be in a pragmatic and scientifically oriented society such as ours. An associate of mine suggested to her husband that they purchase and assemble a pair of square-ended coffins and use them as coffee tables. The husband refused to agree to what he considered a morbid suggestion. A week later he returned to the subject and said, "The idea is sensible and I don't object to it but I don't think we ought to risk it. The funeral home might refuse to bury us if we provided our own coffins."

[6] In our society the octagonal coffin is traditional and a blanket chest or coffee table so shaped would betray its ultimate use and might seem offensive to sensitive guests.

The death avoidance behaviors suggested above have limited the growth of memorial societies and other attempts to organize economically reasonable funerals. During the past decade talk and study of death has become fashionable in academic circles and, among ordinary people, taboos about death have decreased. For example 10 years ago the dead either *expired* or *passed away*, today many of the dead *die*. And there is a rapidly decreasing reluctance to deal openly with death and decide what must be done about it. These changes lead me to suggest that the funeral industry is yielding to social pressures and eventually will supply the public with the service it is asking for at no more than a reasonable profit to the industry. And during this move toward reasonably priced funerals the role of the memorial society is to speak out for the public, for you and me, whose bodies will sooner or later need to be disposed of.

Now let us take a final look at the funeral industry. Despite the adverse publicity it has received, the funeral industry is not intent on gouging the public but is attempting to survive and make a profit at economic odds. On the average the American funeral home handles two funerals a week. The industry's ability to survive and make a profit is enhanced by the vulnerability of the customer. The circumstances under which the customer seeks to buy a funeral are such as to make for maximum customer vulnerability. The purchase must be consummated within a limited period of time. The customer is vulnerable to social and, in some cases, emotional pressures; and the purchaser usually is not an experienced buyer in this particular market. For these reasons the Federal Trade Commission is of the opinion that the customers of funeral homes need to be protected. These circumstances combine to ensure the survival of more funeral homes than the volume of their trade warrants. They also see to it that funerals in our society are more expensive than they should be. As the president of one memorial society put it, "By and large the directors of funeral homes are not villains. They are the victims of their circumstances; and we, in our turn, become their victims because of our circumstances."

The funeral industry has increased the complexity of dealing with bodies after death and by doing so has increased the cost of disposing of our dead. It also has protected its right to decide what should or should not be done to and with dead bodies in our society by encouraging legislation to protect the decision-making rights of the funeral industry. For example, embalming, which became popular during the Civil War because of the demand for corpses delivered in acceptable condition to the home towns of dead soldiers, is a profitable procedure and for this reason has been extensively mandated by the funeral industry's lobby as compulsory. In Florida, for example, a first law was enacted mandating embalming if the body was not finally disposed of within 24 hours. At a later date it was legislated that bodies in Florida could not be cremated before 48 hours after death had elapsed. The second enactment seems excessive. Cremation accounts for somewhere between 5 and 6 percent of bodies being disposed of in the United States.

One funeral director told me that embalming, the vault, and the casket were the cornerstones of the funeral industry, and he went on to explain that because the traditional U.S. funeral included the viewing they had, as he put it, "our customers by the short hairs and a unique technical problem. The viewing exposes the family's selection of a coffin to public comment and makes our customers reluctant to choose one of our cheaper lines." And he went on to explain that most embalmings barely lasted, as a preservative, until the funeral. Apparently an embalming that could be guaranteed to preserve the body (I was assured that this could be done), left the skin looking like leather and, as one funeral director said, "That would never do. Our philosophy is to see to it that the dead when they are viewed look better than they did in life." To this end the mortician becomes an artist and paints the face and hands of the dead he ministers to with great delicacy and enormous skill. One mortician said, "The mouth is our most stubborn problem. Sometimes we are forced to draw protruding teeth; and in most cases we stitch the mouth shut. These techniques cannot be detected by the viewer. We correct injuries inflicted during death, correct nature's faults, and soften the ravages of time. My bodies look on the beautiful side of natural and are a comfort to the bereaved."

CHAPTER FIFTEEN

Death Education for All

J. EUGENE KNOTT

Death's ultimate bequest is to show us a world in which we recognize ourselves.

David Dempsey (1)

INTRODUCTION

Embodied in the above words is the primary rationale for including this kind of chapter in a book called *Dying: Facing the Facts*. That is, one of the unarguable new facts about death is that our society is increasingly recognizing the need for coming to terms with mortality while we are capable of affecting our course toward it. Recent

This chapter is a revised, expanded version of *Educating for death: A prospectus*, copyright 1977 by Forum for Death Education and Counseling, Inc. Gratitude is expressed to Dan Leviton for his valuable critique of an earlier version of this paper.

■■■■■■■■■

In this final chapter Knott deals with a problem that is in the minds of many in the field of death and dying. Knott presents the basic questions that need to be answered if we consider death education for all—why, where, when, how, and by whom? He thoughtfully and diligently answers all these questions by giving various viewpoints. Knott provides a cogent argument for death education for all and offers suggestions that represent the best thinking in this field.

Throughout the chapter the reader is reminded of the need for careful deliberation, for clarity of vision, for well-defined objectives, and for careful selection of means and methods based on the special characteristics of the learner under consideration. As a special feature the author provides an annotated bibliography for death educators.

surveys and informed estimates have indicated that over a thousand courses with death themes currently exist at the postsecondary level nationally, and the influence is beginning to be felt in primary, middle, and secondary schools in the U.S. as well. Further, if one takes into account the expanding number of professional schools of human service and medical education presently giving death curricular address, plus the uncountable community agency and religious group efforts of this nature, the presence and growing interest in death education is quite remarkable. On all levels, teaching has proliferated about the processes of dying and grieving and the "facts" of death and bereavement. While the conversational popularity of death is not fully in the open as yet, it is an undeniable and noteworthy recent phenomenon.

Along with this burgeoning instructional activity has come the production of a number of topical films and other media packages and the publication of an unparalleled wealth of articles and books addressing death-related themes in some manner. Yet, as we have all discovered in recent years with drug education, a surfeit of materials is not itself sufficient for providing a worthwhile learning experience. Then, too, a variety of techniques for augmenting the mere dissemination of information about death and dying have evolved. Included herein are the use of various structured exercises, particularly those that deal with the variety of decisions and value postures that abound in modern medical practice. The many thanatology scenarios that lack absolute answers, those bioethical quandaries that make dying seem anything but absolute, have propelled us further still into courtroom dramas where the "answers" have become secondary to the emotionality elicited by the "questions." In addition, psychodrama methods; visitations to funeral homes, crematoria, and cemeteries; sensitivity group sessions; seminars dealing solely with the affective dimensions of dying and care giving; interviews with dying patients and survivors; and seemingly innumerable programs on isolated aspects of the topic are widely employed in death education efforts today. Indeed, thanatology has come into ubiquity if not maturity.

Death education has become a widely valued topic in formal learning sectors only within the past 10 years. While the various classroom sites may share some techniques and materials, too frequently in this evolution little more than the motivations for high course enrollment and the vogue of currency have prompted the often hasty and ill designed offering of a course on death and dying. Many of these efforts, even when well intentioned, suffer from lack of a thorough consideration of the many issues that influence the dying and postmortem picture.

What is it that has given death a rebirth of public attention, one that gives us the luxury our forebears lacked of being able to view dying objectively and often before it happens to a loved one? Others, in previous chapters, have described many of the factors that provide partial answers to this complex question. In summary, one can note that death education is in the spotlight today as a result of both biomedical revolution and sociocultural evolution. But should death be an educational subject for all to consider? Whether or not it is taught in our schools, death will surely be a common, frequent, and ultimately personal encounter for all! Why, what, where, when, how, and by whom are appropriate queries in exploring this idea of death education for all. These questions and the perspectives their responses offer form the first section of this chapter. Following that, a selected annotated bibliography of printed and other media materials is presented.

DEATH EDUCATION—WHY?

In the plainly stated introductory comments of Ernest Morgan in his latest edition of a death education manual begun 16 years ago, one finds a most appropriate answer to the query, "Why death education?" Morgan (2) writes,

> Death education relates not only to death itself but to our feelings about ourselves and nature and the universe we live in. It has to do with our values and ideals, the way we relate to one another and the kind of world we are building. Thoughtfully pursued, it can deepen the quality of our lives and of our relationships. (p. 3)

Related to this is the view that teachers of sexuality—the public taboo of earlier preeminence—hold regarding contraception. That is the notion that birth control is most effectively taught as *preventive* education, which is best provided prior to the onset of need for its implementation. The lessons for death education contained in this thought have been discussed elsewhere (3) but they merit representation here. The most obvious analogy for death education is the idea that learning about death as a fact of life is probably most beneficial if approached before one is actually bereaved or dying. Although studies of bereavement infer its validity, only recently has there been research of any kind done to assay the contention that death education is a positive preparatory experience (4-10). Unfortunately much of these data remain unpublished and more research is clearly needed. Another lesson is the corollary that contraception is but one aspect of human sexuality and receives its most valid hearing when offered in a context of exploring broader issues of living. The corresponding suggestion for death education is, as Morgan and Dempsey assert, that learning about death and dying is coincident to learning of oneself and one's place and ways of being in the world. Feifel (11) has stated it more expressively:

> ...death makes an authentic statement about life's actuality and meaning. It helps clarify and intensify our images of man and his world. Herein lies the summons to advance our comprehension of how death can serve life. To die—this is the human condition; to live decently and die well—this is man's privilege. (p. 12)

Goals and Objectives

This initial question also begs a consideration of what the goals, objectives, and forms of learning might be in educating for living through teaching about death and dying. A useful point of departure is a statement of the overall goals for death education. Several possibilities come to mind. First and most obvious is the point in Feifel's statement, namely that death is the ultimate reflection on human existence. As the Welsh poet Dylan Thomas has noted, "After the first death, there is no other." The obvious implication is that one's mortality can provide both necessary and sufficient perspective for vital decision making—for career, mate, ethical, and moral choices. Cutter (12), in his excellent but little-noted book *Coming to Terms with Death*, lists two themes à propos of this point. First he cites the compelling Socratic notion that an unexamined life is not worth living. Further, Cutter asserts the inherent value of knowledge for humans, particularly of inevitable and profound life events, the most certain of which is death. Related is the observation that Freud among others has dwelt upon, namely that all of life is a rehearsal for death. However that resonates in one's mind, none can argue that death marks the final drawing of the Shakespearean curtain. As such, we can and should use the fact of our eventual deaths as a practical justification for coming to terms with the ways we spend the time until then and with how our survivors may cope with our absences.

On the matter of survivorship, the why of death education calls for the provision of information to enable individuals to make more provident and purposeful plans for the economic impacts of death-loss. The majority of us are unprepared for the arrangements and costs entailed in a sometimes lengthy dying, the funeral, body disposition, and the often costlier postmortem "bequests," which may affect our well-being physically as well as psychosocially. One would hardly expect such anticipatory preparation if the whole idea of personal death is anathema. Thus death education for all in these times has a strong appeal on intellectual and pragmatic grounds at the least.

At still another level of meaning, learning about the implications mortality has for our ways of living addresses the commonwealth of the larger social systems with which we coexist. Robert Kastenbaum (13) has persistently and eloquently examined this rationale for learning about death's broader meanings. He speaks of the complex interweavings of individuals, organizations, and even countries that contribute in some systematic ways to the phenomena of death. Who, for instance, would fail today to identify Ugandan leader Idi Amin with such a concept on a frightening scale!

From a humanitarian perspective, one can look to formal learning about thanatology as an effective buffer against undue suffering and mental anguish. Surely there is much to be gained from knowing that grief has some predictable properties, including for most a limited time span and thus an ending to its pain. As noted earlier, the effects of enduring significant personal loss can themselves be stimuli to further loss for oneself, including debilitating illness and, in extremis, another death. Whether the so-called survivor-victim is oneself or another, effective assistance with the resolution of loss due to death can be an invaluable facility to acquire and use.

It might be worthwhile to focus on some conceptual handles for what death education for all can entail. A series of triads may offer a helpful schema for looking at this. The first such triad can be viewed as a summary of the foregoing goals for death education. These overlapping areas of focus might be labeled:

1. Information-sharing
2. Values clarification
3. Coping behaviors

Let's look at each of these more closely. First, the *information-sharing* goal is seen to include the dissemination of relevant, often academic types of data about the broad spectrum of what is currently called "thanatology," or the study (approaching a science) of death. Within this information are the several definitions and criteria that qualify dying and death-related phenomena, the particular biomedical dynamics and the various theoretical and empirical statements bearing on bereavement, grief, and mourning. Also, the research evidence amassed on human attitudes and common behaviors reflecting those postures toward dying and death, as well as the varieties of religious and cultural expressions about death, and biostatistics on life expectancy and causes of death constitute a reasonable minimum from the body of knowledge available about the topic.

A second aspect of death education seems to warrant an examination and *clarification of one's personal values* about the many choice points and vital decision-making opportunities involving what might be called "deathstyle." The term is interchangeable with the more common "lifestyle," as either connotes an end attained in a somewhat individualized manner. This goal of instruction involves fostering a climate for considering the death-influencing alternatives incorporated in one's manner of living. In this way then, one can examine social issues such as global conflict, holocaust, violent behaviors of many types, the ever-present threat of "megadeath," and self-destructive behaviors—both the rapidly lethal ones and our more common, slow-acting daily habits.

Further, ecological abuse and increasingly scarce natural resources are important areas of study and personal reflection in learning about the meanings of death. Thinking through such topics systematically and in a group discussion format may have even higher priority in studying death and dying than the mere acquisition of some "static" facts. One is reminded here of Tolstoy's dying Ivan Illych, who contemplates the profound meaning of the Latin inscription "Respice finem" etched on his watch medallion. In this classic piece of fiction is a critical lesson for all and, simultaneously, a compelling argument for death education; that is, an inquiry into the reality of one's final end can be the most effective means for making a necessary and beneficial existential inquiry into one's comportment while alive.

A more specialized learning objective in some ways is the third area of death education, the so-called *coping behaviors*. These skills at problem solving and help giving would seem to be of universal worth whether the object of assistance and need for coping is oneself, a friend, relative, patient, or client. The lack of appropriate sociocultural norms and the absence of mourning experiences during childhood that characterize the experience of most Americans living today are testimony to the need for inclusion of this aspect of death education. Thus, enabling people to master certain types of helping skills, whether the objective is one of effective professional care giving or of dealing with the consequences of anticipated or realized loss for oneself or others, is another important reason for providing death education for all.

A truly thorough education about mortality on both a personal and social plane would seem necessary to encompass all three of these goals of learning. Omission of any would seem to leave matters incomplete. An analogy that comes to mind is that the majority of us experience the frustration of a narrow-minded education that gives us both the means and skills for owning and driving an automobile, while precious few of us can reasonably relate the physics of the engine and propulsion mechanisms let alone repair the thing when it becomes dysfunctional!

DEATH EDUCATION—WHAT?

Another set of three viewpoints that offer a different way of looking at the meaning of death and dying was suggested by a study (14)

The Challenge: Meeting the Issues of Death

done in 1973 of college courses on death at that time. The dominant emphases of instruction found were:

1. Emphasis on death as a *personal* phenomenon (the most frequent focal point for death courses).
2. Examination of the *sociocultural* elements and effects of death.
3. A limited study of all but a *singular aspect of death and dying* (e.g., legal matters, self-destructive behavior, religion, funerary practices, etc.).

While some approaches tend to conceive rather narrowly of a particular way of viewing death, it would seem that altering the death-denying machinations of our culture calls for a broad consideration of all three viewpoints. As this writer (3) has argued elsewhere, we know far too little as yet (if we ever shall) to educate about death and dying from a specialty orientation. A broad, multidisciplinary consideration of the impacts of mortality on our thoughts, feelings, and actions seems called for and potentially of most benefit.

Much has been made thus far of the idea that death education is truly vital learning, that is, an edification of the reasons for and styles of conduct of daily living. Because this goal applies to all age groups and is never put to rest until the body is, the "what" of death education can be seen to involve a variety of ongoing needs. In an earlier paper (15), it was argued that death education is one of the most significant and effective ways of conducting a reasonable instruction in preparation for dying. The point being made once more is that all of us have a definite fate called death, and most of us have the debatably good fortune of dying in some gradual manner rather than suddenly and unexpectedly. And even the rapid losses of life assail many can be seen as strong arguments in themselves for a preparatory learning about death while more involved in living pursuits than dying ones. It would seem a sad case of "too little, too late" to engage in a hurried attempt at reconstructing and reconciling a lifetime in the narrow specter of time afforded many dying patients. As noted in the first section, there are too many important tasks entailed in the final decisions one makes, both for oneself and one's survivors, to leave them to hastily grabbed, emotionally taut moments. Preparation for dying events and postmortem consequences is in itself a solid rationale and substance for death education. And, as a pundit once said, such preparation becomes too late an undertaking *only* after the undertaker has taken one under!

On a less general plane, Leviton (4) has enumerated a set of 12 thorough and realistic goals for death education. Notable inclusions are the elimination of the semantic taboos surrounding death and their attendant anxieties (particularly for the young), as well as promotion of more truthful and comfortable interactions among care givers, patients, families, and other survivor victims, particularly in the service of grief resolution. He notes further that the students dictate to a large degree the emphasis an instructor adopts, with the goals of learning often deriving much of their direction from the intended professional roles of the learners—be they nurses, police, physicians, the clergy, lay persons, or whomever. Any specialized needs and roles for which the students are preparing must certainly color the instructional material. Also, the background and capacities of the students demand thorough consideration. Even though primary responsibility for organizing the formats and general content of the course falls to the instructor, the enrollees too should help influence the nature of material dealt with. This is not to say that all students have a perspective encompassing all of what may be topically salient for death education. But the teacher can benefit from knowing what the students' needs and interests are and can modify the planned course accordingly. Also, in these times of rapid change in the facts of death (for example, frequent statutory revision regarding wills, death criteria, inheritance taxes, and so forth), it may be necessary and even desirable to have outside resources provide some parts of the instruction. This would allow for maximizing the meaning, currency, and relevance of the course and make for a more thorough treatment.

Thus, in summary of the considerations about what should be taught in a relevant death education, three points seem worth considering by all. First, while there may be no fixed curriculum for any group of learners, there should be both personal and professional components to the experience, since death education like death itself is for all. Second, there are several role-related instructional objectives, which take much of their influence from the specific needs of the learners—be they nurses, parents, teachers, physicians, funeral directors, etc. Third, while a number of goals for what should be taught are readily suggested, in the end death education should aim primarily at helping each of us get in touch with what best enhances the purposefulness and satisfaction we derive from living, while securing an acceptance of mortality and the necessity for experiencing loss. Or, as Weisman (16) has put it, ". . . the purpose of studying the dying process is to find ways to . . . attain significant survival" (p. 864).

DEATH EDUCATION—WHERE AND WHEN?

Who should be the recipient of an education about death and dying? In a superficial sense, that answer is an easy "everybody." Yet not all parents or teachers, care givers or other members of the community would accept that response without at least some qualification.

The Challenge: Meeting the Issues of Death

So let's look more closely at where thanatology could or even should be pursued. Here again, a beginning perspective might be gained by looking at a trio of scenarios that broadly describe the settings and students therein for death education. These include:

1. *Formal education*, taken here to include nonmedical schooling at any point from primary through postsecondary classrooms and students, publicly or privately supported.
2. *Clinical education*, encompassing the entire array of health care personnel, particularly as taught in practical professional settings, such as hospitals and clinics.
3. *Lay public education*, meant here to include all other less formal settings and types of learners, whether being educated about death and dying through their religious groups, community agencies, or other such avenues.

With little effort one could justify each of these groups as legitimate students for death education. As indicated at the outset of this chapter, all three broad groups are experiencing a growth in number and scope of educational offerings about death and dying, due to an appropriate combination of public demand and a corresponding recognition of needs. Too often in the not so recent past, death education has been either "institutionalized" or assumed to be accomplished much as sex education was wrongly assumed to be—in the home. While the home would ideally serve as the original and recurrent site for the most effective death education, lingering mythologies and negative parental experiences pose too shaky a foundation for the ideal to occur as yet. If this is the case, then perhaps the most fortuitous target for death education efforts is the family, or, more easily the parents. Much as a recent move has been to educate parents about the vagaries of becoming more effective mothers and fathers, so too should the ultimate and for some the most influential fact of life—death—be taught to parents. After all, they are children too, and must model death-coping behaviors for their offspring as well.

Formal Education

It seems both fitting and appropriate that much of our death education efforts in the coming years be aimed at a primary group of influence and need—the heads of the nuclear family. Nonetheless, Leviton's (17) sentiments on the where and when of death education sound well placed, as he suggests ". . . that formal and informal death education . . . should be developmental and systematic. That is, it should begin when the child, verbally or nonverbally, indicates an interest, and end as death looms near" (p. 46). Several points worthy of mention are hidden in the statement above, for there is minimal evidence reported to date to validate a primary premise of the field in general and this chapter in particular: that learning, verbalization, openness and candor about dying and death are beneficial. What the few studies existing on the matter show is that, indeed, the immediate (short-term) effects of a course on death, dying, and bereavement are to heighten one's awareness and lessen one's fear of death. What is sorely lacking is any available assessments of the enduring effects of such learning experiences. Superficial examination (10) of this matter suggests that subsequent to death education, personal death-loss, the threat of life-endangering circumstances, or sharing the grief of another provide the only acid tests, and those just do not lend themselves readily to post hoc evaluation. Surely we must have more data and more time intervening between course exposure and measurement.

On a related note, there are two prevalent schools of thought about when a young person is developmentally ready or most teachable regarding death and dying. The traditional view as originally promulgated by Nagy (18) and Anthony (19) sees children acquiring a mature, realistic view of death around age 9 and 10 only after some gradual maturation through a pair of earlier stages of thought during younger years. The other outlook, born of more recent study of the issue and reflecting a vastly different cultural milieu, is the notion that children may acquire a valid understanding of mortality at a very young age. The limitation on that understanding is seen as simply a communicative one due largely to the limited symbolic (especially verbal) capacities of the very young (20–22). In either case the lesson appears similar: educating about death and dying has no really inappropriate beginning age and probably varies according to the particular life experiences the child encounters. Otherwise, comprehension levels provide the sole criterion for how much and how one transmits such vital lessons. A noteworthy suggestion on this whole issue came from Toffler (23) in his immensely popular social treatise of some years back called *Future Shock.* In it he urged that the traditional organization for teaching subject matter in schools be discarded. As a replacement he urged an orientation geared to the human life cycle, whereby death and any other critical topic might be more meaningfully presented and integrated into the student's ongoing life experience.

Lay Public Education

All of us are being subjected to a form of death education practically each day, as we are continually bombarded with sensationalistic, usually unnatural and violent death scenes that our media project. Unfortunately, this influence has been a major factor in formulating

The Challenge: Meeting the Issues of Death

our present-day ethos about human mortality. Lamentably, we are learning how un-American it is to die, or even to grow old, as if either were fully avoidable. This kind of death education for all must benefit from a more enlightened public that makes demands for both style and content changes in what is presented as timely and fit to print, hear, or view. This can only happen after the U.S. consumer has learned to defy or deny death less and to respect grief more. This will take time, but it does seem to be coming.

Clinical education

The clinical education category spoken of earlier is another setting that, while changing in more beneficial ways for both care givers and patients, still has plenty of room for progress. Heretofore, the few medical education programs with a course dealing with the terminally ill per se made that exposure to death in one's program of studies, another case of "too little, too late." By exception, nursing education programs have had a record of more intentional and consistent address of dying patient interaction since the advent of the 1970s. This area of education for death and dying is a critical one, and no other single target area for thanatology has the potential to alter societal views of mortality as profoundly and immediately as does effective death education for medical care givers. This too is coming about, however grudgingly.

Sex and Other Differences in Learners

The ways in which the subject of death and its implications are taught might well take into account some very pervasive sex differences at all ages and levels. This is not meant to be sexist, nor to suggest that male and female pupils should have segregated death education, but the large number of variables on which death factors differ by sex alone would seem to call for some very careful consideration in providing instruction at all ages (23a). Perhaps other characteristics of the learning group besides age and sex (e.g., marital status, previous occupational experience, parental status, instructional setting, and so forth) will eventually prove to be significant features delineating what the forms and forums for teaching about death and dying should be in the future.

In general then, the where and when of death education seem to hinge on developmental abilities and needs, as well as the predictable demands of persons at unpredictable times—a statement of the differences between a basically preventive approach and an intervention timed after the emergence of a compelling need. We will all be served best by a comprehensive exposure to death education wherever and whenever it is practical throughout the life cycle.

DEATH EDUCATION—HOW?

This seemingly technical issue is also more probing than first glance or hearing might hint. Unlike some less emotional themes in academia or in daily intercourse, death's implications are such that not just anyone or any way of imparting information will suffice for a satisfactory death education. In addition to a firm grasp of the ever-growing body of published data and opinion of a scientific thanatological nature, death educators should possess a thorough self-knowledge, particularly of their own views and reactions to personal mortality and the loss of others. Also of special importance is an understanding of the elements of bereavement and the modes of grief resolution. Last, but by no means least, the death educator should be willing and able to offer needed counsel or have ready access to a fund of helping resources for such an emotionally charged intrapersonal topic. Just as it is true that not all people seek a death education experience out of mere curiosity, and certainly few do at another's dictation, few (if any) instructors come to teach about dying and death out of some impersonal motivation.

As the mean age of the student body increases, so too does the probable incidence of bereavement among the enrollees. Just to illustrate, rates of death in this decade in America vary from 40 per 100,000 at ages 10 to 14, through 160 per 100,000 for those 15 to 24 years of age, and on up to 730 per 100,000 aged 40 to 55, and 1220 per 100,000 aged 56 plus. By the same token, perhaps younger pupils have greater need for asking questions and even for catharsis about the reactions that death stirs up in them, as they lack a broader experience to provide valuable perspective. Thus the size of the group taught may be of relevance also. To be indeed available for help giving, perhaps a reasonable limit on how many people are taught is called for in death education. It certainly becomes a logistical impossibility to personally serve students in any setting if their numbers far outstrip the available hours to offer them personal access.

In summary then, the particular methodologies and materials employed in teaching about mortality should carefully address the uniqueness of the learners. This may well mean that death educators must be more self-disclosing and become more knowledgeable with thanatology students than is commonly the case in other educational pursuits. As noted earlier, the formats for death education should be predicated on the goals of the particular course. If clarifying individual values is the primary end, ample time and arrangements should be given over to this purpose. If, however, the emphasis is essentially on information sharing, the incorporation of significant time for classroom dialogue may not be so crucial. Again, the ways of learning

The Challenge: Meeting the Issues of Death

about the ultimate fact of life should be a function of the predetermined goals of such a teaching effort and the influences of the learners' characteristics and stated needs as well.

DEATH EDUCATION—BY WHOM?

The final issue is who should teach about death and dying. As noted earlier, as the motivations for becoming a student of death and dying vary, so too do the reasons that move persons to become teachers of this topic. Kennedy (24) put this concern in focus when he observed that "Good things can always be done badly and it is common sense to recognize that not everybody has the sensitivity or depth that is required in dealing with the human issues connected with dying." In addition to the points mentioned thus far, which suggest some basic homework for death educators, formal instruction about the thanatological domain calls for a continual self-assessment. Death educators need to be as fully aware as possible of their own (changing) attitudes and reactions to mortality. This aspect of teacher preparation seems no less important than the material and factual preparation, and in the case of a taboo topic like death it may be all the more critical. The discussion of how and by whom issues are relevant to all, not merely those who would teach about death. Parental and civic concern and responsibility in this matter seem to justify including what appears to be a technical comment to a broader audience. In today's era of credentialing and accountability, certification procedures for thanatologists cannot be far behind the current press for such qualifications for other helping agents.

One is tempted to say that death education is the peculiar province of no one, and yet it should be the active concern of everyone. From being solely responsible for oneself (if that fantasy still beclouds any thinker in this era of modernity) to parental responsibility, as well as for any mature person aware of the tenuousness of life and permanence of death, death education *for* all is an unveiled call for death education *by* all. Simply put, the surest bequest of birth is the legacy of death; a life conducted oblivious of that end is one deprived of its essential humanity. The optimal death educator has to be oneself in this society.

Death education occurs at some level of meaning for all; why not insure its provision systematically and throughout the life span as developmental needs and capabilities allow? Feifel's (25) words offer fitting summary to this thought:

> The time is ripe for "death education" to assume a rightful role in our development. Its pertinence is not only for those in helping

Death Education for All

professions who deal with dying, death and bereavement but for all of us—in the home, school, and in our general cultural upbringing. (p. 353)

REFERENCES

1. Dempsey, D. *The way we die.* New York: McGraw-Hill, 1975, p. 244.
2. Morgan, E. *A manual of death education and simple burial* (8th ed.). Burnsville, NC: Celo Press, 1977.
3. Knott, J. E. Editorial, *Forum Newsletter*, 1976–1977, Vol. 1, No. 2–3, p. 6.
4. Leviton, D. Death education. In H. Feifel (Ed.), *New meanings of death.* New York: McGraw-Hill, 1977.
5. Glick, I. O., Weiss, R. S., & Parkes, C. M. *The first year of bereavement.* New York: Wiley, 1974.
6. Leviton, D. Personal communication, March 25, 1975.
7. Knott, J. E. Some further effects of death education. Unpublished manuscript, University of Rhode Island, January 1977.
8. Bluestein, V. W. Death-related experiences, attitudes, and feelings reported by thanatology students and a national sample. *Omega*, 1975, *6*(3), 207–218.
9. Scott, F. G. Personal communication, July 8, 1974.
10. Knott, J. E., & Prull, R. W. Death education: Accountable to whom? For what? *Omega*, 1976, *7*, 177–181.
11. Feifel, H. The meaning of death in American society. In B. R. Green & D. P. Irish (Eds.), *Death education.* Cambridge, MA: Schenkman, 1973.
12. Cutter, F. *Coming to terms with death.* Chicago: Nelson-Hall, 1974.
13. Kastenbaum, R. *Death, society and human experience.* St. Louis: Mosby, 1977.
14. Berg, C., & Daughtery, G. *Report of the Task Force on Death Education.* DeKalb, IL: Educational Perspectives Associates, 1974, pp. 93–95.
15. Knott, J. E. Death education and the dying patient. Paper presented at annual meeting of the American Psychological Association, Chicago, 1975.
16. Weisman, A. Psychological death. *Psychology Today*, November 1972.
17. Leviton, D. The scope of death education. *Death Education*, 1977, *1*, 41–56.
18. Nagy, M. The child's view of death. *Journal of Genetic Psychology*, 1948, *73*, 3–27.
19. Anthony, S. *The child's discovery of death.* New York: Harcourt, Brace and World, 1940.
20. Vernick, J. Meaningful communication with the fatally ill child. In E. Anthony & C. Koupernik (Eds.), *The child in his family: The impact of disease and death.* New York: Wiley-Interscience, 1973.
21. Rochlin, G. How younger children view death and themselves. In E. Grollman (Ed.), *Explaining death to children.* Boston: Beacon Press, 1967.
22. Bluebond-Langner, M. Meanings of death to children. In H. Feifel (Ed.), *New meanings of death.* New York: McGraw-Hill, 1977.
23. Toffler, A. *Future Shock.* New York: Random House, 1970.
23a. Schulz, R. *The psychology of death, dying, and bereavement.* Reading, Mass.: Addison-Wesley, 1978.
24. Kennedy, E. Death in our culture. *Stress 2.* Chicago: Thomas More Association, 1974.
25. Feifel, H. Epilogue. In H. Feifel (Ed.), *New meanings of death.* New York: McGraw-Hill, 1977.

ANNOTATED BIBLIOGRAPHY

The following selections and comments are solely the choices and opinions of the author and represent in no way an exhaustive or definitive listing of death literature and teaching tools. Rather, these are a collection of recent (since 1974) materials that offer both a unique focus and a quality of expression appealing to this author.

Nonacademic Books for Children

In many ways the best teaching material for death education is literary works wherein the crisis of mortality has served as catalyst for the unfolding of everyday human drama. Children's books in particular often have such a quality, and the following are some recent examples of this genre.

Coutant, H. *First snow.* New York: Knopf, 1974. (Ages 5-8) Presents a Buddhist view of the oneness of life and death, involving a Vietnamese family's first winter in New England. A dying grandmother capitalizes on the first snow to point out that new life replaces that which passes. Interesting illustrations enhance the interwoven themes of closure and renewal, of eager anticipation and sad regret.

Crawford, C. *Three-legged race.* New York: Harper & Row, 1974. (Age 10 and up) Illness and eventual death-loss bind three friends in this well-conceived and effectively presented tale for older children.

Farley, C. *The garden is doing fine.* New York: Atheneum, 1975. (Ages 6-10) A dying father's legacy of intangibles to his daughter and family impresses young Carrie Sheldon with the continuity of living.

Greenfield, E. *Sisters.* New York: Crowell, 1974. (Ages 6-10) Similar in theme to the Coutant book, this story involves a young black girl's loss of her father through death and the resultant unfolding of new meanings of life for her.

Grollman, E. *Talking about death.* Boston: Beacon, 1974. (Ages 6-10) A book to be read and discussed by adult and child together, sharing straightforward thoughts and feelings about death, loss, and separation.

Lichtman, W. *Blew and the death of the mag.* Freestone, 1975. (Ages 6-10) A well-told fantasy of the liberating relationship between the title characters and how much more important sharing living times becomes in the face of losing the chance for ever doing so again. Excellent portrayals of support and empathetic needs in a bereaved child.

Lorenzo, C. L. *Mama's ghosts.* New York: Harper & Row, 1974. (Ages 4-8) Rewarding tale of a youngster's "coming of age" with her dying grandmother's guidance. This book demonstrates how the young and elderly have a uniquely critical role to play in our age where rites of passage are seldom recognized.

Miles, M. *Annie and the old one.* Boston: Little, 1975. (Ages 4-8) Like the Lorenzo tale, this story of a dying Navajo grandmother depicts the bequest of life that the elderly facing death can so eloquently communicate.

Rinaldo, C. L. *Dark dreams.* New York: Harper & Row, 1974. (Ages 10 and up) The title refers to the troubling remembrances of his dead mother by a young adolescent boy, and their impact on his development at that crucial age.

Stein, S. B. *About death.* New York: Walker, 1974. (Ages 5–10) This is another dialogue book, focusing on death's meanings when first a pet bird, and then a grandfather die. It has running twin narratives for adult and child, and some very good photographs, all of which succeed eminently well in conveying the messages and opening a line for communication about death.

Watts, R. G. *Straight talk about death with young people.* Philadelphia: Westminster, 1975. (Ages 12 and up) Straight talk is an effectively presented compilation of some of the common core questions that junior high and older youth are grappling with regarding death. I found it very readable and informative, even for adults.

Zolotow, C. *My grandson Lew.* New York: Harper & Row, 1974. (Ages 5–8) Six-year-old Lew recalls the since dead grandfather he knew at two, who was his "special friend," and who, in his mother's words, ". . . we will remember . . . together and neither of us will be so lonely as we would be if we had to remember him alone."

Nonacademic Books for Adults

For this section I have chosen to describe only a handful of quite different publications.

Ader, C. A., Stanford, G., & Adler, S. M. (Eds.). *We are but a moment's sunlight.* New York: Pocket, 1977. This anthology is of death viewed through many literary artists' eyes and collated under the headings of attitudes, rituals, immortality, suicide, grief, and accounts of dying. It offers interesting perspective on mortality as expressed over time by a variety of writers.

Caine, L. *Widow.* New York: Macmillan, 1974. A widely read account (including a TV movie) depicting one woman unprepared for the death of her husband or the various consequences of being stigmatized as a U.S. widow. *Widow* reads well but models "helpful" behavior only by inference.

Grollman, E. (Ed.). *Concerning death.* Boston: Beacon, 1974. This is a comprehensive set of essays from several religious, legal, medical, educational, funereal, and economic viewpoints. Though somewhat uneven for any single reader's interest, this book is a useful, practical, and informative source for educators and lay readers alike. Some data cited are now out of date, notably the economic information.

Lifton, R. J., & Olson, E. *Living and dying.* New York: Praeger, 1974. This brief work is an interesting exploration of how modern-day humankind has come to the peculiar credo about how "living" and "dying" alternate in prominence and human motivation. It offers a succinct reportage of Lifton's widely printed modes of symbolic self-immortalization.

Phipps, J. *Death's single privacy.* New York: Seabury, 1974. Phipps' book is another first-person "widow" chronicle, however, this one offers a helpful, conscientious view of what can happen and suggests (positively) what could be useful to a young woman whose spouse dies. More of an aid, but not fairly compared to the Caine book.

West, J. *The woman said yes.* New York: Harcourt, Brace, Jovanovich, 1976. A rewarding autobiographical account of what West wrote as fiction in the early 1960s ("A Matter of Time") concerning the effects of life-threatening illness and the losses of her mother and sister. The latter dying scenario forms the crux of the tale, with the author's deft prose cutting to the quick of the quandaries of euthanasia.

Worden, W., & Proctor, W. *PDA* * *(Personal Death Awareness)*. Englewood Cliffs, NJ: Prentice-Hall, 1976. This compact yet full self-help book is an effective product born of the belief that ultimate death provides ample reason to examine one's lifestyle. A highly readable piece, *PDA* is a successful attempt to provide data (about self and society) that might serve as food for thoughtful living in preparation for death.

Academic Books for Students

This grouping is necessarily foreshortened by space demands, as new books of this type have become a monthly routine. At this writing there are another half-dozen known death education texts still in process, but they are not yet available for full review. Inclusion below therefore is predicated on selectivity about the theme, its thoroughness, and a desire not to repeat books that are essentially the same in format or coverage. Thus one can recognize that many exclusions are worthwhile additions to the thanatologist's and student's library.

Ariès, P. *Western attitudes toward death*. Baltimore: Johns Hopkins University Press, 1974. The French social historian's captivating essay addressing the evolution of Western behavior regarding the place of death in life.

Butler, R. N. *Why survive?* New York: Harper & Row, 1975. The award-winning manifesto by the head of NIA, which argues convincingly for reformation of national (read institutional and personal) modes of dealing with the elderly—many of whom are dying "prematurely and tragically" in this country.

Feifel, H. (Ed.). *New meanings of death*. New York: McGraw-Hill, 1977. A most useful and readable new version of the original professional book of thanatology readings. It is up-to-date and comprehensive in most of the areas of possible interest to the neophyte (student) reader.

Fulton, R. (Ed.). *Death and identity* (2nd ed.). New York: Wiley, 1976. Another updating of a classic in the field, this one contains some of the seminal works on several aspects of human mortality.

Kastenbaum, R. *Death, society, and human experience*. St. Louis: Mosby, 1977. As the author suggests in his preface, this is a ". . . responsible, informed, and helpful guide" to the title features. No one does a better job of discussing "developmental" and "systematic" influences on dying and death. Kastenbaum's latest is a thoughtful, suggestive work for student and teacher alike.

Russell, O. R. *Freedom to die*. (Rev. ed.). Human Sciences, 1976. Of the abundance of books recently published on the so-called euthanasia question, this one appeals as a highly reasoned and reasonable presentation of the historical, moral, and legal aspects of the topic. It is comprehensive and yet focused, enlightening and still respectful of bias, scholarly and nonetheless easy to read.

Shneidman, E. (Ed.). *Suicidology: Contemporary developments*. New York: Grune and Stratton, 1976. This is a thorough and current treatment of the many sides of self-destructive behavior. It combines some older perspectives as introduction to many well-written essays in what is a book most appropriately geared to the professional suicidologist.

Shoenberg, B. et al. (Eds.). *Anticipatory grief*. New York: Columbia University Press, 1974. One of this group of thanatologists' better collections on a very crucial topic. While geared toward the care giver, there is much of benefit to be had herein by nonmedical readers in a book that is sometimes inconsistent in caliber of presentation.

Veatch, R. M. *Death, dying, and the biological revolution.* New Haven, CT: Yale University Press, 1976. One of the more recent and scholarly books dealing with the bioethics that pervade the death surround. At times it appears too pedantic for the average reader, but nonetheless it is a significant offering on this theme.

Academic, Including Nonprint Media, for Educators

Frankly, the handful of quarterly journals on death and dying offer the best, most current sources of teaching material in this writer's opinion. Those I am familiar with are *Death Education, Essence* (Canadian), *New Advances in Thanatology, Omega*, and *Suicide.* In addition, there are several recently available education tools for the death educator that can become further resources in one's teaching arsenal. These include the following.

Curriculum guides

Mills, G., Reisler, R., Robinson, A., & Vermilye, G. *Discussing death.* Palm Springs, CA: ETC, 1976. This teacher's resource book is a well-organized compendium of references, activities, and approaches to broaching death in the classroom. Although written for all grades, it succeeds best (of the three herein) with the younger child up through middle-school age.

Stanford, G., & Perry, D. *Death out of the closet.* New York: Bantam, 1976. A secondary school curriculum guide addressing many different focal points and several ways for "living with dying" to be integrated into the high school classroom. Does a good job with an adolescent target group.

Wilcox, S. G., & Sutton, M. *Understanding death and dying.* New York: Alfred, 1977. To my view, a very useful and frequently effective collection of stimuli and readings. Some of the latter are better geared toward college-age students, but most of the material could be applied selectively earlier.

Mixed media

This trio of filmstrip and cassette programs all share the characteristics of being inconsistent in quality, incomplete in themselves, and guilty of trying to say too much in too brief and limited a format. All that notwithstanding, each does have a few units that are both well done and very good in conveying their particular messages.

Loss and grief. Costa Mesa, CA: Concept Media, 1977. This program deals with the generic concept of loss and grief and offers eight depictions of six loss situations (dying, relocation, lifestyle/role change, illness, divorce) as well as how resolution proceeds in each. Aimed at sensitizing care givers, it works best in stimulating discussion about interventive aspects of grief-work. (Available as complete package or in seven parts; technically well done but expensive.)

Dimensions of death. DeKalb, IL: Educational Perspectives Associates, 1977. A collection of 10 tape and filmstrip (or slide) presentations with a varied coverage and utility. Several noted thanatologists consulted on the series, but it has an unnecessary overstatement of funerary themes (as do earlier EPA multimedia programs). The units of widest applicability in this college-age based series are those on sociocultural, developmental, and practical aspects of the topic. (Reasonably priced and available in part or entirety. EPA also has a "flex-test" series of 100 reprints of varying quality to supplement one's assigned readings and a Source Book of AV materials for death education.)

Death and dying: Closing the circle. New York: Guidance Associates, 1976. A set of five filmstrip/sound programs, ostensibly for high school age death education efforts, this package is good though often semantically burdensome. It was originally released with only an introductory tape and additional units on funerary options and meanings as well as a synoptic version of Doris Lund's *Eric*. Recent additions of two segments on the matters of dying and postmortem bereavement have enhanced the scope and usefulness of this package. (Appropriate for secondary level and above and available at a fair price but in the complete set only.)

Films

There are many new and effective noncommercial films becoming available today. Also, collections of audio- and videotapes are now at the public's disposal. My own experience with the three recent releases listed below leads me to recommend them. All are available through several rental outlets, libraries, and universities.

Whose life is it anyway? Distributed by Benchmark Cinema, New York (Released in U.S. in 1974), 53 minutes, color. A very rich British dramatization that has wide relevance for such issues as euthanasia, patient–care giver relations, self-control, and, in the principal character's words, "medical virtuosity" in the service of avoiding death. This film offers much for the death educator and bioethicist, as it raises numerous questions without pretending easy or absolute answers are readily had. (For senior high and above)

Where is dead? Distributed by Life Style Productions, 1975, 19 minutes, color. Realistic presentation of a 6-year-old child's reaction to the death of her 9-year-old brother. Well arranged and not overdone so as to enable viewers to relate to the impact of loss on the young and to how parental influence can be so vital in such times. (For younger audiences through adults)

Dying. Distributed by WGBH–TV, Boston, 1976, 97 minutes, color. A somewhat lengthy but forthright look at three dying cancer patients and their ways of contending with illness, living with dying, and how they each draw on their communities for support. "Dying" is a very contemporary look at the variety of "death-styles" people adopt through a medium that promotes introspection and insight. (For junior high and up)

Author Index

David, H. P., 133
Davidson, G. W. 181
Dawidowicz, L., 42
Dempsey, D. 385, 387, 398
De Paola, T., 233
Descartes, R., 335, 358
Des Pres, T., 369, 374
Deutsch, A., 136
De Vries, P., 374
Dibner, A. S., 205
Dickstein, L. S., 135
Diggory, J. C., 135
Dlin, B. M., 134
Dolan, V., 181
Dorland, W. A. N., 78, 79, 106
Dorsel, T., 232
Dotson, E., 133, 206
Down, J. L. H., 145
Downs, J. F., 156
Dracup, K. A., 157
Ducker, W., 322
Duff, R., 374
Dukeminier, J., 358
Dumont, R. G., 71, 128, 135
Dunbar, F., 274, 281
Durkheim, E., 111, 131, 237, 253

Easson, E. C., 113, 132
Easson, W. M., 232
Edin, S., 220, 231
Edwards, L., 132
Effland, R., 316
Eisdorfer, C., 133, 205
Eliade, M., 259, 280
Eliot, T. D., 111, 131
Elliot, G., 19, 20, 40, 42
Elliott, W., 373
Emerson, R. W., 184
Engel, G. L., 94, 106, 134, 157
English, C. S., 281
Erikson, E. H., 183, 184, 185, 186, 203, 204, 259
Ettinger, R., 51, 71
Evans, A. E., 220, 231
Evans, J., 65, 72
Evans, W. E. D., 107
Evans-Pritchard, E. E., 111, 131, 237, 253

Farley, C., 399
Farr, W. C., 181
Fassler, J., 233
Faunce, W. A., 111, 131, 206
Feder, S., 71
Feifel, H., 40, 43, 71, 72, 116, 121, 130, 132, 133, 135, 136, 157, 181, 183, 194, 196, 203, 206, 207, 231, 253, 388, 397, 398, 401
Feldman, J. J., 254
Feldman, K. A., 134
Fieschi, C., 358
Fischer, H. K., 134
Fisher, R. S., 106, 107
Fleming, S., 133
Fletcher, G., 366, 373
Foley, G. V., 224, 231
Foner, A., 204, 205
Foot, P., 365, 373
Ford, J. R., 254
Formaneck, R., 231
Foss, D. C., 71, 128, 135
Fost, N., 374
Foucault, M., 179, 181
Fowles, J., 52, 71
Franco, Francisco, 111
Frank, C., 205
Frazer, J. G., 111, 132, 259
Frederick, J. F., 254, 274, 281
Frederick, R. S., 357
Freeman, H. E., 42, 157, 205, 206
Freidson, E., 157
Freud, S., 35, 43
Friedman, S. B., 222, 232
Friesen, S. R., 132
Fulcomer, D. M., 251, 255
Fulton, R. L., 8, 42, 111, 121, 127, 131, 135, 206, 254, 255, 278, 281, 401
Futterman, E. H., 226, 232

Garside, R. F., 207
Gartley, W., 231
Garvin, R. M., 207
Geertz, C., 238, 253
Gerber, I., 177, 181
Gianturco, D. T., 207

Kantrowitz, M., 234
Karon, M., 219, 231
Kasper, A. M., 117, 132
Kass, L. R., 349, 351, 352, 353, 358
Kastenbaum, R. J., 44–45, 67, 71, 72,
    115, 116, 121, 132, 133, 135,
    136, 190, 191, 198, 200, 204,
    205, 206, 207, 213–214, 218,
    230, 231, 389, 398, 401
Kay, D. W. K., 207
Keegan, J., 7, 42
Kelly, O., 47, 53, 63, 71
Kelly, W. H., 132
Kennedy, E., 397, 398
Kennedy, I. M., 344n, 348, 349, 350,
    351, 353, 358
Kitagawa, E., 131
Klein, S., 235
Klett, J., 321, 322
Kliman, G., 253
Kline, N. S., 132
Knight, J., 71
Knott, J. E., 398
Knowles, J. H., 157
Knudson, A. G., 219, 231
Kohl, M., 374
Koocher, G. P., 230
Koupernik, C., 181, 255, 398
Knowles, J. H., 157
Ko Hung, 105,
Kraus, A., 254
Kremer, T., 42
Krippner, S., 281
Kübler-Ross, E., 24, 43, 53, 71, 74,
    123, 134, 196, 206, 249, 251,
    255, 275, 281
Kurlychek, R. T., 206
Kushner, J., 232
Kuskin, K., 234
Kutscher, A. H., 134, 205, 207
Kyle, D., 130, 135

Lack, S. A., 166, 167, 181
Lamers, W. M., 71, 72, 237, 253
Langone, J., 71
La Rochefoucauld, F. de, 49, 71
Lascari, A. D., 232
Lassen, N. A., 358

Lawson, R., 233
Lee, V., 235
Lerner, M., 15, 16, 42, 209, 230
LeShan, E., 232
LeShan, L., 54, 55, 71, 274, 280
Lester, D., 133, 205
Leveton, A., 127, 135
Levine, M. D., 374
Levine, S., 42, 157, 206
Leviton, D., 72, 190, 204, 385n, 391,
    393, 398
Lewell, W., 205
Lewis, C. S., 63, 72
Ley, P., 114, 132
Lichtman, W., 399
Lieberman, M. A., 134, 136, 193, 205,
    207
Liegner, L. M., 181
Lifton, R. J., 21, 22, 42, 120, 133,
    400
Lilienfeld, A., 254
Lindemann, E., 181, 249, 255, 260,
    262, 264, 274, 280
Little, S. C., 358
Logan, D. L., 191, 193, 205
Lonetto, R., 133
Lorenzo, C. L., 399
Luke, St., 165, 166
Lumsden, D. B., 183n
Lustig, A., 22, 42
Lutkins, S., 255, 263, 280
Lynch, J. J., 172, 181
Lynn, R., 316

Maddison, D., 207
Mahoney, J., 130, 135
Malinowski, B., 111, 127, 131, 237,
    253, 259
Maloney, L. J., 231
Mandelbaum, D., 237, 238, 239, 253
Marcel, G., 6, 42
Marcuse, H., 128, 135, 182, 203
Marriot, C., 134
Marshall, J. R., 72, 194, 206
Marshall, W., 72
Martin, D., 133
Martin, G., 51, 71
Martinson, I. M., 72, 157, 232

White, E. B., 233
White, L., 71
White, R., 135
Whitehead, A. N., 77, 106
Whitley, E., 189, 204
Wilcocks, C., 157
Wilcox, S. G., 230, 402
Wilson, D. C., 181
Wimmer, M., 213, 230
Winn, M., 36, 43
Wolfenstein, M., 253
Wolff, K., 205
Wolstenholme, G. E. W., 358

Worden, W., 401
Wretmark, G., 255
Wrightsman, L., 133

Young, M., 249, 255
Yudkin, S., 219, 231

Zim, H., 235
Zoger, S., 232
Zolotow, C., 234, 400
Zuehlke, T. E., 129, 135

Subject Index

Federal Trade Commission, 380–381, 383
Fiduciaries, 303–304
Forced retirement, 200
Formaldehyde, 104
Funeral:
  arrangements, 304
  celebration of death, 237
  cost of, 197, 202, 246, 248, 304, 376–381
  customer, 377, 380–381
  customs, 237–238
  family obligation, 247–248
  home, 383
  and guilt, 377
  pagan origin, 242, 243
  for the poor, 379–380
  prearrangement, 382
  purchase and bereavement, 378
  as religious rite, 237, 245
  rite of incorporation, 247–248
  rite of passage, 238, 251, 257
  ritual of disposal, 237
  rituals, extravagant, 376–377
  and status of deceased, 378
  traditional, 245
Funeral ceremonies, 236
  as acting out processes, 271
  ancient Persia, 258–259
  functional and dysfunctional, 238–242
  in Java, 238
  of the Kota, 238–239
  of the Luo and Kikuyu tribes, 239–240
  for President Kennedy, 40, 240–242, 249
  in Shanidar, Iraq, 248
Funeral directors, 59, 242–245, 252–253, 278
  business practices, 378
  claims to be professionals, 377
  conflict of interest, 381
  policing other members of profession, 377
  political activities, 377
  and possession of the body, 378
  training, 377

Funeral industry:
  and claims of grief therapy, 377
  government restraints on, 380–381
  lobby, 383–384
  vs. memorial societies, 382
  in U.S. society, 197, 376
Funeral practices:
  attitudes toward, 197, 242–248
  body disposal and social consolidation, 62
  British and American, 59
  in contemporary society, 59–60, 245–253
  and cremation, 197, 243–244, 384
  deritualization of, 39
  and earth burial, 197
  of Egyptians, 59
  embalming, 59, 104–105, 383–384
  lying in state (viewing the dead) 197, 245, 249, 251, 381
  and Orthodox Jews, 59
Future Shock, 394
Futurity, time perspective and death anxiety, 130–131

Geriatric facilities, 201
Gift tax, 285
Glutaldehyde, 104
Gnosticism, 327
Government support for medical research, 143
Gramp, 362–363
Grief:
  accumulation of losses, 200
  acute: and denial of death, 249–250
    physiological reactions to, 263–264
  anticipatory, 99
    and premature debonding, 97
  counseling, 202–203
  definition of, 257
  distortion of reality, 269–270
  final stage of restoration, 266
  and friends, 277–278
  impact of, 267–269
  management, 266, 269, 270–273, 277, 279–280

Love, need for, 190
Low grief loss, 250
    (*See also* Bereavement; Grief;
        Mourning process)
Lymphatic system, 83
Lyndon Johnson, 94

Make Today Count, 63
Malignant tumors, 87
Malpractice controversies, 180
Marie Curie Homes, 159
Maryland bill, 347
Massachusetts General Hospital
    Optimal Care Committee, 367
Medical College of Virginia Hospital,
    320-323
Medical ethics, 325
Medical euthanasia, 368
Medical-legal consensus, 344
Medical technology, 143-155
Medicare, 161
Medulla, 336
Memorialization, 227
Memorial societies, 58, 243-244, 381-
    383
Meningitis, 87
Mental health professional, 283, 284,
    287, 288
Metabolic disruption, 87
Metastasis, 87
Methodist Hospital in Indianapolis,
    364
"Middle knowledge," 111
Milieu interne, 83
Mind and body association in causa-
    tion of disease, 80, 84, 93-99
Mode of death:
    and age, 110
    and income, 110
    and perceived moral character,
        110-111
    and perceived social deviancy, 111
    and schooling, 110
    and social class in position in
        society, 110
Mongolism, increased life expectancy,
    145
Moral principles, 323, 329, 332

Morbidity, 85
Mortality:
    control techniques, 12
    gain in life expectancy, 81-82
    infant, 12, 109, 209, 224-229
    patterns, 10-15
    statistics, 246, 261, 274, 396
    survivors by age from various coun-
        tries at different time periods,
        81-82
Morticians (*see* Funeral directors)
Mortuary trolley, concealment of,
    118
Mourning process, 173-179, 257
    (*See also* Bereavement; Grief)
Mucopolysaccharide secretions, 83
Multiple sclerosis, 90
Mutilation anxiety, 216
Myocardial infarction, 86, 91, 94
Mythology of death, 373

Nasopharynx, 83
National Funeral Directors Associa-
    tion, 244-245
National Opinion Research Center,
    241-242
Natural death, 202
    (*See also* Euthanasia; Right to die)
Natural Death Act in California, 70
Natural immortality, 120
Near-death experiences, 122-123, 275
Neocortex of the cerebrum, 336, 339,
    340
Neurological decompensation, 88
Neurologically dead, 322, 325
Neurophysiology, 336, 337
Neurotic children, 217
Nomadic peoples, 376
Nurse–patient communications, 115-
    116, 148, 151-152, 169-170
Nurses:
    abandoning patients, 169
    and the bereaved, 278
    conflicting values, 155, 367
    coping mechanisms, 150-151
    education, 148, 156
    feeling trapped, 152
    psychological stresses, 150-155